Starting Strength

Starting Strength

Basic Barbell Training

3rd Edition

Mark Rippetoe

with Stef Bradford

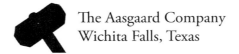

The Aasgaard Company
Wichita Falls, Texas

Editor – Catherine E. Oliver, Plain English Publications
Indexing – Mary Conover
Layout & Proof – Stef Bradford

15 14 13 12   2 3 4 5 6 7 8 9 10

ISBN-13: 978-0-982-5227-4-5 (cloth)
ISBN-13: 978-0-982-5227-3-8 (paper)
ISBN-13: 978-0-982-5227-2-1 (electronic)
ISBN-10: 0-982-52274-6 (cloth)
ISBN-10: 0-982-52273-8 (paper)
ISBN-10: 0-982-52272-X (electronic)

Printed in the United States of America

The Aasgaard Company
3118 Buchanan St, Wichita Falls TX 76308, USA
www.aasgaardco.com
www.startingstrength.com

Contents

Preface

Damned if things haven't changed in the four years since the 2nd edition of *Starting Strength* was written. The Aasgaard Company has changed personnel, I have met lots of people who have taught me many things, and we have had enormous success with what I thought was going to be a book ignored by the industry, academe, and the exercising public. I was right about the fitness industry and the folks with tenured positions, but I was wrong about you. Since 2007 we have taught several thousand people how to do these five lifts in our weekend seminars, and the 2nd edition has sold more than 80,000 copies, making it one of the best-selling books about weight training in publishing history. Thanks.

Now that we've learned some things from you guys – the ones we've been busy teaching for four years – the previous material in the 2nd edition is screaming for an update. Some of it is stale, incomplete, or just plain wrong, and it can't just lay there like a bureaucrat, badly needing something useful to do but making money anyway. This effort is not just the culmination of a top-to-bottom, year-long rewrite. It is the product of an intensive four-year testing program with many of you serving as the experimental population, one which has improved the teaching method for the five lifts, with an extra one thrown in.

It has also been a four-year school for me, as I have tried to find better ways to explain what I know to be true in terms that are understandable, logical, and, most importantly, correct. Much of this material is not in print anywhere else; hopefully, *that* doesn't make it wrong. But you're pretty bright, so you can decide for yourself.

The book needed a new look, too. Our hope is that you enjoy the illustrations by Jason Kelly, in a different style than usually found in a fat messy textbook, and that you appreciate Stef's Herculean efforts to make this a better-looking example of the bookmaker's art than the previous edition.

Many people deserve thanks for their contributions. In no particular order (certainly not alphabetical):

Dustin Laurence, Dr. Dennis Carter, Dr. Philip Colee, Dr. Matt Lorig, Stephen Hill, Juli Peterson, Mary Conover, Catherine Oliver, Bill Starr, Tommy Suggs, Mark Tucker, Thomas Campitelli, Ryan Huseman, Maj. Ryan Long, Maj. Damon Wells, Andrea Wells, John Welbourn, Brian Davis, Justin Ball, Nathan Davey, Travis Shepard, Paul and Becca Steinman, Mike and Donna Manning, Gregg Arsenuk, Michael Street and Carrie Klumpar, Skip and Jodi Miller, Ahmik Jones, Heidi Ziegele, Lynne Pitts, Kelly Moore, Eva Twardokens, Tara Muccilli, Dan Duane, Shane Hamman, Jim Wendler, Dan John, Jim Steel, Matt Reynolds, Charles Staley, Maj. Ryan Whittemore, John Sheaffer, Will Morris, Andy Baker, T.J. Cooper, Doug Lane, Simma Park, Myles Kantor, Phil Hammarberg, Barry Vinson, Gant Grimes, Josh Wells, Shelley Hancock, Terry Young, Ronnie Hamilton, Anil Koganti, MD, Rufus-dog, Ursa-dog, and Mr. Biggles.

—Rip

STRENGTH
WHY AND HOW

Physical strength is the most important thing in life. This is true whether we want it to be or not. As humanity has developed throughout history, physical strength has become less critical to our daily existence, but no less important to our lives. Our strength, more than any other thing we possess, still determines the quality and the quantity of our time here in these bodies. Whereas previously our physical strength determined how much food we ate and how warm and dry we stayed, it now merely determines how well we function in these new surroundings we have crafted for ourselves as our culture has accumulated. But we are still animals – our physical existence is, in the final analysis, the only one that actually matters. A weak man is not as happy as that same man would be if he were strong. This reality is offensive to some people who would like the intellectual or spiritual to take precedence. It is instructive to see what happens to these very people as their squat strength goes up.

As the nature of our culture has changed, our relationship with physical activity has changed along with it. We previously were physically strong as a function of our continued existence in a simple physical world. We were adapted to this existence well, since we had no other choice. Those whose strength was adequate to the task of staying alive continued doing so. This shaped our basic physiology, and that of all our vertebrate associates on the bushy little tree of life. It remains with us today. The relatively recent innovation known as the Division of Labor is not so remote that our genetic composition has had time to adapt again. Since most of us now have been freed from the necessity of personally obtaining our subsistence, physical activity is regarded as optional. Indeed it is, from the standpoint of immediate necessity, but the reality of millions of years of adaptation to a ruggedly physical existence will not just go away because desks were invented.

Like it or not, we remain the possessors of potentially strong muscle, bone, sinew, and nerve, and these hard-won commodities demand our attention. They were too long in the making to just be ignored, and we do so at our peril. They are the very components of our existence, the quality of which now depends on our conscious, directed effort at giving them the stimulus they need to stay in the condition that is normal to them. Exercise is that stimulus.

Over and above any considerations of performance for sports, exercise is the stimulus that returns our bodies to the conditions for which they were designed. Humans are not physically normal in the absence of hard physical effort. Exercise is not a thing we do to fix a problem – it is a thing we must do anyway, a thing without which there will always *be* problems. Exercise is the thing we must do to replicate the conditions under which our physiology was – and still is – adapted, the conditions under which we are physically normal. In other words, exercise is substitute cave-man activity, the thing we need to make our bodies, and in fact our minds, normal in the 21st century. And merely normal, for most worthwhile humans, is not good enough.

An athlete's decision to begin a strength training program may be motivated by a desire to join a team sport that requires it, or it might be for more personal reasons. Many individuals feel that their strength is inadequate, or could be improved beyond what it is, without the carrot of team membership. It is for those people who find themselves in this position that this book is intended.

Why Barbells?

Training for strength is as old as civilization itself. The Greek tale of Milo serves to date the antiquity of an interest in physical development, and an understanding of the processes by which it is acquired. Milo is said to have lifted a calf every day, and grew stronger as the calf grew larger. The progressive nature of strength development was known thousands of years ago, but only recently (in terms of the scope of history) has the problem of how best to facilitate progressive resistance training been tackled by technology.

Among the first tools developed to practice resistance exercise was the barbell, a long metal shaft with some type of weight on each end. The earliest barbells used globes or spheres for weight, which could be adjusted for balance and load by filling them with sand or shot. David Willoughby's superb book, *The Super Athletes* (A.S. Barnes and Co., 1970) details the history of weightlifting and the equipment that made it possible.

But in a development unforeseen by Mr. Willoughby, things changed rapidly in the mid-1970s. A gentleman named Arthur Jones invented a type of exercise equipment that revolutionized resistance exercise. Unfortunately, not all revolutions are universally productive. Nautilus utilized the "principle of variable resistance," which claimed to take advantage of the fact that different parts of the range of motion of each limb were stronger than others. A machine was designed for each limb or body part, and a cam was incorporated into the chain attached to the weight stack that varied the resistance against the joint during the movement. The machines were designed to be used in a specific order, one after another without a pause between sets, since different body parts were being worked consecutively. And the central idea (from a commercial standpoint) was that if enough machines – each working a separate body part – were added together in a circuit, the entire body was being trained. The machines were exceptionally well-made and handsome, and soon most gyms had the obligatory, very expensive, 12-station Nautilus circuit.

Exercise machines were nothing new. Most high schools had a Universal Gladiator multi-station unit, and leg extensions and lat pulldowns were familiar to everybody who trained with weights. The difference was the marketing behind the new equipment. Nautilus touted the total-body effect of the complete circuit, something that had never before been emphasized. We were treated to a series of before-and-after ads featuring one Casey Viator, an individual who had apparently gained a considerable amount of weight using only Nautilus equipment. Missing from the ads was the information that Mr. Viator was regaining size he previously had acquired through more conventional methods as an experienced bodybuilder.

Jones even went so far as to claim that strength could be gained on Nautilus and transferred to complicated movement patterns like the Olympic lifts without having to do the lifts with heavy weights, a thing which flies in the face of exercise theory and practical experience. But the momentum had been established and Nautilus became a huge commercial success. Equipment like it remains the modern standard in commercial exercise facilities all over the world.

The primary reason for this was that Nautilus equipment allowed the health club (at the time known as the "health spa") industry to offer to the general public a thing which had been previously unavailable. Prior to the invention of Nautilus, if a member wanted to train hard, in a more elaborate way than Universal equipment permitted, he had to learn how to use barbells. Someone had to teach him this. Moreover, someone had to teach the health spa staff how to teach him this. Such professional education was, and still is, time-consuming and not widely available. But with Nautilus equipment, a minimum-wage employee could be taught very quickly how to use the whole circuit, ostensibly providing a total-body workout with little invested in employee education. Furthermore, the entire circuit could be performed in about 30 minutes, thus decreasing member time on the exercise floor, increasing traffic capacity in the club, and maximizing sales exposure to more traffic. Nautilus equipment quite literally made the existence of the modern health club possible.

The problem, of course, is that machine-based training did not work as it was advertised. It was almost impossible to gain muscular bodyweight doing a circuit. People who were trying to do so would train faithfully for months without gaining any significant muscular weight at all. When they switched to barbell training, a miraculous thing would happen: they would immediately gain – within a week – more weight than they had gained in the entire time they had fought with the 12-station circuit.

The reason that isolated body part training on machines doesn't work is the same reason that barbells work so well, better than any other tools we can use to gain strength. The human body functions as a complete system – it works that way, and it likes to be trained that way. It doesn't like to be separated into its constituent components and then have those components exercised separately, since the strength obtained from training will not be utilized in this way. The general pattern of strength acquisition must be the same as that in which the strength will be used. The nervous system controls the muscles, and the relationship between them is referred to as "neuromuscular." When strength is acquired in ways that do not correspond to the patterns in which it is intended to actually be used, the neuromuscular aspects of training have not been considered. Neuromuscular specificity is an unfortunate reality, and exercise programs must respect this principle the same way they respect the Law of Gravity.

Barbells, and the primary exercises we use them to do, are far superior to any other training tools that have ever been devised. **Properly performed, full-range-of-motion barbell exercises are essentially the functional expression of human skeletal and muscular anatomy under a load.** The exercise is controlled by and the result of each trainee's particular movement patterns, minutely fine-tuned by each individual limb length, muscular attachment position, strength level, flexibility, and neuromuscular efficiency. Balance between all the muscles involved in a movement is inherent in the exercise, since all the muscles involved contribute their anatomically determined share of the work. Muscles move the joints between the bones which transfer force to the load, and the way this is done is a function of the design of the system – when that system is used in the manner of its design, it functions optimally, and training should follow this design. Barbells allow weight to be moved in exactly the way the body is designed to move it, since every aspect of the movement is determined by the body.

Machines, on the other hand, force the body to move the weight according to the design of the machine. This places some rather serious limitations on the ability of the exercise to meet the specific needs of the athlete. For instance, there is no way for a human being to utilize the quadriceps muscles in isolation from the hamstrings in any movement pattern that exists independently of a machine *designed* for this purpose. No natural movement can be performed that does this. Quadriceps and hamstrings *always* function together, at the same time, to balance the forces on either side of the knee. Since they *always* work together, why should they be *exercised* separately? Because somebody invented a machine that lets us?

Even machines that allow multiple joints to be worked at the same time are less than optimal, since the pattern of the movement through space is determined by the machine, not the individual biomechanics of the human using it. Barbells permit the minute adjustments during the movement that allow individual anthropometry to be expressed.

Furthermore, barbells require the individual to make these adjustments, and any other ones that might be necessary to retain control over the movement of the weight. This aspect of exercise cannot be overstated – the control of the bar, and the balance and coordination demanded of the trainee, are unique to barbell exercise and completely absent in machine-based training. Since every aspect of the movement of the load is controlled by the trainee, every aspect of that movement is being trained.

There are other benefits as well. All of the exercises described in this book involve varying degrees of skeletal loading. After all, the bones are what ultimately support the weight on the bar. Bone is living, stress-responsive tissue, just like muscle, ligament, tendon, skin, nerve, and brain. It adapts to stress just like any other tissue, and becomes denser and harder in response to heavier weight. This aspect of barbell training is very important to older trainees and women, whose bone density is a major factor in continued health.

And barbells are very economical to use. In practical terms, five or six very functional weight rooms – in which can be done literally hundreds of different exercises – can be built for the cost of one circuit of any brand of modern exercise machine. Even if cost is not a factor, utility should be. In an institutional situation, the number of people training at a given time per dollar spent equipping them might be an important consideration in deciding which type of equipment to buy. The correct decision about this may directly affect the quality of your training experience.

The only problem with barbell training is the fact that the vast, overwhelming majority of people don't know how to do it correctly. This is sufficiently serious and legitimate a concern as to justifiably discourage many people from training with barbells in the absence of a way to learn how. This book is my humble attempt to address this problem. This method of teaching the barbell exercises has been developed over 30 years in the commercial fitness industry, the tiny little part of it that remains in the hands of individuals committed to results, honesty about what works, and the time-honored principles of biological science. I hope it works as well for you as it has for me.

This York Barbell model 38 Olympic Barbell set was obtained from the Wichita Falls Downtown YMCA. It was used for nearly 50 years by thousands of men and women. Among them was Bill Starr, famous strength coach, Olympic weightlifter, and one of the first competitors in the new sport of Powerlifting. Bill was the editor of Hoffman's "Strength and Health" magazine and Joe Weider's "Muscle" magazine. He was he coach of numerous national, international, and Olympic teams as well as one of the very first full-time strength coaches at the collegiate and professional level. He is one of the most prolific writers in the Iron Game, with books and articles published over 5 decades. His influence is still felt today through the accomplishments of his many athletes and training partners. His first weightlifting was done on this set.

From the Bill Starr Monument in Wichita Falls Athletic Club, Wichita Falls, Texas.

THE SQUAT

The squat has been the most important, yet most poorly understood, exercise in the training arsenal for a very long time. The full-range-of-motion exercise known as the squat is the single most useful exercise in the weight room, and our most valuable tool for building strength, power, and size.

The squat is literally the only exercise in the entire repertoire of weighted human movement that allows the direct training of the complex movement pattern known as *hip drive* – the active recruitment of the muscles of the posterior chain. The term *posterior chain* refers to the muscles that produce hip extension – the straightening out of the hip joint from its flexed (or bent) position in the bottom of the squat. These muscle groups – also referred to as the *hip extensors* – are the hamstrings, the glutes, and the adductors (groin muscles). Because these important muscles contribute to jumping, pulling, pushing, and anything else involving the lower body, we want them strong. The best way to get them strong is to squat, and if you are to squat correctly, you must use

Figure 2-1. Three views of the squat. *Middle,* Depth landmarks for the full squat. The top of the patella (A) and the hip joint, as identified by the apex in the crease of the shorts (B). The B side of the plane formed by these two points must drop below parallel with the ground.

hip drive, which is best thought of as a shoving-up of the sacral area of the lower back, the area right above your butt. Every time you use this motion to propel yourself out of the bottom of the squat, you train the muscles in the posterior chain.

All styles of squatting tend to make the quads sore, more so than any of the other muscles in the movement. This soreness occurs because the quads are the only knee extensor group, while the hip extensors consist of three muscle groups (hamstrings, glutes, adductors). They comprise more potential muscle mass to spread the work across – if they are trained correctly. Given this anatomical situation, we want to squat in a way that maximizes the use of all the muscle that can potentially be brought into the exercise and thus be strengthened by it. So we need a way to squat that involves the posterior muscle mass, making it operate up to its potential for contributing to strength and power. The low-bar back squat is that way.

Done correctly, the squat is the only exercise in the weight room that trains the recruitment of the entire posterior chain in a way that is progressively improvable. These are the things that make the squat the best exercise you can do with barbells and, by extension, the best strength exercise there is. The squat trains the posterior chain muscles more effectively than any other movement that uses them because none of the other movements involve enough range of motion to use them all at the same time, and none of the other movements train this long range of motion by preceding their *concentric*, or shortening, contraction with an *eccentric*, or lengthening, contraction, which produces a stretch-shortening cycle, or *stretch reflex*.

The squat's stretch-shortening cycle is important for three reasons:

1. The stretch reflex stores energy in the viscoelastic components of the muscles and fascia, and this energy gets used at the turnaround out of the bottom.

2. The stretch tells the neuromuscular system that a contraction is about to follow. This signal results in more contractile units firing more efficiently, enabling you to generate more force than would be possible without the stretch reflex.

3. Because this particular loaded stretch is provided by the lowering phase of the squat (which uses all of the muscles of the posterior chain over their full range of motion), the subsequent contraction recruits many more motor units than would be recruited in a different exercise.

The conventional deadlift, for example, uses the hamstrings and glutes, but it leaves out much of the adductors' function, and starts with a concentric contraction in which the hips start out well above the level of a deep squat. No bounce, shorter range of motion, but very hard anyway – harder, in fact, than squatting, due to the comparatively inefficient nature of the dead-stop start – yet not as useful to overall strength development. Plyometric jumps can be deep enough and might employ the requisite stretch reflex provided by the drop, but they are not incrementally increasable the way a loaded barbell exercise is, they can be damned tough on the feet and knees for novices, and they are not weight-bearing in the sense that the whole skeleton is loaded with a bar on the shoulders. In contrast, the squat uses all the posterior chain muscles, uses the full range of motion of the hips and knees, has the stretch-shortening cycle inherent in the movement, and can be performed by anybody who can sit down in a chair, because we have very light bars that can be increased in weight by very small increments.

The term "posterior chain" obviously refers to the anatomical position of these muscular components. It also indicates the nature of the problems most people experience under the bar, trying to improve their efficiency while squatting. Humans are bipedal creatures with prehensile hands and opposable thumbs, a configuration that has profoundly affected our perception as well as our posture. We are used to doing things with our hands in a position where our eyes can see them, and we are therefore set up to think about things done with our hands. We are not used to thinking about our nether regions, at least those unrelated to toilet functions. The backside of your head, torso, and legs are seldom the focus of your attention unless they hurt, and they remain visually unobservable even with a mirror. The parts you can see in the mirror – the arms, chest, and abs, and the quads and calves if you're wearing shorts – always end up being the favorite things for most people to train. They are also the easiest parts to learn how to train because they involve or are facilitated by the use of our hands, and we are very "handsy" creatures.

The hard parts to train correctly are the ones you can't see. The posterior chain is the most important component of the musculature that directly contributes to gross movement of the body, as well as being the source of whole-body power. The posterior chain is also the hardest part to learn how to use correctly. This would be easier if you didn't have any hands: how would you pick up a table without the ability to grab the edge of the thing and lift it? You'd get under it and raise it with your upper back, or squat down and drive up with your hips against the undersurface of it, or lie down on your back and drive it up with your feet, because those

would be the only options open to you. But your hands shift your focus away from these options and enable you to avoid thinking about them at all. So posterior chain matters remain largely unexplored by most people, and this makes their correct use a rather groundbreaking experience.

You will find that the posterior aspects of squatting and pulling present the most persistent problems, require the greatest amount of outside input from coaches and training partners, and will be the first aspects of form to deteriorate in the absence of outside reinforcement. For coaches, the posterior chain is the hardest part of the musculature to understand, to explain, and to influence. But it is also the most critical aspect of human movement from the perspective of athletic performance, and the mastery of its lore can determine the difference between an effective coach and a slightly-more-than-passive observer, between an effective athlete and one who merely moves.

Much is made of "core" strength, and fortunes have been made selling new ways to train the core muscles. A correct squat perfectly balances all the forces around the knees and the hips,

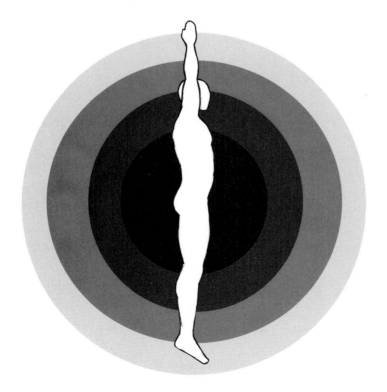

Figure 2-2. Total-body power development originates in the hips, and the ability to generate power diminishes with distance from the hips. Note also that the farther from the center of the body a body part is, the greater the angular velocity with which the body part can move, enabling the application of power through acceleration. From a concept by David Webster, versions of which have been used by Tommy Kono and Bill Starr. This concept has recently gained new traction under the names "core strength," "core stability," and "functional training." It seems rather obvious to the author that an athlete with a 500-pound squat has a more stable "core" than that same athlete would with a 200-pound squat.

using these muscles in exactly the way the skeletal biomechanics are designed for them to be used, over their full range of motion. The postural muscles of the lower back, the upper back, the abdominals and lateral trunk muscles, the costal (rib cage) muscles, and even the shoulders and arms are used isometrically. Their static contraction supports the trunk and transfers kinetic power from the primary force-generating muscle groups to the bar. The trunk muscles function as the transmission, while the hips and legs are the engine.

Notice that the "core" of the body is at the center of the squat, that the muscles get smaller the farther away from the "core" they are, and that the squat trains them in exactly this priority (Figure 2-2). Balance is provided by the interaction of the postural muscles with the hips and legs, starting on the ground at the feet and proceeding up to the bar. Balance is controlled by a massive amount of central nervous system activity under the conscious direction of the athlete's mind. In addition, the systemic nature of the movement, when done with heavy weights, produces hormonal responses that affect the entire body. So not only is "the core" strengthened, but it is strengthened in the context of a total physical and mental experience.

The squat is poorly understood because it involves the use of many muscles – more than most people realize – and most of the people who don't understand it have never done it correctly themselves. This means that they can't appreciate the true nature of the movement and the interactions of all the muscles functioning in a coordinated manner, since to truly understand a thing, you must experience it personally. The more people who learn to squat correctly, the more people there will be who understand the squat, and then, like ripples in a pond, knowledge and strength will spread. This process starts here, with you.

Loaded Human Movement

A basic understanding of the nature of loaded human movement – the ways that the skeletal system translates the force of muscle contraction into movement as the body interacts with its environment – is essential to understanding barbell training. A few simple lessons, which can be learned through observing the squat, are equally applicable to all other barbell exercises. The most basic of observations is that when a barbell is loaded,

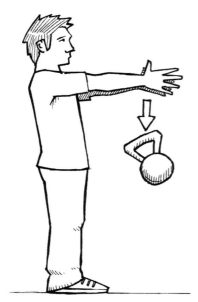 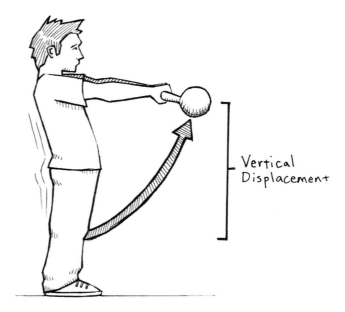

Figure 2-3. Gravity acts vertically, and only vertically. Any work done against gravity will be done in a direction opposite to its force, i.e. straight up. Any horizontal component to a barbell movement is not work done against gravity.

the force that provides the weight of the barbell is gravity. And gravity – always, everywhere, every time – operates in a straight line perpendicular to the surface of the earth. Gravity is generated by mass. In this particular case, we are concerned with the mass of the planet, which has conveniently organized itself into the general shape of a sphere – ignoring minor surface features like mountains and valleys – under the influence of this gravity. So the surface of the earth is assumed to be horizontal for this definition; after all, a rock dropped on the side of a hill still falls in the direction we define as *down*. This fact has yet to be disputed, and the principle has risen to the status of Physical Law: there are no known examples of unimpeded objects falling in a path described as "non-vertical." The force of gravity acting on the bar is always acting straight down in a vertical line. Therefore, the most efficient way to oppose this force is by acting on it vertically as well. So not only is a straight line the shortest distance between two points, but a straight *vertical* line is also the most efficient bar path for a barbell moving through space in a gravitational framework.

In fact, the work done on a loaded barbell must be analyzed on the basis of this framework. *Work* is defined as the amount of *force* (the influence which causes a change in motion or shape) multiplied by the *distance* the barbell moves. Pounds on the bar being a unit of force, work can be expressed in foot-pounds. But since gravity operates in only one direction, straight down, the work done against gravity consists only of the distance the barbell moves vertically. Any other motion imparted to the bar – i.e., horizontal motion, in a direction either forward or back relative to the lifter – cannot be considered work against gravity, although force will be utilized when the motion is produced. Rolling the barbell around the room constitutes work against gravity *only if the elevation of the barbell changes,* because gravity influences the mass of the barbell in only one direction – down.

Next, when a barbell is supported by a human body, the lifter and the barbell must be considered as a system for any analysis that applies to their combined mass. The center of mass (COM) of the human body in the standing "normal

anatomical position" is a point in the middle of the hips, approximately level with the sacrum. When you squat down below parallel, the geometry of the system changes to place the COM in the air somewhere between your thighs and your torso. The COM of the loaded bar is in the middle of the bar on your back. The *lifter/barbell system* has a COM somewhere between the two. As the weight of the bar increases, the system's COM moves closer to the bar until, at very heavy weights, the barbell itself approximates the system's COM. For practical purposes, we will assume that the barbell will be loaded with heavy weights and that the barbell is usually the object that we must be concerned with balancing as we move it through the range of motion of the exercise.

Notice that in Figure 2-5, a dashed line illustrates a vertical relationship between the barbell on the back and the middle of the foot against the

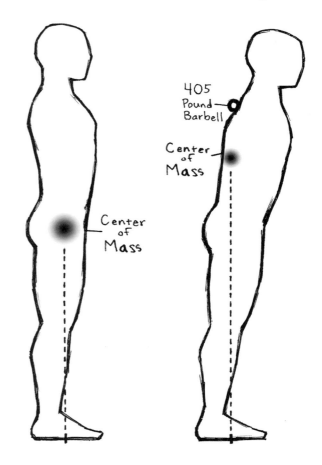

Figure 2-4. The COM shifts up toward the bar as the mass of the barbell increases.

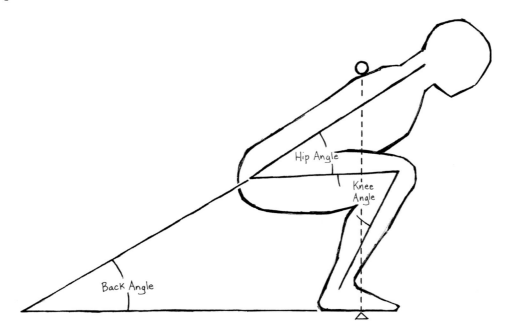

Figure 2-5. The diagnostic angles for the squat. The hip angle is formed by the plane of the torso and the femur. The knee angle is formed by the femur and the tibia. The back angle is formed by the plane of the torso and the floor. Note that the barbell is directly over the mid-foot and is therefore in balance.

floor. It should be intuitively obvious that the lifter/barbell system will be in balance when it is directly over the middle of the foot, with the *mid-foot* position – right under the arch of the foot – being the point of interaction with the ground that is the farthest away from both the forward and rearward edges of contact. Very simply, the mid-foot is exactly halfway between either end of the sole of the shoe. It is therefore the most stable position, the one which would take the most movement to disrupt, and therefore the one naturally favored by the body, loaded or not. The heavier the weight on the bar, the more precisely the bar position calibrates to the mid-foot. In other words, at light weights, where the mass is primarily that of the body itself, the bar may be forward of the mid-foot in a position of stability, and as the weight increases, the bar comes into balance more directly over the mid-foot.

The body prefers stability to pretty much everything else. For example, the ankle joint – the actual point of rotation – is behind the mid-foot, and the calf muscles attach at the heel at about the same distance behind the ankle as the mid-foot is in front of it. The calf muscles exert tension on the heel behind the ankle to counter the effects of the leverage between the ankle and the mid-foot (Figure 2-6). The body selects the mid-foot as the balance point by inclining the shins and doing the calf work necessary to maintain this more stable position. In addition, the gastrocnemius, the hamstrings, and the quadriceps all cross the knee joints, stabilizing the position of the knees relative to the ankles, and the hips are embedded in a web of muscle, tendon, and ligament that permits the upright body to squat down under load and maintain a position of balance over the mid-foot.

Consider the unloaded lifter: if you stand up straight with your hands on your hips and lean forward, even a little, you can feel the weight shift to the balls of your feet and feel the increased tension in your calves as you apply some force to the mass of your body above your feet to keep from falling forward. If you lean back, you can feel the shift onto your heels – lean back far enough, and you will have to actually hold your arms out in front of you to change your center of mass so that you don't fall back. (Our bodies have evolved to move forward, and forward imbalances are more naturally handled by our anatomy.) You settle into a position of balance when the greatest amount of force is needed to perturb the position, or when the least amount of force is needed to maintain the position. When you stand, this position is where your COM is over the mid-foot, and when you squat down and stand back up, your body's COM is in balance when it travels in a vertical line directly over this point. Since you will do most barbell exercises (except the bench press) while standing on your feet, this mid-foot balance point becomes a critically important concept in the analysis of good exercise technique.

Let's assume that the bar in Figure 2-5 weighs 315 pounds. Were the bar forward of this balance point, it would still weigh 315 pounds, but the effort required to move it through its range of motion would be greater. The eccentric and concentric work done on the 315 pounds would be harder due to the bad leverage position generated by the distance the bar was out of balance. And the isometric stress of stabilizing the load in the bad leverage position adds quite significantly to the effort. Keeping the 315-pound bar directly over the mid-foot through the complete range of motion (ROM) constitutes the most efficient way the work *should* be done during the lift. When the bar is off-balance, the added energy you must expend due to the leverage of the off-balance load makes 315 much harder to lift.

It doesn't take much of an imbalance for the leverage to increase to the point where the rep is missed. Imagine the bar on your back in a position 12 inches in front of the mid-foot as you try to squat; this is an awkward position with even 30% of your 1RM (1 rep max), and the heavier the weight gets, the smaller the imbalance you can deal with. You can easily see that this continuum ends up with essentially *zero* amount of deviation tolerable at 1RM loads. This concept applies to every barbell exercise where the load must be balanced. So, "good technique" in barbell training is easily and understandably defined as the ability of the lifter to keep the bar vertically aligned with the balance point. The ability to maintain this balanced relationship between the bar and the ground is one of the many things trained with barbells that are not trained in other exercise methods. Since balance is an important characteristic of most human physical endeavors, this is one more reason to base your training on barbell exercises.

Figure 2-5 also shows the angles we use to analyze the movement of the body under the bar during the squat. The *hip angle* is the angle formed by the femur and the plane of the torso. Even though the spine is curved when held in the correct position to bear weight under the bar, it is held rigid during the squat, so we can use the concept of "the plane of the torso" to describe the mechanical behavior of this segment under the bar. The *knee angle* is formed by the femur and the tibia, effectively illustrating

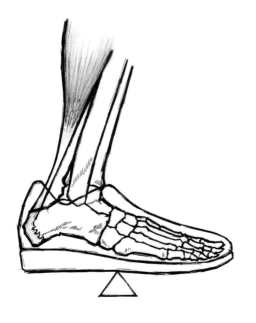

Figure 2-6. The mid-foot balance point is the position favored by the body for balance. The point of rotation at the bottom of the leg – the ankle – does not function as the last piece of the kinetic chain due to the stability provided by the anchoring system of the lower leg, calf muscles, and foot; this system maintains the tibial angle and transfers force to the sole of the foot. Considering the system this way allows us to calculate balance from the mid-foot position, the point of greatest stability against the floor.

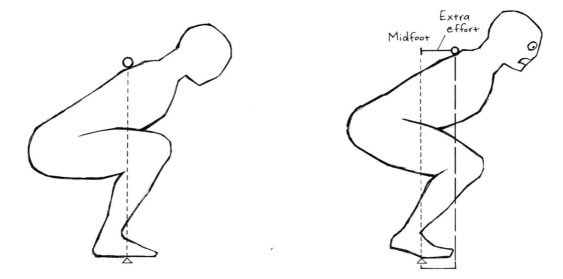

Figure 2-7. Extra work that must be done on an out-of-balance bar.

the relationship between the thigh and the "shank" (as the lower leg segment is called). The *back angle* is formed by the plane of the torso and the floor, which is assumed to be horizontal (meaning *level*, perpendicular to the force of gravity).

These angles describe the relationships of their constituent segments to each other under the load of the barbell. The back angle is said to be either more *vertical* or more *horizontal*, while the knee and hip angles are either more *open* or more *closed*. Control of the position of these angles depends on the muscles operating the bones that form the angles. We know that the lifter/barbell system will be in balance when the bar is directly over the middle of the foot, and the heavier the bar, the more precisely this position must be kept. Even if the weight is light enough to remain in a position of imbalance, the lifter will expend more energy than he would if the bar were in balance.

If the bar is on the front of the shoulders, as in the front squat, this bar position will require a very vertical back angle if the bar is to be kept over the mid-foot, as Figure 2-8 illustrates. Notice the knee angle made necessary by this position: it is very closed. And notice the hip angle: it is much more open than it would be with a more horizontal back angle. In this position, the hamstrings are shortened because their proximal attachments on the pelvis and their distal attachments at the knee are as close

together as they can be at the bottom of a squat. Here, the hamstrings are functioning isometrically to hold the torso in the nearly vertical position required of the front squat, a much easier position to hold than a more horizontal back angle because of the reduced leverage against the hips (much more on this later). But when the hamstrings are shortened, there is not enough contractile capacity left to contribute much to hip extension. In essence, the hamstrings are already contracted in the bottom of the front squat and can't contract much more. This leaves the glutes and adductors on their own to produce hip extension, and this is why your butt gets so sore when you front-squat heavy: it's having to do all the work the hamstrings normally help with in a squat.

The upshot of this situation is that the front squat leaves out much of the hamstrings' function, and we'd like to use the hamstrings when we squat so that we can get them strong. The front squat is therefore a poor choice for training the posterior chain. To best recruit the hamstrings, and let them contribute the most they can to hip extension, we need to use a squat form that produces a more closed hip angle and a more open knee angle. At the bottom of this squat, the hamstrings are contracted isometrically – that is, they are stretched out proximally, by the attachments at the pelvis, even as they are shortened distally because of the

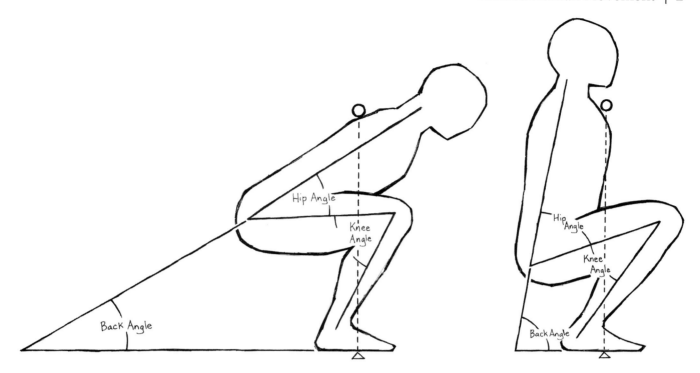

Figure 2-8. Squat variations commonly seen in the gym. *Left,* The low-bar squat, our preferred position and the form referred to in this text as "the squat." *Right,* The front squat, used to catch and recover from a clean and as an assistance exercise by Olympic weightlifters.

flexing knees. As the knees and hips extend during the ascent, the hamstrings have to work hard to maintain tension on the pelvis, and to control the effects of the increased leverage demands of the more-horizontal back angle. The back angle largely determines the hip angle, and the back angle enables the hamstrings to contribute more force to the squat.

And when we use that more horizontal back angle, the bar must be placed on the back such that the bar is over the middle of the foot. The lower the bar is on the back, the more horizontal the back angle can be. The bar should therefore be in the lowest secure position it can occupy on the back, right below the spine of the scapula – that bump on your shoulder blade you can feel when you reach across and touch the back of your shoulder. Any lower than this, and the bar scoots down a little every rep of the set.

If the adductors – the groin muscles – get their share of the load, too, that adds muscle mass to the exercise. When we use a moderate stance with shoulder-width heels, toes pointing out at about 30 degrees, and knees shoved out so that the thighs stay parallel to the feet, then the groin muscles stretch out as the hips are lowered. If the muscles are stretched out, they are in the position they must be in to contract and contribute force to the hip extension. The muscles that hold the knees out – the external rotators of the hip – are engaged as well, thus adding to the muscle mass involved in the squat.

The low-bar squat, or in this book, just the Squat, is not the same form used by suit-and-wraps-equipped powerlifters, who are trying to get the most out of their squat suit, an expensive, very tight singlet that is designed to resist hip flexion and store elastic energy in the eccentric phase, and therefore aid hip extension. To this end, some powerlifters use a very wide stance and as vertical a shin position as they can produce. Some lifters use a high-bar position with low elbows, a more vertical back angle, and an upward eye gaze (quite different from the squat style used in this book). A wide stance and vertical shins open the knee angle and close the hip angle, thus permitting the more effective use of the suit/hip extension. Knee wraps are used to resist knee flexion, and like the squat suit, they store elastic energy during the eccentric phase. Our stance, which is not nearly as wide, permits more forward travel of the knees and more use of the quadriceps. In fact, every aspect of the technique used in our version of the squat has been chosen specifically to maximize the amount of muscle mass and the range of motion used so that we can lift as much weight as possible through that range of motion and thus get stronger.

If the bar is placed high on the back – on top of the traps, where most people start off carrying it because it's an easier and more obvious place for a bar – the back angle must accommodate the higher position by becoming more vertical to keep the bar over the mid-foot. If the back angle is more vertical, the knee angle must become more closed because the knees get shoved forward when the hips open up (Figure 2-8 again). In other words, the higher bar position makes the back squat more like the front squat, and we don't want to front-squat for general strength development because it doesn't effectively train the source of whole-body power: the posterior chain.

The high-bar, or "Olympic," squat has been the preferred form of the exercise for Olympic weightlifters for decades. This seems to be largely a matter of tradition and inertia, since there are compelling reasons for weightlifters to use the low-bar position, too. Since the squat is not a contested lift in weightlifting, and since Olympic lifters front-squat to directly reinforce the squat clean anyway, the reasons for weightlifters to use the low-bar squat in training must involve other considerations. The squat makes you strong, and weightlifting is a strength sport; even if it is terribly dependent on technique, the winner is still the one who lifts the most weight. The high-bar position may be harder, but the low-bar position uses more muscle, allows more weight to be lifted, and consequently prepares the lifter for heavier weights.

If an argument on the basis of specificity is to be made, the low-bar squat is also more applicable to the mechanics of Olympic weightlifting than the high-bar squat. The low-bar position, with the weight sitting just below the spine of the scapula, much more closely approximates the mechanics of the position in which the bar is pulled off of the floor. As the discussions of pulling mechanics in the Deadlift and Power Clean chapters illustrate, the shoulder blades are directly above the bar when it leaves the floor in a heavy pull, and they stay there until the bar rises well above the knees. This is true for both the clean and the snatch, with the snatch being done from a position even less similar to the Olympic squat than the clean is. Low-bar squats done with this similar, relatively horizontal back angle train the movement pattern more directly than does the high-bar version, which places the back at a higher angle due to the higher position of the bar on the traps. And they do it through a nice, long range of motion due to the fact that the squat goes to a deeper hip position than the start position of either the snatch or the clean and jerk.

If the back angle is kept constant for both the low-bar squat and the pull from the floor (which it must be, see pages 127-131), they are very similar movements – more similar than a high-bar squat and a pull of any type. If an argument is to be made for squatting with a form specific to the motor pathway requirements of the sport, the low-bar position would be that form. And if an argument is made that the squat need not be similar, the low-bar squat still makes more sense because it can be done with heavier weights.

Squat Depth – Safety and Importance

The full squat is the preferred lower-body exercise for safety as well as for athletic strength. The squat, *when performed correctly*, not only is the safest leg exercise for the knees, but also produces more stable knees than any other leg exercise does. Correctly is deep, with hips dropping below level with the top of the patellas (see Figure 2-1). Correctly is therefore full range of motion.

Any squat that is not deep is a partial squat, and partial squats stress the knees and the quadriceps without stressing the glutes, the adductors, or the hamstrings. In full squats, the hamstrings, groin muscles, and glutes come under load as the knees are shoved out, the hips are pushed back, and the back assumes the correct angle on the way down for hip drive to occur on the way up. At the very bottom of the squat, the hips are in flexion and the pelvis tilts forward with the torso. In this deep squat position (Figure 2-9), several muscle groups reach a full stretch: the adductors (attached between the medial pelvis and various points on the medial femur), and the glutes and external rotators (attached between the pelvis and the lateral femur). Here, the function of the hamstring muscles (attached to the tibia and to the ischial tuberosity of the pelvis), is primarily isometric, since they don't necessarily change length on the way down. In the bottom of the squat, the tightened hamstrings, adductors, glutes, and external rotators provide a slight rebound, which will look like a "bounce"; this is the stretch reflex we discussed earlier. The tension of the stretch

pulls backwards on the tibia, balancing the force produced by the anterior quadriceps attachment on the tibial tuberosity. The hamstrings finish their job, with help from the quads, adductors, and glutes, by extending the hips.

A partial squat done with an upright torso and vertical back angle is typical of most people's attempts to squat, because we have all been told that the back must be vertical to reduce *shear*, the sliding forces that occur along a segment in rotation. Shear between the vertebral segments is supposed to somehow disarticulate your spine, despite the fact that this cannot and has not ever occurred. But in a misinformed effort to protect the back, this advice results in a lot of unnecessary stress on the knees. As we've already discussed, however, the vertical back angle fails to fully load the hamstrings. Therefore, they cannot exert the posterior force needed to

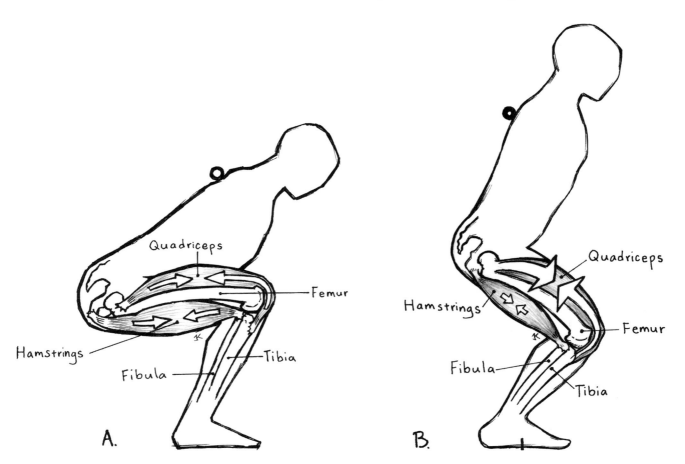

Figure 2-9. Muscular actions on the knee. In the deep squat position (A), the anterior force provided by the quadriceps is balanced by the posterior force provided by the hamstrings. The depth is the key: partial (high) squats (B) predominantly work the quadriceps and therefore lack balance.

oppose and balance the anterior force exerted by the quadriceps and their attachments to the front of the tibia, below the knee. (In other words, there's no force pulling backwards to balance the forces that are pulling the knees and tibias forward.) The result is an actual anterior shear on the knee. And like a front squat, the partial squat also forces the knees quite forward of the mid-foot – much more so than the low-bar squat form we will be using, which keeps the knees back and uses the hips as the primary mover of the load. This lack of posterior support produces an anterior-dominant force distribution on the knee: the further back the hips are, the more hip muscle you use, and the further forward the knees, the more quad you use. Many cases of patellar tendinitis have been caused by this incorrect squat technique. Even when partial squats are done with the correct back angle, they fail to work the full range of motion and therefore fail to perform to their potential as an exercise.

The hamstrings benefit from their involvement in the full squat by getting strong in direct proportion to their anatomically proper share of the load in the movement, as determined by the mechanics of the movement itself. This fact is often overlooked when the medical community considers anterior cruciate ligament (ACL) tears and their relationship to conditioning programs. The ACL stabilizes the knee: it prevents the tibia from sliding forward relative to the femur. As we have already seen, so does the hamstring group of muscles. Underdeveloped, weak hamstrings thus play a role in ACL injuries, and full squats strengthen the hamstrings. In the same way the engaged hamstrings protect the knees during a full squat, hamstrings that are stronger due to full squats can protect the ACLs during the activities that we are squatting to condition for. With strong hamstrings and the knees-back position provided by the low-bar version of the squat, the hips bear most of the stress of the movement. So athletes who are missing an ACL can safely squat heavy weights because the ACL is under no stress in a correctly performed full squat (see Figure 2-11).

Another problem with partial squats is the fact that very heavy loads can be moved due to the short range of motion and the greater mechanical efficiency of the quarter-squat position. A trainee doing quarter-squats is predisposed to back injuries as a result of the extreme spinal loading that comes from putting a weight on his back that might be more than three times the weight that he can safely handle in a correct deep squat. A lot of football coaches are fond of partial squats because they allow the coaches to claim that their 17-year-old linemen are all "squatting" 600 pounds. Your interest is in

Figure 2-10. The variation in squat depths commonly seen in the gym. *Left to right:* Quarter-squat, Half-squat, a position often confused with parallel, where the undersurface of the thigh is parallel with the ground, Parallel squat according to the criteria established in Figure 2-1, and "Ass-to-grass" squat.

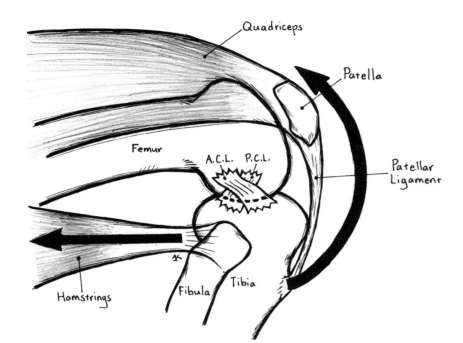

Figure 2-11. Forces on the knee in the squat. The hamstrings and adductors exert a posterior tension on the tibia, and the net effect of the anterior quadriceps tendon insertion is an anterior force against the tibial plateau. With sufficient depth and correct knee position, anterior and posterior forces on the knee are balanced. The anterior (ACL) and posterior cruciate ligaments (PCL) stabilize the anterior and posterior movements of the distal femur relative to the proximal tibia. In a correctly performed squat, these ligaments are essentially unloaded.

getting strong (at least it should be), not in playing meaningless games with numbers. If it's too heavy to squat below parallel, it's too heavy to have on your back.

There is simply no other exercise, and certainly no machine, that produces the level of central nervous system activity, improved balance and coordination, skeletal loading and bone density enhancement, muscular stimulation and growth, connective tissue stress and strength, psychological demand and toughness, and overall systemic conditioning than the correctly performed full squat. In the absence of an injury that prevents its being performed, everyone who lifts weights should learn to squat, correctly.

Learning to Squat

We will approach the squat in two phases: first unloaded, to solve problems associated with the bottom position, and then loaded, to learn how to apply the bottom position to the hip drive used for heavier weights. Since the majority of the problems with the squat happen at the bottom, this method expedites the process quite effectively.

GENERATING HIP DRIVE

We will use a fairly neutral foot placement, with the heels about shoulder width apart and the toes pointed out at about 30 degrees. An excessively wide stance causes the adductors to reach the end of their extensibility early, and excessive narrowness causes the thighs to jam against the belly. Both of these problems prevent you from reaching proper depth. Shoulder width is proportionate to pelvic width in most people, and experience has shown that this width works well for most of the population. **Many people will assume a stance with toes pointed too forward, so you may need to point them out more than you want to.** Look down at your feet and make a mental picture of what you see.

Now comes the crucial part of learning the movement. You are going to assume the position you will be in at the bottom of a correct squat, without the bar. This method works well because you can easily correct any errors in position before the bar adds another variable to the system. And if you've already been in the correct bottom position *without* the bar, getting into that position again *with* the bar is easy. Assume the correct stance and squat down, all the way. Don't even think about stopping high; just go on down to the bottom. Sometimes a lack of flexibility or a failure to point your toes out enough will alter your stance on the way down, so make sure you have assumed the correct foot position.

Next, put your elbows against your knees, with the palms of your hands together, and shove your knees out (Figure 2-13). This will usually be a decent bottom position, and if your flexibility is not great, the position will act as a stretch if you maintain it for a few seconds. Remember, **proper depth is essential in the squat**, and this low bottom position lays the groundwork for your attaining good depth from now on.

Stay in the bottom position for a few seconds to allow for some stretching. If you get fatigued by holding the position, your flexibility might not be quite what it should be. Stand up and rest for a few seconds. Then go back down to get some more stretching done and to reinforce your familiarity with the bottom position. This is the most important part of learning to squat correctly because good depth is the difference between a squat and a partial squat.

Now is the time to notice some important details about the bottom position. Your feet are flat on the floor, your knees are shoved out to where they are in a parallel line with your feet, and your knees are just a little in front of your toes. Your back should be as flat as you can get it, but if it's not perfect, we'll fix it later. Also notice that your back is inclined at about a 45-degree angle, not at all vertical. You may think it's vertical, but it won't be and it's not supposed to be. And your eyes are looking down at the floor a few feet in front of you.

After you've established the bottom position, come up out of the bottom by driving your butt straight up in the air. *Up,* not forward. This movement keeps your weight solidly over the whole foot instead of shifting it to the toes. Think about a chain hooked to your hips, pulling you straight up out of the bottom (Figure 2-14). Don't think about your knees straightening out, don't think about your feet pushing against the floor, and don't even think about your legs. Just drive your hips up out of the bottom, and the rest will take care of itself.

This important point should not be missed. Our previous discussion about hip drive and the use of the hamstrings in the squat applies here. The squat is not a leg press, and the idea of pushing the floor

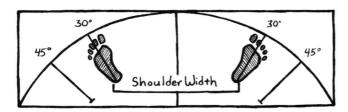

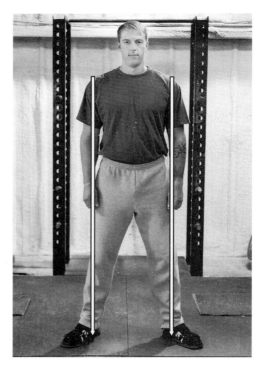

Figure 2-12. *Left,* Map of foot placement in the squat, as seen from above. *Right,* Heel placement by shoulder width.

Figure 2-13. Use your elbows to stretch into the correct position at the bottom. The femurs are parallel to the feet, the feet are flat on the ground at the correct angle, the hips are back, the knees are just a little forward of the toes, and the back is at an angle (about 45 degrees) that will place the bar over the middle of the foot.

with the feet provides an inadequate signal for the hamstrings, adductors, and glutes to provide their power out of the bottom. Hip extension is the first part of the upward drive out of the bottom. When you think about raising your butt up out of the bottom, the nervous system has a simple, efficient way to fire the correct motor units to initiate hip drive.

Eye gaze direction plays an important part in this process of driving the hips, and it is introduced even before the bar becomes part of the squat. Looking up at the ceiling when squatting has so many detrimental effects on proper technique that it

is absolutely amazing that so many people still advise their lifters to do it. It interferes with the correct bottom position, with hip drive out of the bottom, and with correct chest position. It changes the focal point from a close, manageable spot to one that is farther away. And the neck position that results from looking at the ceiling is inherently unsafe: to place the cervical spine in extreme overextension and then to place a heavy weight on the trapezius muscles directly underneath it is, at best, imprudent. The normal anatomical position for the cervical spine is the preferred position when the weights get heavy.

Figure 2-14. An interesting way to visualize hip drive in the squat.

Figure 2-15. Blocking the hips to learn the effect of eye gaze direction. An upward-directed gaze quite effectively diminishes the ability to use the posterior chain during the drive up from the bottom.

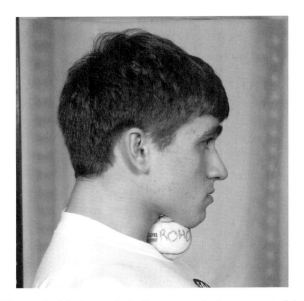

Figure 2-16. A tennis ball can teach the correct chin/neck relationship.

The habit of looking up is also a very difficult problem to correct if it has existed for any length of time. Lifters whose high school football coaches taught them to look up during the squat often have a very difficult time with changing the eye gaze direction, even when we have effectively demonstrated that looking down works so much better. An embedded movement pattern is always easier to perform than a new one, and it will be the default movement pattern if conscious control is shifted to another aspect of the new technique.

Do an experiment or two to demonstrate for yourself the effect of gaze direction. Assume the bottom position with knees out, toes out, and heels down. Put your chin down slightly and look at a point on the floor 4 or 5 feet in front of you. Now drive your hips up out of the bottom, and take note of how this feels. Now do the same thing while looking at the ceiling. If you have a training partner or coach, get in the bottom position and have him block your hips, with a hand placed firmly on your lower back and pushing straight down, so that you have something to push up on, but not so that he pushes you forward. Push up against the resistance while looking down at your floor focus point, and note the effectiveness of your hip drive and the power it produces. Then try this movement again while looking up. You will discover an amazing thing – that the chin-down (looking down keeps the chin down), eyes-down position enables your hip drive to function almost automatically. In contrast, the upward eye gaze pulls the chest forward, the knees forward, and the hips forward – just a little, but enough to produce a profound effect. It slacks the hamstrings and all the posterior muscles we are trying to keep tight so that we can use them to drive the hips up. The first time you do this experiment will convince you that looking down is more efficient.

Looking at the floor also provides the eyes with a fixed position reference. Using this reference, you can easily identify any deviation from the correct movement pattern and adjust it as it happens. The ceiling also provides a reference, but the neck position is unsafe, and anything you're looking at upward will be farther away than the floor when you're at the bottom of the squat. It's hard to imagine a room in which the floor isn't closer to the eyes than the ceiling is; the floor is therefore more useful as a reference – smaller movements can be detected against the closer point.

Most people will have more trouble with this change in their eye gaze direction than with any other aspect of this squatting method. To correct the error of looking up, fix your eyes on a position on the floor 4 or 5 feet in front of you. If you're training close to a wall, find a place to look at that is low on the wall and results in the same neck position. Stare at this point, and get used to looking at it so that it requires no conscious effort. Most people, if they are looking down, will not raise their heads to the point where neck position is affected. Inventive coaches have used tennis balls for the purpose of demonstrating a chin-down, chest-up position (Figure 2-16).

ADDING THE BAR

Now you're ready to squat. You have already been in the position you will go to at the bottom, and now you're just going back down there with the bar. First, chalk your hands. Chalk is always a good idea because it dries out the skin. Dry skin is less prone to folding and abrasion than moist skin and therefore is less prone to problem callus formation. If the weight room is not equipped with chalk, bring your own. If the gym complains, change gyms.

The squat begins at the power rack or the squat stands, whichever is available. Set the rack height so that the bar in the rack is at about the level of your mid-sternum. Many people will perceive this as too low, but it's better to be a little low taking the bar out of the rack than to have to tiptoe back into the rack with a heavy weight. Often, this position in the empty rack will look low because the diameter of the bar sitting in the hooks tells the eye a different story about its true height in the rack. When the bar is placed in the rack, the eye will be more comfortable with the setting. And remember, we are placing the bar in a lower position than the top of the traps, so you'll need the rack lower than you think. You'd rather have the rack set a little too low than a little too high, and most people are not as tall as they think they are. *Most people will want to use a position in the rack that is too high.* If your shoulders are not flexible enough to assume the low-bar position at first, they should stretch out over a couple of weeks.

Face the bar. Always an empty bar at first. ALWAYS. There will be plenty of time very soon to add weight. Take an even grip on the bar, measured from the markings placed on the bar for this purpose. A standard power bar has 16–17 inches between the ends of the outside knurl, and 32 inches between the finger marks, those ⅛-inch gaps in the knurl indicating a legal bench-press grip. Grip width for the squat will obviously vary

Figure 2-17. A comparison of wide and narrow grips. Note the difference in tightness of the upper back muscles and the resulting difference in bar support potential.

Figure 2-18. Wrist alignment on the bar. The correct grip keeps the hand above the bar and keeps all of the weight of the bar on the back. An incorrect grip intercepts some of the weight, loading the wrists and elbows. Note that the thumb is on top of the bar and the hand is between the outer ring and the inner edge of the knurling.

with shoulder width and flexibility, but in general, the hands will be between these two markings on this type of bar. A narrower grip allows a flexible person to better support the bar with the posterior muscles of the shoulders when the elbows are lifted, and a wider grip allows an inflexible person to get more comfortable under the bar. In either case, a narrower grip tightens your shoulder muscles so that the bar is supported by muscle and doesn't dig into your back. The thumbs should be placed on top of the bar so that the wrists can be held in a straight line with the forearms. The elbows should be cranked up to trap the bar between the hands and the back. If a lack of flexibility in the chest and shoulders prevents your achieving this position, use the high-bar position until proper stretching can make you flexible enough to get the bar down to a better position. If you're flexible enough now, take a grip wide enough to permit straight wrists under the bar, and then with each set, narrow your grip a little until it is tight and secure. Mark this position as the grip you will use.

With your grip in place, and your hands and thumbs on top of the bar, dip your head under the bar, and come up into position with the bar on your back. Place the bar in the correct position, just immediately under the bone you feel at the top of the shoulder blades – the spine of the scapula – and then secure it in place by lifting your elbows and chest at the same time (Figure 2-20). It should

feel as though the bar is resting on a "shelf" under the traps and on top of the posterior deltoids. This action tightens the muscles of your back and lifts your chest, placing the thoracic spine in an extended, straight position and thereby fixing many of the problems encountered with a round-back position. Enormous weights can be safely handled this way later. *Most people starting with this method will place the bar too high on the back*, perhaps just above the scapular spine instead of just below it. Check to make sure the bar is in the right position.

First and foremost, **ALWAYS STEP BACK OUT OF THE RACK. ALWAYS. NEVER PUT THE BAR BACK IN THE RACK BY STEPPING BACKWARDS. NEVER.** This cannot be done safely. You should never be in a position to have to step backwards and rack a weight at the end of a set. You cannot see the hooks, and even if you have spotters, there will eventually be a wreck. If you do this, or permit it to be done by someone you're training, you are a fool.

Take the bar out of the rack in the same position in which it is to be squatted, with the torso and shoulders tight, the chest and elbows up, the head position down, and both feet under the bar. Everything should be the same as it is for the full squat, so take the bar off of the hooks by extending the knees and hips, just as in the top of a squat. In this way, any weight can be taken safely out of the rack. Many problems are caused by doing this

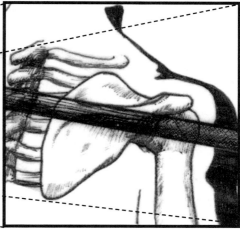

Figure 2-19. Position of the barbell relative to the scapular anatomy. The bar is just under the spine of the scapula.

improperly. It is very common to take the bar out of the rack with a loose back and chest, and then attempt to tighten everything just before squatting. It is obviously much more effective to tighten the muscles and *then* take the weight onto tight muscles than it is to take the weight, let it mash down into your back through loose muscles until it stops on some crucial skeletal component, and then try to tighten everything up underneath it. Likewise, taking the bar out with one foot back and only one foot under the bar, like a lunge, is a bad habit, one

that everybody gets away with when the weight is light but that can cause back problems from the unevenly stressed hips when the weight gets heavier. Unrack the bar exactly like it is in a squat, even when it is light, and you'll have no problems later when it is heavy.

Once the bar leaves the rack, don't take a hike with it, backing up three or four steps before setting up to squat. This is unnecessary, and it could become a problem if the set is heavy, the spotters are unreliable, or the trip back to the rack is just too

Figure 2-20. Simultaneous lifting of the elbows and the chest "trap" the bar between the hands and the back, creating a stable back and chest position and a tight bar placement on top of the posterior delts.

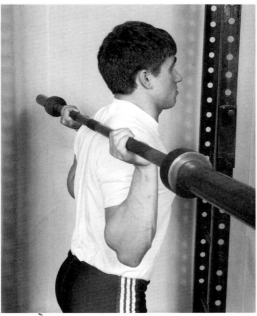

Figure 2-21. The proper position in which to receive the bar from the rack.

far on this particular day. One step back out of the rack with good form is enough to clear the rack and allow the spotters to do their job while minimizing the trouble of getting the bar back home.

The stance should be the same as the one used during the stretch. Again, heels should be about shoulder width apart, with toes pointed out about 30 degrees. *Most people will change the stance at this point, rotating the toes back in.* Make sure you are using the same stance you previously used during the unweighted part of this teaching method.

At this point, you are ready to squat with the empty bar. THE EMPTY BAR. All of the groundwork has been laid, the correct bottom position is fresh in your mind, and you are now in the correct starting position. Everything you are about to do is the same as you did during the stretch. Only two things are different: one, you don't have your elbows available to help push your knees out, so you need to do this with your brain. And two, don't stop at the bottom. Just go down and immediately come back up, driving your butt straight up, not forward, out of the bottom. Now, take a big breath and hold it, look down at a spot on the floor about 4–5 feet in front of you, and squat.

You should be in good balance at the bottom of the squat, having already been there

when you stretched. Your weight should stay evenly balanced over the middle of your feet. The reference point your eyes have on the floor should help you maintain position all the way down and all the way up. Balance problems usually indicate a back angle that is too vertical, so make sure you're sitting back and leaning forward enough. *Most people have a picture in their minds of a vertical torso during the squat.* Remember that the back angle will not be vertical at all; sit back, lean forward, and shove your knees out.

Get someone to verify that your depth is good, and DO NOT accept anything less than full depth, ever, from this point on. If your impartial critic tells you that you're high, check your stance to make sure that it's wide enough but not too wide, that your toes are out enough, and that your knees are tracking parallel to your feet. While he's being helpful, get him to check your eye gaze direction and to remind you to look down every rep. If you're sure the form is fairly good, do a set of five and rack the bar. If the form is good except for the depth, the squat itself will act as a stretch IF YOUR KNEES ARE OUT. And most of the time, if you are high, it is because your knees are not out. *Most people who have problems with the squat — at this rank novice level as well as later on — do not shove their knees out*

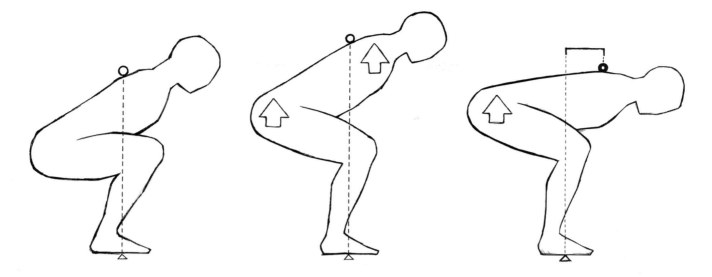

Figure 2-22. The back angle during the drive up from the bottom is critical to the correct use of the hips. The correct angle is produced when the bar is just below the spine of the scapula and directly over the middle of the foot, the back is held tight in lumbar and thoracic extension, the knees are parallel to the correctly placed feet, and the correct depth is reached. Flopping forward allows the bar to drop forward of the mid-foot.

enough. If the squat is crazy bad, rack the bar and repeat the pre-squat procedure, focusing on the knees-out part.

To rack the bar safely and easily, walk forward until it touches the vertical parts of the rack. Find the uprights, not the hooks. You can't miss the uprights, and if you touch them, you'll be over the hooks. If you try to set the bar directly down on the hooks, you can and will eventually miss it on one side. Big wreck.

The general plan is to do a couple more sets of five reps with the empty bar to nail down the form, and then add weight, do another set of five, and keep increasing in even increments until the next increase would compromise the form. Sets of five are a good number to learn with – not so many that fatigue affects form during the last reps, but enough to establish and practice the technique while handling enough weight to get strong. Increments for increasing the weight between sets will vary with the trainee. Lightweight, unconditioned kids need to go up in 10–15 lb or 5–7.5 kg jumps. Older or stronger trainees can use 20–30 lb or 10–15 kg increments. Decide which jumps best fit your situation, being conservative since it is your first day. *Most people will*

try to increase the weight by increments that are too large for this point in the teaching method. Go on up in weight, practicing good form and making sure to keep good depth, until you can tell that the next jump up would alter your form. Then do two more sets at the current weight, for a total of three sets across with the heaviest weight. And that is the first squat workout.

The Important Things You're Going to Do Wrong

Depth: You're probably going to squat to a position above parallel. This will occur because you're not looking down, you're not shoving your knees out, you have a stance that is either too narrow or too wide, or you have not committed to going deep.

Knee position: You will fail to shove your knees out as you start down. This will make correct depth hard to attain and will kill your hip drive.

Stance: Your stance will be either too narrow or too wide, with your toes usually pointed too forward. This will result in a squat that is not below parallel.

Figure 2-23. The squat.

Eye gaze: You will fail to look down. This will kill your hip drive.

Back angle: Your back will (usually) be too vertical, due to a faulty mental picture of what your hips do when you squat or due to the incorrect placement of the bar on your back, or your back will be too horizontal, due to your failure to keep your chest up. Either error will adversely affect hip drive and depth.

Hip drive: You will lift your chest instead of driving your hips up. This will kill your power out of the bottom by making your back angle too vertical.

Bar placement: You will place the bar too high on your back. This will adversely affect your back angle and your hip drive.

Rack height: You will set the bar in the rack in a position that is too high. This will make the preferred position on the back difficult to attain.

Notice that all of these problems are extremely interrelated. The squat is a complex, multi-joint exercise whose correct execution depends on all the components of the entire system functioning together. An incorrect placement of any component will perturb the entire system to its detriment. A

Figure 2-24. Don't do this, you fool.

working knowledge of the functional mechanics of the system is important if you are to understand the contribution of each component to the system, and the workings of the system as a whole.

Leverage and Moment – The Basis of Barbell Training

If the system of barbell training you are about to study is to be more than just another collection of opinions about the subject, it must proceed from more than just the history of the activity, the preferences of the author, and the observed habits of those people who happen to be performing at a high level. History is filled with examples of less-than-efficient behavior that is nonetheless effective; personal preferences quite often reflect an unquenchable bias; people are often good at things without knowing exactly why, and these folks might be even better at them if they did. It seems likely that barbell training would be more efficiently performed if it had more in common with engineering than with astrology – more like physics class than birthday party – and it would be more effectively coached if it were developed from mechanics rather than from folklore.

An understanding of the forces affecting the lifter and the barbell is essential to forming an accurate analysis of the movements used in barbell training. The squat, bench press, deadlift, press, and power clean are potentially complicated multi-joint exercises that form the basic movements employed in barbell training. The complexity of these movements is mitigated by the fact that they are all quite natural expressions of loaded human movement – the ways that the skeletal system translates the force of muscle contraction into movement as the body interacts with its environment. But if these natural movements are to effectively and efficiently function as exercises, they must be tailored to specifically cause the use of the most muscle mass over the longest range of motion so that the most weight can be lifted and thus produce the most effective strength adaptation.

If we develop an accurate description of each exercise based on an understanding of what each one is supposed to accomplish in terms of movement against a loaded bar, how this movement is most efficiently accomplished using muscular contractile force translated through the skeletal components that transfer the force to the load, and which physical adaptations will accompany an ability to handle increasing loads in each particular movement pattern, we will have what can be described as a *model* of the exercise.

This model must be grounded in an understanding of the principles that govern the motions within a physical system. And a grasp of each model makes the performance and coaching of each movement more straightforward, logical, and understandable. The science of *classical mechanics* studies the effects of forces on the motions of material bodies. An extensive treatment of this science is obviously outside the scope of our discussion, but a basic understanding of a few of its concepts is critical to the development of an accurate model for each exercise in this method of barbell training. These concepts are important to understand because the system of levers you will use to lift the barbell – your muscles moving your skeleton, loaded by the barbell in a gravitational framework – obeys the laws of mechanics, and you must know them before you can analyze your lifting to optimize the way you do it.

So, let's start with the most basic concept and build on it. As noted previously, the agent that produces the weight of the loaded barbell is *gravity*. It is produced by the mass of the planet, and for our purposes the planet is assumed to be a uniform sphere. Every unimpeded object will fall in a direction perpendicular to the surface of this sphere. The term "level" is used to denote a surface parallel to the surface of the planet, so that if an object is dropped, it always falls perpendicular to "level," and we describe this path as *vertical*. The force exerted by the weight of a loaded bar is therefore always vertical and down, and the only way to oppose the force of a freely moving barbell is with a force that is vertical and up. Horizontal force may be applied to the bar during its trip through the rep, but none of the horizontal force can contribute to the vertical

motion of the bar. So, to the extent that squatting, pulling, or pressing a loaded bar works against gravity, the vertical components of the force do the work. This means that the most efficient bar path for a barbell moving in a gravitational framework is always a straight vertical line; not only is this path the shortest distance between the two points, but any force applied in any other direction is not work against the force of gravity (see Figure 2-3, page 10).

Gravity is expressed as three primary forces that affect the lifter/barbell system: tension, compression, and moment.

Tension is the force transmitted along an object that would elongate *if* it were deformable (not every object is deformable under normal gym circumstances). An example would be the body of a lifter hanging from the chin-up bar.

Compression is the force transmitted along an object that would get shorter if it were deformable. Compression is the opposite of tension, and an example would be the body of a lifter standing under the loaded squat bar.

Both tension and compression are said to be *axial* forces because they are expressed parallel to the axis of the force that generates them, gravity.

Moment is force that tends to cause a rotation about an axis. It is the force that is transmitted down a wrench handle to turn a bolt. Moment can also be thought of as "leverage" or bending force.

When the bar is carried on the back, or overhead in the lockout position of the press, the force it applies is compression. When the bar hangs from the arms in a deadlift or a clean, the force along the arms is tension. The bones transmit compressive force, and the connective tissues and muscles transmit tension. Both the connective tissues and the bones working together transmit moment (leverage). If the bar is supported overhead and then lowered in an arc to the hang position of the deadlift, all three forces – compression at the

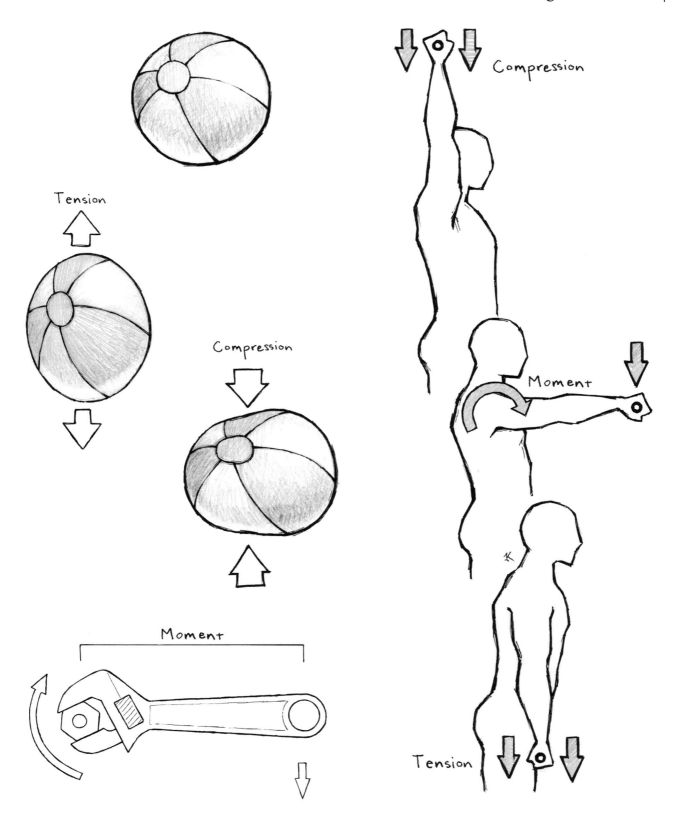

Figure 2-25. Tension, compression, and moment are the expressions of the force of gravity across the lifter/barbell system.

Figure 2-26. Compression, moment, and tension expressed through the upper body with a loaded bar.

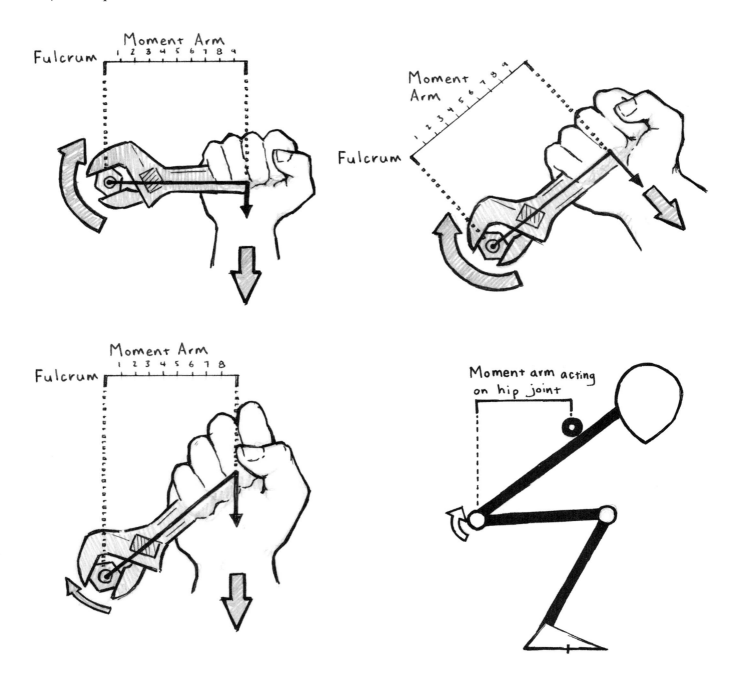

Figure 2-27. The moment arm is the distance between the point of rotation and the point of the application of force along a rigid segment, measured at 90 degrees from the point of force application. In barbell training, gravity provides the force, and gravity always acts vertically and down.

top, moment as the arms travel through the arc to the body, and tension as the bar comes to rest on the legs – can be experienced in that order.

A *moment arm* is the distance between a point of rotation and the point at which the rotational force is applied, measured at 90 degrees from the point of the force application. When you're using a wrench, for example, the moment arm is the distance along the handle, between the point of rotation (the bolt) and the force that causes the rotation (your hand), *measured at 90 degrees to the force.* Moment is the force transmitted along a rigid bar to act on a pivot, or *fulcrum*. The moment arm (the term "lever arm" is synonymous) is essentially a way to calculate the amount of moment force generated by a lever: *the moment force is the force applied to the bar multiplied by the length of the moment arm.* At one end of the system, force is being applied to the bar. At the other end of the system, the turning force is being resisted by the object being turned, so that along the rigid bar, force is acting in two directions. (For this reason, moment is a *shear* force, in contrast to the axial forces of tension and compression.) The "moment arm" is the effective distance over which the system operates. The longer the moment arm is, the more turning force is produced by the actual force applied to the bar.

The most effective angle to pull on the wrench handle is perpendicular to it. This is intuitively obvious to anyone who has ever used the device; you adjust the position of the jaws on the conveniently designed hexagonal head – shaped this way for just this purpose – so that you can pull on the wrench at right angles to it, regardless of the angle at which the job causes the wrench to fit on the bolt. *If you pull at any angle other than 90 degrees, some of the force will be either compression or tension along the wrench handle* – 90 degrees is the only angle at which *all* of the pulling force causes the wrench to turn the bolt. Since 90 degrees is the most effective angle at which to pull, any other angle is only as effective as the distance along the moment arm measured at 90 degrees, thus the convention of measuring its length at this angle (see Figure 2-27).

The amount of turning force that can be applied to the bolt varies with the length of the moment arm (the distance from the working end of the wrench to your grip, measured at 90 degrees to your pull) and the amount of force applied to it (how hard you pull on the wrench). You can increase the amount of turning force either by pulling harder or by lengthening the handle – by getting a longer wrench or extending its length with a "cheater pipe."

In barbell training, the turning force is the force of gravity acting on the barbell, and the moment arms are the horizontal distances between barbell and joint along the segments of the body over which this force acts. The instant the knees and hips

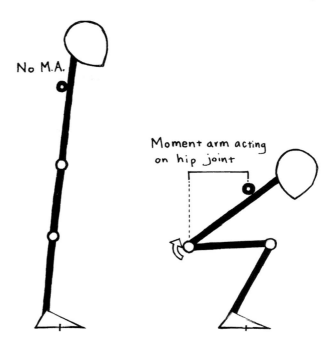

Figure 2-28.The moment arm along the back segment in the squat. (*M.A. = moment arm*)

are unlocked and our diagnostic angles come into existence along the back, thigh, and shank segments in the squat, moment arms come into existence between the end points of these segments and the location of the barbell relative to the segment and the balance point under the mid-foot. The force of gravity always operates straight down – the hand turning this particular wrench is gravity, and it's always pulling straight down from the bar. So we can calculate the moment arms along the segments as measured perpendicular to the bar.

This means that the length of the moment arms along the back segment in the squat will always be the horizontal distance between the bar and the hips. For the thigh segment, the moment arms will be the horizontal distance between the bar and the hips, and the bar and the knees, since the femur is bisected by the gravity vector, and the moment arm can be considered from either hip or knee. The hip extensors "see" the femur moment arm between the hip and the bar, and the knee extensors "see" the femur moment between the knee and the bar. Likewise, along the shank segment between knees and ankles, the moments can be regarded as between bar and ankles, and between bar and knees.

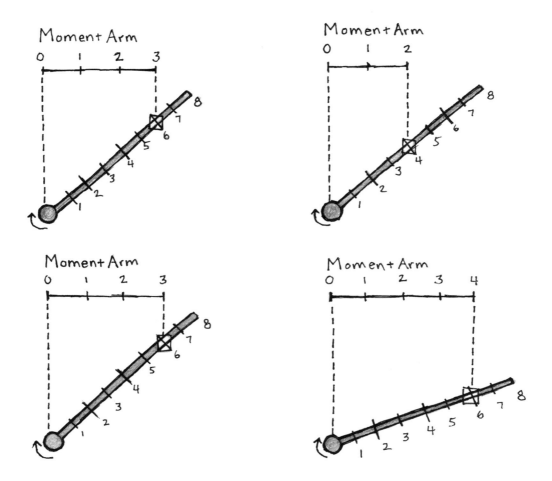

Figure 2-29. The moment arm varies in length with angle and segment length. If the segment length changes and the angle is held constant (*top panels*), or if the angle changes and the segment length is held constant (*bottom panels*), the moment arms can be varied.

The moment arm between the bar and the hips will thus vary with the bar position on the back and the angle at which the back is inclined. If the bar is in the low position advocated here, the distance between hips and bar is shorter than it would be if the bar were in the higher position. But since the bar must be maintained over the mid-foot balance point, the lower bar position requires a more horizontal back angle. And for the same reason, the more vertical back angle compensates for the longer distance between bar and hips in the high-bar position. The moment arm – the horizontal distance – between hips and barbell in both positions may indeed be the same length. But we don't use the low-bar position because it reduces moment force on the back segment; **we use it because the more horizontal back angle, closed hip angle, and open knee angle place the hips further behind the mid-foot balance point, so the hamstrings, glutes, and adductors have to work harder to maintain the angle and come up out of the bottom than they do when the knees are farther forward and the hips are closer to the bar.** This anatomical manipulation adds their mass to the muscles moving the load, and thus also enables heavier weight to be used.

There is another way to consider the moments active in the lifter/barbell system. In each case, a moment arm involves a force on one end, a point of rotation on the other end, and a segment transmitting the force in between. Consider the effect of the bar on your shoulders as it relates to the balance

Figure 2-30. "Balance" defined as the absence of a horizontal moment arm along a vertically-oriented system.

point at the mid-foot. If the bar moves forward or backward from its ideal position directly over the mid-foot – i.e., you apply any force horizontally to the bar – and the mid-foot balance point is thought of as a point of rotation, then between the bar and the mid-foot, a rotational force is created that acts along the whole system. This horizontal force creates a moment arm that is expressed *vertically* along the body between mid-foot and barbell.

Now, it is true that the foot is a flat surface (the sole of your shoe) in contact with another flat surface (the floor), and the actual point of rotation nearest the floor would be the ankle. But given that the calf stabilizes the ankle, that the load shifts in relation to the mid-foot if the bar and your body move forward or backward, and that the greater the weight and distance, the larger the effect, the system behaves like a moment arm acting on a point of rotation at the mid-foot. This leverage has the potential to add quite a bit to the force needed to overcome the weight of the bar, which happens as the bar moves forward of the balance point.

Forward is the usual direction of off-balance movement due to the vagaries of human anatomy – the ankle is behind the mid-foot, the knees articulate forward, and the eyes are forward-directed. Most people who have been training for more than a couple of weeks will not put themselves

in the rather awkward position of moving back with the bar on the shoulders. And since the body is in an asymmetrical position at the bottom of a squat or a deadlift, with more of the body behind the bar than in front of it, it would be simplistic to conclude that the same amount of movement forward and backward from the mid-foot would affect the system symmetrically, i.e., that a forward bar movement of 3 inches would have to be reacted against with the same force as a backward bar path deviation of the same 3 inches.

Considered in this context, the term "out of balance" means that a moment (rotational force) exists between the bar and the mid-foot vertically along the body, and this moment must be controlled with an amount of force necessary to cancel its effects. This is force that could be more productively used to lift more weight on the bar if it were "in balance." So your ability to control the moment between bar and mid-foot – your ability to maintain a vertical relationship between barbell and mid-foot – is your ability to use good technique in lifting.

We must consider the effects of two systems of leverage while we squat. The moments operating horizontally along the segments of the body are produced by the force of gravity acting on the load. They are inherent in squatting down and standing back up under a heavy barbell; they make up the

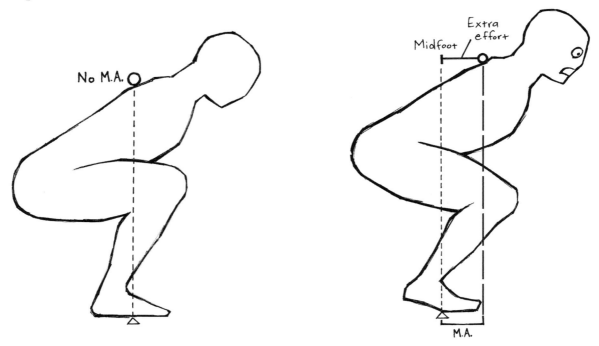

Figure 2-31. Good technique in the squat is the ability to maintain zero moment between the bar and the mid-foot balance point. This completes the concept presented in Figure 2-7 – the extra effort is due to the existence of the moment arm between bar and midfoot. (*M.A.* = *moment arm*)

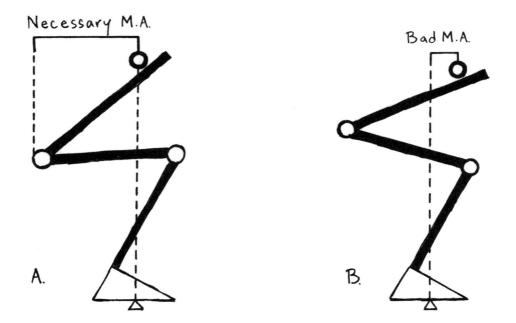

Figure 2-32. The concepts of moment force applied to the body during the squat. (A) The moment force A, along the segments, is inherent in performing the motion of squatting and is thus the force against which we exercise. (B) The moment force B, between the bar and the mid-foot balance point considered vertically, must be kept to ZERO for greatest efficiency. Moment force B adversely affects the work done against moment force A. (*M.A.* = *moment arm*)

resistance against which we work to get strong. The moment operating vertically between the bar and the mid-foot balance point, however, must be kept at ZERO to avoid wasting force that could otherwise be used to lift more weight. Both of these moments must be considered when you're analyzing the biomechanics of the system.

Common Problems Everyone Should Know How to Solve

A correct squat will always have certain identifiable characteristics controlled by skeletal anatomy and muscle function. For any squat, back or front, these conditions will be satisfied, making it relatively easy to determine whether form and position are correct. At the top, all the skeletal components that support the bar – the knees, hips, and spine – will be locked in extension so that the muscular components have to exert only enough force to maintain this position, in which compression is the primary force on the skeletal components. The job of the muscles here is to keep the bones lined up correctly so they can hold up the load. The bar will be over the middle of the foot. The heavier the weight, the more critical this position will be.

When the squat begins its eccentric phase, all the muscles that will ultimately extend these joints – or in the case of the spinal erector muscles, isometrically maintain extension under increasing stress – come under mechanical load as they resist the leverage along the segments on the way to the bottom position. During this ride to the bottom, the bar must maintain its position over the mid-foot. The correct bottom position is identified by definite anatomical position markers:

- The spine will be held rigid in lumbar and thoracic extension.

- The bar will be directly over the middle of the foot.

- The feet will be flat on the ground at the correct angle for the stance width.

- The thighs will be parallel to the feet.

- The hip joint will be in a position lower than the top of the patella.

Any deviation from this position will constitute bad technique, as will any movement on the way down or back up that causes a deviation from this position. And actually, if you keep the bar in the correct vertical position over the mid-foot on the way down and back up – as if the bar were riding in a narrow slot directly plumb to the mid-foot – you will have done it right. Your skeleton will have solved the problem of how to most efficiently use your muscles to get the job of squatting done. It will have done so within the constraints imposed upon it by the mechanics of the barbell/body/gravity system.

The position of the bar on the torso will control the angle of the back, and the angle of the back and the stance will control the forward or back position of the knees. When the bar is in the front squat position, the back will be quite vertical because this angle is necessary to keep the bar over the mid-foot and to prevent it from falling forward off the shoulders. When the back is this vertical, the hips are nearly directly under the bar, a position which forces the knees well forward in front of the toes and which the ankles must accommodate by allowing the tibias to incline (Figure 2-33). This means that for the front squat, the back angle will be nearly vertical, the hip angle will be open, and the knee angle will be closed. For the back squat, when the bar is in the position advocated here, just below the spine of the scapula, the back will be at a much more horizontal angle, and the knees will be at a point just in front of the toes (depending on your anthropometry), so that the hip angle will be more closed and the knee angle more open. A high-bar squat would place the back and knees in the middle of these two more useful positions.

Every barbell exercise that involves the feet on the floor and a barbell supported by the body will be in its best balance, both during the movement and at lockout, when the bar is vertically plumb to the middle of the foot, as discussed earlier. An assistance exercise like the barbell curl or the goodmorning intentionally moves the bar out of line as a part of creating the resistance for the exercise.

GRIP AND ARMS

Grip errors are common even among experienced lifters. The grip on the bar is the first part of your temporary relationship with the barbell that is referred to as a *set*. If that grip is wrong, none of the reps in that set will be optimal because the relationship of the body to the bar is determined first by hand position on the bar. For instance, an uncentered placement of the bar on your back results in an asymmetrical loading of all the components under the bar – that is, more weight on one leg, hip, and knee than on the other – as well as a spinal shear. A careless approach to grip placement can result in problems with heavy weights. Most people, as discussed earlier, will need to take an even grip somewhere between the score mark and the end of the knurl.

There is, however, an important exception to this rule: for a trainee whose shoulders have significant differences in flexibility – as might result from an injury – a symmetrical grip on the bar will result in an asymmetrical bar position on the back. A tight shoulder on the left side, for example, prevents the upper arm from assuming the same angle as that used on the uninjured right side. The tight shoulder thus drags the bar out toward that side, resulting in the bar's being off-center left and out-of-level on the back. If this is your situation – and it might require a third party or a mirror to identify this, since it is not always easy to feel – you will need to experiment with your grip until you find the right position for each hand. Centered loading of the back should be your primary concern at this stage.

As we discussed earlier, the thumb should be placed on top of the bar so that the wrist can be held in a straight line with the forearm. The vast majority of people, however, will prefer to hold the bar with a thumbs-around grip. At lighter weights, this is fine because the load is easy to keep in place. But when heavier weights are being used, the grip that results from thumbs-around can create its own

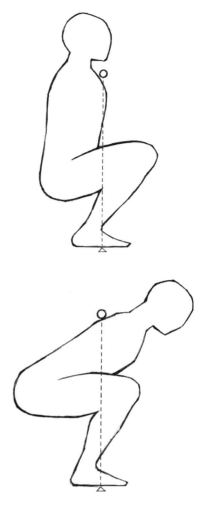

Figure 2-33. Bar position ultimately determines back angle, as seen in this comparison of the front squat and the squat. Note that the bar remains balanced over the mid-foot in each case, and this requires that the back angle accommodate the bar position. This is the primary factor in the differences in technique between the two styles of squatting.

problems. Most people have a mental picture of the hands holding up the weight, and this usually ends up being what happens. The bar sits in the grip with the thumbs around the bar, the wrists are bent back, the elbows end up directly below the weight, and nothing really prevents the bar from sliding down the back from this position. People who do this will eventually have sore elbows, a horrible, headache-like soreness in the inside of the elbow that makes them think the injury occurred doing curls. If the elbows are underneath the weight, and the force of

Figure 2-34. Incorrect (*left*) and correct (*right*) use of the hands and arms under the bar. Elbows should be elevated to the rear with the hands on top of the bar, not placed directly under the bar, where they intercept part of the weight.

the weight is straight down (the nature of gravity is sometimes inconvenient), then the wrists and elbows will unavoidably intercept some of the weight (Figure 2-34). With heavy weights, the loading can be quite high, and these structures are not nearly as capable of supporting 500 pounds as the back is.

If the thumbs are on top of the bar, the hands can assume a position that is straight in line with the forearms when the elbows are raised. If you are accustomed to letting your wrists relax into extension and letting your elbows drop, your grip might be too narrow for your shoulder flexibility, and a slightly wider grip would make straight wrists easier to maintain. You might also need to actively "curl" the wrist into what will feel like flexion if you have been passively allowing it to extend. In the correct position, the wrist is straight, neither flexed nor extended; none of the weight is over any part of the arm, wrist, or hand; and all of the weight is on the back (Figure 2-34). Learn to carry all of the weight of the bar safely on your back before your strength improves to the point where this same weight carried in your hands – and thus on your wrists and elbows – can become a problem.

Occasionally a person gets misled into thinking that it is okay to put the hands out so wide on the bar that the fingers or even the palms of the hands are in contact with the plates. Bizarre as this sounds, you will eventually see this in the gym. As grip width increases, upper-back muscle tightness decreases and muscular support for the bar is diminished, as previously discussed. If the

posterior deltoids, rotator cuff muscles, traps, and rhomboids relax due to a widened grip, the skeleton becomes the default support structure. This is less than desirable. To add to the problem by placing the hands on the plates – a ROTATING pair of objects at the far end of the bar – is just silly. You must be in control of the bar, and this means that it must be secure on your back and therefore in your grip.

As is often the case in athletics, one problem is intimately associated with another, and the solving of one fixes the other. A lack of shoulder tightness and failure to keep the chest up are related problems and must be corrected together. If your elbows drop, your shoulders relax; if you lift your elbows, your shoulders tighten. Likewise, lifting the chest requires a contraction of the upper back muscles, especially the superior portion of the longissimus dorsi complex. Lifting the chest is *thoracic spinal extension*, a back movement. The act of tightening the shoulders and lifting the elbows aids the thoracic extension muscles by helping to support the bar at the point where it is mashing down into the back. If you do both of these things at the same time, all the muscles under the bar tighten. And if you do this before you take the weight of the bar onto your back, the bar cannot sink down through loose muscle, unsupported against the skeletal components of the shoulder. Lifting the elbows and the chest together tightens the supporting muscles under the bar, so do this before you let the weight bury itself in your back.

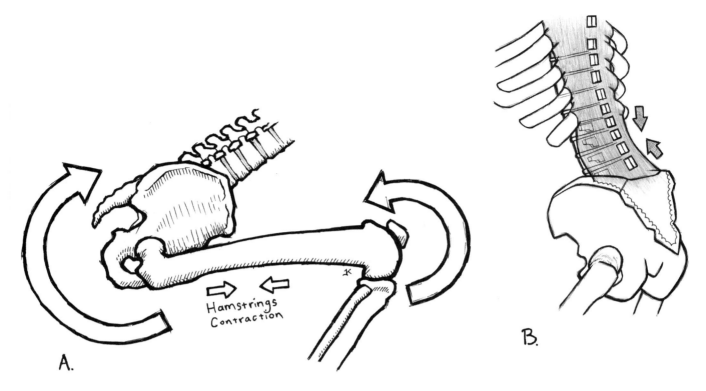

Figure 2-35. (A) The relationship of the bones of the lumbar spine, pelvis, femur, and upper tibia and the actions of the muscles that move them, in profile. The squat has the reputation of being a quadriceps exercise, but the hamstrings are also strongly developed during the full squat. (B) The spinal erectors attach to the pelvis, ribs, and vertebrae, and extend the spine when in contraction. This "arching" action is accomplished in conjunction with the underlying multifidis, rotators, interspinales, and intertransversarii muscles. When contracted, these muscles move the spine into the position shown by the arrows.

Many people seem to be making a flat, level spot for the bar to sit on by keeping their chest parallel to the floor. It is as if they think that bending over into a position of spinal flexion makes the bar less likely to roll off the back. The bar will not roll off your back if you properly grip the bar, with your hands in the right position, and raise your elbows. When the elbows come up and the chest comes up, the hands are pushed forward and the bar is actually forced forward into the back, trapped between the hands and the rack position, so it cannot go anywhere. This jamming effect creates a tight, secure bar position that can tolerate changes of angle, acceleration, and deceleration.

BACK

Although the squat has an undeserved, baseless reputation for knee injury, its greatest danger is to the spine. Lower-back injuries – usually due to form problems – are more common by far than knee injuries, and care must be taken to prevent them. It's not hard to hurt your lower back, and back injuries are the most common workplace injury, amounting to many billions of dollars per year in treatment costs and lost productivity. Lifters are susceptible as well, although our problems with lower-back injuries are most often associated with activities outside the gym. We know this because hundreds of thousands of young lifters at the mercy of inexperienced, pigheaded coaches are permitted to lift heavy weights with bad spinal mechanics every day, and the rate of injury in the weight room remains low. The most dangerous movement for the spine is flexion with rotation under a load, and we don't do this in barbell training – we do it when putting the lawn mower in the back of the truck. So barbell training, even done incorrectly, is comparatively safe. But doing it wrong is much more dangerous than doing it correctly. Our primary concern is that doing it wrong is also *inefficient*, so we'll do it right because that ultimately allows us to lift more weight and get stronger, and safety will be a welcome side effect.

Understanding the role of the lower back in lifting mechanics requires an understanding of the anatomy of the hip and leg musculature, as well as of spinal anatomy. Remember from our previous discussion that the spine acts as a rigid bar to transmit moment force generated by the muscles that extend the hips and knees. The spine is held rigid by the musculature of the trunk, and it is moved through space by the muscles that extend the pelvis, into which the spine is locked by the muscles of the low back.

The hamstring group consists of the biceps femoris, the semimembranosus, and the semitendinosus, all three of which attach to the ischial tuberosity of the pelvis. They all insert at various points on the tibia, behind the knee on the lower leg. This configuration means that the

hamstring group crosses two joints, the hip and the knee, and therefore technically has two functions: the proximal function (hip extension), and the distal function (knee flexion). The hamstrings can also act isometrically against both attachments to control the back angle. When you squat, ultimately it is hip extension – straightening out the hip joint, their proximal function – that you produce with the hamstrings, along with the glutes and adductors. (In reality, the hamstrings can control hip extension, knee flexion, and back angle while functioning eccentrically, concentrically, and isometrically; the definitions of these functions are blurry, and are really significant only when we isolate joints on exercise machines. The complexities of normal movement do not lend themselves to such constructed distinctions.)

Squatting power is generated by the hips and legs and is transmitted up the rigid trunk segment to the load resting on the shoulders. The spinal column is held rigid in its normal anatomical position by the muscles of the back, sides, rib cage, and abs so that the force can be safely transmitted through the trunk to the load. Before you lift anything heavy, you squeeze your abs (really, you squeeze everything in the vicinity of your abs) into contraction. This squeezing transforms your trunk into what is essentially a rigid cylinder that surrounds and supports the spine. The effect is that of a hydrostatic column – an uncompressible column of fluid that is therefore capable of transmitting compressive force – between the contracting abdominal wall and the spine. The force of contraction transmitted through this fluid medium braces the spine into the position set by the back muscles until the load overcomes your ability to stay in position. These muscles contract isometrically – that is, they stay in contraction but *cause* no movement to occur – and in doing so, they *permit* no movement to occur.

The pelvis articulates with the spine in the L5/S1 area of the lower back, the area above the tailbone. The muscles of the lower back – the erector spinae group, or "spinal erectors" – insert on the pelvis and at numerous points along the spinal column. When these muscles are contracted, the pelvis remains in a constant position relative to the

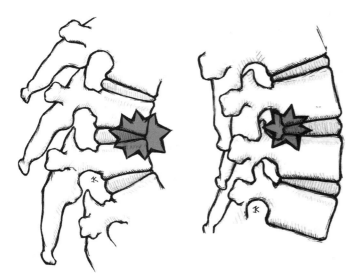

Figure 2-36. Proper spinal alignment ensures the anatomically correct distribution of forces across the intervertebral discs during loading. Improper vertebral position under load can result in either anterior or posterior squeezing of the discs and the injuries that accompany this bad position.

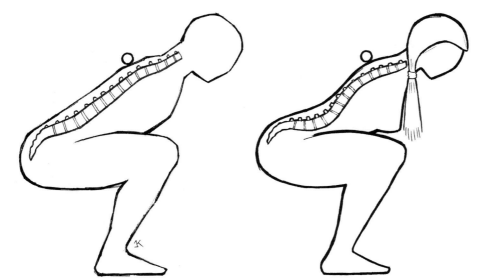

Figure 2-37. Lumbar overextension (*right*) is not the correct back position to use in the squat. It indicates a failure to engage enough abdominal contraction to support the spine from the anterior.

lumbar vertebrae. The spinal erectors and associated lower back ligaments serve to lock the pelvis and spine into a rigid structure – to protect the vertebral column from movement under load and to hold all these joints in their normal anatomical positions when you're lifting heavy loads – so that the intervertebral discs are not damaged. This area needs to stay arched to stay safe when you're lifting. And this is why the pelvis must tilt forward at the same angle as the lower back as you lean forward.

However, as the squat approaches the bottom position, the necessary forward lean of the trunk can have a tendency to make the lower back assume a flexed, rounded position. This tendency is caused by the hamstring anatomy and the position of the thighs. As squat depth increases and the torso assumes a more forward tilt, the bottom of the pelvis (the origin point of the hamstrings) comes under tension from the direction of the proximal tibias (the insertion point of the hamstrings just below the knees). As the hamstrings reach the limit of their ability to stretch, they become tighter and begin to exert more pull on both the knees and the muscles' pelvic attachments. If your knees are not far enough apart, your thighs will also crowd your torso as you approach the bottom.

There are two problems. First, your back muscles attach at the top of your pelvis, your hamstrings attach to the bottom, and the pelvis can pivot around the hips. So both the lower back muscles and the hamstrings can cause pelvic movement around the hip joints. The back muscles and the hamstrings are thus competing for control of your pelvis, and the back muscles must win if your spine is to stay efficiently rigid and safe. Second, if the femurs are too close together as you approach the bottom, there is not enough space between them for the torso to drop down low enough for a deep squat. The key is to position the femurs, the pelvis, and the low back so that the erectors and the hamstrings complement each other's function.

By shoving the knees out as you squat, while locking the spine into extension, you remove the tendency for the lower back to round. Shoving them out as you unlock at the top places the femurs in external rotation, and then the muscles that perform external rotation just keep the femurs in this position on the way down and up. The muscles that are stretched out when externally rotated then become active in the squat. If the knees are shoved out of the way, hamstring extensibility plays a minor role in the ability to assume a deep squat position. Since the hamstrings do not stretch out that much, most people are flexible enough to squat below parallel if they do it correctly.

Usually, the biggest problem with back position is the trainee's inability to identify which position the lower back is in. A lack of *kinesthetic sense* – the ability to identify the position of the

Figure 2-38. The easiest way for a coach to identify spinal extension – arching the back – is to look for wrinkles that appear in the cloth of the shirt as the top and bottom of the back get closer together.

body or a body part in spatial relation to the ground or the rest of the body – is very common. Some people have absolutely no idea that their lower back is rounded at the bottom of the squat, or that it is arched correctly at the top of the squat, or have any idea at all of what position their back is in. They cannot tell an upper-back arch from a lower-back arch, and the line between upper and lower seems to be blurred. If you ask someone with this problem to arch his lower back, he lifts his chest, or bends over from the waist, or performs a number of other interesting movements that have nothing to do with lumbar extension. Many people with inflexible hamstrings exhibit this problem, but not much hamstring flexibility is actually required to squat correctly, and many perfectly flexible people cannot assume a position of lumbar extension and hold it through a squat. Some people – mostly female, as a general rule – can place the lumbar spine into a position of *overextension*, and this is bad, too, perhaps potentially more dangerous than loaded lumbar flexion. This occurs when you fail to use your abs to provide the anterior support necessary to counter the extension provided by the erectors. But this overextension is far less common than the simple inability to maintain lumbar extension against a heavy load in the squat or deadlift. As it turns out, if you can't make a voluntary concentric contraction of the lumbar erectors – the movement commonly understood as arching the lower back – then you have no voluntary way to *keep* the lower back in

extension when this position gets hard to maintain. Please read this again, and understand this point: **an overextended lumbar spine is not the position you use to squat. But if you can't voluntarily arch your lower back, you can't control the erectors well enough to keep the spine from flexing at the bottom of the squat or the start of a deadlift or clean.**

The key to learning the correct position for the lower back is to assume a position that is correct, and then memorize the way it feels so that you can reproduce it every time. The best way to do this is to lie down on your belly on the floor, put your hands behind your head, lift your elbows, and raise your chest up off of the floor. This is how it feels to produce a thoracic, or upper back, extension. We want to train the lower back, so lie back down, straighten your knees, and then lift your knees up off the floor. To increase the sensation, try to get your quads off the floor, too. (Don't push your toes down into the floor to lift the knees up.) When you do this movement correctly, you'll be using your glutes, your hamstrings, and most important, your lower back muscles. This is how it feels to have your lower back in contraction. Feel this arch. Relax and do it again. By placing your back in a position where you have to contract your spinal erectors repeatedly, without trying to do anything else at the same time, you can embed this new movement pattern quickly and easily, without having to try to distinguish it from the other elements within an unfamiliar

Figure 2-39. *Top to bottom,* The progression from identifying the lower-back arch while lying on the ground, the same arch while standing, the same arch as the bottom position is assumed, and the arch at the start position of the pull.

movement. A set of 10–15 reps causes a burn in these muscles, and when you stand up, you can feel the muscles quite well, the movement pattern is fresh on the mind, and you can then duplicate the movement that caused the burn.

Assume this arched position again immediately while standing, and repeat it several times. Now, just to be sure, unlock your knees and hips to about a half-squat position and see if you can still perform this lumbar extension. Since you can now identify the correct back position, you should be able to keep your back arched through the whole squat *if you keep your knees out of the way.*

HIPS

The squat is an important exercise because of the intricate interplay between the skeletal and muscular components of the *kinetic chain* of the movement. The feet against the floor, the lower legs, the thighs, the hips, and the spine supporting the bar are woven together and controlled by a web of anterior and posterior muscles and connective tissues that continually adjust their positions relative to the balance point over the mid-foot. Several of these muscular components – the gastrocs, the hamstrings, and the rectus femoris – cross two joints. The roles of these muscles are especially complex, as they operate against both proximal and distal attachments at the same time, providing the fine adjustments necessary for the production of force in the context of balance.

"Hip drive" is the term used for this complex interplay as it relates to the pelvis. The hips provide the power out of the bottom as the glutes, adductors, and hamstrings start opening the hip angle. As you rise above parallel, the quads assume a larger role in the upward drive as the hamstrings anchor the back angle. At the top, the glutes, adductors, hamstrings, and quads finish their simultaneous extension of the hips and knees.

Knees and hips are tied together conceptually, as well as by the femurs. If your knees are too far forward, your hips are, too. And if your hips are too far forward and your knees are too far forward, either you are off-balance forward or your back angle is too vertical, the hip angle is too open, the knee angle is too closed, and you can't drive up out of the bottom. Hip drive is the basis for squatting power, and even though it is anatomically complex, hip drive can be learned easily and quickly.

Look carefully at Figure 2-40. As you assume the bottom position, imagine a hand placed on your sacrum, right at the base of the spine, and imagine pushing this hand straight up in the air with your butt. This is as clear a picture of the process of driving the hips up as can be drawn. If you have a training partner, revisit the hip drive lesson from the first part of the chapter: get him to place his hand as shown in the picture and provide some resistance to your hip drive so that you can feel the effect. (This is also a good time to refresh your head/eye-position lesson. Look both down and up at the ceiling while driving against the hand, and see which direction you prefer. Twenty bucks says it's down.) There is only a subtle difference in appearance between good strong hip drive and a squat that lacks this, but you will be able to feel the power of this technique the first time you do it correctly.

A common error is the tendency for some lifters to drive the hips forward instead of upward (Figure 2-41). If your hips go forward, your knees will too, causing the weight to shift forward to the toes. This shift is bad for power because anytime the knee angle closes, the hamstrings have shortened from the distal end, and a slack muscle is not a source of contractile power. If the rebound out of the bottom depends on hamstring and adductor tightness, then any relaxation of tension in these muscles represents a loss in stored elastic energy, not to mention a loss in the ability to contract and generate force.

Likewise, it is common to see the hips shift backwards instead of straight up out of the bottom. When this happens, the back angle will have become more horizontal, the hip angle more closed, and the knee angle more open, all in the absence of upward movement of the bar. This means that the hamstrings have not done their job of anchoring the back angle at their proximal attachments on the pelvis, the knee angle has opened because the gastrocnemius failed to anchor it, and the quads can't contract the

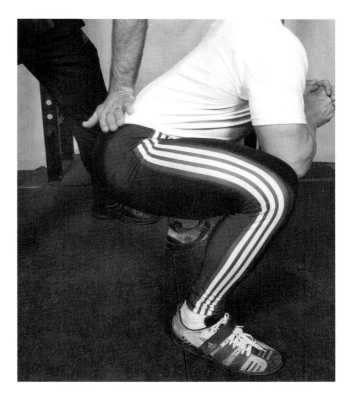

Figure 2-40. Learning hip drive with the aid of a coach.

already opened knee (Figure 2-42). As we will see often, form errors in many exercises represent the loss of the ability to generate force due to a loss in the position required for force production. Your best power is achieved when your hips continue straight up out of the bottom, with your tibias, anchored by your gastrocs, serving as anchors for your hamstrings; your glutes and external rotators holding your femurs out; your hamstrings, glutes, and adductors contracting against the pelvis to produce hip extension against a constant back angle; your quads producing knee extension; and then your knees and hips locking out simultaneously at the top. Let's examine the role of these muscles and skeletal components in detail.

Squat depth has been emphasized since the beginning of this chapter, so let's begin our analysis of hip function with its relationship to squat depth. When we squat, the standard range-of-motion criterion for the exercise is "below parallel," defined as the hip joint (identified at the apex of the hip angle, the "corner" in your shorts over the hip) as

Figure 2-41. Driving the chest up instead of the hips kills hamstring tension in the middle of the squat. The closed knee and open hip angles at right shorten the distance between hamstring origin and insertion, removing much of the hamstrings' contribution to hip drive.

Figure 2-42. Allowing the back angle to go horizontal on the way up from the bottom produces bad mechanics and inefficient use of the hip and leg musculature.

it drops below the knee (identified as the top of the patella). Most people who have trouble with the squat are having trouble getting good depth while preventing their low back from rounding. Pretty much anybody can get deep if they allow the lumbar spine to relax into flexion. But almost every single human being on this planet can squat below parallel with pretty good lumbar extension if their stance is correct and if they simply shove their knees out to the sides as they squat. At the bottom of the squat, a type of *impingement* – a trapping of soft tissue between two bones – occurs, and it is relieved by shoving out the knees. This simple skeletal-position adjustment allows for a below-parallel squat, and at the same time, a drastic improvement occurs in the way the hips function.

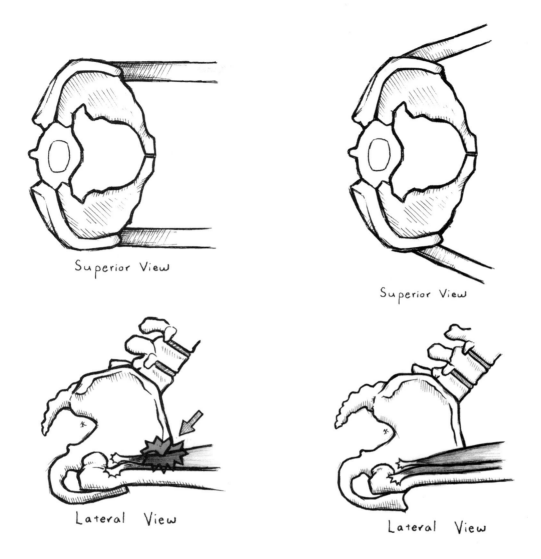

Figure 2-43. Hip impingement, the primary factor limiting squat depth. This contradicts the conventional wisdom of the hamstring-flexibility theory of squat depth, and it pleases us to do so.

Most people think that the main problem with squat depth is hamstring extensibility, more commonly referred to as "flexibility" – the ability of the hamstrings to lengthen as the depth of the squat increases. This is not really the case, and loose, elastic hamstrings are not the key to a deep squat. Optimal skeletal mechanics is.

If you stand with your heels at shoulder width apart and point your toes out at about 30 degrees, squat down, and keep your thighs parallel to your feet, then as your hip angle closes and your thighs approach your torso, your femurs will track to a position that is *outside* of the anterior superior iliac spine (ASIS), the "hip pointer" that you feel right below your waistline. But if you point your toes straight forward and let your knees follow your toes, or even if you point your toes out but still let your knees cave in toward the middle when you squat, then your femurs will approach the ASIS as you approach the bottom of the squat. So as your thighs crowd your hip pointers, they tend to trap any soft tissue or muscles that may be in the area in between, making it harder to go deep. (See Figure 2-43.)

Squat depth is a function of hip angle, the angle formed between the generalized plane of the torso and the femur. If you try to drop down to get better depth without adjusting the position of your femurs, you'll get depth at the expense of a rounded lower back because the hip angle cannot become more closed if the femurs are impinged. The pelvis is supposed to be locked in line with the lumbar vertebrae and held rigid by the erector spinae muscles. If the pelvis can't tilt forward to maintain this position because it rams into an obstruction, the only way to keep going deeper is to round the low back. Everybody, big belly or not, will experience this phenomenon to one degree or another, so if you're having depth problems, shoving the knees out fixes these problems so often that it is a waste of time to do anything else first.

Most people won't do the job of keeping their knees out unless they're coached; the knees want to track more medially because of the tension felt on the inside of the femurs. This tension is produced by the adductors – the groin muscles. These five muscles (the adductor magnus, adductor brevis, adductor longus, pectineus, and gracilis) attach at various points along the medial and posterior aspects of the femur, and on the ischium and pubis of the pelvis. Tension is produced between these two bones as you squat down and keep your knees out; this is an eccentric action for these muscles because they lengthen on the way down – *if* the femurs maintain their position parallel to the feet. As you come up out of the squat and the hip angle opens up, the distance between the inside of the femur and the medial pelvis shortens, so the concentric action of the adductor muscles thus produces hip extension. (See Figure 2-44).

Visualize the function of the adductors by imagining a point at the end of the inside of your thigh down by your knee, and another point on your "seat bone," under your butt and behind your crotch. These points represent the attachments of the adductor magnus. Your spinal erector muscles lock your back in extension and lock your pelvis in line with your back, so as you squat down and make your back more horizontal, your seat bones rotate back and away from your knees. If your knees stay in position, pointed in the same direction as your feet – out at about 30 degrees – the distance between the point on the inside of your thigh and your seat bone increases. And if this distance increases as you go down and decreases as you come up, the muscles that get longer on the way down make the "up" part happen as they get shorter. This is how the adductor muscles function in a correctly performed squat and why they are considered hip extensors, along with the glutes and hamstrings, as part of the posterior chain.

Since the adductors tend to pull the knees in, what keeps them out when you use your hips correctly? If *ad*-duction of the thighs means pulling the distal end of the femurs (the knees) toward the midline of the body, it seems like *ab*-duction would be the movement used to keep the knees out, and that the abductors would be the muscles that did this. But the abductors consist of only the tensor fascia latae (TFL, a small muscle that connects the hip at the anterior iliac crest to the lower leg), the gluteus medius, and the gluteus minimus. Together they create hip abduction if you raise your leg out to the side, away from your body. Since nobody actually does this, except to demonstrate the definition of abduction in biomechanics class, this is probably not what is going on when we squat.

External rotation occurs when you make your right femur rotate clockwise and your left femur rotate counterclockwise, as when you stand up and pivot on your heels to rotate your toes away from each other. There are at least nine muscles that perform this function: the gluteus medius, minimus, and maximus, the adductor minimus, the quadratus femoris, the inferior gemellus, the obturator internus, the superior gemellus, and the piriformis. (Notice that the external rotators include two of the abductor muscles.) External rotation is critical to stabilizing gait mechanics through the stride. As it relates to our analysis, the action of rotating the femurs out is what actually occurs when you shove your knees out on the way down to the bottom of the squat. Prove this to yourself by sitting in a chair and rotating your femurs the same way you would if you were standing up and pivoting on your heels to point your toes out. Using the external rotators to set the knees in a position parallel to the feet makes all kinds of sense when you consider that they are

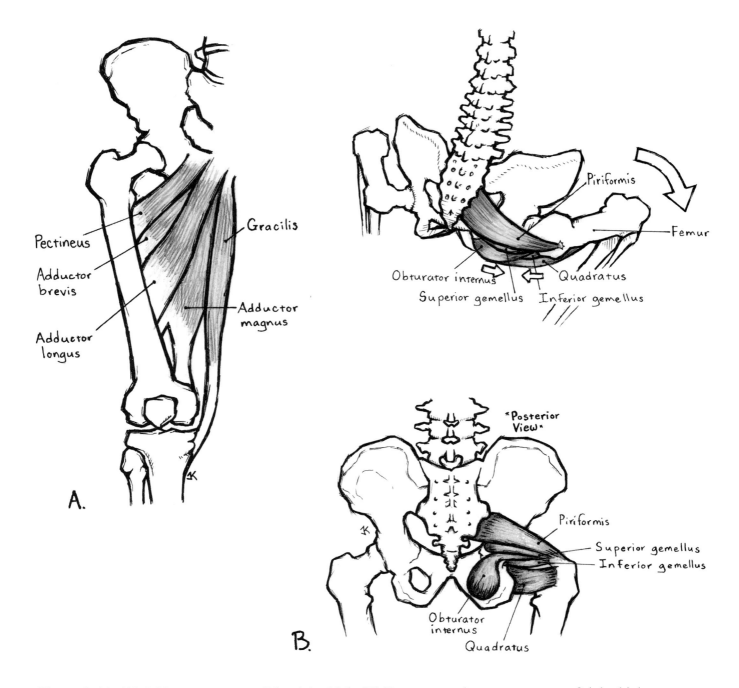

Figure 2-44. (A) Adductor anatomy of the right thigh. (B) Deep external rotator anatomy of right thigh.

in an effective position to do it and the TFL is not. So shoving the knees out at the top of the squat, and keeping them there so that the adductors can do their job, is accomplished by the muscles that rotate the hips externally. These muscles anchor the thigh position that allows for both good squat depth and the more effective use of all the muscles of the hips.

When you intentionally shove your knees to the outside as you come down into the bottom of the squat, not only do you get the femurs away from the ASIS and the gut, but you also allow the adductors to stretch tighter and position themselves to more effectively contract as they reach the limit of their extensibility. A tight, stretched muscle contracts harder than a looser, shorter muscle does because the stretch tells the neuromuscular system that a contraction is about to follow. A more efficient firing of more contractile units always happens when preceded by a stretch. This stretch reflex is an integral part of all explosive muscle contraction, and better athletes are very good at making it happen. Test this by trying to do a vertical jump without any drop before the jump; you will find this virtually impossible to do because the stretch reflex is such an integral part of the sequence of any explosive muscular contraction. When we squat, the hips' external rotators position the femurs so that the adductors and the external rotators themselves can participate with the hamstrings in the bounce, and the whole hip musculature can contribute to squatting efficiency – *if* you shove your knees out.

The bounce you feel when you stretch out the hamstrings, glutes, and adductors at the bottom of the squat is *not* due to knee ligament tightness or rebound. The correctly performed squat is an ACL/PCL-neutral event. You bounce off of the stretched and tightened components of the posterior chain and the now correctly loaded quadriceps, and it is absolutely safe for the knees.

Your timing here is important. If the bounce is used correctly, it will be immediately followed by a hard drive up of the hips. It is important that the bounce is not followed by a pause and then a drive up. The bounce must be incorporated into the drive – it must be *anticipated as the first part of the drive.* Think about the "up" drive all the way down during the descent. Don't think about going down while you're going down – think about coming up the whole time. Doing this will reduce the tendency to separate the drive from the bounce, because the drive is being anticipated even before the bounce occurs. The timing of your descent and rebound is critical to the performance of good squats. Bounce occurs optimally at the correct speed of descent. If your descent is too fast, the bounce will be less effective, and much less safe, because the only way to drop too fast is to relax something. Muscles tightened in the squat descent store elastic energy; tight muscles also keep your back, hips, and knees in the correct, safe positions. If you are loose enough to drop into

the bottom of the squat much faster than you can come up, you need to tighten up more – and it may help to think of this as slowing – on the way down. A loose descent can allow joints to be jammed into positions they should not occupy, and this is how most people get hurt squatting: getting out of good position by going down so fast that they cannot maintain proper technique. This may be how squats got an undeserved bad reputation. Don't contribute to the problem by dive-bombing into the bottom.

The limit of the adductors' and hamstrings' extensibility will almost always be below parallel, as defined earlier. The hamstrings' length does not change that much anyway, since the knees and hips come into flexion together during the descent. Tension builds on the isometrically tight hamstrings as they approach the bottom; in this way, they control the back angle and contribute to the stretch reflex effect as the rebound occurs. A few people lack sufficient extensibility in the posterior chain muscles, and some people have tight joint capsule ligaments, but not nearly as many people need stretching out as merely need the correct stance, the correct knee position outside the ASIS, and a loud reminder to keep their knees out. The weighted squat has few superiors in the realm of things that go *stretch*, anyway, and what little stretching is actually needed can usually be done within a few sets of weighted squats that incorporate a correct knees-out descent.

Our previous discussion of low-back position can now be understood in a more complete context. A developed kinesthetic sense of spinal position is necessary for efficient force transfer and for effective athletic performance in general. Relying on ligament tension and general trunk tightness is fine with very light weights, but is really a handicap at work-set loads. If the lumbar spine and the pelvis do not stay perfectly rigid in what can be called "pelvic lock," force transfer is not as efficient up the spine, and posterior chain rebound is soft because of the less-than-efficient relationship that a loose lumbar spine has with the pelvis and the muscles attached to it. Rigid lumbar extension places the pelvis at a better angle to tighten the hamstrings at the bottom, making a more efficient rebound possible because force isn't being absorbed by a loose lumbar spine. And the hamstrings produce a more efficient stretch reflex with a rigid lumbar spine at the back angle used in the low-bar squat. Think of it this way: there is a war between the erectors and the hamstrings over control of the pelvis, and the erectors *have to win* if the back is to stay rigid and the hamstrings are to be used effectively.

If you do not know how to contract your erector muscles in order to arch your lower back, with no tension from the hamstrings interfering, this means that you do not know how to assume this position voluntarily. You do not have the kinesthetic sense to know when the arch is there and when it isn't, and you can't put your back in this position at the bottom of a deadlift or keep it there at the bottom of a squat when hamstring tension is at its highest. If this is you, make it a priority to learn how to control your lower back position.

To recap: The complete concept of the correct use of the hips in the squat is best understood as the use of both an actively locked lumbar extension and actively shoved-out knees, resulting in a below-parallel squat that incorporates a stretch reflex, using all the muscles of the posterior chain in the most optimal way possible. This movement pattern gets the thighs out of the way of the pelvis so that good

depth can be more easily obtained. At the same time, it makes the squat stronger because the active use of the external rotators holds the femurs in a position that enables both the external rotators and the adductors to contribute to hip extension. This hip extension produces a more effective use of more muscles over a wider range of motion.

KNEES

In a correct back squat of the style advocated here, there is one correct place for the knees: directly in line with the feet so that the femurs and the feet are parallel. This position will, for most people, be slightly out in front of the toes, with the exact distance being determined by the anthropometry of the individual. This basically means that the femur and the foot should be in a straight line as seen from directly above, so there is no twisting of the knee. Depending on your femur, tibia, and trunk dimensions, your knees could be anywhere from very slightly behind your toes, with short femurs and long tibias, to 3 or 4 inches in front of the toes, with long femurs and short tibias. Since your knees will be directly in line with your toes, the angle of your feet in your stance will determine the angle of the knees as well. As shown in Figure 2-12, an angle of

Figure 2-45. The differences that anthropometry can produce in the appearance of the bottom position of the squat. Both are correct, but both are different due to variations in leg and trunk length.

Figure 2-46. *Top,* The knees-in position most people will assume unless coached to do otherwise. *Bottom,* The way to coach knees-out.

about 30 degrees out from the perpendicular works for most people, although this varies as well. This angle allows the hips to function as discussed above.

By far, the two most common knee errors are 1) knees caved in too much, and 2) knees too far forward, either early in the descent or at the bottom. It is actually unusual to see novices not make one or both of these errors the first time they squat. Both errors are related to hip function and positional awareness.

If you allow your knees to come together at any time during the squat, you dilute the function of the muscles both medial and lateral to the femurs. But this problem cannot be corrected if it is not identified. When you squat, look down even more than usual, to a point on the floor right between your toes, where you can clearly see your knees, and check your position. If your knees move toward each

other at any point during the squat, shove them out. You will probably have to exaggerate this shoving-out in order for it to put your knees in the correct position, since you thought they were in the right position when they were coming in. When you get them back out to parallel with your feet and keep them there for a couple of sets, you will notice later that your adductors, and perhaps your most lateral glutes, get sore. From our previous discussion, you know why.

Letting your knees travel too far forward presents a different challenge. The problem with this position is not so much that it destroys the knees (although it is not particularly good for them), but that it has a detrimental effect on hip drive out of the bottom. A knees-forward position produces a more acute knee angle, and the resultant distally shortened hamstrings have less room to contract from the other end. When the hamstrings are already contracted, their contribution to hip extension is much less efficient than it would be with longer, stretched-out hamstrings. It also means that there is more moment force against the ankle/mid-foot balance point because of the more horizontal angle of the tibia. The obvious consequence of this difference in hamstring utilization and lower-leg mechanics is that less weight can be used. This is what happens in the front squat.

To maintain the vertical back angle required by the bar position, you must close the knee angle and open the hip angle; the front squat therefore involves inherently shorter hamstrings in the bottom position. A primary difference between the front squat and the squat is that the knees drive forward in the front squat. And if the knee angle gets too closed, some of the knee problems inherent in the front squat – the impingement of the posterior aspect of the meniscal cartilages between the acutely squeezed femoral and tibial condyles – start to show up where they shouldn't. The cause of this knee-position error is often an incorrect understanding of where the back should be in the squat.

If your concept of the low-bar back squat involves a mental image of your doing the movement with your back in a vertical position, your perception of what you're supposed to be doing is wrong, and it will cause your knees to be too far forward. If your torso is too vertical, your knees will be forced forward to maintain the bar/mid-foot balance position. The layman's advice to "lift with your legs, not your back" might be part of the problem because most people interpret this advice as involving a vertical torso and the legs pushing the floor. The saying should be "lift with your hips, not your back," because "lifting with your back" is what happens when you bend over to pick something up and round your spine into flexion. Leaning over is a normal part of the squat; it is required if the bar is to remain in balance over your mid-foot. The correct mental picture, discussed on page 58, usually fixes this problem.

If it doesn't, there are other things that can get the knees back. If the weight is on the heels during the squat, the knees can't be too far forward. Think about your heels, and how it feels to have your weight balanced on them. Assume your squat stance, pick up your toes, and rock back onto your heels. Once your weight is on your heels, shove your knees out and squat. When you squat from the heels, your knees stay back, and if you stay in balance, your back angle will have adjusted to a more horizontal position as well. Now, you will not be able to continue to squat on your heels because this is also an unbalanced position. But after three or four reps, this trick will have done its job and you will have settled into the middle of your feet with your knees in the correct position, not too far out over the toes. This position will feel balanced and strong, and done correctly a few times, it will be the one you favor from then on.

A different problem, often encountered in more advanced trainees, is the tendency to let the knees slide forward as the bottom approaches. This problem usually develops over time, and the embedded movement pattern can be hard to fix if you let it go uncorrected too long. And it is potentially complicated. If your knees move forward at the bottom of the squat, you may have relaxed your quads, which hold the knees open; the closed knee angle in turn shortens the hamstrings, which then are slacked distally and therefore cannot be used effectively for proximal hip extension. Quads

Figure 2-47. Quite often, the mental image of the squat involves a vertical torso like a front squat, a position that kills posterior chain involvement. The correct back angle is horizontal enough that efficient hip-drive mechanics are used, and this back angle awareness involves the correct mental image of where your torso actually is during the squat. Don't be afraid to lean over, sit back, and shove your knees out.

maintain the knee angle, which in turn anchors the hamstrings as they tighten with greater squat depth and a more closed hip angle so that they can extend the hips on the way up. Or you may have relaxed the hamstrings' tension on the tibias, dorsiflexed your ankles, and shifted forward to your toes from the bottom. The soleus anchors the knee angle from the distal end, and the gastrocnemius adds to this effect by crossing the knee joint to the distal femur, to anchor the knee to the ankle. The squat is essentially an interaction with the ground and your balance point over the mid-foot. All these muscles, if relaxed at the bottom of the squat, have to be retightened to be used effectively, and this is hard to do from what are now terribly inefficient skeletal positions.

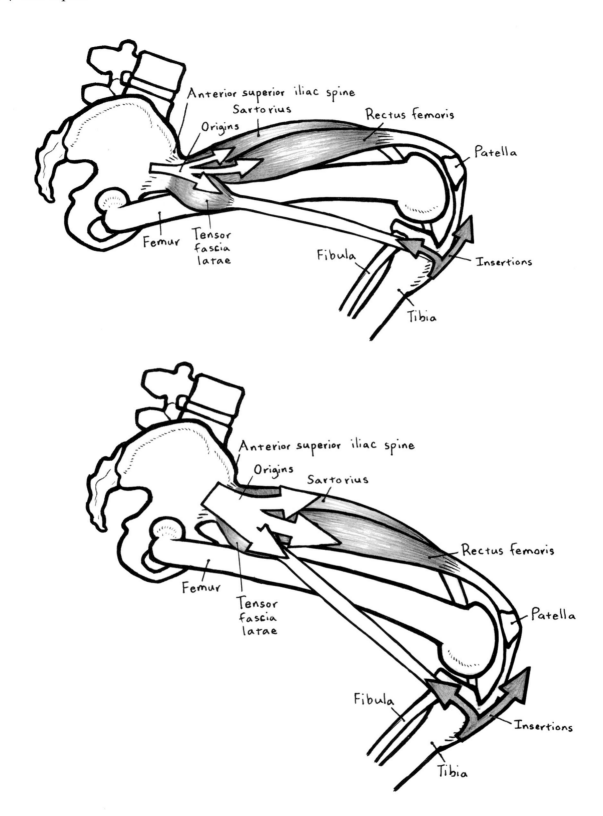

Figure 2-48. If the knee slides forward – note the partial squat and the inclination of the tibia – the increased pull from the knee develops high tension against the attachments on the pelvis. This can cause an interesting type of tendinitis.

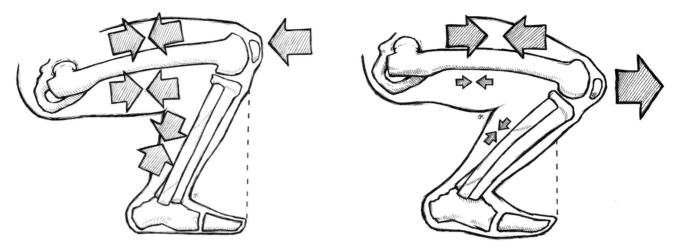

Figure 2-49. The relationship of the quads, hamstrings, and gastrocs at the bottom of the squat. All work together to maintain the knee angle, and letting the knees slide forward indicates a failure in this relationship.

The fact is that most people don't like to maintain tension in the quads, the calves, and the posterior chain as they approach the bottom of the squat. It is indeed a lot of work to maintain tension in these components as the angles become more closed, the muscles reach the end of their ability to extend, and the tendons become stretched and tight. Tempting as it may be to relax forward, doing so is obviously inefficient because it eliminates the possibility of storing elastic energy in the extensible components as they stretch out and get nearer to the point of activating the stretch reflex as the direction of the movement reverses. Relaxing forward also

increases the risk of injury because low-back relaxation often comes along for the ride.

The answer is to learn to squat with the knees in the proper place and to move them correctly during the descent. If the knees are moving out as the femurs externally rotate, their forward travel will be limited to that which is normal for your anthropometry in a correct squat, where all of the forward knee travel occurs in the first third or half of the descent. After that, the knees just stay in place and the hips account for the rest of the movement. So, from the very top, shove the knees forward *and* out to the place where they will end up, just

Figure 2-50. Note that the knees, once they move forward to their position over the toes, do not move during the remainder of the squat until the ascent carries them back up to this point.

Figure 2-51. A terribly useful block of wood. Touch the block, but don't knock it over.

in front of the toes, and stop them there; the rest of the descent will consist of the hips moving back and down. Make two movements out of this for a couple of reps, and then reduce this sequence to a smooth single motion (Figure 2-50). A useful way to learn this is to place a block of wood in front of your knees, as illustrated in Figure 2-51.

In order for this knee-control technique to work, you'll need to actually look down at your knees so that you'll know what they are doing in response to your direction. In your squat stance, at the top with the bar in position on your back, look straight down at a point on the floor between your toes. You will see a picture of your knees relative to your feet, and the movement of your knees relative to your toes will be apparent as you descend. Look at your knees all the way down and back up a couple of times with the empty bar. You will need to practice this because it will seem awkward at first. But as you watch your knees change position through the movement and as the sets get heavier, you will see exactly what the problems are and you will have immediate feedback on what you need to do to correct them. If your concept of the squat is correct, this technique is the best way to fix your knee problems.

FEET AND STANCE

As previously noted, the interaction with the feet against the floor is central to the entire concept of the squat. The middle of the feet is the point of balance against the floor, and the bar must remain directly above this point for the system to be in balance. Remember that in our recommended stance, the heels are about shoulder width apart, with the toes pointed out at about 30 degrees. Stance is a highly individual thing and will vary with hip width, hip ligament tightness, femur and tibia length and proportion, adductor and hamstring flexibility, knee joint alignment, and ankle flexibility. Everybody's stance will be slightly different, but shoulder-width heels, with toes at 30 degrees, is a good place to start.

As noted earlier, stance width will influence knee position. For example, if you are tall with very long femurs and relatively narrow shoulders, you need a wider stance than is usually recommended. If you have a long torso and short legs (not that uncommon a body type), you will need a bit narrower stance than our rule of thumb would predict. Sometimes the foot angle needs to be adjusted for individual situations: if you are pigeon-toed, your foot angle will need to be slightly more forward-pointing than our model recommends, or more commonly, in the case of out-toeing, the feet will need to be pointed out more. These corrections are necessary to keep the correct neutral relationship between the femur and the tibia so that no twisting occurs in the capsular, medial, and lateral ligaments of the knee. Expect a closer stance to place the knees more forward relative to the toes, and a wider stance

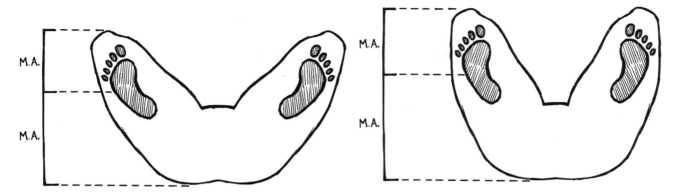

Figure 2-52. The relationship between stance width, stance angle, and knee angle. The wider the stance, the more the toes point out, due to the changing angle of the femurs at the pelvis as width increases. The feet keep the tibias rotated in line with the femurs – and keep the stress off the knees – by changing their angle to accommodate the rotation. As explained on page 33, the moment arm along the femur is calculated from the position of the bar over midfoot. The knee "sees" the moment arm from knee to bar and the hip "sees" the moment arm from hip to bar. (*M.A. = moment arm*)

to place them farther back (see Figure 2-52). But again, shoulder-width heels produces the best effect for general strength training.

A narrow-stance squat, such as that frequently pictured in the muscle magazines, develops an aesthetically pleasing set of quads. But since we plan to use the rest of the hip musculature, too, it seems unwise to omit it from the training program. It is very difficult for people of normal flexibility to get deep enough with a narrow stance, so the hamstrings are never engaged as fully as they would be with a more generalized wider stance. Also, the narrow stance does not involve the groin muscles, as discussed earlier. For this reason, it can be useful in the event of a groin injury and can be used for several weeks while the adductors are healing. If used all the time, however, narrow-stance squatting predisposes you to a groin injury due to the lack of conditioning for these muscles.

One occasionally sees powerlifters squatting with a wide stance and their toes pointing almost forward. Some really strong powerlifters do this to increase the joint tightness and resultant rebound obtained by placing an additional twist on the knee and hip ligaments. Some of the others do it because they are merely copying what they've seen the strong guys do. This is a practice best left to very experienced powerlifters. For you, it will be very important to

have all the bones of the legs and hips in the best position to generate force without causing tendon and ligament problems. Here is a way to see this relationship: sit in a chair with your knees slightly bent and your feet out in front of you, without pushing hard on the floor. Put your legs together, and note that your toes are pointing straight forward. Spread them out wide and note that your toes are pointing out. In both positions, your feet naturally assume a position parallel to your femurs, and your knees are in an anatomically neutral position, with no twisting (Figure 2-52). As your knees point out, your toes point out. The wider the knees, the more the toes point out. As the knees widen, the femurs rotate externally, the tibias follow to keep the knee ligaments in their normal anatomical position, and the toes point out more because they are attached to the end of the tibias. This anatomical relationship must be understood and respected so that avoidable knee injuries don't happen.

The practice of placing a block or a 2×4 under the heels is common. Most gyms keep one lying around somewhere. People use the block to make the full squat position easier to reach, and understanding why this works is necessary for understanding why you should not do it. A block under the heels tilts the shins forward by lifting the ankles and allowing the knees to move forward without stretching the ankle joints. This shin angle closes the knee angle and causes the hamstrings' attachment point on the back of the tibia to move closer to their origin on the pelvis, loosening the muscle a little and thus decreasing the amount of stretch necessary to get to full depth. Weightlifting shoes with a heel height of between ½ and ¾ inches provide a little lift that helps tilt the shins enough to involve the quads a little more, but a heel height of 1½ to 2 inches is as bad as a 2×4. If you are having "flexibility" problems severe enough that you need a block under your heels in order to squat deep, your problem is most likely your stance and your knee position, as discussed earlier.

The Master Cue

There is an important mental trick that you can use to fix most things wrong with the bar path in the squat and all the resultant errors made by the body. The trick is amazingly simple, and it corrects a wide variety of technique problems, from knees to back angle, from air under the heels to a wobbly bar path. This trick is simply keeping the barbell over the mid-foot by thinking about doing so.

The case for barbell training was built around the idea of balance by observing that the most efficient form to use was that which keeps the bar in a vertical relationship with the middle of the foot. If you do this, the back angle will be determined by the position of the bar on the back. Furthermore, if you keep your spine rigid, and the bar travels up and down in the imaginary slot directly above the mid-foot, then the knees, hips, and ankles will do what they must do to maintain this vertical relationship, and the body will solve all the problems associated with doing so at a level beneath any requirement for micromanagement. In a similar fashion, if you make the bar path vertical when you are deadlifting, the biomechanics of the pull will be correct because the task of making the path vertical causes you to solve the problem with your "body," not your "brain." This concept is an example of a *bar cue*, which enables the body itself to sort out complex motor problems by jumping past the analysis to the result. You have

Figure 2-53. The Master Cue.

been solving movement problems your whole life, and if you're a natural athlete, you've been doing it well. By giving the body a general task instead of a specific one, you move your brain out of the way and allow your accumulated motor skills to solve the problem. If you command the bar to move in a vertical line, it will do so, and you will move your back, thighs, and shins in a way that makes it do so without your having to analyze the exact problem.

For the squat, you do this by constructing a mental image of an actual slot in the air for the bar to travel within. Visualize this narrow slot over the mid-foot, extending up into the air above you. Then visualize the bar traveling within this slot. An amazing thing then happens: it does. With varying degrees of precision based on your visualization skills, the bar will tend to line up vertically with the balance point because your knees and hips will have done the things needed to make it happen. And your visualization skills are just as trainable as everything else. This trick is a useful tool for all the pulls from the floor and for the press because the mechanics of balance and bar path are the same.

Breathing

Much controversy exists about breathing patterns during exercise. It is thought by some that "inhaling on the way down and exhaling on the way up" is a good way to lower the peak blood pressure during the rep and thereby eliminate the possibility of cerebrovascular accidents occurring during exercise. Such advice reveals a misunderstanding of the mechanisms involved, overrates the likelihood of an exercise-related cerebrovascular injury (a breathtakingly uncommon event), and underrates the likelihood of an orthopedic injury, an all-too-common occurrence. If we are to put this controversy to rest, it behooves us to understand the function of the Valsalva maneuver during the squat. The *Valsalva maneuver* is the proper term for holding the breath against a closed glottis while pressure is applied by the abdominal and thoracic muscles.

If your car runs out of gas in an intersection, and you have to push it out of the way or get killed, you will open your car door, put your shoulder on the door frame, take a great big breath, and push the car. You will probably not exhale except to take another quick breath until the car and you are out of the way. Furthermore, you will not even think about this because the many millions of years your ancestors have spent pushing on heavy things have taught your central nervous system the correct way to breathe while pushing. Or you might find yourself grunting aloud during the effort, a vocalization produced by a marked restriction in the airway at the glottis; this restriction produces a similar increase in pressure during the partial exhalation. This is perhaps the origin of the "kiyah" in martial arts, the vocalization that allows for an increased focus of power at the instant of the striking of a blow.

When you inhale, your diaphragm contracts and the volume of your thoracic cavity increases.

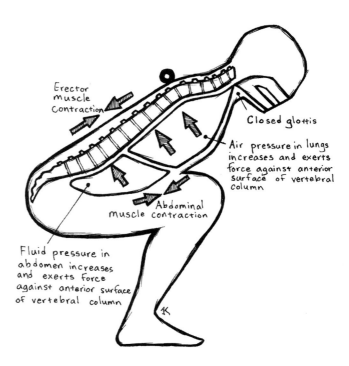

Figure 2-54. The combined effects of increased lung (intra-thoracic) pressure, intra-abdominal pressure produced by abdominal muscle contraction, and spinal erector contraction on spinal stability during loading. The Valsalva maneuver increases the ability to produce this pressure and stability. Exhalation during heavy efforts prevents the development of sufficient pressure to stabilize the spine. Best is a big, held breath during a heavy effort.

As air flows into your now larger lungs, pressure equalizes between the outside and the inside. When you clamp down to hold your breath and tighten your trunk muscles, you create a pressure gradient between the inside and the outside. This pressure increases markedly with the intensity of the squeeze. Since your thoracic and abdominal cavities are separated by only your diaphragm, abdominal pressure increases, too. The spinal vertebrae are being held in the correct anatomical position by your back musculature. This correct position is reinforced by static pressure transmitted to the spine across the essentially non-compressible contents of the abdominal cavity (Figure 2-54). Pressure in your abdominal and thoracic cavities is therefore transmitted to your spine from the anterior and lateral directions, and the spinal erectors are

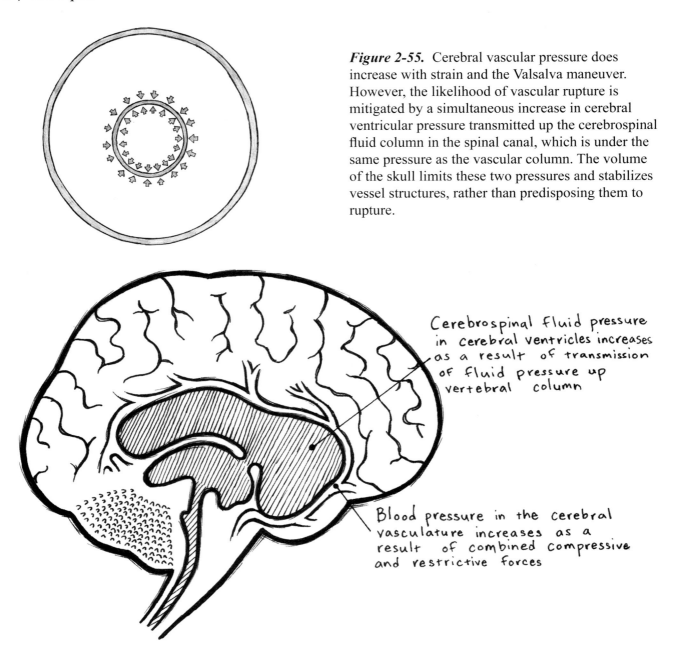

Figure 2-55. Cerebral vascular pressure does increase with strain and the Valsalva maneuver. However, the likelihood of vascular rupture is mitigated by a simultaneous increase in cerebral ventricular pressure transmitted up the cerebrospinal fluid column in the spinal canal, which is under the same pressure as the vascular column. The volume of the skull limits these two pressures and stabilizes vessel structures, rather than predisposing them to rupture.

Cerebrospinal fluid pressure in cerebral ventricles increases as a result of transmission of fluid pressure up vertebral column

Blood pressure in the cerebral vasculature increases as a result of combined compressive and restrictive forces

generating pressure from the posterior. When pressure in the thoracic cavity increases with a big held breath, and this pressure is increased by the tightening of the abs and obliques, support develops for the spine as if a rigid cylinder were surrounding the spinal column. A weightlifting belt adds to this effect, its main function being to add support to the cylinder from the front and sides, rather than to apply pressure from the back.

The conventional wisdom is that this thoracic and abdominal pressure is also being applied to the cardiovascular system embedded in the trunk, that the increase in pressure is being transmitted up the vascular column to the head, and that this increase in pressure has the potential to cause a cerebrovascular accident (CVA), such as a stroke or a blown aneurysm.

This assumption ignores several facts, most important among them the fact that for pressure across a membrane to breach it, there must be a *pressure gradient*, a difference in the pressure on either side of the membrane, or movement cannot occur. When we use the Valsalva maneuver while lifting weights, the whole system is pressured up so that no gradients exist across any barriers. The same pressure being applied to the arteries in the vascular column up the neck and into the head is also being applied to the cerebrospinal fluid (CSF) in the spinal canal; this fluid transmits pressure up through the subdural space in the skull and throughout the cerebral ventricular system, balancing cardiovascular pressure across the blood/brain interface (Haykowsky, MJ et al., *Medicine & Science in Sports & Exercise*, 35(1):65-68, 2003) (Figure 2-55).

Conventional wisdom also ignores the fact that the cranium is essentially a pressure vessel, like a propane tank, that is quite capable of containing high pressures. Imagine inserting a balloon into a glass milk bottle and trying to blow the balloon up so that it pops – obviously impossible unless you're capable of making the milk bottle explode, too. The pressure vessel prevents a pressure gradient from developing between balloon and bottle. The pressure across the membranes within the skull is contained by the capacity of the bony encasement to control and prevent changes in pressure, and pressure changes are required for the inter-membrane disruptions of a CVA. The pressure will thus remain the same across all the structures inside the skull – unless you exhale.

Conventional wisdom further ignores the fact that aneurysms are vessel wall defects associated with genetic predisposition and, rarely, with the response to a disease state, like tertiary syphilis, that produces chronic inflammation of the vascular walls. People with aneurysms have them for reasons other than the fact that they train with weights, and the likelihood of such a person rupturing an aneurysm while under the bar is approximately the same as the likelihood of its happening while the person is walking across the front yard.

Now, a little empirical evidence to help make the case for breathing correctly under the bar. The actual rates of cerebrovascular accidents versus orthopedic injuries provide ample evidence that the greater risk is orthopedic. In Risser's 1990 study (*American Journal of Diseases of Children*, 144(9):1015–7, 1990) of junior high and high school athletes from all sports, 7.6% of all athletes incurred injuries that kept them out of training for seven days. The rate of injury from all causes was 0.082 injuries per training year; 74% of all injuries were simple sprains and strains, and *59% of all injuries were classified as back injuries.*

In contrast, the death rate from cerebrovascular accidents in 2004 was about 0.000512 (150,074 total) for the *entire population of the U.S.* (293 million in 2004). The rate of survivable CVAs in 2004 was 0.00305 (895,000). So even if we compare the rate of orthopedic injury in a specialized small population engaging in exercise with the rate of CVA in the population of the entire United States, orthopedic injuries are still 27 times more common than survivable strokes, and you are still 94 times as likely to hurt your back in sports as you are to die from a CVA even if you don't exercise.

In reality, the difference is much greater because athletes are far less likely than the general population to have cerebrovascular problems they have not inherited. There are no actual data for the rates of CVA in the weight room *because they occur so infrequently as to be statistically unmeasurable.* More people drown in 5-gallon buckets each year than have had barbell training-related strokes since the invention of barbells.

The spinal support provided by the anterior thoraco-abdominal pressure is precisely why it is natural for us to use the Valsalva when we lift or push. Fighter pilots perform the Valsalva when they are subjected to high G-forces in acrobatic maneuvers; the increased support maintains an open vascular column, which supplies blood to the brain, so that consciousness can be salvaged under momentary high-G conditions that would otherwise cause a blackout due to a drop in blood supply to the brain. The same conditions exist under a heavy bar; the back must be supported, and the increased blood pressure provided by the Valsalva maneuver serves to maintain blood supply to the brain when pumping that blood gets harder under a bar weighing 405 pounds.

What is most important is that no one gets under 405 pounds and squats it without having trained enough to be able to do so. The cardiovascular

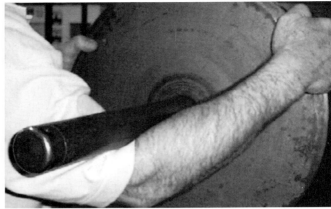

Figure 2-56. Spotting the squat requires attention, teamwork, and some finesse. Spotters should assume their positions prior to the start of the set. If the lifter misses the rep, the spotters use both hands and the crook of one elbow to catch each end of the bar. This effort must be balanced and coordinated, or the lifter gets uneven de-loading of the bar and a possible torsion injury. Any lifter who bails out of the missed rep and leaves the spotters holding the bar needs to be beaten with a hammer.

system adapts to resistance training, just like all of the other tissues and systems in the body, and this adaptation occurs as strength increases. Anyone who is capable of squatting extremely heavy weights is adapted for it in all the necessary ways. And no lifter has ever pulled 800 pounds off the floor while exhaling. For any trainee – and certainly any athlete – it is incalculably more likely that following the advice to "inhale on the way down and exhale on the way up" will actually cause an orthopedic injury, rather than prevent a stroke.

In fact, it is a good practice to take and hold the biggest breath you can before each rep of your heaviest sets. Get in the habit of breathing correctly during your lighter sets so that the pattern is well established by the time the weights get heavy. The Valsalva maneuver will prevent far more problems

than it has the potential to cause. It is a necessary and important technique for safety in the weight room.

Spotting the Squat

Spotters in the weight room can often be more trouble than help. Inexperienced, inattentive, stupid spotters can get you hurt. The squat and the bench press are the only two exercises in this basic program that require spotters, and if they do it wrong, it's almost better to just take your chances without them. Almost. Squats and benches can be dangerous when they're heavy, so good spotters become an important commodity at some point in everybody's training.

Figure 2-57. Left, The incorrect way to spot. Single-person spotting of the squat is tricky. The purpose of the spot is to take some of the weight off the rep so that it can be completed by the lifter. This cannot be safely accomplished by applying force to the lifter's body. *Right,* A better way to perform a one-person spot if necessary. Spot the bar, not the lifter.

Weights used in the squat can be sufficiently heavy and are in such a position that it is not safe for one spotter to work alone. Any squat attempt or set of squats you are uncertain you can do, or you're even a little worried about, should be spotted by two people. **The squat requires two spotters.** They have to learn to watch each other and work carefully together to minimize the effects inherent in having two people apply force to the same object. The differential loading caused by one spotter jerking the bar up while the other one doesn't is a potential wreck, and it has caused many back injuries. But this situation can be managed by having spotters learn how to do it correctly. Spotters should apply force to the bar in a balanced way, coordinating their efforts to keep the bar as level as possible while minimizing the chance of hurting themselves in the process (Figure 2-56).

A one-person spot for a squat cannot be safely accomplished. When one spotter stands behind the lifter, leaning over with his arms wrapped around and under the lifter's chest, this is not only an embarrassing position but also a terribly ineffective and unsafe one. After all, if the lifter is so ungracious as to drop the bar off of his back, what will a single spotter do? Catch it in his elbows? If you are the ungracious lifter, any help the spotter gives you from this position will be applied to your chest with his hands, thus altering your position at precisely the worst time it could be altered. So put embarrassing, ineffective, and unsafe together, and you can see why using a single spotter for the squat is always a bad idea (Figure 2-57, left).

In a *dire* emergency, a spotter might be able to help by standing directly behind you and pushing up on the bar with as even a hand position as can be managed around your grip and bar placement (Figure 2-57, right). This method will not work if the weight is heavy or the miss is profound; in either case, everybody needs to take care of himself by getting away from the bar as safely as possible. In fact, some coaches teach their athletes to dump the bar off their backs – when they're using rubber bumper plates and no spotters – in the event of a miss. You can't hurt spotters this way, since there aren't any, and spotters can't hurt you, either. But this action requires practice, bumper plates, and the permission of the gym owner. Don't try it without being shown how by a good coach.

But this is a completely avoidable situation, one that indicates that either the wrong weight is on the bar or there is not enough help in the weight room. Things should be changed so that it does not happen again, because the potential for injury is high. Either come prepared to squat weights that require spotters, by having them with you, or change your training plans for that day.

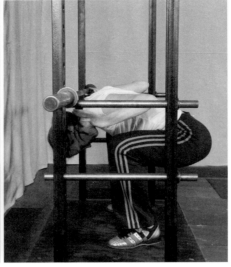

Figure 2-58. Squatting inside the power rack. If necessary, the bar can be lowered to the pins.

THE POWER RACK

Squatting inside a power rack is sometimes necessary. If the weight room is not set up correctly – i.e., the surface of the platform against the power rack is not flush with the inside floor of the rack so that you can walk the squat back across a level surface, or if your rack lacks a floor – you will need to stay inside the rack to avoid stepping down or over things with the bar on your back. And if there are absolutely no spotters and it is squat day, you might have to squat inside the rack with the pins set at the correct height for the bar: low enough that a below-parallel squat doesn't touch them, and high enough that a missed rep doesn't drive you into the floor.

Power racks should be designed 1) with a heavy floor inside that can be made flush with an adjacent platform so that most of the time, squats can be walked out; 2) with uprights built using the correct depth dimensions so that people can squat inside the rack; and 3) with the pin holes spaced at a 2½- to 3-inch interval so that lifters can set the pins at the right heights for their personal dimensions (a 4-inch or greater interval is not useful). Squatting inside the rack as a matter of regular practice might be required because of a poorly designed rack and platform, or if you train alone, but when you're squatting heavy in the normal gym environment, it creates a potential risk for the spotters and their

hands. For the lifter, having the uprights visible peripherally might be distracting; their presence might alter the bar path as the lifter tries to avoid touching them. You can get accustomed to having them there, but squatting outside the rack is preferable, since available spotters remove the only reason to squat inside a rack in a properly equipped weight room.

"Squatting" in a Smith machine is an oxymoron. A Smith machine is not a squat rack, no matter what the girls at the front desk tell you. A squat cannot be performed on a Smith machine any more than it can be performed in a small closet with a hamster. Sorry. There is a gigantic difference between a machine that makes the bar path vertical for you and a squat that is executed correctly enough to have a vertical bar path. The job of keeping the bar path vertical should be done by the muscles, skeleton, and nervous system, not by grease fittings, rails, and floor bolts.

A leg press machine – the "Hip Sled" – is even less useful to a lifter who is already strong enough to squat. By restricting the movement of joints that normally adjust their position during a squat, this device eliminates the expression of your normal biomechanics. The leg press may be useful for geriatric trainees or for special populations that cannot effectively use the squat as an exercise. But it is particularly heinous for healthy younger people because it allows the use of huge weights and therefore facilitates unwarranted bragging by those who should be squatting. A 1000-pound leg press is as irrelevant as a 500-pound quarter-squat.

Personal Equipment

Supportive apparel, such as squat suits, squat briefs, power socks, bench press shirts, and other such items, is designed to help powerlifters lift more weight at a meet where such equipment is permitted. Powerlifting is an extremely technical sport due to the use of this equipment, but it has no place in a program of strength training for athletics and fitness. Remember: *lifting more weight is not always the same thing as getting stronger.* This should be obvious in light of the principles already discussed regarding squatting and strength.

BELTS AND WRAPS

Less obvious is the role of belts and knee wraps. A properly designed and adjusted belt is useful as a safety device when you're squatting heavy weights. A belt protects the spine by increasing the amount of pressure that can be applied to it by the muscles that support it. The belt itself reinforces the "cylinder" of the ab muscles around the spine. At the same time, the belt acts as a proprioceptive cue for a harder abdominal muscle contraction: you can actually squeeze harder with a belt on than you can without one, just as you can push harder against a loaded barbell than you can against a broomstick. This effect ultimately produces both stronger abs, due to the stronger isometric contraction facilitated by the belt, and a stronger squat, due to the heavier loads made possible by the more stable spine.

A suit is different in that it actually enables you to lift weights that are heavier than those you can lift without the suit. With a suit, some of the kinetic energy of the descending, bar-loaded, eccentric contraction is stored as elastic energy in the suit material and in the compressed skin and muscle under the suit. That energy is then made available to the lifter as he rebounds up, so the suit is in fact an artificial aid. It has been argued that

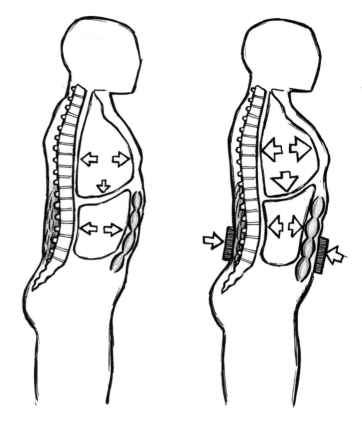

Figure 2-59. Increased pressure against the spine is necessary for the safety and efficiency of the lift. The belt facilitates this increase by providing a platform for proprioceptive feedback for increased abdominal muscle contraction. Pushing against the resistance of the belt makes for a harder abdominal contraction. And the volumetric containment it provides allows an increase in pressure in the abdominal and thoracic cavities.

the belt is too, but a belt does not function across a joint going into a sequence of flexion, stretch reflex, and extension, like a suit does. Spinal support and safety are necessary for our general strength training purposes, while a squat 30% heavier than that which can be done unaided is not. Leave the squat suit for later, when you're entered in the meet.

A properly designed belt is the same width, usually 4 inches, all the way around. Many millions of cheap, junky belts have been produced with 2-inch buckles and fronts, and either 4- or 6-inch backs. These belts were designed by someone who did not understand how a belt works. For the belt to function correctly, it must act around the complete circle, and there is no reason for it to be wider in the

Figure 2-60. Different types of weightlifting belts. They can be constructed in various ways, but useful belts are the same width along their entire length. Belts that widen in the back are designed by people who do not understand the function of a belt.

back than in the front. Four inches is about the widest belt that most people can get between their ribs and hips. If you're shorter, or short-waisted, you may need to find a 3-inch belt. Thickness is important in that a very thick, laminated suede belt feels very good under a big weight. Its almost complete lack of stretch makes for a comfortable ride. Such belts are expensive, though, and any good single-ply 4-inch leather belt with a good buckle will suffice. Even a well-made Velcro belt is still better than no belt.

You may not need a belt at all for the early part of your training career, and if your abs are strong and your back is uninjured, you may prefer to never use one. Very heavy weights have certainly been lifted without one. This is a judgment call, but it is probably prudent to err on the side of safety if there is any question at all about it or if you have previously injured your back. When a belt is used, it should be used judiciously, possibly restricted to the last warm-up set and the work sets. As a general rule, do not introduce a new variable into the work set – if you're going to wear a belt in the work set, make sure you use it in the last warm-up set so that your movement pattern will not be altered or your attention diverted under the heaviest weight of the day.

Using the belt correctly is a matter of practice. It must be worn in the right place at the right tightness to be effective, and if it's wrong, it can actually screw up the lift it's designed to support. Put it on around your natural waist (higher than you wear your pants) at a comfortable tightness, take your squat stance, and squat down into the bottom position. The belt will adjust to the position it wants to settle into, the place where it functions most effectively, and it will have done so before the weight is a factor. In other words, don't let this position adjustment take place at the bottom of the first rep you need the belt for – do it in advance. Stand back up and tighten the belt to the point at which it adds a little pressure to the gut.

There is a common misconception about the use of a belt. Many people have heard that you push the "stomach" out against the belt. Doing this, however, will usually result in spinal flexion, the very thing we wear the belt to prevent from happening under a load. Just put the belt on tight, forget it's there, and use your abs the way you would without it. The belt functions without your having to actually "use" it, because the tightness it provides against the abs causes them to work harder without your micromanagement of the situation.

The right amount of tightness is a matter of individual preference, but as a general rule, more experienced lifters can wear a tighter belt than novices can. It is also quite possible to have a belt on too tight. If you have to stretch up to get the belt's prong in that last hole, you will be less able to exert pressure with your own abdominal musculature, since it must be contracted to actually generate force. Try this once to see for yourself; when you do, you'll find that there is an optimum tension on the belt, and that too tight is worse than too loose. You'll eventually find that your belt adjustment varies with your body weight, your underlying clothing, and even your hydration level; if your belt is designed with holes close enough together to allow for fine adjustment, it will come in handy.

Contrary to the new conventional wisdom regarding this, a belt will not prevent your trunk from getting and staying strong. It is hard for the layperson – or for that matter, a coach who lacks personal experience with very heavy squats – to understand this, but there is not one single relaxed muscle group in the entire human body under a 600-pound squat; this statement most especially applies to the muscles that are busy stabilizing the spine. It's not as if your trunk muscles just go to sleep when you put on your belt. What actually happens is that the abs contract harder against the external resistance provided by the belt than they can without it, in the same way that your arms can contract harder when you curl a barbell than when you curl a broomstick. A belt does in fact help you safely lift more weight than you would without one, since a tight back better supports more weight when you're squatting, and squatting more weight allows you to do more work through the range of motion and thus get stronger.

Knee wraps are another matter. When a lifter uses tight wraps, the one-meter or longer heavy kind with the various-colored stripes, he is doing so to lift more weight. The mechanism is the same with wraps as with squat suits. In the absence of an injury, knee wraps must be considered supportive gear and should not be worn. But in the event of certain knee injuries, wraps can be very helpful IF USED CORRECTLY. If you have an old ligament injury that has healed as well as it's going to, wraps are useful to add some compression, and thus stability, to the knee. A light wrap adds just enough circumferential pressure to the whole knee assembly to act almost like an external joint capsule, as well as maintaining warmth and providing proprioceptive input to the

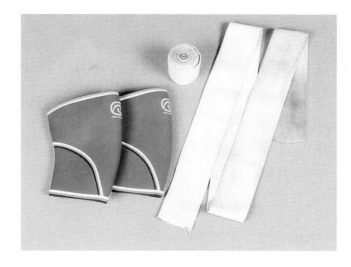

Figure 2-61. Knee wraps are used to help lifters train with minor injuries by providing capsular support to the knees. Knee sleeves are made of cloth-covered rubber and are used primarily to provide warmth.

skin and superficial structures. The caveat is this: if your wraps are so tight that they must be loosened immediately after the set, then they are acting as aids and not as support. If you can keep the wraps on for the whole workout without cutting off circulation to your lower legs, the wraps are loose enough to be considered as only supportive.

Some older lifters with older-lifter knees find that wraps a little tighter than loose support wraps make pain-free squatting possible. By adding more support to knees that have aged ungracefully, wraps can make the difference between a productive exercise and a source of irritation. The compression provided by properly applied wraps seems to prevent some of the inflammation that unwrapped older knees experience when the lifter is training the squat heavy.

Some heavier powerlifting wraps are so heavy that they cannot actually be used as loose support wraps; their elastic is so heavy that when it is stretched into position over its entire length, even applied loosely, it is too tight to leave on, and therefore too tight to consider as just supportive. Lighter wraps are available at most sporting goods stores, and they're fine for our purposes. Rubber and cloth knee sleeves can be used if warmth is the primary objective.

Figure 2-62. Weightlifting shoes are the most important personal equipment a lifter can own. They provide solid contact with the floor and eliminate sole compressibility and the instability of squishy footing. Get a pair. It will be the best money you spend on your training gear.

SHOES

Shoes are the only piece of personal equipment that you really need to own. It takes only one set of five in a pair of squat shoes to demonstrate this convincingly to anybody who has done more than one squat workout. A good pair of squat shoes adds enough to the efficiency of the movement that the cost is easily justified. For anywhere from $50 for a used pair to more than $200 for the newest Adidas weightlifting shoes, a pair of proper shoes makes a big difference in the way a squat feels. Powerlifting squat shoes have relatively flat soles, and Olympic weightlifting shoes have a little lift in the heel that makes it easier to get the knees forward just in front of the toes. Your choice will depend on your squatting style and your flexibility. Avoid shoes with heels higher than 1 inch because these are difficult to use for pulls from the floor, using the kinematics advocated here, and they produce the same problems as using a 2×4 under the heels. Most squat shoes have metatarsal straps to increase lateral stability, provide some very important arch support, and suck the foot back into the heel of the shoe to reduce intra-shoe movement.

The primary beneficial feature of a squat shoe is its lack of heel compressibility. The drive out of the bottom starts at the floor, where the feet start the kinetic chain. If the contact between the feet and the floor is the squishy gel or air cell of a running shoe, a percentage of the force of the drive will be absorbed by the compression of the cell. This compression reduces power transmission efficiency and foot stability. Unstable footing interferes with the reproducibility of the movement pattern, rendering virtually every squat a whole new experience and preventing the development of good technique. Squatting in running shoes is like squatting on a bed. Many people get away with it for years, but serious lifters invest in squat shoes. They aren't that expensive, especially compared to brand new name-brand athletic shoes, and they make a huge difference in the way a squat feels.

We have spent a lot of time developing a model of barbell training from the perspective of balance. Poorly designed or incorrectly utilized footwear completely undermines your application of this rather elegant model. Just buy the damn shoes.

CLOTHING

A brief word about clothing is in order. It is best to squat in a T-shirt, as opposed to a tank top, because T-shirts cover more skin than tanks do. Skin is slick when sweaty, and slick is not good for keeping the bar in place. The shirt should be 100% cotton or 50/50 poly/cotton, not all synthetic, because these high-tech materials are always slick under the bar. Shorts, sweats, or training pants should always be made of stretchy material. This is very important because if your pants grab your legs, and they will because of the sweat, a non-stretch garment will restrict the movement of your legs and

Figure 2-63. Training clothes should fit in a way that does not hinder the performance of the lifts or the ability of a coach to observe your technique. Baggy pants and shirts may be fashionable, but they are not terribly useful in the weight room. T-shirts are preferred over tank tops, and shorts and sweats should be chosen for function, not appearance. But clever logos are always good.

interfere with your ability to shove your knees out and use your hips. The same thing is true for shorts that stop right below the knee, even if they are stretchy. Mid-thigh stretchy shorts or simple gray sweats are the best pants for training. And make sure your pants are pulled up; if the crotch hangs down in the middle of your thighs, this will interfere with your knee position. Clothing should not affect your movement in any way and should never, ever make it harder for you to do a thing that is hard already – squat correctly.

MIRRORS

Squatting in front of a mirror is a really bad idea. Many weight rooms have mirrors on the walls and have conveniently placed the squat racks near the walls, too, making it impossible to squat without a mirror in front of you. A mirror is a bad tool because it provides information about only one plane of the three: the frontal, the one that gives you the least information about your position and your balance. Forward and backward movement is extremely difficult to detect when you're looking straight forward into a mirror. Depth is also very difficult to judge from this direction; some obliqueness of angle is required to see the relationship between the patella and the hip, but a mirror set at an oblique angle would require that the neck be twisted a little under the load to see it. Cervical rotation under a heavy bar is as bad an idea as cervical overextension under a heavy bar.

A mirror can also be distracting because it shows any movements occurring in what should be your invisible, uncluttered background when you're looking down. The human brain being quite sensitive to visual movement, this is not useful when you're trying to concentrate on squatting a heavy weight and some Bozo looking at his massive biceps walks behind you during the set.

The most important reason to squat without a mirror in front of you is that you should be developing your kinesthetic sense while you squat. When you pay attention to all of the proprioceptive input provided by focusing on your balance point on the floor in front of you, the pressure on your feet, the feel of your back angle, the bar in your hands and against your back, and your general sense of the balance of the movement, your sensory input is much richer than that provided visually by the mirror image. Learn to feel the correct position, not to merely see it.

Coaching Cues

One more thought: Throughout this book, the term "cue" will be used. A *cue* is a movement signal, and it is an important concept in sports pedagogy. Cues are used both by coaches with the athletes they are handling and by athletes for themselves.

For a coach, a cue is a signal that causes the athlete to correct some part of the movement he is about to do, as previously discussed with the coach. It has been built into the athlete's understanding of the movement during the process of learning it with the coach. The cue focuses the athlete's attention on the thing he should be thinking about at that time, instead of all the other things he is probably thinking about. A cue is not a long, detailed explanation that introduces a brand new concept just before the lifter performs a PR (personal record) attempt. Rather, a cue is a word or two, maybe three, seldom four, that *reminds* but does not explain. A cue should not have to be processed much by the mind that receives it; it should be heard by the ear and sent on down to the place that was waiting for it to trigger the action to which it refers.

An example of a cue is "chest up." In contrast, "lift the chest so that your back gets flat" is not a cue. The former can be used after the lifter has assumed the starting position, right before he starts the pull. The latter must be used well before he assumes the starting position, when he can give some thought to what he is about to do.

Cues are worked out between the athlete and the coach during training. Cues evolve naturally as the two people communicate with each other about the movement. A coach will develop his favorite ways of explaining key concepts to his athletes over his coaching career. He will tailor these explanations to fit the needs of the individuals he is working with, and cues will develop. Some cues, like "chest up," are almost universal due to their usefulness, brevity, and sound. They almost bark the correct position at the athlete. Other cues, which appear to be so non-specific as to be useless (like "Now!"), are in fact specific to a thing decided upon between coach and lifter and are extremely individual to that particular situation. Cues must be given in the right circumstances and at exactly the right time, or they do not trigger anything useful.

A cue can also be a reminder that you give yourself. It will not necessarily be spoken aloud, although this sometimes helps. It will be the same thing that a coach would say to you under the same circumstances, a reminder of a position problem that you have already worked out but that you need to pay attention to just before doing the movement. As you learn the exercises covered in this book, you should develop your own set of cues that will serve to reinforce good form. As you become more experienced, you will find it necessary to build cues into your approach to each lift, to solve your own individual problems with each movement pattern. You will find that each lift responds to its own reminder, and if you train alone, you'll have to remind yourself.

You will find that there are two basic types of cues: body cues and bar cues. *Body cues* are references to parts of your body interacting with the bar, like "chest up," "look forward," or "long, straight arms." These cues draw awareness to the thing doing the moving: the muscles or body part needing a correction. In contrast, *bar cues* refer to the object being moved. For instance, if your problem is jerking yourself out of position while coming off the floor in a deadlift, a problem that usually happens when you're in a hurry to get the bar moving fast, the bar cue might be "pull it slow" or "squeeze it up."

As a general rule, body cues draw the lifter's attention to a component of the movement, while a bar cue refers to the whole movement or to a part of it that several components are engaged in. "Straight elbows" may fix a problem by calling attention to the specific problem addressed. In contrast, "Keep the bar vertical" describes a complicated process of adjusting the three diagnostic angles, which the lifter can easily do by visualizing one simple thing. A bar cue generally means that if you do certain things to the bar correctly, your body will solve the problem. Some people process bar cues better than body cues, and what works for one exercise might not work for another. Deciding which cues to use is just one of the skills that you will develop through experience.

THE PRESS

The press is the oldest upper-body exercise done with a barbell. The day the barbell was invented, the guy who invented it figured out a way to pick it up and shove it over his head. After all, it is the logical thing to do with a barbell. Equipment has changed quite a bit over the past hundred or so years. We now have barbells that load with plates, racks we can set our bars in and adjust to various heights so that we don't always have to clean the weight to our shoulders first, and even plates made out of rubber in case we need to drop the weight. But pressing the barbell overhead is still the most useful upper-body exercise in the weight room.

Prior to the rise of bodybuilding, the standard test of upper-body strength was the press or, more correctly, the *two-hands press*. The popularity of the bench press has changed this to the detriment of athletes and lifters who never obtain the benefits of the press, which is the more balanced exercise. Bench pressing, a contest lift in powerlifting, actually became popular among bodybuilders first, when large pectorals ("pecs," or maybe "chesticles") became the fashion in physique contests, starting in the 1950s. Powerlifting incorporated the bench press as a standard contest lift in the mid-1960s, thus diminishing the importance of the overhead version of the press among those training primarily for strength. The final nail in the coffin was the elimination of the clean and press from Olympic weightlifting competition after the 1972 Olympics. This unfortunate development changed the nature of Olympic weightlifting training, effectively removing upper-body strength training from the list of exercises perceived as necessary by most weightlifting coaches. The exercise has continued its decline in both popularity and familiarity, to the extent that today you are quite likely to hear a seated behind-the-neck press described as a "military press" by the personal trainers in big-box gyms.

Figure 3-1. Bill Starr, the father of modern strength coaching, presses 350 pounds in the gym.

Figure 3-2. Tommy Suggs demonstrates a moderate amount of layback in this 1968 National Championships photo. The press was eliminated from Olympic competition due to "judging difficulties" – a reluctance on the part of the international governing body to establish and enforce adequate criteria about layback. It is likely that the press was actually eliminated due to a desire to shorten the meet and to avoid the political complications that arose from the lack of uniformly applied judging standards.

So, a terminology lesson is in order. A *press* refers to a movement performed while standing, whereby a weight is extended to arms' length overhead with the use of the shoulders and arms only. If a barbell is used, the exercise is properly a *two-hands press*, although it is understood that the unqualified term "press" refers to a barbell press done with both hands (since lifting a barbell one-handed is not the normal use of the equipment). Any deviation from this description warrants a qualifier. A *seated press* is a barbell press done in a seated position – an exercise that requires a special bench, unless the lifter is capable of cleaning the weight and sitting down with it on his shoulders, and then lowering it to the floor after the set. This restriction limits the amount of weight that can be lifted, and thus the ultimate usefulness of the exercise. A *dumbbell press* is a standing simultaneous two-hands movement, unless the alternated or one-hand version is specified. Any press performed supine on a bench is a *bench press*, the barbell being understood as the equipment unless a *dumbbell bench press* is specified. If the barbell is used behind the neck, this position is part of the name. "Military press" refers to the strictest form of the exercise. A *military press* is performed without any bend of the hips or back used to start the weight, sometimes with the heels together. A *behind-the-neck press* is a harder movement than a press; still harder is a *seated behind-the-neck press*. The use of the flexed and extended knees as an aid in starting the bar off the shoulders means that a *push press* has been performed.

One of the reasons the press was eliminated from Olympic weightlifting was the difficulty most judges had in bringing themselves to red-light an excessively weird press. Referred to by the term "Olympic press," the form of this movement that developed over the last few years of its presence in the meet was such that the bar was driven up from the shoulders by the use of a combination of a sharp hip flexion from overextension and a shrug of the traps. Some very adept practitioners could lean back to a point almost equivalent to a bench press, rendering the description of the lift as a "press from the shoulders" rather inaccurate. An inexperienced or unconditioned lifter attempting this movement ran the risk of a spinal hyperextension injury, although such injuries were not that common: experienced, conditioned lifters had very strong abs.

The press is the most useful upper-body exercise for sports conditioning, primarily because it is not just an upper-body exercise. Except for powerlifting and swimming, all sports that require the use of upper-body strength transmit that force along a kinetic chain that starts at the ground. Any time an athlete pushes against an opponent, throws an implement, uses a racquet or club on a ball, or transmits force to an object, that force starts at the feet against the ground. In a press, the *kinetic chain* – the components of the musculoskeletal system involved in the production and transmission of force between the base of support and the load being moved – starts at the ground and ends at the bar in the hands.

The kinetic chain in a bench press, in contrast, begins at the point on the bench where the upper back contacts it directly under the bar, and ends at the bar in the hands. Proficient bench pressers involve their legs all the way down to the

ground, using their lower body as a brace for the kinetic chain. But this does not mean that the kinetic chain extends to the ground, since the bench press can be performed with the feet on the bench or even up in the air. As in the squat, where the hands are an important component of the exercise but do not actually move the bar, the lower body is an important part of the bench press without actually being part of the kinetic chain. Even a very proficient bench presser, using the trunk and legs as efficiently as possible, is still pushing against a bench, not balancing the load with his feet and

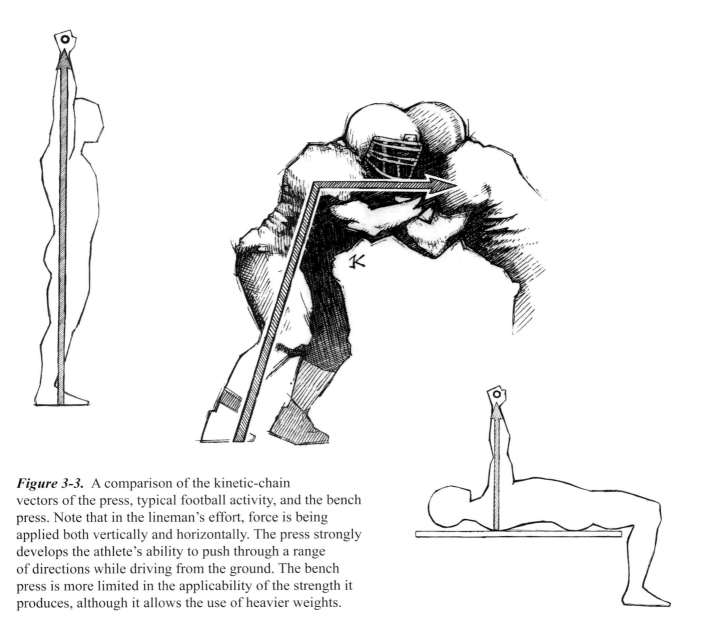

Figure 3-3. A comparison of the kinetic-chain vectors of the press, typical football activity, and the bench press. Note that in the lineman's effort, force is being applied both vertically and horizontally. The press strongly develops the athlete's ability to push through a range of directions while driving from the ground. The bench press is more limited in the applicability of the strength it produces, although it allows the use of heavier weights.

not using his entire body against the ground as he presses. For the press, using the whole body as the kinetic chain is inherent in the movement.

Basic bench press performance is different from the press in that it is primarily an upper-body exercise. It is an unusual thing in sports to actually place the back against an immovable object and use it to push against something else; it happens after the play is dead in American football if you're under the pile, but not in many other situations. The press involves the entire body, down to the feet against the floor, using all of the trunk musculature (the abs and back muscles) and the hips, legs, ankles, wrists, and feet to stabilize the body while the shoulders, upper chest, and arms press the bar overhead. This kinetic chain, from overhead at full arms' length down to the floor, is the longest possible one for the human body. And this makes the press an excellent tool for training your stability under a load.

Another difference lies in the basic nature of the movement pattern and its use of the muscle contraction. The bench press starts from the top down, with an eccentric contraction, and thus has the advantage of a stretch reflex out of the bottom to assist the concentric contraction, the up phase of the lift. In contrast, the press, like the deadlift, starts the drive up (in this case, from the shoulders) with the bar at rest; the hardest part of the movement is the first part. A multi-rep set can be modified so that the reps after the first one can start at the top – you drop down and rebound up out of the bottom position, utilizing a stretch reflex, and breathe at the top, as you do in a bench press or a squat. But the basic movement, the one done with the heaviest weights, starts at the shoulders from a dead stop.

For an exercise to be useful as a conditioning tool for a sport, it must utilize the same muscles and the same type of neurological activation pattern as that sport. *It need not be an identical copy of the sport movement.* In fact, it has been demonstrated that if the motor pathway of a slower conditioning exercise is too similar to that of the faster sport skill – as in throwing a weighted basketball – interference with correct skill execution can result. You would, in effect, be practicing throwing the ball slower than you actually throw it. And since you don't

throw objects of different weights exactly the same way, you'd also get to practice throwing it slightly wrong. Effective strength training for a sport should incorporate all the muscles involved in the sport in a coordinated way, so that strength is produced in the generalized patterns of movement used in barbell training – *and specific to nothing else*. Then, sports practice incorporates the newly acquired strength as it develops. A sport such as football requires the use of all the muscles in the body because force is generated against the ground by the hips and legs, transmitted up the trunk, and applied to the opponent through the arms and shoulders. Presses, squats, deadlifts, bench presses, and power cleans develop that strength through progressive *training*, and as the athlete gets stronger, football *practice* precisely applies the strength in the actual pattern of its use.

Specifically for the press, it is important to understand that the force is not produced solely and independently by the upper body. The shoulders and arms participate in the production of force, but they are completely dependent on the hips and legs to react against the ground through the feet as they work. In football, the kinetic chain begins at the ground because the feet move first; in pressing, it begins at the bar. Both movements transfer force along this kinetic chain through the trunk, and its isometric function is the same in both. The press provides the pattern of kinetic similarity required of a useful, applicable exercise (Figure 3-3). The bench press does not, but it does allow the use of heavier weights. We will do them both in this program, but we must realize the strengths and limitations of each exercise.

As a general rule, the more of the body involved in an exercise, the better the exercise. The press produces strength in the trunk muscles – the abs, obliques, costals, and back – as well as in the shoulders and arms. It trains the whole body to balance while standing and pressing with a heavy weight in the hands and overhead. It uses more muscles and more central nervous system activity than any other upper-body exercise. And it produces force in a more useful direction than does the bench press, in which force is directed at about 90 degrees away from the trunk. In football, the arms are usually used at an angle well above 90 degrees. The press, producing force vertically overhead, is not an exact match, but it is much closer to a useful direction than the bench press is. More important, if football players put their backs against solid objects positioned at an inclined angle and pushed against them, the incline bench press would be a pretty good exercise. They don't. Programs that have switched to the incline because of the supposedly improved carryover ignore the important kinetic-chain element of the press that makes it such an important exercise.

It is in fact possible to press a lot more weight while lying on the bench than while standing with the bar in the hands. So for simple upper-body strength, the bench press is the better exercise. Doing both exercises enables the strength developed from the bench press to be applied in a more useful way for sports. Athletes who never do anything but bench press tend to have more shoulder problems than those who include overhead training. With all the pressing emphasis directed to the anterior side of the shoulders, the posterior side gets relatively weak. Since it is possible to bench very heavy weights with years of training, this strength imbalance can be very pronounced.

The posterior shoulder musculature includes the very important rotator cuff group of external rotators, the muscles responsible for decelerating internal humeral rotation during throwing movements (Figure 3-4). The rotator cuff basically consists of the muscles on the anterior and posterior sides of the shoulder blade. The subscapularis covers the front of the scapula between it and the rib cage, and functions as an internal rotator. The supraspinatus, the infraspinatus, and the teres minor attach various points on the posterior scapula to the humerus, and provide for its external rotation as well as deceleration of internal rotation (as when

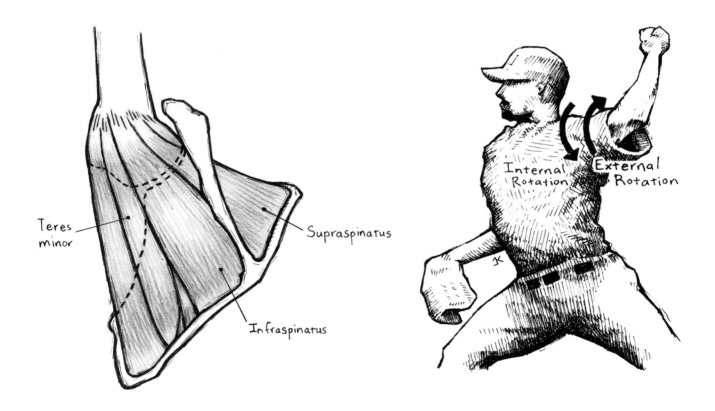

Figure 3-4. *Left,* Posterior view of the rotator cuff muscles. *Right,* They decelerate internal rotation of the humerus during throwing.

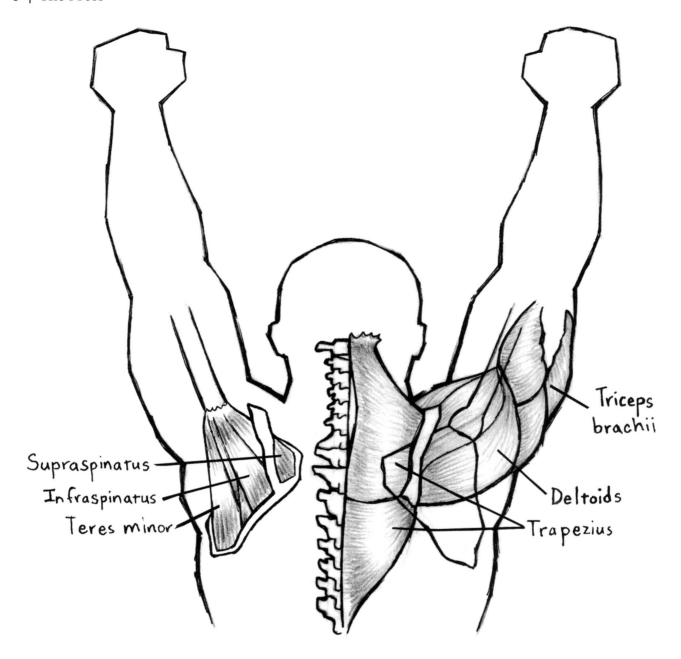

Figure 3-5. The anatomical relationship of the traps, the scapulae, the arms, and the bar in the press.

a thrown ball is released). In a press, they do not work directly as the primary muscles producing the movement, but they are used as stabilizers and are therefore strengthened in this capacity. In contrast, the bench press does not work the external rotators much, certainly not much in comparison to the loads being handled by the pectorals and anterior deltoids, which function as the main internal rotators of the humerus. If the internal rotators become disproportionately strong, enough to exceed the capacity of the external rotators to decelerate the humerus during a throw, injuries can and often do occur.

An injury usually attributed to the press by physical therapists and other medical types is the situation called *shoulder impingement*. Most of the time, PTs advise against using the press because of the supposed tendency of the tendons of the rotator cuff muscles to become trapped between the head of the humerus and the bony projections on the scapula – the coracoid and acromion processes. These bony knobs function as attachment points for the biceps, the pec minor, the coracobrachialis muscle, and the ligaments that hold the scapula and the clavicle together at the acromioclavicular (AC) joint. The coracoid and acromion processes overhang the head of the humerus where it articulates with the glenoid. Because the external rotators, specifically the supraspinatus and the infraspinatus, overlay the head of the humerus and underlay the subacromial bursa and these bony knobs, most PTs believe that the potential for mashing the bones together and trapping the tendons in between (impinging the tendons) is so high that the exercise is dangerous and should not be performed.

This dogma ignores the anatomical facts about a properly performed press. The scapula is attached to the rest of the shoulder girdle at only one point, the clavicle at the AC joint. Except for the acromioclavicular ligament, the scapula essentially "floats" freely through its range of motion in a sheath of fascia and muscle, so that its position can change relative to all the other structures of the back and the humerus. The scapula can move from a position of extreme adduction, as in the bench press, to being pulled forward, as with the start position of a barbell row (see page 272), to the shrugged-up, rotated-in-at-the-top position used at the top of the press.

When you press overhead, you finish the movement by shrugging your shoulders up toward the bar. This motion engages the trapezius muscles that connect the spinous processes of the vertebral segments in the neck and upper back to the scapulas, and this actively reinforces the traps' support for the shoulders and the bar. In effect, the bar is supported overhead by the locked-in-line arms, the scapulas hold up the arms, and the traps hold up the scapulas, so the shrugged traps actively support the weight of the bar. When the traps contract, they pull the scapulas together at the top so that they rotate medially, and the shrug pulls them upward. This motion points the glenoid cavity upward to directly support the humerus from below, and pulls the acromion and coracoid processes *away* from the

Figure 3-6. The lockout position in the press. The force of gravity drives the humerus into the glenoid.

humerus. If you press properly, the shrugged-upward scapulas are thus positioned to support the arms and the bar overhead while making impingement of the cuff tendons impossible (Figure 3-5, 3-6).

The claim that presses impinge the shoulder is therefore not correct. Pressing *incorrectly* is not the same thing as pressing – you don't get to redefine the exercise and then claim that it's dangerous. Driving a car is dangerous if you drive it into a great big rock.

There are several excellent ways to impinge the shoulder, none of them involving the press. All you have to do is hold the scapula in position while letting the humerus wedge itself into the bony processes. Bench pressing with an incorrect elbow position and certain gymnastic movements, like ring dips and ring pushups in the absence of adequate strength preparation, are good ways to put the shoulder in an anatomically or mechanically dangerous situation that you cannot control. Powerlifting is hard on the shoulders' long-term

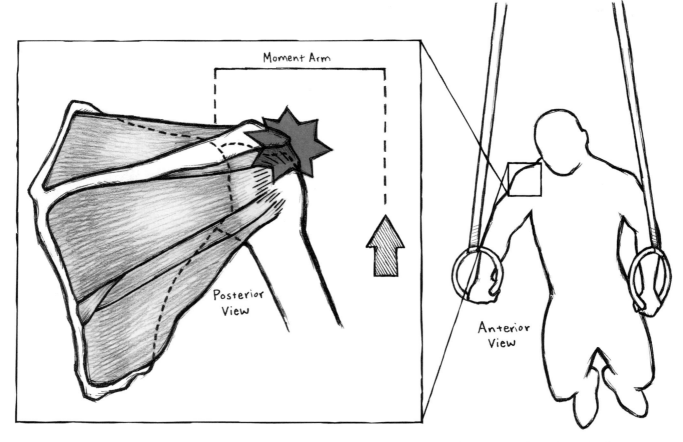

Figure 3-7. Impingement of the shoulder with incorrect position of the shoulder in the ring dip. The force of gravity drives the A/C joint down into the humerus, and moment force created by the lateral motion of the arm can produce severe shoulder problems.

health, and the recent fascination with gymnastic exercises by novice athletes has been responsible for many surgical procedures that would otherwise not have been necessary. Sports that use an overhead position, like tennis, swimming, and volleyball, but which do not typically use the press to prepare the body for the stress of that position, experience high rates of shoulder injury and surgical repair. But amazingly enough, shoulder injuries are quite uncommon in Olympic weightlifting, where the point of the sport is to put as much weight overhead as possible. Weightlifters learn very quickly how to hold a weight overhead, while tennis players have perhaps been actively discouraged from learning the safe way to work in this position.

Shoulder injuries do occur with significant frequency, and the press has been used for decades to rehabilitate injured shoulders, particularly injured rotator cuffs. Rehabbing this way works for the same reason that it is safe to press, and for the same reason that pressing actually strengthens the rotator cuff muscles. Physical Therapy usually addresses shoulder rehab with direct exercises on the rotator cuff involving rubber bands and 2-pound dumbbells, an interesting approach considering that these isolation movements do not occur as a normal part of typical human movement patterns. But when you press overhead and finish the lockout correctly, all of the muscles of the shoulder are tight and contracted. As the weight goes up over time, the strength of the finish must increase and the force produced by all of the contracting muscles must therefore increase as well. Since the press uses the rotator cuff muscles isometrically to stabilize the lockout position at the top, and since proper form ensures that they are active in this capacity *as well* as safe relative to a position of impingement, it seems as though the logical way to strengthen the cuff muscles – even cuff muscles weakened by injury and surgical repair – is to press correctly. In the correct press lockout, the weaker muscles are supported by the healthy ones, and as the injured muscles heal, they are able to resume an increasing amount of their normal functional load *if* correct technique is utilized with weights light enough to permit it. In this way, the injured muscles can be brought back to normal function *while performing* their normal function, in effect given no choice but to heal by doing what they normally do.

Since the press strengthens the shoulders, the key to shoulder health for your whole athletic career and your life as an active adult is to press correctly as an integral part of your training. Most lifters who have shoulder problems have failed to take this advice and have paid for ignoring this

Figure 3-8. Grip width, just outside the shoulders, to produce vertical forearms.

most important upper-body exercise. In fact, before the bench press became the sole focus of upper-body training in the gym, shoulder injuries were uncommon. Rotator cuff problems can be addressed in training, before they ever start, by making sure that bench press work is balanced by an equivalent amount of overhead work. For every bench press workout, there should be a press workout.

The surprising thing about the press is that it is very technically demanding. It is a very hard lift to do with a lot of weight, and most people work for many years to develop their ability to do it well. We'd better get started.

Learning to Press

The press starts at the rack with the empty bar. It should be set at the same height as for the squat, at about the middle of the sternum. If you are a female, a younger trainee, or an older or injured person, be aware that a 45-pound bar may be too heavy to start with on this exercise. Take steps to ensure that the proper equipment is available, or you will never have a chance to learn the exercise properly.

The grip for the press is determined by the simple mechanics we already know. The width is such that it places the forearms in a vertical position as seen from the back or front (Figure 3-8). This grip places your index fingers somewhere between the edge of the knurl and a half-inch out from the knurl. There are exceptionally large people who need a wider grip to keep the forearms vertical, but not many. Too wide a grip creates moment arms between the grip position on the bar and the elbows, between the elbows and the shoulders, and between the grip and the shoulders; and these moment arms are leverage you will have to overcome that need not be there at all (Figure 3-9). The choice of equipment may not be up to you here, and most people will need to work with what they have, so note that a standard Olympic weightlifting bar has about 16.5 inches (42 cm) of space between the knurls (there is no standard center marking for a powerlifting bar, but most are close to this). It might make things easier if you mark your oddball bar to this standard so that you can use the same grip width every time.

The grip should position the bones of the forearm directly under the bar, to eliminate any leverage produced against the wrist from having

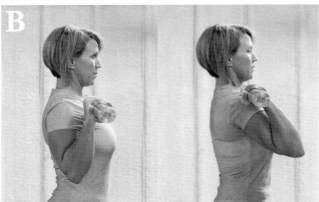

Figure 3-9. Moment arms that are created by an incorrect grip. (A) Between hand and shoulder, and between elbow and shoulder. (B) Between elbow and shoulder along the sagittal plane. (C) Between wrist and bar.

the bar too far back in the hand. The best way to position the grip efficiently is to set the grip width at your index fingers, and then rotate your hands into pronation by pointing your thumbs down toward your feet. This setup aligns the bar with the *radial longitudinal crease* and between the *thenar eminence* (the high spot adjacent to the thumb) and the medial palmar (*hypothenar*) eminence on the other side – parallel to your "life-line," to use a more familiar term. Then, just lay your fingers down on the bar and squeeze the fingertips into the bar. When you take it out of the rack, the bar will be on the heel of your palm and directly over your forearm bones, as shown in Figure 3-10. The thumbless grip is never used when pressing, not because of the danger – which is obviously not there when the bar can be dropped to the floor. Rather, the thumbs-around grip permits the "squeeze" in the forearms that increases the tightness of the muscles, making the drive from the start position more efficient and increasing motor unit recruitment throughout the arms and upper body. Except for the squat, *there is no thumbless grip in barbell training.*

Take the bar out of the rack – the EMPTY BAR, at the correct weight for your ability. Your grip will have placed the bar on the heel of your palms, and your elbows should now move to a position just in front of the bar when viewed from the side. This placement creates a vertical position for the radius bone of the forearm. (Most people place the elbows under or behind the bar, positions that tend to make the bar drive away from the body when you press.) Shrug your shoulders up and forward just a little; the idea is to have the bar resting on top of your anterior deltoids, the meaty part of your shoulders, at the start of the movement.

Inflexible people may not be able to get the shoulders far enough forward and up to put the bar in this position at first; if flexibility is the problem, you will quickly stretch out. Some people have long forearms relative to the length of their upper arms, and this anthropometry makes getting the bar on the deltoids impossible with the elbows in the correct position and a narrow grip. Sitting on the delts is the ideal position for the bar, but the movement can be done from a less-than-perfect position without any

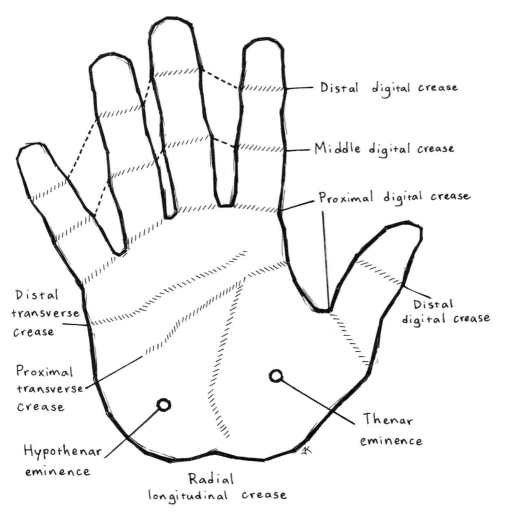

Distal digital crease

Middle digital crease

Proximal digital crease

Distal digital crease

Distal transverse crease

Proximal transverse crease

Thenar eminence

Hypothenar eminence

Radial longitudinal crease

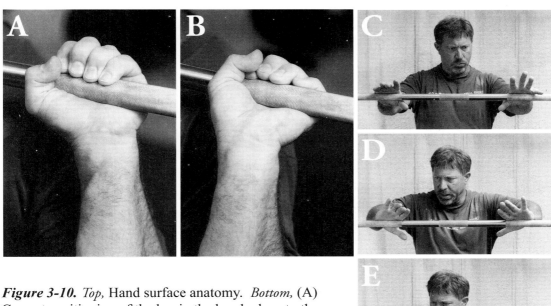

Figure 3-10. *Top,* Hand surface anatomy. *Bottom,* (A) Correct positioning of the bar in the hand: close to the heel of the palm, not back in the fingers (B). The method for taking the grip correctly (C–E).

real problem. Very flexible people should make sure not to raise the elbows too high; doing so pulls the scapulae forward and produces a lack of tightness and stability across the shoulder blades that is not conducive to an efficient press.

Your stance in the press is not as precisely critical as it is in the squat. Take a comfortable stance, and you will usually end up with something that will work. Your squat stance actually works well for the press. Too close a stance creates a balance problem, and much farther apart than the squat stance feels pretty weird. We will not be using a ground reaction in this lift (since it is not a push press), so don't worry about trying to simulate a vertical jump stance for this lift. In fact, when in doubt, go a little wider.

Many initial position problems can be prevented with a correct positioning of the eyes. Look straight ahead to a point on the wall that is level with your eyes. (This assumes that you are in a facility with walls. If the walls are too far away, a piece of equipment will do.) Stare at that point for the whole set. You might need to give yourself a point to look at. If you need to, draw a big dot on a sheet of paper and hang it up at the point that causes your eyes to hold the correct position.

Now lift your chest. This is actually accomplished by placing the upper part of the erector spinae in contraction. Think about lifting your sternum up to your chin or showing off your boobs. (Sorry for the coarse analogy, but you'll have to admit that it's useful.) Refer to Figure 3-13 for this position. "Chest up" is really a back contraction, and the press and the front squat are the two best exercises for strengthening and developing control of these muscles. Lifting your chest produces tightness in the upper back and in the entire kinetic chain, making your connection to the ground more stable and improving your pressing mechanics overall.

When your elbows are up correctly and you have lifted your chest, you are ready to press the bar. The press is learned in two stages: First, you will put the bar where it is going to be in the finished position. This step consists of learning the lockout position and the anatomical and mechanical reasons for using it. Second, you will learn how to get the

Figure 3-11. The elbows are in front of the bar. This position places the radius in a vertical position and provides for the correct direction of upward drive.

Figure 3-12. The bar rests on the meat of the shoulders – the anterior deltoids – if possible. *Top,* Normal forearm dimensions. *Bottom,* A long forearm relative to the humerus. This lifter will press from a bar position that "floats" over the delts. An attempt to set the bar down on the delts will adversely affect the mechanics of the start position.

Figure 3-13. *Top*, The correct upper back position, providing a firm platform from which to drive the bar. *Bottom*, A relaxed upper back.

Figure 3-14. The skeletal landmarks of the press. The lockout position is correct when there is a perfectly vertical relationship between the bar, the glenohumeral joint, and the mid-foot.

bar there correctly. This step consists of learning how to produce a mechanically efficient bar path and how to use your whole body to do it.

Step 1: Take a big breath, hold it (our friend the Valsalva maneuver), and drive the bar up over your head. The vast majority of people will press the bar up to lockout but in a position just in front of the forehead. Make sure that you have the bar directly above the back of your neck, a point that should have the bar, the glenohumeral joint, and the mid-foot in a straight vertical line (Figure 3-14). This is the position in which there is minimal leverage operating against the primary segments of the kinetic chain – the bar to the shoulder, and the shoulder down to the mid-foot. If the bar is directly plumb to the shoulder joints, the load applies no leverage to the shoulders. If the shoulders

plumb to the mid-foot, the back and legs apply no leverage to the balance point. If the bar is plumb to the mid-foot, the entire kinetic chain is in simple compression, with no leverage against the primary segments.

Once the bar is over your head correctly, lock your elbows and shrug up your shoulders to support the bar. The bones of the arm are lined up in a column by the triceps and deltoids; the shoulders are shrugged up with the trapezius; and the arms and the traps must work together to support heavy weights overhead. Imagine someone behind you gently pushing your elbows together and pulling them up at the same time, as illustrated in Figure 3-15. The combination of locking the elbows out and shrugging the traps up at lockout, with the bar directly over the ears, produces a very firm, stable

Figure 3-15. Cues for the lockout position. (A) The bar is back in a position over the shoulder joints, a point that will be well behind the forehead if the neck is in the normal anatomical position. You might find it helpful to think of the bar being pulled back into this position from behind. (B) The bar is then supported in this position with the triceps, deltoids, and traps. To learn this position, you might find it helpful to feel a gentle upward and inward squeeze on the humerus from either side, along with hearing a reminder to "shrug" the bar up.

position at the top that involves all of the shoulder-girdle muscles and prevents shoulder impingement.

It is helpful to think about the lockout as a continuation of the upward drive, as though you are never finished pressing the bar upward. When the load is heavy, this cue provides the last little push necessary to get the bar into the lockout position. Think about pressing the bar up to the ceiling.

Step 2: After this lockout position is correct, it is time to learn how to best drive the bar to this position. This step involves making the bar path correct and establishing the proper movement of your body in relation to the bar. Since the bar is sitting on your deltoids, in front of the neck, and it must move up to a position above the shoulder joints, several inches behind the starting position, there must be a relative lateral movement of several inches on the way up (Figure 3-16). But barbells like to travel in straight vertical lines up and down, especially when they're heavy. Our vertical bar path must therefore be produced in a way that takes the load from a position in front of the shoulders to the lockout position plumb to the shoulder joints. We do this with motion of the torso.

Lean back slightly by pushing your hips forward. This slight movement must not be produced by bending the knees or the lumbar spine. Rather, the movement is a function of only the hips. Without the bar and with your hands on

Figure 3-16. The lateral distance between the initial position of the bar on the shoulders and the final position overhead. This distance is covered by the movement of the torso as it drives forward after the bar crosses the level of the forehead on its way up.

Figure 3-17. The hip movement used in the press. With hands on the hips, shove your pelvis forward and backward to simulate the torso movement used in the press. Do not unlock your knees or your lower back.

your hips, push your pelvis forward and back a few times, keeping your knees and your low back locked in position. Try to do this rocking motion with just your hip joints. When the weight gets heavy, your abs will lock your low back and your quads will lock your knees, involving both of these muscle masses in the exercise isometrically. It's easy unweighted, but later it becomes a huge part of this challenging exercise (Figure 3-17).

When you understand this motion, take the bar out of the rack, making sure that your grip and elbow position are correct, and then push your hips forward and drive the bar up straight. As soon as it crosses the top of your forehead, *get under the bar*. Move your body forward under the bar and drive it to lockout. Don't move the bar back – slam yourself forward under the bar (Figure 3-18). When you do this correctly, you will find that the forward torso movement contributes to lockout at the top: as the shoulder drives forward, the contracting deltoid and tricep bring the upper arm and the forearm into alignment, thus driving up the bar.

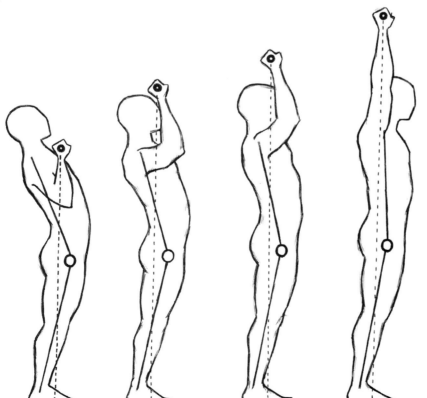

Figure 3-18. The torso drives forward as the bar drives up.

Do this for a set of five, and rack the bar. Do as many sets as necessary with the empty bar to clarify the concept of moving yourself forward under the bar, as opposed to moving the bar back to the shoulder joint. Make sure you're leaning back *before* you start to press, because it's very common to start the press with a vertical torso and then lean back as the bar starts up. Hips-forward must occur before the press starts, or the bar will travel *forward* around your chin, not *up* in an efficient vertical path.

To further reinforce the vertical bar path, think about keeping the bar close to your face on the way up. Aim for your nose as the bar leaves your shoulders. Then, as you lower the bar for the next rep, aim for your nose on the way down as well. You may actually hit yourself in the nose before you figure this out, but you'll probably do it just once. By establishing a bar path close to your face on both the concentric and eccentric halves of the movement, you practice it starting from the very first sets of the exercise.

After as much practice with the empty bar as is necessary, start up in 5-, 10-, or 20-pound jumps, whatever is appropriate for your age and strength, until the bar speed begins to slow markedly on the fifth rep of the set, and call it a workout.

Faults and Corrections

There won't be nearly as many problems with the press as there are with the squat or deadlift, because there are fewer joints actively participating in the movement of the bar. Most problems are either starting position problems or bar path problems, and they result in a missed press for really just two reasons:

• You fail to get the bar off your chest.

• The distance between the shoulder and the bar becomes too long a moment arm to overcome: bar path problems.

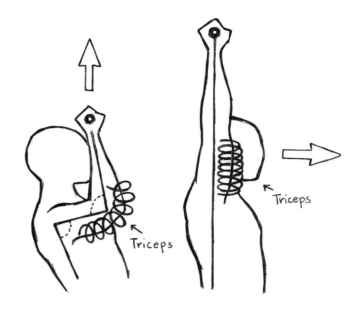

Figure 3-19. The forward movement of the torso aids in the lockout. As the shoulder and the elbow extend, the forward motion of the shoulder drives the distal end of the humerus up, helping to straighten the elbow.

The first problem happens because you have lost your *tightness* in the start position due to breathing errors, positioning errors (chest not up, elbows not up, etc.), or a focus error or because you have just gotten tired or the weight is too heavy. The second problem occurs because you have produced *an incorrect bar path*. You pushed the bar forward instead of up, you failed to hold your position under the bar as you pushed it up, or you failed to get back under the bar after it crossed your forehead. Let's look at the conditions under which these errors occur and figure out how to prevent them.

LOSING TIGHTNESS

There are two types of upper back looseness that commonly screw up the press. The first type, caused by letting the chest cave in so that the upper back rounds, is very common. Heavy weight on a press is uncomfortable enough already, without your exacerbating the problem with a lack of good support. Keeping the chest up holds the thoracic spine in proper anatomical position, and this is primarily accomplished with the upper back muscles and your breathing pattern. When the upper erector spinae muscles contract, they rotate the rib cage up, holding it in place against the load on the shoulders. Remembering to "lift the chest" is usually all that is required, but most people will need to really focus on this in every rep for a while. The attention span can be short under a bar, especially a heavy bar on the front of the shoulders, and focusing on technique gets more difficult as the weight gets heavier. A big held breath – the same Valsalva maneuver that is used for all barbell exercises – is your friend during the press. Air is support, in this case for the rib cage as well as for the spine, and the act of tightening and lifting the chest is so enmeshed in the action of taking a big breath under a heavy load that the two are essentially inseparable. They happen at the same time and they signal each other to happen.

You will have to take a new breath before each rep, at least for a while, or you risk a "blackout" at heavier weights. *Vasovagal syncope* is the term applied to a blackout or fainting. It can be caused by a sympathetic/parasympathetic nervous system response to 1) pressure on the neck from the bar, 2) the shrugged lockout position, and/or 3) the general effects of the anterior bar position's load on the vascular structure in the neck that is known as the *carotid sinus*. Pressure applied to the carotid sinus by any of these three mechanisms can produce a blackout in susceptible people by reducing the heart rate at exactly the wrong time (interestingly enough, this seldom happens in women). The phenomenon is not directly related to the Valsalva itself because a loaded Valsalva is not a problem for healthy people in the squat, bench press, or deadlift, in which the loaded Valsalva results in *increased* blood flow to the brain. The chances of a blackout happening increases markedly if you do not release the pressure between each rep by taking a new breath.

Blackouts under the bar can be a problem because if you fall, your weight room surroundings are never a comfortable place to land in a big heap with a loaded barbell. The press and the rack position of the clean are the only two places that blacking out is usually a problem, so be prepared if it happens. You will feel a change in perception before the event occurs. If possible, rack or drop the bar. If the feeling persists or gets worse (your knees will begin to wobble), take a knee so you'll have a shorter distance to fall. The blackout itself is harmless and will pass in a few seconds with no lasting effects; the fall is the problem, so be careful.

The other way to be loose is to let the elbows and the shoulders slide down, or to never get them up in the correct position. When you fail to hold the elbows up, the shoulders drop, too. This combination not only places the elbows in a bad mechanical position to press, but also lets the bar drop down the chest a little, thereby adding to the distance the bar must be pressed. A longer bar path means more work done on the weight from a worse position, thus decreasing the weight you can lift that way. Keep your shoulders up and your elbows just in front of the bar so that the bar path is shorter and more efficient and the bottom position is better supported between reps.

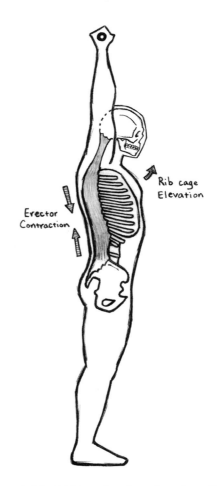

Figure 3-20. Lifting the chest is primarily a function of the upper back muscles.

USING AN INEFFICIENT BAR PATH

The second major problem is an inefficient bar path. Barbells like to move in straight vertical lines, and your job is to arrange your body movements so that the bar can do this. You have to lean back before the press starts, and 95% of people will not lean back enough to enable the bar to clear the chin without introducing forward movement into the bar path. Leaning back enables you to perform the press efficiently. Make up your mind that you are going to lean back *before* you start every rep of the press.

The heavier the weight, the greater the tendency for the bar path to head away from the shoulder joints. When the distance between the shoulder joints and the bar gets to the point where the leverage created by this moment arm exceeds your strength – even if the load itself does not – you will get stuck on the way up. It is critical to keep the bar close. Three common bar path problems cause this to happen; pushing the bar away, failing to get under the bar after it passes the forehead, and leaning back away from the bar are all different problems, but they all affect the press the same way.

First, the most common form problem with light weights is having the bar out in front too far, away from the face; this problem is produced by a bar path that curves away from the face (Figure 3-22). Heavy weights like to move in straight vertical lines because they represent less energy expenditure than do longer, curved bar paths. This is true for all barbell exercises, from the simple press to the more complex snatch and clean and jerk. Heavy weights must follow a straight vertical bar path in the press because heavy weights can't be pressed in a curve. And if the bar moves forward, your back must go backward so that the system's center of mass stays balanced over the mid-foot. This loss of control erodes the position necessary for a powerful press, with the delts and triceps driving up on the elbows held close to the body, in a position of increased mechanical efficiency with a shorter lever arm. Sometimes allowing the elbows to drop into a lower position is what makes the forearms less than vertical. This is an easy thing to correct if you catch

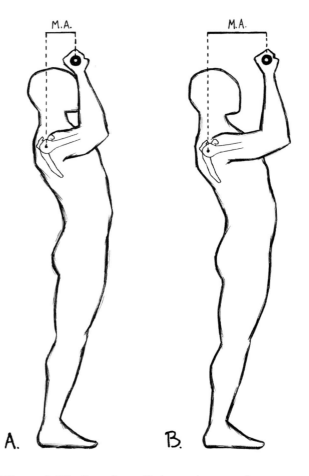

Figure 3-21. Pressing efficiency is strongly influenced by the mechanics of the pressing position: the shorter the distance between the bar and the shoulders, the shorter the moment arm. *Left*, Driving up close to the face provides this good mechanical position. *Right*, Any movement of body or bar that increases the moment arm length is detrimental to pressing efficiency. (*M.A. = moment arm*)

it early: raise your elbows until they are just in front of the bar, and aim the bar at your nose. After you lock the bar out at the top, aim for your nose on the way down so you can practice keeping the bar close *10* times per set of 5 reps.

Second, leaving the bar out in front – not "getting under the bar" – is a different problem, and it most definitely will occur with heavy weights. When the bar has been started perfectly straight up but the lifter fails to move forward under the bar after it clears the head, the same position problem occurs at a higher point in the bar path. You have

Figure 3-22. Problem 1: Pushing the bar away from the face produces pressing inefficiency and a curved bar path. This error often happens if the bar is pushed forward to clear the chin due to insufficient lean-back.

Figure 3-23. Problem 2: The failure to get under the bar after it crosses the top of the head leaves the long moment arm between the bar and shoulders intact and unmanageable. With this error, the lifter fails to take advantage of the torso driving forward to help lock out the elbows.

to get in the habit of slamming your body forward under the press just as soon as the bar passes your forehead. This pattern must be embedded early in the process of learning the exercise, and it must be consciously revisited each workout, from the empty bar on up.

There is another way to make the body get forward under the bar at lockout. As is so often the case in athletics, a thing can be conceived of and understood in many different ways. The lockout of the press can be thought of as the shoulders moving forward under the bar, but it can also be approached from the opposite direction, *as the hips moving back* as the bar crosses the forehead. These are obviously two different ways to explain the same concept. If the lift starts with a slight hip extension, lockout is facilitated when the hips are straightened

fast and the shoulders and elbows are driven up, as previously illustrated. Both the chest and shoulders moving forward or the hips moving back produce the same net effect relative to the bar; use the cue that helps you best. As you become experienced as a lifter, you should get better at understanding the mechanics of what is happening under the bar and be able to visualize more solutions for movement problems you may be experiencing.

An emphasis on getting forward under the bar can result in a balance problem, noticeable as a tendency to be on the ball of the foot during the drive and lockout. A good connection with the ground requires that the weight be evenly distributed over the whole foot even as the bar is centered over the middle of it. Any shifting forward during the press must be done in the context of the entire body staying in balance under the bar. If the forward shift is sufficient to actually alter the center of gravity of the lifter/barbell system, you will have to compensate by moving a foot or both feet forward to avoid losing balance. Getting under the bar comes from a shift in torso position, not from a shift affecting the body all the way to the ground. Excessive movement disrupts the kinetic chain and the lift. For some people, the initial forward hips position can be cued by thinking about shifting the weight to the toes and squeezing the glutes, but as soon as the drive upward starts the system must return to balance over the mid-foot. Thinking about the mid-foot and its relationship to the bar as a vertical slot in which to drive the bar upward is the best cue for correcting a balance problem.

The third bar path problem is the tendency to push yourself away from the bar. Leaning back during the drive off the shoulders is a problem that gets worse as the weight gets heavier. Hips are a vital part of the press, with a little hip extension established to "cock" the drive off the shoulders. Timing gets off, and you drive the bar up and then lean back from the hips, instead of leaning back first and then driving the bar up. The distance between the bar and the shoulders increases, not much at first but enough to kill the press when the weight gets heavy. The bar path itself may start out vertical, but as the leverage decays, the bar will drift forward.

This problem usually occurs due to a loss of control over the lower back position, when the lean deteriorates into a lumbar overextension instead of being a hip movement. Since extreme loaded hyperextension of the lumbar spine is dangerous, it's best to never lose control of the back at all. The problem here will be abdominal muscle control, and may simply be weak abs. The rectus abdominis acts directly against lumbar hyperextension by providing tension between the rib cage and the pubis, counteracting lumbar hyperextension and increasing intra-abdominal pressure to reinforce correct lumbar curvature from the anterior side of

Figure 3-24. Problem 3: Excessive layback is not the same as pushing the bar forward. Note the position of the bar over the mid-foot, except that the torso is too far behind the bar, contributing to moment arm length and an excessive horizontal distance to make up during lockout.

the trunk (Figure 3-25). Weighted sit-ups can be helpful to develop a strong set of abs.

Heavy weights tend to blur awareness of the fine points of technique and position, as anyone who has trained heavy knows. We depend on our training, which has embedded the correct motor pathways, and coaching – when we can get it – to keep our form correct and efficient. Most often, when you miss a heavy press in front, you won't know why: a position error of a couple of inches is hard to feel under a heavy weight. Most often you didn't get under the bar. You must drill this movement pattern during the warm-up sets, both in the drive up and when lowering the bar, so that you can do it without a lot of thought and conscious direction during the work sets.

There are two breathing patterns that can be used during the set. The first pattern, which seems to be more useful for novices using lighter weights, is to breathe at the top of the press, at lockout. It has to be a quick breath, taken without relaxing anything that is supposed to be tight. It has the advantage of allowing you to rebound the bar quickly off of your shoulders after the first rep, making the press analogous to the bench press with the stretch reflex at the bottom. This use of a stretch reflex is fine at first, but most lifters tend to outgrow this and adopt the pattern of breathing at the shoulders between reps. This second method requires that the lifter stay very tight, with chest up during the breath, a thing learned with experience. Breathing at the top allows a novice to handle heavier weights while learning the skills necessary to maintain control during the press, and it will work better for flexible people who can get in a good forward lockout position to catch a breath. Breathing at the shoulders allows the more experienced lifter the luxury of a second or two of rest between heavy reps and maintains the breathing pattern of the first rep throughout the set. Try both methods and see which works better for you.

As mentioned earlier, eye position is important for good body position. It is also the key to good neck positioning, and your cervical spine will appreciate the attention. If you are having problems of any kind, especially an unpredictable bar path or lockout position, always check to make sure your eyes are looking at the right place. Or get someone else to check you during a set; it is often hard to remind yourself to do this after the bar is out of the rack. Correct eyeballs solve lots of problems with all the lifts in this program.

CHEATING WITH A PUSH PRESS

Another common problem is that when the weight gets heavy, most people try to turn the press into a push press, by starting the bar up with a push from the knees. This is a logical way to cheat

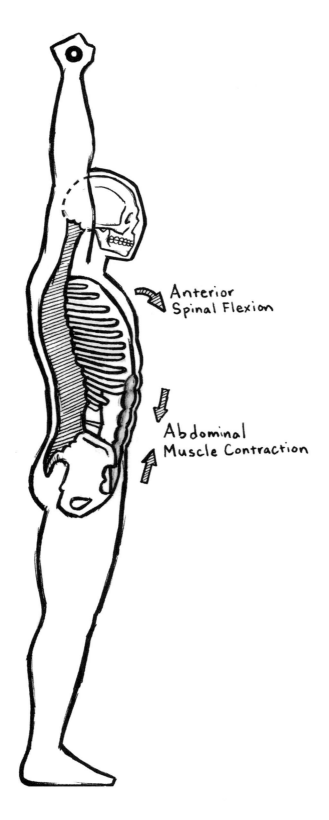

Figure 3-25. Weak abdominal musculature can account for excessive layback. Very strong pressers have very thick sections of rectus abdominis.

– after all, the hips and legs are much stronger than the shoulders and arms, and a little sharp squat-like bounce generates a lot of power. If a push press is the intended exercise, then at least do it correctly, with the bar resting firmly on the deltoids for a firm transfer of power to the bar, and a sharp dip and drive using a knee and hip bounce, not a slow push out of the knees. The push press can be done with more weight than the press can, much more with practice. But if you are trying to do a press, you must do it with correct press technique, which uses the quads to squeeze the knees into lockout and uses the hip thrust to start the bar up. If the weight is too heavy to do with correct press technique, take some off.

Some people are reluctant to admit they have too much weight on the bar, in the same way that they are likely to take too big an increase in weight each workout. The ego interferes with thinking, causing an attempt to handle weights that cannot be lifted with correct form. As with all exercises, correct form is necessary for real progress and for safety. The push press enables heavier weight to be handled, true, but the shoulders are doing less of the work while the triceps are getting better at locking out the bar. This is fine if kept in proper perspective: push presses make a good assistance movement for the press, but they are no substitute for it. Strict work with good form causes strength to be developed in the target muscle groups. More important, you need to learn how to bear down on a hard rep and finish it without cheating so that you develop the mental discipline to stay with a hard task and finish it correctly. This is one of those indirect benefits that can be obtained from physical education. If you learn nothing else from training, it is very important to learn that your limits are seldom where you think they are.

Figure 3-26. The press.

THE DEADLIFT

Lower-back strength is an important component of sports conditioning. The ability to maintain a rigid lumbar spine under a load is critical for both power transfer and safety. The deadlift builds back strength better than any other exercise, bar none. And back strength built with the deadlift is useful: while the bar is the most ergonomically friendly tool for lifting heavy weights, a 405-pound barbell deadlift makes an awkward 85-pound box more manageable.

The basic function of the lumbar muscles is to hold the low back in position so that power can be transferred through the trunk. They are aided in this task by all the muscles of the trunk: the abs, the obliques, the intercostals, and all of the many posterior muscles of the upper and lower back. These muscles function in isometric contraction – their main task is to prevent skeletal movement in the structures they are supporting. When the trunk is held rigid, it can function as a solid segment along which the force generated by the hips and legs can be transferred to the load, which will lie on the shoulders, as in the squat or the press, or go across the shoulder blades and down the arms to the hands, as in the deadlift. There is no easy way to do a deadlift – one which doesn't involve actually picking up the bar – which explains their lack of popularity in most gyms around the world.

Figure 4-1. The deadlift, as performed by brutally strong men. *Right to left*, John Kuc, Doyle Kenady, and Andy Bolton.

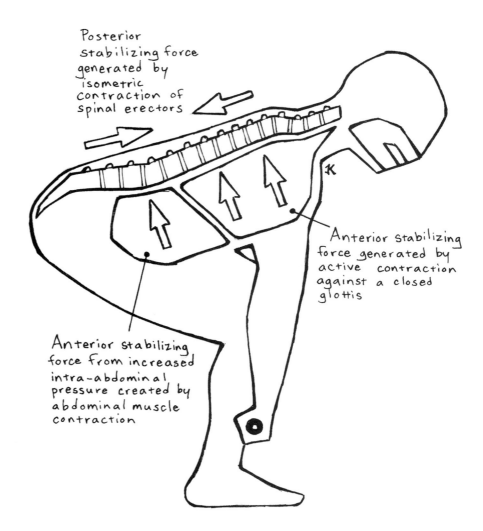

Posterior stabilizing force generated by isometric contraction of spinal erectors

Anterior stabilizing force generated by active contraction against a closed glottis

Anterior stabilizing force from increased intra-abdominal pressure created by abdominal muscle contraction

Figure 4-2. Stabilization of the spine during the deadlift is essential and is accomplished the same way as in the squat. Intra-abdominal and intrathoracic pressures increase in response to the contraction of the trunk musculature coupled with the Valsalva maneuver.

The deadlift is a simple movement. The bar is pulled, with straight arms, off the floor and up the legs until the knees, hips, and shoulders are locked out. Immense weights have been moved in this way by very strong men. In powerlifting, the deadlift is the last lift in the meet, and the expression "The meet don't start till the bar gets on the floor!" is very telling. Many big subtotals have been overcome by strong deadlifts, especially in the days before squat suits and bench shirts. The meet was often won by a lifter with a bigger deadlift than his squat. It is hard to overstate the strength of a man with an 800+ lb deadlift, a feat accomplished by only elite lifters. Nine-hundred-pound contest deadlifts are more common than they used to be, although many more lifters have done them with straps (which eliminate the grip-strength aspect of the lift).

The deadlift is brutally hard and can therefore complicate training if improperly used. It is very easy to do wrong, and a wrong deadlift is a potentially dangerous thing. There will be a few trainees who simply cannot perform this movement safely with heavy weights, due to a previous injury or an inability to perform the movement correctly. The deadlift is also easy to overtrain; a heavy workout takes a long time to recover from, and you must keep this fact in mind when setting up your training schedule.

For the vast majority of lifters, the deadlift should be an essential part of training. It is the primary back strength exercise, and it is an important assistance exercise for the squat and especially for the clean (for which it is an important introductory lesson in position and pulling mechanics). The deadlift also serves as a way to train the mind to do things that are hard.

There are two ways to perform the deadlift used in competition: the conventional, with the feet inside the grip; and the "sumo" style, with the feet outside the grip. The sumo-style wide stance produces the effect of shorter legs, thereby allowing for a more vertical back angle and a shorter moment arm along the trunk segment, thus reducing the effective load on the trunk segment (Figure 4-3). This shortening is similar to the effects of a snatch grip in Olympic weightlifting, which produces artificially "shorter" arms for the purpose of reducing the distance the bar travels to lockout overhead. Since our purpose is the development of lower back strength through the effective use of exercises that work the lower back muscles, the sumo deadlift will not be used in this program.

First, some general observations about the deadlift, in no particular order. It can be used as a leg exercise if injury prevents squatting. It is not nearly as effective as the squat for this purpose, due to the lack of hip depth used in the starting position (Figure 4-3, top). But this is the very reason it can be used if a knee or hip injury makes squats too difficult or painful, and at least some leg work can be done while healing takes place. A high-rep deadlift workout can provide enough work to maintain some leg conditioning, even if the injury is something – such as a groin pull or a not-too-severe quad tear – that would prevent the lifter from doing heavier, low-rep deadlifts.

Tremendous leg power can be exerted in the deadlift starting position, which uses essentially a half-squat depth, so the challenge is usually to keep your back tight to break the bar off the floor. Quad strength is seldom the limiting factor in the deadlift, although the hamstring strength often is. If the bar gets past the knees with the back staying flat enough, the legs can lock out what the back can support. If the bar stays on the floor, the problem is either the grip, an injury producing sufficient pain to distract from the pull, a lack of experience with pulling a heavy weight that would rather stay where it is, or just too much weight on the bar.

Figure 4-3. The mechanical effects of stance and grip width on the lifter's relationship with the bar. *Top*, Conventional deadlift start configuration. *Middle*, A wide (snatch) grip shortens the distance the bar has to travel overhead, but because this grip essentially produces artificially short arms, it also changes the back angle of the pull. *Bottom*, Likewise, a wide stance in the deadlift (sumo, with the grip inside the legs) produces artificially short legs.

A deadlift requires the production of force from a *dead* stop, thus the name. Deadlifts differ from squats in more than just depth at the bottom: the deadlift starts with a concentric contraction and ends with an eccentric contraction. The squat begins eccentrically, as the bar is lowered from lockout, and then returns to lockout with the concentric contraction, as in the bench press. To review, an eccentric contraction occurs when the muscle lengthens under tension, and a concentric contraction occurs when the muscle shortens during tension. (Muscles don't "flex"; they contract. Joints flex and extend.) Sometimes referred to as the "negative," the eccentric phase usually lowers a weight, whereas the concentric phase raises it. The stretch reflex occurs at the transition between lowering and raising, and many studies have shown that a muscle contracts harder concentrically when this contraction is preceded by a stretch, which is the very thing provided by an eccentric contraction. Demonstrate this to yourself by trying to do a vertical jump without dipping down to start the jump. Or try applying this principle to barbell curls by starting them from the top instead of from the bottom. The down phase, if used skillfully, makes the up phase much easier. But a deadlift is not preceded by any loaded stretch reflex, no matter how much drama and hip movement the lifter engages in before the pull. Much of the effect provided by the eccentric/concentric transition comes from the viscoelastic energy stored in the muscles and tendons that are elongating under a loaded trip to the bottom of the range of motion; if there is no loaded trip, there is no energy to store. The deadlift starts at the mechanically hardest part of the movement and requires the lifter to generate the entire explosion necessary to break the bar off of the floor and get it moving up, without any help from a negative or anything else.

Grip strength is crucial to the deadlift, and the deadlift works grip strength better than any other major exercise. It is the limiting factor for many lifters with smaller hands or short fingers, or for lifters who rely too much on their straps when training. The lift is famous for its alternate grip to the extent that many people use it just because they

Figure 4-4. The alternate grip. Most people prefer to supinate the non-dexterous hand.

are deadlifting and they think that's just what you do when you deadlift. Using the double-overhand grip as much as possible makes for stronger hands, though, and keeps the stress on the shoulders symmetrical. The alternate grip prevents the bar from rolling in the hands, since it is always rolling up into one hand as much as it's rolling down out of the other. In contrast, the straight double-overhand grip makes you squeeze the bar. So if all the warm-ups possible are done with a double-overhand grip, and the alternate grip is reserved for the really heavy sets, grip strength develops quickly. Novices are often able to pull their heaviest sets with a double-overhand grip because their hands can be stronger than their backs. More advanced lifters find that they need to flip a hand over to an alternate grip when the weight gets very heavy. (Most lifters prefer the non-dexterous hand for the supine, or underhand, side of the alternate grip.)

For those not intending to deadlift at a meet, straps may be a logical choice for the heavy sets, since using one supine hand and one prone hand produces asymmetrical stress on the shoulders, can cause or aggravate biceps tendon problems on the supine side in some people, and has a tendency to push the bar forward of the mid-foot on the supine side due to bicep tension. Your decision to strap the heavy sets will be based on personal preference, flexibility, and training goals. If you do your warm-ups without straps and go as heavy as you can that way, your grip will still get most of the benefit of

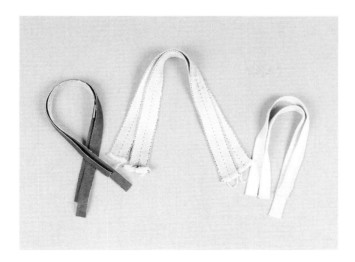

Figure 4-5. When properly used as training aids, straps can remove grip strength as a limitation. Used inappropriately, they can prevent the development of improved grip strength.

the exercise, but without the supine-side shoulder problems that sometimes accompany the alternate grip.

Anybody who has trained the deadlift for a few months has had the experience of pulling on a weight that seemed too heavy even to break off the ground when tried with a double-overhand grip, only to find that it goes up surprisingly easily when the grip is alternated. The back will not pull off the floor what the hands cannot hold, due to proprioceptive feedback that tells the back that the weight is too heavy. When the grip is flipped and the hands don't slip as the load increases off the floor, the back doesn't receive the signal that makes it stop the pull. A long, heavy deadlift can get dropped from higher up the legs with any style of grip, but most lifters cannot even break a weight off the floor that is so heavy that it opens the hands at the start of the pull. Deadlift straps have a place in training, but judgment must be exercised here; they can cause as many problems as they solve. Straps can allow heavier back training if grip is the limiting factor, or they can cause grip to *be* a limiting factor by preventing it from getting strong if they are used too often with too light a weight.

The hands are prone to callus formation as a normal part of training. All lifters have calluses, and need them to protect the hands from blisters and tears. Skin adapts to stress like all other tissues do; skin thickens precisely where it receives the stress of abrasion and folding. Calluses are bad only if they are excessive, and gripping the bar incorrectly causes excessive callus formation. Most lifters do this and have never considered the role of the grip in callus formation. Heavy calluses tear frequently, usually

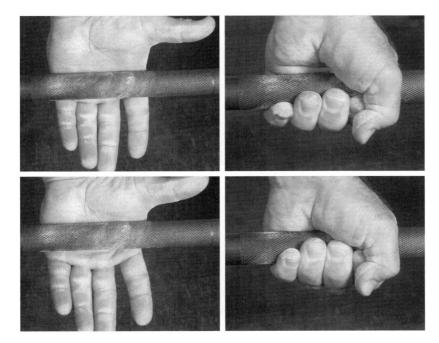

Figure 4-6. Top panels, Gripping the bar correctly, well down into the hook of the fingers, will reduce the amount of callus development. *Bottom panels,* Gripping the bar too high in the hand will allow the bar to slide down into the fingers, folding the palm skin as it goes. This folding along the area between the distal transverse crease and the proximal digital crease causes most callus formation. If they become excessively thick, calluses can tear off during heavy lifts and ruin the rest of your day.

on the distal palmar crease (and most often into the base of the ring finger because ring wearing has already produced a starter callus there). A torn callus makes the rest of the meet a challenge, eased only by some lidocaine gel that you might have in the gym bag if this has happened to you before. But if the bar is gripped correctly, callus buildup is kept minimal and the problem is not nearly as bad.

When you're setting the grip, if you place the bar in the middle of your palm and wrap your fingers from there, a fold forms at the distal end of your palm, right before the area where your fingers start. When you pull the bar up, gravity shoves this fold farther down toward your fingers, increasing the folding and stress on this part of the skin. A callus forms here as a result, and the presence of the callus amplifies the folding problem by making the fold even thicker. If you grip the bar farther down toward your fingers to begin with, it can't slide down much because *it's already there*. This is actually where the bar needs to be, since gravity will pull it there eventually. And since the bar should stop there anyway, you might as well start in this position. You also get the advantage of having less far to pull the bar; if it is farther down in your fingers, then your chest is up higher, your position off the floor is easier, the bar locks out farther down your thigh, and the bar has a shorter distance it has to move before being locked out.

Equipment can contribute to callus formation, and this fact applies to all the lifts. A bar with an excessively sharp knurl is an annoying thing to have to use in the weight room. Older bars usually have better knurls than newer bars; either the older ones are worn smooth or they were made more correctly (it seems that companies decided to start making *Texas Chainsaw Massacre* knurls in about 1990). Bad knurls can be improved with a big mill file and about an hour's work.

Chalk is important for hand safety. It keeps the skin dry and tight, making folding under a load less of a problem. You should apply chalk before you start training every day, for all the lifts. If your gym is one of those that do not allow chalk, for reasons of cleanliness or perception, you need to reevaluate your choice of gyms.

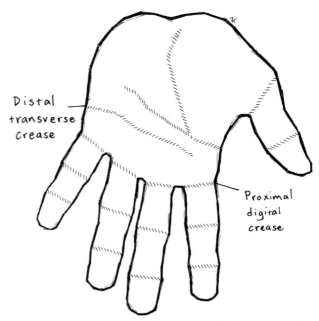

Figure 4-7. Hand surface anatomy. The bar should be between the distal transverse crease and the proximal digital crease.

Gloves have no place in a serious training program. A glove is merely a piece of loose stuff between the hand and the bar, reducing grip security and increasing the effective diameter of the bar. Gloves make bars harder to hold on to. The gloves that incorporate wrist wraps prevent the wrists from getting used to training. The only legitimate use for a glove is to cover an injury, like a torn callus or a cut, when the workout is important enough to do with the injury and it cannot be done without the covering. A desire to prevent callus formation does not constitute a legitimate use. If your gym makes a lot of money selling gloves, you have another reason to look for a different gym. And if you insist on using them, make sure they match your purse.

Deadlifts are hard. Many people don't like to do them. Most people, even the ones who will squat heavy and often and correctly, will leave deadlifts out of the workout at the slightest provocation. This is the reason most powerlifters squat more than they deadlift – there was often no "time" to do them in the program. But doing them adds back strength, and back strength is necessary for the other lifts, and for other sports, work, and life. So let's learn how to do them.

Figure 4-8. The standard plate diameter provides a standard height for the bar above the floor. Different weights in this standard diameter allow people of different strength levels to pull from this standard height, 8⅛ inches or 20.5 cm between the bottom of the bar and the floor.

Learning to Deadlift

The bar should be loaded to a light weight relative to your capability. A light weight for a novice 55-year-old woman will be different from that for an 18-year-old 205-pound athlete. Your gym should be equipped to load weights as light as 55 pounds, or possibly even lighter, to accommodate people of all levels of ability. This makes it necessary to obtain 5–10 lb plastic training plates that space a "45" lb (20 kg), 15 kg, or even 10 kg bar off the floor to the same height as a standard plate: 17¾ inches, or 45 cm. If you cannot get these light plates, you can place blocks under 10 or 25 lb iron plates, or set the bar at the correct height in the power rack; the small iron plates place the bar closer to the floor than most people's flexibility can accommodate in a correct starting position. Judgment must be exercised here; the starting weight must be light enough so that if your form is bad, you cannot hurt yourself, just in case these instructions are not followed closely enough. So 55 pounds or lighter will be the starting weight for some people, 40 kilos (88 pounds) will work for most women and lighter-bodyweight novices, and 135 pounds will work for athletes and more experienced trainees. There is never a reason for anyone other than a competitive lifter to start heavier than 135 pounds.

This method for learning the deadlift proceeds in five steps. Pay careful attention to each step as you are learning. As the steps become more practiced and familiar, they will merge into a continuous pattern of movements.

STEP 1: STANCE

The stance for the deadlift is about the same as the stance for a flat-footed vertical jump, about 8–12 inches between the heels, depending on anthropometry, with the toes pointed out. Bigger, taller people with wider hips will use a proportionately wider stance. This stance is much narrower than the squat's stance because of the difference between the two movements: the squat is done from the top down, with the hips lowered and driven up; the deadlift starts at the bottom, with the feet pushing the floor, the back locked in place, and the legs driving the floor away from the bar. The difference in stance is due to this difference in hip and knee mechanics and the need to accommodate a narrow grip for pulling efficiency (Figure 4-9).

The bar should be 1–1½ inches from your shins. For almost every human being on the planet, this distance places the bar directly over the middle of the foot, the position over which the bar stays on its way up to lockout. Most people are reluctant to keep the bar close enough to their legs during the pull, as well as when setting it down, and for that matter before the bar leaves the ground. This reluctance is often due to the fear of marring the beauty of the shins and thighs and a lack of appreciation of the significance of balance in the pull. Efficient bar paths are straight vertical lines, and if the bar starts from a position directly over the mid-foot and travels vertically to lockout directly over the mid-foot, the most efficient pull will have occurred. It is common to mistake the middle of the *forefoot* – between the tibia and the end of the toes – for the middle of the *whole* foot, the place the bar should actually be. The bar should be positioned with half the foot forward of the bar and half the foot behind it, so that the bar is directly over the middle of the arch of the foot, the

Figure 4-9. The starting stance for the deadlift places the heels approximately 8–12 inches apart, with the toes pointed slightly out.

point directly under which the weight of the lifter/barbell system is centered across the sole of the foot against the ground.

When you have the bar in this position, point your toes out. The angle will be at least 10 degrees and maybe as much as 30 degrees (see the picture of George Hechter in Figure 4-39, page 134).

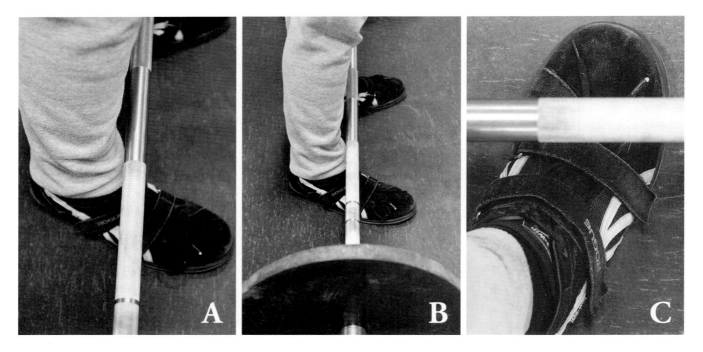

Figure 4-10. The difference between the middle of the whole foot – seen from the side (A), and from the coach's perspective (B) – and the middle of the forefoot (C), seen from the lifter's perspective from above, the most common mistake in stance placement.

Your toes might be more pointed out than you want them to be. This stance places the hips in external rotation just as it did for the squat, providing the same benefits: more adductor and external rotator involvement in the movement, as well as clearance between the femurs for the torso so that a good start position can be obtained.

STEP 2: GRIP

After you have assumed the correct stance, grip the bar, double-overhand and thumbs around, at a width that places your hands in a position in which your hands are close to your legs, without being so close that you rub your thumbs against them as you pull. This grip results in the shortest distance to lockout for the barbell (as should be obvious from our discussion of the snatch grip earlier). Bar markings are the knurling on a standard Olympic bar, which will always have a smooth space in the middle (and which may have a 6-inch center knurl in the middle of this space). Standard bar markings are at about 16½ inches for this middle space, so the grip can be set according to this dimension. Most people's hands will be about an inch into the knurl, or about 18½ inches between hands. Bigger people will need to use a proportionately wider grip to

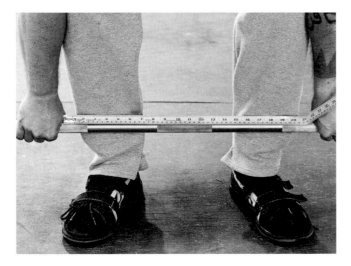

Figure 4-11. The grip width should be just outside the legs when the feet are in the correct position. This placement allows the thumbs to just clear the legs on the way up.

match their stance, while most women will need to put their hands closer together than this, with their index fingers on the edge of the knurl. Be aware that most people tend to take too wide a grip. If your grip is 3 inches into the knurl and your hands are touching your legs, your stance is too wide unless you are very broad through the hips.

Take your grip on the bar by bending over at the waist, stiff-legged, without lowering the hips. Most important at this point and for the following steps is that you **DO NOT MOVE THE BAR**. You have gone to considerable trouble to place the bar directly above the mid-foot for pulling efficiency, and if you move it during this or any subsequent steps, you will have undone Step 1.

STEP 3: KNEES FORWARD

With your grip secure, bend your knees and drop them forward just to the point where the shins touch the bar. Again, **DO NOT MOVE THE BAR,** since it is already where you want it over your foot. Hips do not drop down during this movement — *only the knees and shins move*. Once the shins are touching the bar, the hips freeze in position. They do not drop any farther. Now shove your knees out just a little to establish the slight angle of the thighs and knees that keeps them parallel to your feet. Knees will be in contact with elbows after this happens, and that is fine. The correct grip width will have the clearances very close during the pull, and if the grip is correct and the thighs are externally rotated a little, the knees will touch the elbows. Most people will try to lower their hips during this step. If you do this, you will push your knees forward, thus pushing the bar forward. Just touch the bar with the shins and shove your knees out just a little.

STEP 4: CHEST UP

This will be the most difficult step for most people: squeeze your chest up into the deadlift start position. Lifting the chest is accomplished by using the muscles of the upper back, and this starts a process of spinal extension that finishes at the pelvis. While gripping the bar, being careful

NOT TO MOVE IT, shove your rib cage up so that your chest rotates up between your arms. Let this contraction continue down your back until your lumbar spine is tightened into contraction as well. In this way, your back is properly positioned for you to pull without dropping your hips – the back will have positioned itself correctly so you can pull from the top down instead of by lowering the hips, which would shove the bar forward. DO NOT try to squeeze your shoulder blades together in the back; scapular adduction will pull you down closer to the bar into a position that you cannot maintain with a heavy weight because that's not where your shoulder blades actually stay during a pull. When you are in the correct position, stare at a point 12–15 feet in front of you on the floor so that your neck can assume its normal anatomical position. You might need to think about keeping your chin down, too.

This step will be difficult because of hamstring tension fighting against the proper extension of the lower back. Remember: The back muscles and the hamstrings are in a war for control over your pelvic position, *and the lower back must win*. During this step, most people will try to drop their hips. If you do this, the bar will roll forward of the mid-foot. Your hips will probably be higher than you want them, especially if you have been deadlifting using another method. Keep your hips up, and compensate for this weird feeling by squeezing the chest up even more. After you do a few deadlifts and your hamstrings get warm, the movement will feel better and more familiar.

STEP 5: PULL

Take a big breath and drag the bar up your legs. This means exactly what it says: "drag" implies contact, and the bar *never* leaves contact with your legs on the way up to lockout. This step will be the first time that the bar actually moves at all, and if you do it correctly, the bar path will be a straight vertical line, starting at its position directly over the mid-foot and ending at the top at arms' length with your chest up, knees and hips in extension, spine in the normal anatomical position, and feet flat on the floor. If at any time during the pull the bar leaves

your legs – which often happens as the bar gets above the knees and near the thighs – it will be off balance, forward of your mid-foot.

If the bar loses contact with your shins as you start the pull, it has traveled forward. Leaving the bar out away from the legs may be due to the perfectly natural desire not to scrape the shins, but the bar must remain close to the legs to avoid getting it out of balance. Make up your mind that you're going to keep it close, and wear sweats or thin shin guards to protect your shins if you have to. If the bar moves forward anyway and you're sure you are squeezing your chest up, chances are that you were not in balance over the mid-foot when you started the pull. This problem is commonly encountered with people who are wearing weightlifting shoes with heels that are too tall, or with people who have long legs and a short back. If this happens, you will need to insert another step, **Step 4.5: before you start the pull, get your weight back off of your toes**. Don't exaggerate this by trying to get back on your heels; just rock back a little and get the weight off of your toes and back onto your mid-foot, and then think about pushing the mid-foot straight down into the floor.

At the top of the pull, just lift your chest. That's all; don't shrug your shoulders either up or back, and don't lean back. Just raise the chest. Seen from the side, this position will be anatomically normal, with both lordotic and kyphotic curves in unexaggerated positions, your eyes looking slightly down, your hips and knees fully extended, and your shoulders back. This is the position your body must assume to safely bear weight, and the correct back position during the pull provides a safe way to transfer the load from the ground to this upright position. Refer to Figure 4-12, 5d, for this position.

Down should be the perfect opposite of up, the only difference being that the bar can go down faster than it went up. It is just as easy to injure the back by setting the bar down incorrectly as it is by picking the bar up incorrectly, and it is extremely common to set the bar down wrong, with a round back and the knees forward, even if you have pulled it correctly off the floor. A non-vertical bar path makes no more sense on the way down than it does

Figure 4-12. The five steps for a perfect deadlift. 1) Take the correct stance. 2) Take your grip on the bar. 3) Drop your shins forward to touch the bar, pushing your knees out slightly and without dropping your hips. 4) Squeeze your chest up, with your weight on the mid-foot. 5) Drag the bar up the legs.

on the way up. Be sure that you lower the bar by first unlocking your hips and knees, and then shoving your hips backward and letting the bar slide down your thighs in a straight vertical line, with your lower back locked in extension, in a movement that is the opposite of the upward bar path. As the bar passes your knees, bend them to finish setting the bar down, never unlocking the back. If your knees go forward before the bar passes them on the way down, the bar will obviously have to go forward to get around them, and this usually means that you will have also released your tight back position.

Fix your eyes on the floor at a point that is 12–15 feet in front of you, to put your neck in

Figure 4-13. Become familiar with the position the back should assume during the pull. Lifting the chest toward the hand of a coach places the upper back in extension, and arching the lower back around a hand in contact with the muscle bellies of the lumbar spinal erectors puts the lower back in extension.

the normal anatomical position, and pull a set of five. Think very hard and pay close attention to your form, concentrating especially on your back position and keeping the bar close to your legs. If you're sure your form is good enough, add weight for a few sets until it feels like the next increase might be a problem, and that's the first deadlift workout.

Back Position

Everything else can be wrong with the deadlift and nothing really bad will happen, but if your low back is round under a big load, safety will be compromised. So now is the time to learn the most important part of the deadlift: setting the back correctly. After you set the bar down, stand up without the bar and lift your chest. At the same time, arch your lower back by thinking about sticking your butt out. Refer to Figure 4-13 and imagine a coach touching you on the chest to cue your chest-up position, and touching you at the small of your back to cue your lumbar arch. The touch on your lower back gives you a point to "curl" your low back

around as you stick out your butt, the net effect of which is to cause the erector spinae muscles to contract under your conscious direction.

The arched position in which the contracted spinal erector muscles place the lower back is referred to as *lumbar extension*. You will probably not be able to maintain this degree of lumbar extension at the starting position with the bar on the floor because hamstring tension will pull your pelvis and lumbar spine out of this position to some extent, depending on your flexibility. A few people – usually women and underweight men – are so flexible that they can produce lumbar *overextension* at the bottom (Figure 4-14). This is not desirable at all because an over-arched lower back is just as bad – and perhaps much worse – a position for the lumbar discs and their normal weight-bearing ability as a rounded one. A loaded, overextended lumbar spine can not only harm the intervertebral discs but also damage the facet joints and the close-by nerve roots. The desirable position is an anatomically normal lordotic curve or normal anatomical arch. But to achieve this, most people will need to concentrate on an exaggerated extension, because even the correct arch will test the

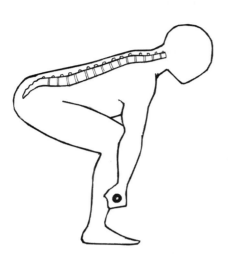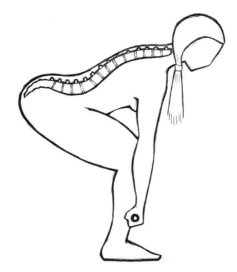

Figure 4-14. *Left*, The correct starting position for the lower back uses a normal anatomical arch. *Right*, A hyperextended lordotic curve is both unnecessary and counterproductive, as well as being difficult for people of normal flexibility to attain. The idea that the lumbar spine must appear to have a visible lordotic curve in order to be in the correct position is a misconception based on the appearance of skinny people in this position. Muscular men will be in the correct position when the low back appears flat due to the muscle mass of the erectors. Be aware that a hyperextended position is not actually desirable, but an inflexible person might need to *try* to hyperextend just to get into a correct lordotic position.

limits of most people's flexibility. The point here is to learn to set your back and identify and control the muscles you must use to do this, so that you can quickly develop the correct position. Once again, just to be sure you understand: **an overextended lumbar arch is NOT the position to use to start the deadlift. Normal anatomical position is.** But it may be necessary to *try* for overextension in order to produce normal anatomical position.

The majority of the problems encountered in the deadlift will involve an incorrect lower back position. Most novice trainees who exhibit the most common incorrect back position in the deadlift – a round lower back – are completely unaware of their back position. They are unable to identify the correct position, the incorrect position, or any position in between. This may be your problem if you struggle for more than a couple of workouts with your deadlift form. You may lack the *kinesthetic sense* – the ability to identify the spatial position of your body or a body part – required to perform the movement correctly. The cause of this may be related to visual perception: you can't see your lower back, and you haven't even attempted to look at it. You can tell if your elbows are flexed or extended, but you have no idea if your low back is flexed or extended, probably because you haven't thought about it before, because you can't see the muscles involved. Arms are in view, both in a normal field of vision and in a mirror, and it is natural to relate voluntary control to an observed, observable movement. In contrast, the lower back is behind you, and it would require a truly innovative mind to think of an excuse to look at the action of the lower back in a mirror from profile while picking up stuff in the garage.

Fixing low back problems requires an awareness of what the lumbar muscles do, what it feels like when they are doing these things, and what must be done to do them every time. Repeat the action of lifting your chest and sticking your butt out several times to practice the voluntary contraction of these muscles. Just to be sure, get on your belly on the platform and do the drill described in the "Back" section (page 40) of the Squat chapter a few times, too. Setting the back is essentially the opposite of a sit-up, which is an active flexion of the spine. Active extension of the spine activates the muscles on the other side of the torso, and thinking about it this way can help.

Once you know what an extended low back feels like, you can get yourself into a good position at the bar in steps. Take your correct starting stance, set your back, and lower yourself into position a little at a time by shoving your butt back, your knees out a little, and your shoulders forward, going down until you feel your lower back break out of extension. Then come back up as high as necessary to set it in extension again, and then try to get a little lower than the last time. In this incremental way, you can eventually get into a reasonably good starting position at the bar.

Back injuries are fairly common in the weight room, and unfortunately this is a part of training with heavy weights. Both squats and deadlifts, as well as cleans and all other pulling exercises, can produce these painful, inconvenient, and time-consuming problems. But knowing what actually causes them can lend a whole new perspective on how necessary it is to prevent position errors that result in these injuries.

If you go to the doctor when you have a back injury, nine times out of ten she will tell you that "You just tore a back muscle. Take these drugs and quit lifting so much weight." This diagnosis and recommendation reflect a lack of personal experience with these types of injuries and a lack of understanding regarding how and when muscles actually get torn and how they heal.

Torn muscle bellies bleed. They are vascular tissues, and a tear of any significance disrupts the connective-tissue components of the muscle belly to the extent that the contractile and vascular components burst; blood then begins to accumulate in the area of the tear, producing a hematoma. This looks like a large bruise and goes through the same processes that bruises do as they reabsorb and heal. Bad tears will leave a visible gap in the muscle belly. Minor tears hurt like hell, too, but they don't bleed enough to make a noticeable bruise. Little ones heal quickly, while a major tear can take several weeks.

The majority of muscle tears occur in the thighs and legs, with bench pressing accounting for

Figure 4-15. A rounded lower back is the most common problem encountered for most people learning the deadlift. Step 4 in the setup is where this must be corrected.

quite a few torn pecs. These muscles are attached to long bones that either move heavy weights over a long range of motion or accelerate the bones themselves very quickly over a long range of motion. In tears that occur during the bench press or the squat, the weight itself provides more resistance than the muscle can temporarily overcome and the rupture strength of the contractile tissue is exceeded. These tears can occur at any velocity of movement, even after sufficient warm-up. More commonly, running injuries occur in which the contractile strength of either the agonist or the antagonist muscle exceeds the rupture strength of the opposing component. Hamstrings, quads, and calves are torn with unfortunate frequency, and this becomes more common as athletes age and lose both muscle and connective tissue elasticity.

The common feature of muscles that are the most subject to belly rupture is the job they do: they accelerate long bones around an angle. To do this, they produce long ranges of motion and relatively high angular velocities. Contrast this to the job of the spinal muscles: they produce and hold an isometric contraction. They are postural muscles, and their primary function is to hold a column of small bones in a constant position relative to each other. Their morphology reflects this task: the spinal muscles are long muscles, true, but they all have multiple origin and insertion points on a closely spaced, segmented, bony structure that is designed to be held in place while the appendicular structures – the arms and legs – propel it through space. The vertebral column depends on stability for its structural integrity, and though it features a relatively limited amount of flexure, it must be held rigid as it bears a load. Lifting weights requires this rigidity, and the postural muscles of the trunk provide it.

Back injuries often occur during lifting, and most usually occur when someone is lifting incorrectly. But even when this does occur, the circumstances are markedly different from those in which a hamstring tears. A leg muscle tears during a long angular contraction that involves a significant change in the muscle belly's length over a long ROM, whereas a back injury occurs over a small intervertebral ROM that may involve little or no movement within the erector belly. Even if the entire lumbar musculature completely relaxes, not much movement will have occurred, certainly not when compared to a sprint stride. This makes it highly unlikely that you will actually rupture a back muscle belly while picking up a sack of groceries, yet these low-force, low-velocity types of activities are precisely where most back injuries happen. In the absence of blunt trauma, true back muscle ruptures are quite rare.

Most back injuries are, unfortunately, spinal in nature. Think of them as joint injuries, like a knee injury. The intervertebral discs and facet joints are quite susceptible to loaded abnormal intervertebral movement, the kind of movement that back muscle contraction is supposed to prevent. Strong back muscles developed through correct lifting technique are perhaps the best preventative for back injuries, since the habits you form while lifting correctly contribute to spinal safety just as much as the

strength it produces does. Knowing this, pay extra attention to form while learning to pull off the floor; it will come in handy. That's a promise.

Pulling Mechanics

First, let's make a few general observations about the behavior of the physical system we're working with here. *Moment*, or rotating force (sometimes the term *torque* is used), is the force applied along a rigid bar that makes an object at the end of the bar turn around an axis. Moment is at its maximum when applied at 90 degrees to the thing being rotated. Think about turning a nut with a wrench; your hand placed at a weird angle to the wrench is not strong, and the strongest position is one in which your hand is at a right angle to the wrench. This is why a mechanic always wants to have enough room to get his arm at right angles to his wrench on a stuck bolt.

Moment also increases with distance away from the thing being turned. A grip on the wrench turns the bolt more easily the farther it is from the bolt. The *moment arm* is the distance between the bolt and your hand on the wrench, measured at right angles between the bolt and the direction you're pulling on the wrench. A longer wrench works better than a shorter one because the longer length creates a longer moment arm if the angle of the pull remains efficient. The moment arm's length

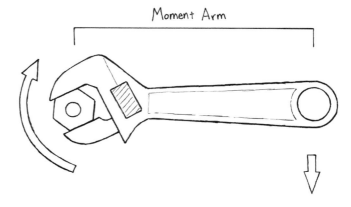

Figure 4-16. The important mechanical concept of the moment arm, as illustrated by the wrench and bolt.

is determined by both the length of the segment and the angle of the pull. A long wrench pulled from an angle that is less than 90 degrees will not turn the bolt well because the horizontal distance between the pull and the bolt is not as long as the wrench; i.e., you have created a short moment arm. Likewise, a short wrench pulled at 90 degrees is not an effective tool for a tight bolt because of the short moment arm.

This fact applies to all situations where a weight is lifted by the back, i.e., pulling or squatting. Gravity operates in a straight vertical line in the direction we call "down." A bar in the hands always pulls straight down, so the moment arm in this system is always measured from the bar horizontally. A short back at a more horizontal angle might have the same moment arm length as a longer back at a more vertical angle. The best setup would *seem to be* a short back at a vertical angle, but we are, unfortunately, limited by the other physical constraints on the system in our ability to make our pulling mechanics more favorable. If the back is short relative to the legs, making the back vertical will drop the hips, which shoves the knees forward, which inclines the shins, which pushes the bar forward. This sequence puts the bar forward of the mid-foot and puts the shoulders behind the bar, neither of which will work at heavy weights, for reasons we shall soon investigate.

A wrench-and-bolt model works just fine for simply describing a moment arm, but it's not really an accurate depiction of what happens at the hip joints in a deadlift. There is another way of describing the mechanics of the pull. The hip and the spine held rigid by your trunk muscles form a Class 1 lever. To refresh your memory, a Class 1 lever places the fulcrum between the load and the force that moves it, with the rigid member being the object that transmits the force, like a seesaw (Figure 4-17). The moment arms are the segments of the rigid member on either side of the fulcrum. If they are the same length, the force applied to the load is the same as the weight of the load if the system is in balance, and the distance each side moves is the same. If one side is shorter and the other side longer, the short side moves a shorter distance, more slowly,

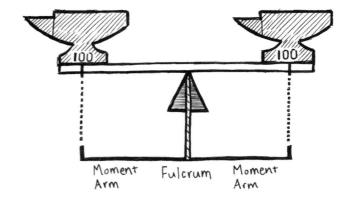

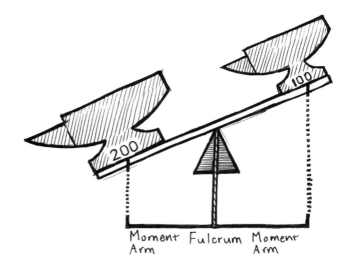

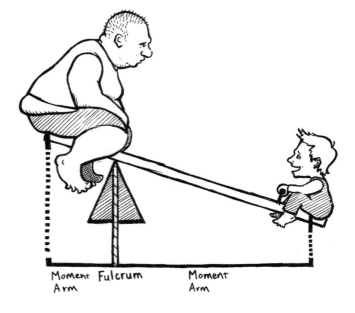

Figure 4-17. The Class 1 lever.

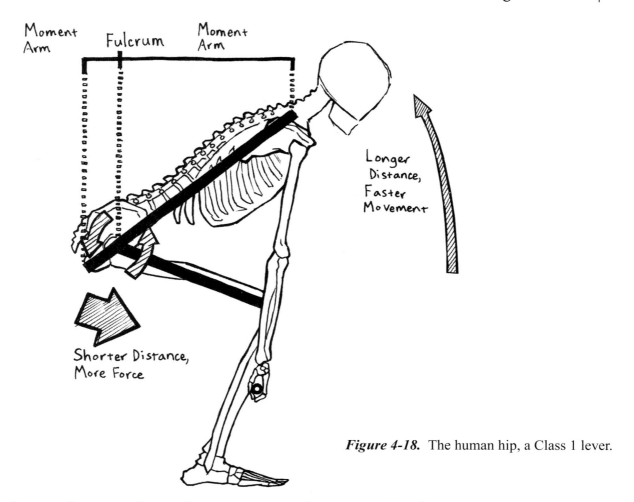

Moment Arm   Fulcrum   Moment Arm

Longer Distance, Faster Movement

Shorter Distance, More Force

Figure 4-18. The human hip, a Class 1 lever.

while the longer side moves a longer distance more quickly. But the speed at the longer end comes at the expense of higher force at the shorter end, with the force at the short end being multiplied by the length of the bar at the long end. So, a Class 1 lever can move a heavy weight a short distance more slowly if you push (or pull) down on the long side, like a crowbar prying loose a nail. Or it can move a light weight faster if you push (or pull) down hard on the short side, like stepping on a rake and having the handle hit you in the face, or the way a trebuchet worked in the olden days of siege warfare.

Because our muscles can contract only a small percentage of their length, our skeletal system is composed of levers that multiply the distance of their contraction at the expense of an increased force production requirement. The human hip is a Class 1 lever. The back and the pelvis form the rigid segment; the hip joint is the fulcrum; the hamstrings, glutes, and adductors of the posterior chain are the force pulling down behind the hips (the short segment); and the load in your hands is the force pulling down in front of the hips (the long segment) (Figure 4-18). If the force generated by the posterior chain is high enough – if you are strong enough – the short segment behind the hips can lever up the long segment in front, even with a heavy weight. The simultaneously extending knees complicate the system, but not much. If we could design the system to deadlift heavy weights, we'd put the hips closer to the bar. But since we can't, we have to design the pull to make the most of the mechanics we have, and this is why we keep the bar as close to the hips as we can get it. Some advanced lifters use an intentionally rounded upper back to shorten the distance between their hips and the bar. As we'll see, this is properly the job of the lats.

This leverage system operates when you deadlift. But if you're strong enough, the moment arm works the other way, too; the short side moving

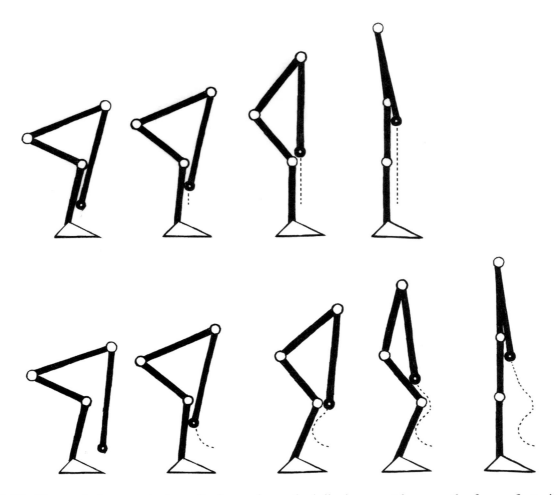

Figure 4-19. The work done against gravity is purely vertical displacement because the force of gravity acts vertically. Any other movement of the bar is horizontal motion that does not represent work done against gravity and is therefore effort spent inefficiently.

a short distance with enough force can make the long side accelerate its load over a long distance. This is what happens in a clean or snatch.

The bar path in a heavy deadlift should theoretically be straight, because that is the shortest, most efficient way to move an object through space from one point to another, and vertically up, because that is opposite to the direction in which gravity is pulling the barbell. *Work* is defined as force (in the case of work against gravity, the force of gravity acting on the mass of the loaded barbell) multiplied by distance (the measured distance the barbell has to travel), and can therefore be expressed in foot-pounds. Since gravity operates straight down, the only work that can be done *against gravity* is straight up, and any other movement represents

energy expended doing something else. Force can be applied to the bar horizontally – in a direction either forward or backward relative to the lifter – and cause the bar to move forward or backward on its way up, but this horizontal force cannot cause work to be done against gravity. In other words, you can walk around the room with the bar if you want to, but the deadlifting part consists of the work done to change the vertical distance between the bar on the floor and the bar in your hands at lockout. The shortest distance a deadlift can travel is a straight vertical line, and a longer bar path is therefore less efficient. Most sports-related movement – think of judo, downhill skiing, or football – is not as simple as a straight vertical line, but the movements involved in lifting barbells can be, so they *should* be.

The deadlift places the bar in front of the legs, creating a different situation than exists in the squat and, to a lesser extent, the press: the bar is not balanced on the shoulders and directly over the mid-foot, with a roughly equal amount of body mass on either side of the bar that can remain in balance during the lift. A deadlift must stay in balance with most of the body behind the bar. This requirement creates a situation in which the center of mass (COM) of the lifter/barbell system must be considered. During the deadlift, this COM will vary slightly, and cleans and snatches are more complicated than deadlifts due to their longer range of motion and increased musculoskeletal complexity. Light deadlifts actually balance differently than heavy deadlifts – the heavier the weight, the closer the loaded barbell approximates the COM of the body/barbell system, and the less important the body mass behind the bar becomes. A light deadlift can therefore leave the ground from a position more forward of the exact middle of the foot than a heavy deadlift can, and the same is true of a snatch or a clean.

It should also be obvious that the closer the barbell is to the body's own COM, the shorter the moment arm will be between them, and the less leverage there will be between the components of the lifter/barbell system. The closer you can get the bar to the body's COM without getting behind the mid-foot, the less leverage between them you must overcome while lifting the load. Any distance between the bar and the balance point at the mid-foot constitutes a moment arm as well, one that has a profound effect on pulling efficiency, as we will see. And as mentioned earlier, the greater the distance between bar and hips, the longer the moment arm is against the hips. So, as is the case with all other barbell exercises that involve standing with the bar in the hands or on the back, leverage is optimal and the bar is in balance when it is right over the middle of the foot. And it should never deviate from this bar path where it is in balance: right over the middle of the foot in a straight vertical line. This bar path should be recognized as the ideal physical model we try to approach; a good deadlifter gets very close.

The deadlift uses force generated by the extension of the knees and hips to drive the bar off the floor to lockout. The force is transmitted along the rigid spine, acting as a moment arm rotating at the hip between the hip extensors and the weight of the bar. This moment force is transmitted to the scapulas (more correctly, *scapulae*) and to the arms, and then down the arms to the bar. The scapula, a flat bone with a comparatively large surface area, interfaces with the rigid back as it lies against the rib cage, and is anchored in place by the extremely strong trapezius as well as by the rhomboid major and minor, the levator scapulae, and other muscles. The trapezius originates at the base of the skull and – by the *nuchal ligament* – all along the spinous processes of the cervical spine to C7, and from the spinous processes of C7 to T12, making this muscle origin the longest one in the human body. All of these fibers have an insertion point on some part of the shoulder: either the long bony ridge that runs down the length of the scapula (this ridge is called the *spine of the scapula*) or the superior aspect of the clavicle. The traps can therefore transfer force from a very long line of attachment on the spine to a very long line of attachment on the shoulders. (This is why the deadlift is such a good builder of traps and why good deadlifters have bigger traps than other athletes.) Although the traps can concentrically shrug the shoulders, adduct the scapulas, and depress the scapulas, their function in the deadlift is isometric – they hold the scapulas in place. When you are in position to pull the bar off the floor, with a back angle of somewhere between 20 and 30 degrees, depending on your anthropometry, the scapulas lie flat against the Valsalva-supported rib cage. They are held in place there by the traps and rhomboids, and are thus in a well-supported position to receive the force coming up the rigid trunk from the extending hips and knees.

The humerus is attached quite thoroughly to the scapula at the *glenoid,* or shoulder joint, by several ligaments, the deltoids, the rotator cuff tendons and musculature, the long head of the triceps, the biceps, and the teres major muscles. The delts have a long origin all along the inferior side of the spine of the scapula, directly across the bone

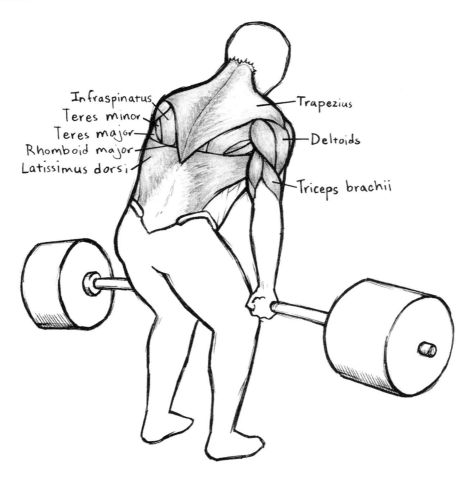

Labels: Infraspinatus, Teres minor, Teres major, Rhomboid major, Latissimus dorsi, Trapezius, Deltoids, Triceps brachii

Figure 4-20. Muscles involved in force transfer between the arms and the spine, posterior view.

from the trap attachment, and they wrap around to the front along the acromion and the outside one-third of the clavicle. The delts insert on the *deltoid tuberosity* on the lateral side of the humerus, a large bump almost halfway down the shaft. This assembly – of spine to trapezius to scapula/clavicle to deltoid to humerus – produces a very robust, effective piece of force-transfer architecture. The teres major ties the bottom of the scapula to the front of the humerus, close to the glenoid, adding to the musculature connecting the two bones.

The latissimus dorsi muscles have a very important role to play here, too: they arise from a very broad origin on the lower back, starting for most people (there are variations between individuals) at the T7 spinous process and sweeping down with the *thoracolumbar fascia*, a broad sheet of connective tissue with fibers on the sacrum and the iliac crest of the pelvis. The insertion of the lat is on

the front of the humerus at the top, very close to the pectoralis major insertion, so its function is to pull the humerus back; this function is very important to the mechanics of the pull. So the humerus has attachments both from the scapula and directly from the spine, and every spinous process in the spinal column, from skull to sacrum, is connected by either lats or traps to the humerus, with both overlapping from T7 through T12. All of these attachments form a rather thorough and effective connection between the back and the arms.

The correct position from which to pull will be one in which the scapulas, the bar, and the mid-foot are aligned vertically. The back will be held rigid in its normal anatomical position, the elbows will be straight, and the feet will obviously be flat against the floor. This is the position in which the skeleton most effectively and most efficiently transfers force – produced by the muscles that extend the hips

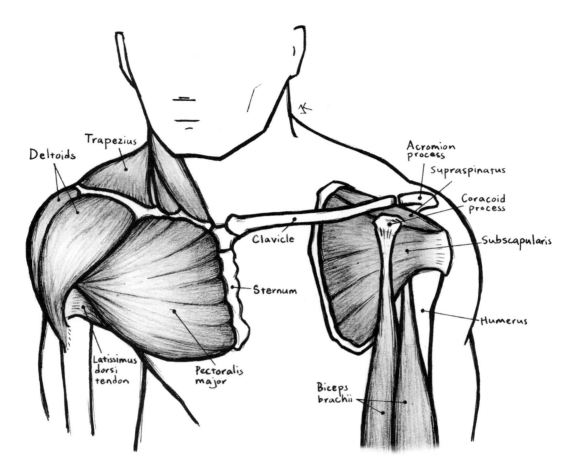

Figure 4-21. Muscles of the upper body involved in the deadlift, anterior view.

and knees – up the back and down the arms to the loaded barbell. Furthermore, this principle is true for any pull off the floor, with any grip or stance. This alignment produces optimum balance between the lifter/barbell system and the balance point in the middle of the foot.

Any other bar position has the potential to create two problems. The first problem, occurring when a barbell is pulled from a position forward of the mid-foot, is a moment arm between the barbell and the balance point. The lifter must compensate for this moment arm in some way, either by moving the bar back into balance or by applying the extra force needed to act against both the load on the bar *and* the effect of the moment arm. The distance also has a detrimental effect on the hip, knee, and back angles, causing them to assume less-than-optimal relationships with each other and the bar. This is intuitively obvious if you stand with the bar

a couple of feet in front of you – the distance is a huge problem, and when it is exaggerated in this way, the reason is clear. Cut the distance in half by stepping forward, and pulling will be easier but still not correct. Halve the distance again and the trend becomes apparent: the closer you are to the bar, the easier it is to pull; and the reason is the distance's effect on the leverage against the mid-foot.

Even a casual examination of the bar paths of heavy deadlifts, cleans, and snatches demonstrates a tendency for a barbell pulled from a position forward of the mid-foot to move back into balance, producing a curved bar path off the floor. The heavier the pull, as in deadlifts, the smaller the curve in height and amplitude. The lighter the pull, as in snatches, the larger the horizontal displacement that can be tolerated, and the higher the bar can go before settling into balance over the mid-foot. (Some snatches may be so light relative to

Figure 4-22. The correct start position in the standard pulling model. Note the angle at which the arm hangs relative to vertical.

the lifter's absolute strength that they can be pulled through their entire bar path out of balance.) You can see, then, that balance exists directly over the mid-foot, and that it makes sense to design your pulling technique to conform to this physical reality by pulling the bar off the floor in a straight vertical path.

The second problem, occurring with any bar position that is not slightly behind the front of the shoulders, is a lack of equilibrium between the bar and the lifter's arms and spine; to obtain this equilibrium, people tend to move into the correct position during the pull. In this position, your shoulders will be slightly in front of the bar, and your arms will *not* be perpendicular to the floor. It is a common feature of all pulls from the floor that after the back angle stops changing – i.e., the back has settled into a stable angle as the knees and hips extend at the bottom of the pull – the arms do not hang vertically. They hang at an

angle of somewhere between 7–10 degrees behind vertical, placing the shoulders just in front of the bar and, perhaps coincidentally, directly under the scapulas. Most Olympic weightlifting coaches teach this position, shoulders in front of the bar, and a quick online search through the many thousands of available videos of deadlifts, cleans, and snatches, viewed frame by frame, will quickly demonstrate the universal nature of the shoulders-forward position during the pull.

A continuum can be observed from light to heavy pulls: snatches, being very light relative to deadlifting capacity, can be observed to poorly conform to this model for some inefficient lifters. Cleans, being heavier than snatches but still lighter than deadlifts, are more likely to conform, and heavy deadlifts almost always conform as soon as the bar leaves the floor. Furthermore, the tendency of the lifter/barbell system to seek equilibrium in the shoulders-forward position is so inherent in pulling the barbell that if someone tries to pull with vertical or behind-vertical arms, the back angle will change – either before the pull starts or during the first part of the pull – in order to produce this position. The tendency to do this varies with weight in the same way the tendency of the bar to move toward the mid-foot balance point does, with snatches showing a lot of back-angle change over a longer portion of the pull, cleans showing much less, and deadlifts almost always starting the plates right off the floor with the same back angle used until the bar approaches the knees.

Keep in mind that a straight vertical bar path is the most physically efficient expression of barbell movement in a gravitational framework. Starting positions that place the bar forward of mid-foot or that involve vertical arms will either cause the bar to be pulled in a non-vertical path or cause a shift in back angle, both of which are costly in terms of unnecessary energy expended on the lifter's body or the barbell. Not only is a bar that is farther away from the hips harder to pull because of the longer moment arm between bar and hips, but movements that do not contribute to the vertical displacement of the load also represent wasted work capacity. Although some very good lifters may excel at

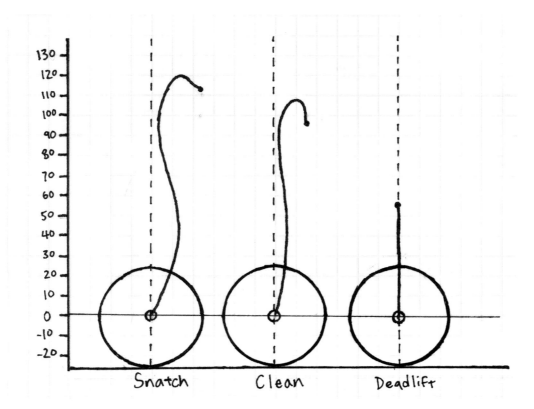

Figure 4-23. Bar path tracings of a typical heavy, snatch, clean and deadlift.

performing the lifts inefficiently, this does not mean that their method is efficient. The most efficient way to pull a barbell off the floor will be the way that produces the most straight vertical bar path, because that's the way that comports with the fact that the actual work to be done against gravity in a deadlift is the energy spent vertically displacing the weight as close to the hips as possible.

Furthermore, the center-of-mass considerations described earlier explain many aspects of this curved bar path. Think of the two ways the bar can move: vertically and horizontally. In a very general sense, vertical movement is accomplished by muscular force generated along the rigid segments of the body interacting with the load, and horizontal movement is accomplished by manipulating the body's mass in relation to the barbell. So pulling force comes from the muscles that extend the knees and hips, and from the muscles that keep the back rigid and keep the bar in the hands and correctly positioned under the spine. Horizontal movement, made necessary by the incorrect positioning of the

body/barbell system over the balance point, results from movement of the body's mass in an attempt to influence the position of the bar.

Some coaches teach that the hips should be dropped, the shoulders should be positioned behind the bar, and the back should be as vertical as possible. This start position will always create a lot of movement in both lifter and barbell before the weight actually leaves the floor, because this position places the bar forward of the mid-foot as the hips drop and the knees drop forward, pushing the shins and the bar forward, away from both the mid-foot and the hips. It also places the lifter's COM behind the bar. At heavy weights, the bar out-masses the lifter by perhaps more than 300% in strong lifters. The lifter can move the bar horizontally by manipulating the mass of his body relative to the bar, as evidenced by the layback at the top of a clean or snatch, where the bar is forward of the balance point. Since the barbell is much heavier than the part of the lifter's body behind it, the reaction between the bar and body positions will be proportionate to

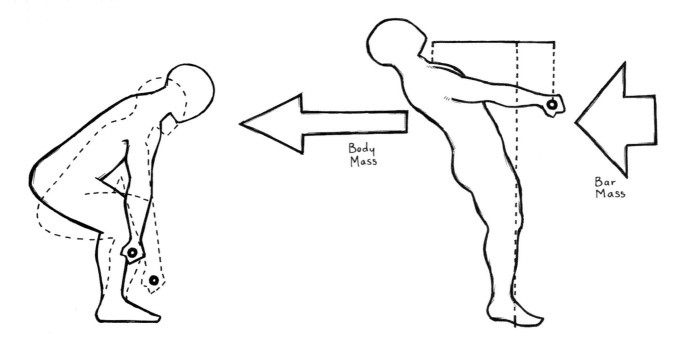

Figure 4-24. Use of the body's mass is necessary to produce a horizontal bar path component. The body's pulling machinery can efficiently move the bar upward, but the vertical orientation of the lifter/barbell system cannot effectively move the bar horizontally. For that, we make the mass of the body move horizontally to react against the mass of the barbell. Since the heavy barbell out-masses the lifter, his body must move further horizontally to effectively react against the barbell.

the differences in the mass. If the bar is forward of the balance point by 3 inches as it passes the hips in a clean, the layback will have to be *much greater than that* since the body is lighter than the bar. And if the layback does not sufficiently dampen the forward displacement, the lifter will have to jump forward to make the catch.

The same thing happens when the bar is on the floor: if you shove a heavy bar forward, your body mass behind it reacts against the bar's forward displacement by acting as a cantilever for the horizontal motion necessary to bring the bar back into balance over the mid-foot and closer to the hips. The feet are pinned to the ground by the load, so as the pull starts, the mass of body behind the bar reacts against the mass of the bar which is forward of the balance point. The bar rolls back and leaves the ground in a curve as the body swings forward around the hands and positions itself in equilibrium, with the shoulders forward of the bar. As this position settles in, the bar path becomes vertical. This movement is, of course, completely

unnecessary if the bar starts out in balance with the body's preferred position of pulling equilibrium so that a vertical bar path can be produced.

The non-vertical arm angle is perhaps the most poorly explained phenomenon in weightlifting. Why does the back angle become stable for the first part of the pull when the shoulders are in front of the bar and the arms assume their characteristic angle of 7–10 degrees from vertical? Why is there an apparent equilibrium between how far the shoulders are in front of the bar and how far the hips are behind the bar? Our working theory is that the critical relationship is the interaction between the lats, and the teres major, the triceps, and the humerus. There is a back angle at which the lats can best stabilize the arms and shorten the distance between bar and hips in order to facilitate a vertical bar path, and a heavy deadlift settles into this angle because it cannot do otherwise.

The humerus is suspended from the scapula by lots of muscle and ligament, and it would seem as though the arms should just hang vertically, as a weight on the end of a rope hanging from the ceiling hangs vertically, or "plumb" as it is called. But the arms don't hang vertically, not with a weight that is actually heavy enough to force you to tighten your back and arms. Check the videos yourself. If you want that rope to hang from the ceiling at any angle other than vertical, you will have to apply another force to the system from a different direction – you'll have to tie *another rope* to the one hanging plumb. And that second rope will work best against the first one if you pull at a right angle to the loaded rope, because a right angle is the configuration that allows the force to be applied most efficiently. Like pulling on a wrench at any angle other than 90 degrees, pulling on the rope from anything other than a right angle fails to generate the maximum turning force. It's easier to see this when the first "rope" is your humerus, and the second rope is your lat.

So, there is another rope after all; there are actually several of them. The teres major and the triceps control the angle between the scapula and the humerus. The teres major connects the inferior part of the scapula to the proximal end of the humerus on the anterior side, only millimeters away from the lat attachment under the armpit on the arm side. The triceps attaches the superior scapula, up high on the shoulder side of the armpit, to the elbow, although its leverage position is weak. More important, the lats connect their large origin along the low back directly to the shaft of the humerus, up under the armpit on the anterior side, so it pulls across   the full thickness of the shaft. These muscles add to the large number of attachments from the shoulder joint area, which, working together, transfer force from the trunk to the arms.

This posterior pull is responsible for the non-vertical angle of the arms as they hang from the shoulders under a loaded spine, and must equal the tendency of the weight to rotate the arms forward to a vertical position. If the arms rotate forward, this will place the bar forward of the mid-foot and thus off-balance, unable to be pulled if it is heavy enough. Since the triceps and the teres major are actually minor contributors to the situation due to their poor positions of leverage, the total contribution of the lats, teres major, and triceps averages out to approximately the same as just the lats. When the shoulder is in front of the bar and the back angle is stable in a pull, the angle of attachment between the lat and the humerus is about 90 degrees, since *this is the angle at which the least muscular force is required to produce a rotation force that is equal and opposite to the weight*. It is the angle at which these muscles can exert their tension on the humerus most efficiently and thus provide the maximum force transfer and stability during a pull from the floor in which the bar needs to stay over the mid-foot and as close to the hips as this stable "hang" will allow (see Figure 4-25). And the back angle adjusts to produce the 90-degree lat angle in equilibrium between the shoulders and hips.

The fact that several muscles are contributing to this posterior pull makes the angle hard to calculate precisely, and some variation with anthropometry would be expected, but the lats appear to be the major factor in the system, and the angle of attachment in a stable configuration is probably very close to 90 degrees. What is absolutely clear is that through the bottom of the pull, there exists a back angle in which the shoulders are in front of the bar, the arms do not hang straight down, the hips are closer to the bar than they would be if the arms did hang straight down, and pulling the bar off the floor in this position results in a vertical bar path. With this path, the lifter can most efficiently maintain the balance point over the mid-foot and use the lats and related muscles to maintain a vertical bar path.

Stated more succinctly, **the arms are not plumb in a deadlift because the lats do not attach to the arms at 90 degrees when the arms are plumb**. The arms must slant back to achieve a position of stability as they hang from the shoulders. So the body must assume a position that allows the arms to be at 90 degrees to the lats and for the bar to be pulled in a straight vertical line off the floor. If the hips are too low, the lat attachment angle will be less than 90 degrees, and the hips will rise as the back angle adjusts to the stable position. If the hips are too high, the angle is greater than 90 degrees, and the lifter cannot as efficiently prevent the bar from continuing forward.

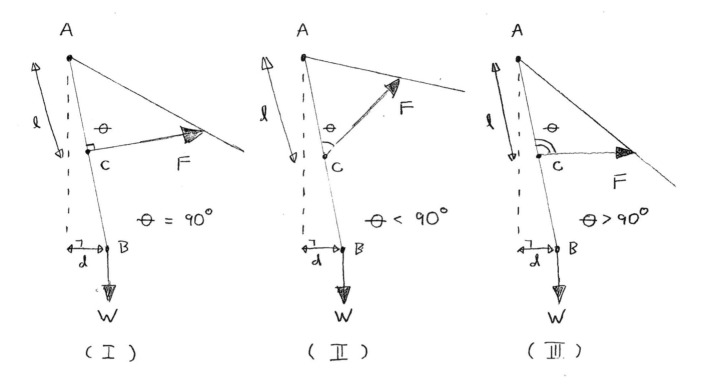

In each of the drawings above the arm hangs at an angle that places the shoulder (point A) a horizontal distance d in front of the weight. The weight pulls downward on the arm at point B with a force W producing a clock-wise moment about point A. The magnitude of this moment is W·d.

The lats attach to the arm at point C and pull on it with a force F. This produces a counter-clockwise moment about point A. The magnitude of this moment is l·F·sin θ. The back angle controls the angle θ.

In order to prevent the arm from rotating about point A the magnitude of the two moments must be equal.

$$l \cdot F \cdot \sin \theta = W \cdot d \qquad \Rightarrow \qquad F = W \cdot d / (l \cdot \sin \theta)$$

F will be smallest when sin θ reaches its maximum, which occurs at θ = 90° (I). Any other angle will require a relatively larger force F (II and III).

Matt Lorig

Figure 4-25. A proof of the theory that the lat stabilizes the humerus most efficiently at 90 degrees, from our friend Matt Lorig, Ph.D. This is the kind of analysis you get when you ask a physicist to think about barbell training.

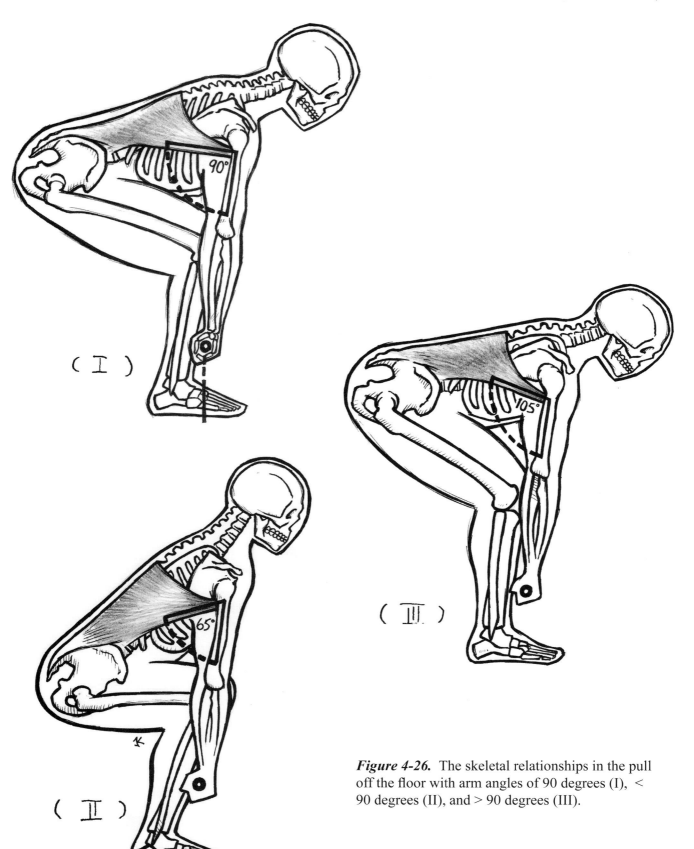

(I)

(II)

(III)

Figure 4-26. The skeletal relationships in the pull off the floor with arm angles of 90 degrees (I), < 90 degrees (II), and > 90 degrees (III).

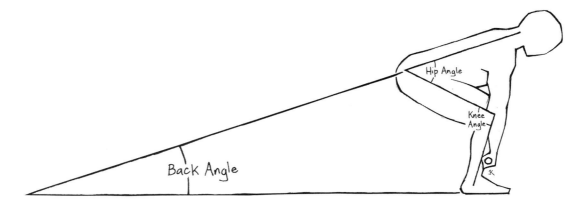

Figure 4-27. The three reference angles: knee angle, hip angle, and back angle.

The reference angles used in analyzing the deadlift are the same as those used in analyzing the squat. The *hip angle* is formed between the femur and the plane of the torso. The *knee angle* is formed between the femur and the tibia. The *back angle* is formed between the plane of the torso and the floor, which is assumed to be horizontal. In a correct deadlift, the knees extend as the bar comes off the floor, indicating that the quadriceps extend the knees under load. The back angle should be constant until the bar approaches the knees; the hamstrings "anchor" the pelvis so that this angle can be maintained (more on this later).

The hip angle opens up only slightly as the tibias get more vertical. As the bar approaches the bottom of the knees, the back angle – and consequently the hip angle – begins to change significantly (Figure 4-28). Some people start this transition at mid-shin, some higher, as there appears to be quite a bit of individual variability in the precise position of the beginning of this shift. Anthropometry is probably an important variable; arm length, for example, obviously influences this balance relationship. In most snatches and cleans, this back-angle shift appears to start a little higher up the tibia – very close to the knees for most good lifters – than it does in deadlifts, so it may be a function of the relative load. The "shorter" arms and wider grip in the snatch may mitigate the lighter weight used relative to the clean. The function of the lats changes here, as the back angle becomes more vertical and keeping the lifter/barbell system

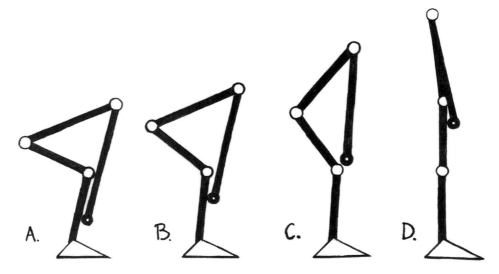

Figure 4-28. The correct sequence off the floor. (A) The starting position. (B) Knees extend, opening the knee angle. (C) The hip angle opens, bringing the bar up to the finish position (D).

in balance over the mid-foot becomes a function of the increasing back angle, and less dependent on lat tension. In all pulls from the floor, this is seen in the bar path, which always tends to come back over the mid-foot even if the bottom of the pull has been inefficient.

As the hips extend more, the hip extensors – the glutes, adductors, and hamstrings – become the predominant movers of the load, the quads having finished most of their initial job of extending the knees before the bar gets to them. The role of the back muscles during the pull is to hold the trunk rigid and keep the shoulder blades back in their normal anatomical position so that the force generated by knee and hip extension can be transferred up the back, across to the arms, and down to the bar. Lockout at the top occurs when the knees and the hips reach full extension simultaneously, with the chest up and the shoulders back. If this pulling sequence is followed, the bar will come up the legs in a vertical path.

If the back rounds during the pull, some of the force that would have gone to the bar gets eaten up by the lengthening erectors. If the weight is sufficiently heavy, the rounded back cannot be re-straightened and the deadlift cannot be locked out; the spinal erectors are designed to hold an extended position isometrically, not to actively extend a flexed spine under a compressive load. The knees and hips are already extended – the knees in this position are straight and the pelvis is in line with the femurs – and their extensors cannot help since they are already fully contracted.

The question of exactly what these three angles should be is answered for each person individually since it depends on individual anthropometry. People with long femurs, long tibias, and relatively short torsos will have a more horizontal back angle and a more closed hip angle than people with long torsos and short legs, who will have a more vertical back angle and a more open hip angle. Each person will have a different set of knee, hip, and back angles, but the correct starting position for everyone will have the previously discussed things in common: the shoulders will be slightly in front of the bar; and the bar will be touching the shins directly over

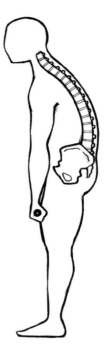

Figure 4-29. A rounded lower back is difficult to straighten when the weight is heavy. The muscles that hold the lumbar spine in extension are postural and are not designed to change the relative positions of the vertebrae; their job is to maintain extension, not to concentrically extend under compressive loading. And if the spine is in flexion, the hips are, too. If the hip extensors have finished their job, the pull is essentially finished. The only way to continue the pull would be to "hitch" the bar with a knee re-bend that would allow the hip position to reset a little. Many heavy deadlifts have been missed this way.

the mid-foot, resulting in the vertical alignment of the scapula, bar, and mid-foot. If this alignment is correct, and if the arms are straight, the feet are flat on the floor, and the back is in good thoracic and lumbar extension, the resulting reference angles are correct for that person's anthropometry. Of the three angles, the back angle will exhibit the most obvious individual variability, easily seen by an informed observer.

Arm length must also be considered when you are analyzing these angles. All other segment lengths being equal, short arms produce a more horizontal back angle and long arms produce a more vertical back angle. Long arms tend to mitigate the effects of a short torso, while short arms and a short

Figure 4-30. A comparison of different anthropometries in the deadlift start position.

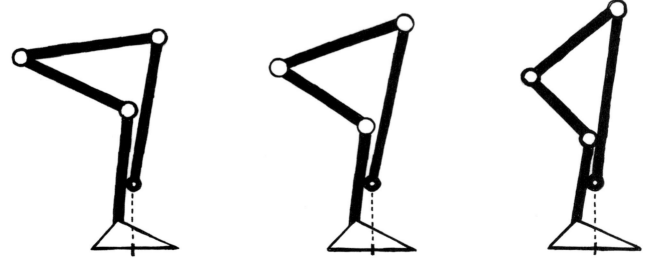

Figure 4-31. The effect of different variations of back and leg dimensions on the back angle in the starting position. From left to right, back length increases as leg length decreases.

Figure 4-32. The correct down sequence is the opposite of up (Figure 4-28). The last thing that happens on the way up is the first thing that happens on the way down: the hips and knees unlock simultaneously; then the hips move back and lower the bar to below the knees; then the knees flex and lower the bar to the floor.

torso make for a nearly perfectly horizontal back. To balance the effects of short arms and a short torso, people with this build might need to use a sumo stance, since a wide stance produces the more vertical back angle typically seen in people with more typical proportions.

Most of the problems you will have with deadlift form can be analyzed with a good understanding of pulling mechanics. Consider, for example, the problem of lowering the bar with a round back, caused by unlocking the knees first: the down phase is the exact reverse of the pull. If the last thing that happens at the top of the deadlift is the simultaneous extension of knees and hips, with a locked back and the chest up, then the first part of lowering the bar has to be knee and hip "un-extension" with a locked back and the chest up (Figure 4-32). The knees unlock just enough to take the tension off the hamstrings, at exactly the same time that the hips unlock. Then the butt travels back with the lower back locked, as the lifter closes the hip angle and uses the hamstrings and glutes

eccentrically as they lengthen. As the bar slides down the thighs, further closing the hip angle, it reaches a point as it passes the knees where the knee angle can begin to close with the hips. As the bar is lowered past the knees, they bend and the quadriceps add to the hamstrings' eccentric function, and the bar gets to the floor. This sequence of movements – the opposite of the pulling-up sequence – allows the bar to drop down in a vertical line (Figure 4-32).

Any deviation from this order will not work. If your knees move forward first when you are lowering the bar, they will be in front of the bar, and the bar cannot go straight down because it has to go forward to get around the knees (Figure 4-33). Your knees can move forward only so far before your heels get pulled up, so you round your back to let the bar go forward far enough to clear your knees. This action places the bar off-balance, forward of the mid-foot. If you find yourself progressing forward across the floor from the start to the finish of a set of five, this is why.

As you pull the bar off of the floor, your knees and hips extend together while your back angle stays

Figure 4-33. This is the wrong way to set the bar down. The knees have moved forward first, and this places them in a tragic position where kneecaps often pay a high price. And if the kneecaps somehow remain unscathed, the lower back might not.

constant, meaning that the quads initiate the push off the floor while the hamstrings hold the back angle constant, resulting in an opening of the knee and hip angles. If you attempt to extend your hips first, the result will be a non-vertical bar path. This happens when you lift your chest first, thus opening the hip angle first and leaving the knee angle in the start position. If this happens, the bar goes forward around your knees, which have not pulled back out of the way. This actually occurs only with very light weights; heavy weights like to move in straight vertical lines. If you try to pull heavy weights chest-first, you will be dragging the bar back into your shins, and the blood on the bar will tell you this is wrong. And when it's very heavy, the bar will not travel forward around your knees anyway because you can't pull a heavy weight off-balance forward.

When the knee angle opens first, as it should, the shins get more vertical and move back relative to the front of the feet, allowing the bar to travel in a vertical path up the legs. If the knee angle changes first, the bar can move up in a straight line, the way heavy bars like to move. If you feel the weight go to your toes, or if your coach sees your

heels come up, you know what you're doing wrong. Get your weight back off your toes, keep your chest up, and pull the weight straight up your shins as you push the floor. This forces the bar back into the correct path, which lets your knees straighten out and lets your quadriceps extension start the deadlift correctly. It might also be helpful to think about pushing the bar back into your legs with your lats, reinforcing the close-to-the-shin position a second way (Figure 4-34).

When the weight gets heavy, it is a common error to let the bar come forward, away from your shins, before it even leaves the floor. When this happens, your hips will have lifted, also before the load moves. Using our pulling model, we can see that when this occurs, the knee angle has opened, the hip angle has probably stayed constant, and the back angle has become more horizontal, all before the load has moved (Figure 4-35). In this situation, your quadriceps have extended your knees, but have not moved any weight while doing so. In opening the knee angle unloaded – pushing your butt up in the air without moving the bar – the quads have avoided participating in the lift and have placed the

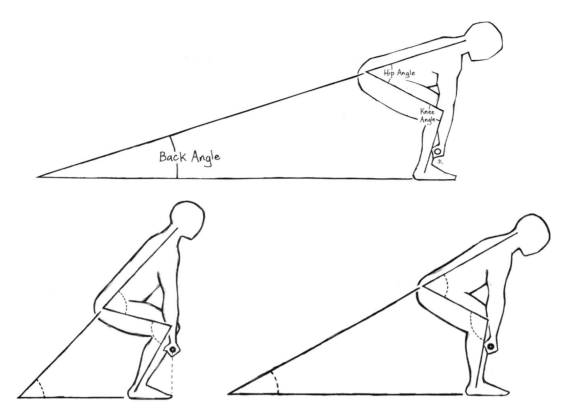

Figure 4-34. The order in which the angles open up off the floor is important for correct technique. *Top,* Reference angles in the start position. *Bottom left,* When the hip angle opens first, the bar must travel forward to clear the knees, and usually the shins get scraped when this happens. *Bottom right,* The correct order – knees first, then hips – allows for a vertical bar path.

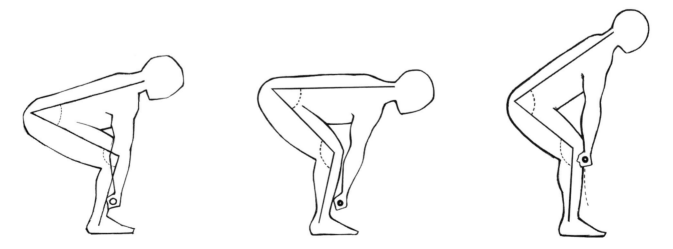

Figure 4-35. When the knee angle opens before the bar leaves the floor, the quadriceps have not been used to move the load. When the hamstrings fail to control the knee angle (their distal function) the back angle goes horizontal. This leaves the bar away from the shins, and the work of lifting the weight becomes predominantly hip extension. Technique errors that involve one group of muscles failing to make their contribution to an exercise are a common phenomenon in barbell training.

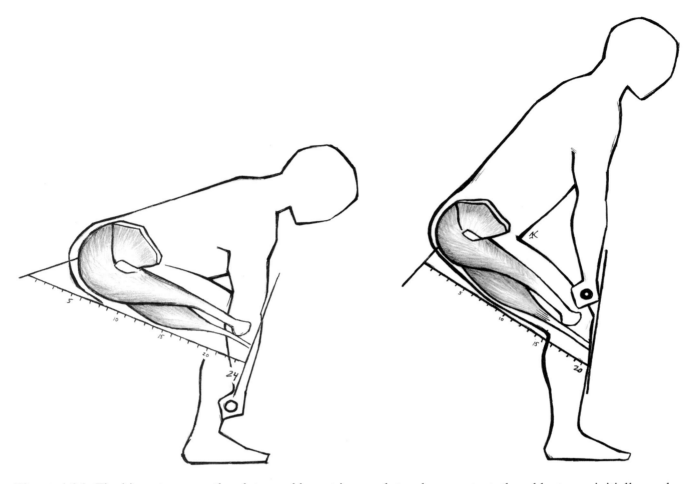

Figure 4-36. The hip extensors – the glutes and hamstrings and, to a lesser extent, the adductors – initially work only to maintain the back angle as the bar rises from the floor. As the bar approaches the knees, the hip extensors continue to contract, but at this point they begin to actively open the hip angle.

entire job on your hip extensors, which now have even more to do since they must move through a greater angle to extend. In addition, since your back is now almost parallel to the floor, your back muscles are in a position of decreased mechanical advantage: they have to stay in isometric contraction longer while rotating through a greater angle, starting in the worst mechanical position they can occupy – parallel to the floor.

The reason for this is not immediately apparent. In the deadlift, the clean, and all other pulling exercises from the floor, raising the hips before the chest is a common enough problem that we should analyze it here. The quadriceps straighten the knees, and if the back angle stays constant while this happens, the bar comes vertically up the shins.

But it is the hip extensors – the glutes and hamstrings and, to some extent, the adductors – that act as stabilizers during the initial phase of the pull and maintain the back angle by exerting tension on the pelvis from the posterior, at their insertion points on the ischium and the ilium. If the spinal erectors keep the back flat, the hip extensors anchor the back angle by pulling down on the bottom of the pelvis. The pelvis and the spine are locked in line by the erectors, so the hamstrings actually keep the chest up and the back angle constant, allowing the quads' function of straightening the knees to push the bar away from the ground. During this phase, the hip angle will open slightly, but the back angle should stay constant relative to the floor. It is as the bar approaches the knees that the hip extensors begin to actually change the back angle by actively opening the hip angle. So, the function of the hamstrings and glutes changes during the pull: initially they act to maintain the back angle as the quads straighten the knees; then they change the back angle as they extend the hips and finish the pull (Figure 4-36).

If the hamstrings fail to maintain the back angle, then the butt comes up and the shoulders drift forward, allowing the quads to avoid their share of the work since the knees have extended but the bar has not moved. The bar, however, must still be pulled, so the hip extensors end up doing it all, and in a much more inefficient way. They should be working with the quadriceps through the initial phase of the pull, instead of having to open a much more horizontal back angle at the end of the pull. Either way, the hip extensors work, but their job is easier if the initial contraction controls the back angle and the last part is active concentric hip extension, instead of the whole movement being a long, mechanically hard hip extension. The problem is not that the hamstrings are not strong enough; it is one of *motor learning*, teaching the muscles to move the bones correctly, in the right order at the right time. The only way to correctly address this problem is to take weight off the bar and make sure you do the deadlift with proper form, with all the angles correct, so that all the muscular contributors to the pull learn to do their jobs in the right order. If you know the actual cause of the problem – and you do now – you can fix it by thinking about squeezing your hamstrings and glutes tight before you pull, thus making them better at doing their job of holding your ass down. If this doesn't work, think about making your chest move up *first*, which causes you to fire the muscles that would make this happen; the hamstrings and glutes try to make the chest rise, and this action averages out to a constant back angle.

An interesting thing happens when all the pulling mechanics are correct: the deadlift feels "shorter," as if the distance the bar has moved has been reduced, compared to an uncorrected, sloppy deadlift. It obviously hasn't, since the bar moves the same distance either way, but the increased efficiency obtained from the improvement in pulling mechanics is significant enough that the perception is one of a shorter movement. This perception is largely due to the reduction in extraneous hip and knee movement and a consequent reduction in the time the lift actually takes. **A correct pull that results from a correct setup will show no change in back angle as the pull starts and for at least the first couple of inches of bar path off the floor.**

One of the most common technique errors in the deadlift is using a starting position that attempts to hold the back in a too-vertical position. The method detailed earlier for learning the deadlift eliminates this problem, but hard-headed folks may require further explanation. This misunderstanding of the correct starting position may have several possible causes. One cause might be confusion about the actual role of the back muscles in the deadlift. Some resources on deadlift instruction available in the mainstream certification agency material – intended for fitness/wellness audiences that are not interested in strength – advocate a more vertical back angle than is actually possible for a lifter to use in a deadlift of any significant weight. According to these sources, in an attempt to reduce *shear*, or sliding forces, between the vertebral segments, you should make the back as vertical as possible so that most of the force on the vertebrae becomes compressive rather than shear. However, shearing cannot occur because the vertebral segments overlap at the facet joints, and sliding between the segments is not anatomically possible. When the erectors and abdominal muscles do their job of maintaining intervertebral rigidity, no movement takes place, and when the load gets heavy enough that the erectors cannot hold rigid extension, spinal flexion occurs, not shear. The back functions as a rigid segment, and its job is to stay flat. Sometimes this is hard, and this is why the deadlift is a back exercise.

Another cause of the confusion might be the idea that the deadlift is somehow just a squat with the barbell in the hands, and that driving with the legs is best accomplished with a more squat-like starting position. But the deadlift is *not* a squat with the bar in the hands – it is a pull, a completely different piece of mechanics. And if it were a squat,

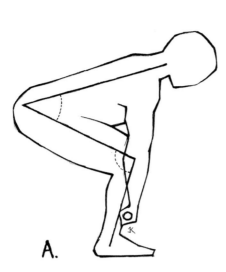 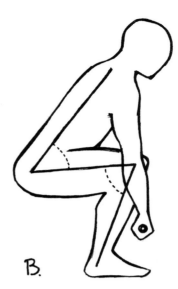

A.   B.

Figure 4-37. The correct starting position (A), and the position that often gets used instead (B). The correct position reflects proper pulling mechanics; from this position, the bar can leave the ground and travel in a straight path up to lockout. From the incorrect position, the bar cannot leave the ground with a heavy weight, yet many people think it is the correct position from which to pull. What actually happens is that the lifter "sets up" in position B, thinking that the bar leaves the ground from there, but he then raises his hips into position A before the bar leaves the ground. Even a cursory video analysis of any heavy deadlift clearly shows that this is always the case. This shift from setup to pull leaves the bar out in front of the shins as the knees pull back, producing a bar path that curves back toward the legs before it becomes vertical. The most efficient pull is a straight vertical line over the mid-foot, with the shoulders just in front of the bar. The closer to this model your setup position allows you to be, the better.

you'd want your hips to be as high as you could get them because you can half-squat more weight than you can squat from a deep position since you don't have to travel as far.

Confusion about the correct starting position might also be due to the idea that the weight on the bar should not be allowed to pull you forward, and *back* is therefore the direction the bar should be pulled. But it should be obvious that the bar cannot be pulled back through the legs. Or the problem might be that an observation of the sumo-style deadlift as performed by competitive powerlifters has created an incorrect impression of the proper back angle in the conventional deadlift. Sumo technique employs a much wider stance, which produces the correct pulling position with a more vertical back angle. When a lifter tries to assume this position and back angle with a close stance, he lowers his hips to a point where he achieves the angle, but only at

the expense of placing his shoulders behind the bar. Since the bar cannot leave the floor in this position, when the pull starts, the lifter's hips will rise and the back angle will adjust itself to the point where the shoulders are in front the bar, and only then will the plates break off the floor.

It is an error in understanding the mechanics of the start position to try to assume a back position more vertical than the relationship between the back, the arms, and the bar allows. The lifter's shoulders will be in front of the bar when it leaves the ground, and an artificially vertical back angle will decay as the pull is started, leaving the bar out in front of the shins, off-balance, with a horizontal displacement to cover before it leaves the ground. The best position that can be assumed at the start is the one already described: with the bar over the mid-foot, and the scapulas directly over the bar. When this alignment exists, the bar is easier to pull.

Figure 4-38. The different bar heights produced by different grip widths. A narrower grip reduces the distance the bar has to travel. Note the position of the bar relative to the lower rack pin.

Make sure the bar is touching your skin or your socks before it leaves the floor. It is not necessary to bump your shins with the bar or to scrape the meat off of them on the way up. You do need to maintain good control of the weight, because if you scrape your shins, you can get sores that will be a problem for a long time; then every time you deadlift, you will break the sore open and make a big mess on your socks or the bar. You might need to cut a shin guard out of a one-liter plastic bottle and place it inside the front of your socks until the sore heals. Sweats help eliminate this scraping problem, and allow the bar to slide up the thighs better as well.

The knurl of the bar might also be a problem for your shins if it starts in too close to the middle. A standard Olympic weightlifting bar and most power bars have an opening in the knurl that is about 16.5 inches wide, and this is usually sufficient to accommodate the stance widths of all but the tallest people. Some bars are manufactured with no thought given to the possibility that they might someday be used to deadlift. Don't use these bars.

Foot placement has been discussed above. In a deadlift, you are pushing the floor, not lowering the hips as in a squat, and you must set your stance accordingly. If your stance is too wide, your legs will either rub your thumbs on the way up or force your grip out wider to avoid being rubbed. The wider the grip, the farther the bar has to travel to lock out at the top. The grip and the stance are interrelated in that your stance must be set to allow the best grip, and the best grip for the deadlift is one that allows your arms to hang as straight down from the shoulders as possible when viewed from the front, i.e. the closest grip possible, in order to make the shortest possible distance from the floor to lockout for the bar. Too wide a stance necessitates too wide a grip and confers no mechanical advantage. If you're thinking that since we squat with a wider stance, we should pull with a wider stance, don't think that. We are not squatting; we are pushing the floor with the feet, an entirely different thing.

Too narrow a stance is not a thing encountered very often. There have been great deadlifters – Vince Anello and George Hechter come to mind – who pulled with a very narrow stance, with heels nearly touching and knees out. This is called a "frog stance," and many lifters have used it effectively. We learned the knees-out position in Step 3 of our deadlift method. In the Squat chapter, we discussed at length the advantages of externally rotating the femurs for its effects on depth, the ability to lock the pelvis and the lower back together, and the stretch reflex (see pages 45-51). This concept is also applicable in movements – such as starting a pull from the floor – that don't elicit a stretch reflex. If a hip extension is involved in the movement, the lower back obviously needs to be locked with the pelvis and in hard extension, but what is less obvious is the role of the adductors and external rotators. If the knees-out position can

Figure 4-39. Note the toes-out position of the stances of both Vince Anello *(left)* and George Hechter *(right)*. The knees-out position this stance enabled these massively strong men to get more out of their pulls.

tighten up the groin muscles, they can function more effectively as both back-angle anchors and hip extensors in the pull. Since hip extension is involved in any pull, a knees-out position can improve the extensors' participation in the pull. Olympic weightlifters often employ this knees-out starting position to fix problems off the floor and to allow for a better back angle.

A more knees-out position also effectively shortens the distance between the bar and the hips when the knees are shoved out of the way a little. This modification of the effective length of the thighs – similar to the effects of a snatch grip or a sumo stance, where the angle acts to shorten the effective length of an otherwise fixed segment – makes a more vertical bar path easier to obtain off the floor. This may be very important for lifters who have longer femurs and are trying to get into a better start position. (Some very good competitive deadlifters have learned to use a round upper back to produce this same shortening of the distance between hips and bar, producing a better set of pulling mechanics at the hips. This method is NOT recommended for novices.) But even for lifters with normal proportions, a little external rotation of the femurs alters the balance of muscle action around the hips in a positive way, helping to produce a more effective hip extension off the floor.

The easiest way to identify and reproduce the stance every time is to note the position of the bar and its knurling marks over your shoelaces as

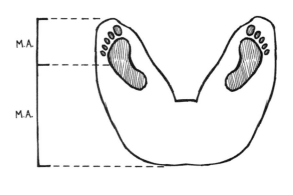
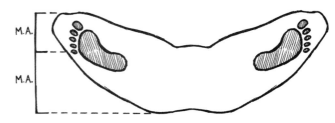

Figure 4-40. The angle of the stance affects the horizontal distance between knees and hips, with a toes-forward stance producing a longer moment arm between the hips and the bar, and a toes-out stance shortening the effective distance and thus the moment arm. This shortening effect is magnified by the lifter's widening into the sumo stance. (*M.A.* = *moment arm*)

Figure 4-41. You can easily duplicate the stance every time by establishing a reference position for the bar against the shoelaces when looking down at your feet.

you look down at your feet. Use this landmark on your shoes to quickly and consistently produce the same stance.

The Little Details

Just in case you were thinking that the deadlift was not rife with picky details, here are a few to consider.

Breathing is the kind of detail that is often ignored in lifting instruction. The details of the Valsalva maneuver and its importance to spinal support were discussed in Chapter 2. To implement this procedure for a pull from the floor, inhale while the bar is on the floor, before you start the pull, not while you're supporting a heavy weight at the top. And exhale after you're finished with the rep, which happens when the bar is back on the floor. The top of a deadlift is a poor place to lose back support, and it is unnecessary since setting the bar down doesn't take very long. You can breathe much more safely when the floor is supporting the bar than you can when your back is supporting the entire weight at the top.

A set of deadlifts should start at the floor, meaning that each rep begins and ends at the bottom, with the back getting set and a new breath being taken between reps while the bar is on the floor. Many people like to pull the first rep off of the floor, breathe at the top at lockout, and finish the set by bouncing the bar off the floor for the remaining reps. It is easier to do the set this way, true, but *easy* and *strong* are usually opposing concepts. You need to develop the ability to set your back and control your position each time you pull the bar, because these things use precisely the skills and the muscles you are doing this exercise to develop. The point here, as is so often the case in the weight room, is not to simply do the deadlifts by moving the barbell through space, using a deadlift-like movement; the point is to use deadlifts to get strong by doing them correctly, the way they are best used to develop strength. They have to be done right, not just done.

AVOIDING A BOUNCE

One of the key features of the deadlift is that it requires the production of force from a dead stop. In contrast, a key feature of efficient squatting is the use of the controlled "bounce," which takes advantage of the stretch reflex that occurs at the transition between an eccentric and a concentric contraction. Any muscular contraction is more powerful if it is immediately preceded by a stretch, as always occurs when you jump. One of the reasons a heavy deadlift is so brutally hard is that it starts up out of the bottom without the benefit of the bounce that helps the squat change the direction of the force from down to up. Up to down without a bounce is quite a bit harder. If a bounce is incorporated into all the reps of a set of deadlifts except the first one, much of the value of doing them is lost.

The energy expended in resetting the spine into extension and holding it there through the first part of the pull is a major part of the energy expended during the deadlift. It has been suggested that if the bar is traveling through the complete ROM of the deadlift, then all of the work of the deadlift is being done since the work is being done on the barbell. The *work* – defined as force times distance – done against gravity consists of the vertical distance the bar moves. But the *total energy expended* in a deadlift cannot be expressed by merely calculating the work done on the barbell. The deadlift occurs within the lifter/barbell system, and force must be

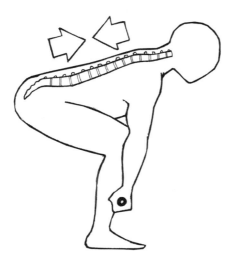 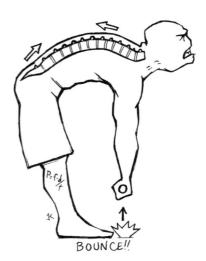

Figure 4-42. The work of the deadlift is understood to include the force necessary to maintain the correct intervertebral relationships in lumbar extension, so that the pulling force all gets to the bar. If you substitute plate-to-platform rebound for the work you should be doing with your back, you are a pussy.

produced isometrically to control the positions of the skeletal components that transfer the force to the bar. The isometric effort of keeping the vertebral column rigid for efficient force transfer is obviously significant; you can miss a heavy deadlift if your low back gets round and your hips extend before the bar is high enough up your thighs, thus sabotaging your ability to transfer force to the bar for the top of the pull. It may be harder to calculate than the simpler force-times-vertical-distance equation used for the work done on the bar itself, but no one – or at least no one capable of a truly heavy deadlift – would argue that the ATP expended in isometric control of the back is an insignificant contribution to the movement. A set of "deadlifts" in which the first rep is pulled from a dead stop and the last reps are bounced is, in reality, one deadlift and a set of RDLs (about which more, later). Training this way, you will never develop the strength needed to hold the lumbar position for heavy weights, because for 80% of your set you are relying on plate rebound and the elastic energy stored in the elongating muscles and fascia, instead of on dead-stop pulling strength. So don't trade the ability to develop long-term strength for the immediate gratification provided by cheating your deadlifts.

Another problem with bouncing your reps is that any back position problems that develop during the set cannot be addressed as effectively. If your back begins to round during the set, it tends to stay round or get worse unless you reset it, which you must do at the bottom, when the bar is sitting on the floor and your back can move into the correct position unloaded.

There are a couple of ways you can think about setting the back before starting the pull. Positional awareness has already been discussed, and for some people it is sufficient to think about arching the lower back. This is, after all, most of what setting the back is about. But really and truly, you set the entire torso before you pull, and you may find it helpful to think about it in this way – squeezing your low back and abs and chest all at the same time on a big breath, not as separate muscle groups but taken as a whole unit. This approach increases the effectiveness of the Valsalva and causes all the muscles participating in it to contract harder and provide more stability.

LOOKING IN THE RIGHT DIRECTION

Eyeball position is also often overlooked when you assume the starting position. If you look straight down at the floor when you pull, the bar will usually swing out away from your legs. It is easier to keep your chest up and your upper back

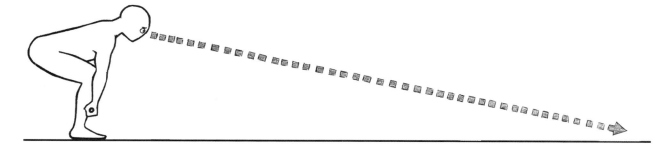

Figure 4-43. Eye gaze direction in the deadlift, for neck position safety and balance.

tight if your eyes are focused on a point that places your neck in an anatomically neutral position; this point can be on the floor (if you're in a big room) or on the wall facing the platform. If the floor is your gaze point, look about 12–15 feet in front of you. Looking up is not any better for the deadlift than it is for the squat, as we discussed at length in that chapter. Actually, looking straight down is not terribly detrimental to the squat, but it will make the deadlift harder most of the time. The functions of correct eye gaze direction are to keep the neck in a safe, useful position during the movement, to aid in placing the back at the correct angle for the mechanics of the lift, and to provide a visual reference for balance purposes. Looking up never works well except in the bench press.

KEEPING YOUR ARMS STRAIGHT

Your arms must stay straight during the deadlift. There is no better way to produce a really lovely elbow injury than to let 500 pounds straighten out your elbows for you. The physics of this is not difficult to understand. The force produced by the hips and legs is transmitted up the rigid torso, across the scapulas, and down the arms to the bar. Seen from the side, the shoulders will be in front of the bar and the arms themselves will not be vertical, but they must be straight.

Just as the back must stay locked to facilitate force transfer, the elbows must stay straight during this whole process, too. A bent elbow is a thing that can be straightened out, if the weight is heavy enough, and the straightening out is done by force

that should have gotten to the bar. Deadlifting with bent elbows is like towing a car with a spring instead of with a chain: the chain transfers all the pull to the car, whereas the spring absorbs some of the force as it changes length. The elbow is flexed by the muscles of the forearm, the brachialis, and the biceps. If your elbows are bent, these muscles are working unnecessarily, since they add nothing to the lift; in fact, bent elbows actually increase the distance the bar has to travel because they cause the bar to lock out at an unnecessarily higher position. It is important to convince yourself that your arms are not involved in the deadlift and that straight elbows are the best way to pull. This will also be important when you learn how to power clean.

Figure 4-44. Bent elbows in the deadlift are the fault of the part of the brain that tells you that "All things must be lifted with the arms." In a deadlift, the only function of the arms is to connect the shoulders to the bar; straight arms must be learned early so that this very bad habit does not become embedded.

Figure 4-45. An overzealous lockout that produces lumbar hyperextension is both dangerous and unnecessary.

FINISHING THE LIFT

Once the bar has completed the trip up the legs, there are several ways you can finish the deadlift, only one of them correct. You lock out the bar by lifting your chest and bringing your knees, hips, and lumbar spine into extension simultaneously. Many people insist on exaggerating some of these things, performing the movement inefficiently and, if the exaggerations are carried to the extreme, unsafely. For example, you don't need to roll your shoulders up and back at the top, creating an active concentric shrug. The deadlift is not finished until the shoulders are back and the chest is up, and finishing this part of the movement is important. But the traps get sufficient work from their isometric role in heavy deadlifts without your attempting to add additional trap work by exaggerating the shrug and possibly causing a neck injury in the process. Heavy barbell shrugs are a good assistance exercise for an advanced lifter who knows how to perform them correctly, but novice deadlifters have no business trying to add an extra movement to an exercise that is sufficient without it.

Likewise, it is unnecessary and unwise to exaggerate the hip-extension part of the lockout

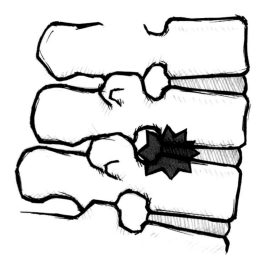

Figure 4-46. Unnecessary arching, as shown in Figure 4-45, asymmetrically loads the spine to the posterior, setting up the conditions that may result in disc or facet joint injury.

into a lumbar overextension (Figure 4-45). Since it is virtually impossible to overextend your hip joints in an upright position with a loaded bar lying on the anterior side of the thighs, what actually happens is that you overextend the lumbar spine, sometimes as almost a separate movement after the deadlift is actually finished. This is a very dangerous habit to acquire: uneven loading of the lumbar discs is as harmful from the posterior as it is from the anterior.

Knees sometimes get forgotten in the rush to lock everything out from the hips up. Many contest deadlifts have been red-lighted because of the lifter's failure to lock out the knees. This always produces a flurry of bad language from the lifter when the lights are explained to him, because anybody who can lock out a 622-pound deadlift can also straighten out his knees the final 5 degrees. Once the deadlift is finished at the top, it requires no more work – you just have to remember to lock your knees out. Make sure you are finishing each deadlift with locked knees, and remind yourself occasionally to check them. This last little movement is an important part of the lift, even if a powerlifting meet is not the goal of your training.

Get in the habit of holding the bar locked out at the top for just a second before you set it down, so that you achieve a stable position first. If you are in the process of falling backwards as you attempt to lower the bar, there will be a significant wreck. The bar should be lowered only after it is locked out and motionless for just a second, indicating a correctly finished lift with the bar under control. Don't exhale; just pause a second and then set the bar down.

Setting the bar down fast in the deadlift is actually okay. Since the deadlift starts as a concentric movement, much of its training effect is due to the hard initial position and the lack of help from a stretch reflex during the lift, as discussed above. Setting the bar down slowly will make it harder, and some people might benefit from the extra work, but the emphasis in the deadlift is on picking up heavy weights. As the weight increases and the lift gets difficult, upward bar speed will decrease. Setting the bar down slowly uses up too much gas that could

Figure 4-47. Our very strong friend Phil Anderson has forgotten to lock his knees at the top. The fix for this is better coaching and a cue to "Stand up!" Phil has since had his knees replaced with the apparently very good Stryker prosthetics, and he deadlifted 600 pounds 11 months post-op.

be better used in picking up your next rep. As long as some modicum of control is exercised, the bar can be dropped as fast as you are capable of doing safely with your back in good position according to our previous analysis. Going down fast with poor control is, of course, hard on your kneecaps and shins. And depending on the type of plates being used and the nature of the platform surface, a poorly controlled bounce can cause problems. But in general, a deadlift can, and usually should, go down faster than it comes up.

PLATFORMS

A platform is a good thing to have in your weight room: use multiple layers of plywood or particle board glued and screwed together, with rubber mats under the area of plate contact or the whole thing surfaced with rubber; horse-trailer mats work just fine and are relatively cheap (Figure 4-48). Failing that, rubber mats placed under the plates on the floor will work, but the room really needs to be set up correctly for you to train the pulling movements. Bumper plates, a necessary expense for the clean and the snatch, can be used for the deadlift

Figure 4-48. The basic components of a cheap and durable training platform. Three layers of 4 foot × 8 foot × ¾ inch plywood or particle board, laid in alternate directions each layer and then covered with horse-trailer mats, provide a durable, inexpensive training station. It works well on a concrete floor. This particular platform has been in service in a commercial gym for 16 years.

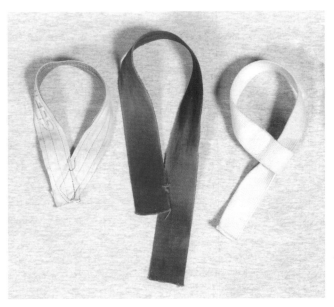

Figure 4-49. Several types of straps are commonly seen in the gym. The kind most commonly available commercially (*right*) is junk: the design does not work well, these straps do not last long, they hurt the hands, and they can break with a heavy weight. The black one in the center has been in use since 1984 and has never failed.

as well, but the more reasonably priced ones take up so much space on the bar (they are very wide) that iron plates will eventually need to be used as you get stronger. Your gym should be equipped for this. And if your gym is one of those places that doesn't allow deadlifting, find a better gym. Sorry to have to keep saying this, but there may come a time when your training becomes more important than the reasons that caused you to originally choose the inadequate facility. It's a sign that you're becoming a lifter.

STRAPS AND BELTS

Straps will be useful on occasion. Use the kind made from seat belts (it's probably best not to take the ones out of your car for this purpose) or some other nylon-type strapping material, about 1½ inches wide. Cotton will not work, no matter how thick and strong it looks; it will tear at an inconvenient time. Straps can be left as simple pieces of material, about two feet long, or the ends can be tacked together. Straps go around your hands, not your wrists. And do not use the kind with a loop

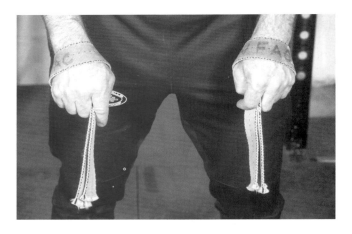

Figure 4-50. Our favorite straps are simple pieces of seat-belt webbing or other 1½-inch strapping. They are 2 feet long, are never made of cotton, and ride down on the hands, not on the wrists.

sewn into one end, where the rest of the strap passes through the loop. They will continue to tighten on your wrists during the set. Loop-ended straps are never really secure with a heavy weight, tend to wear out quickly and tear during a heavy set, and never

Step 1: non-dominant hand.

Step 2: dominant hand.

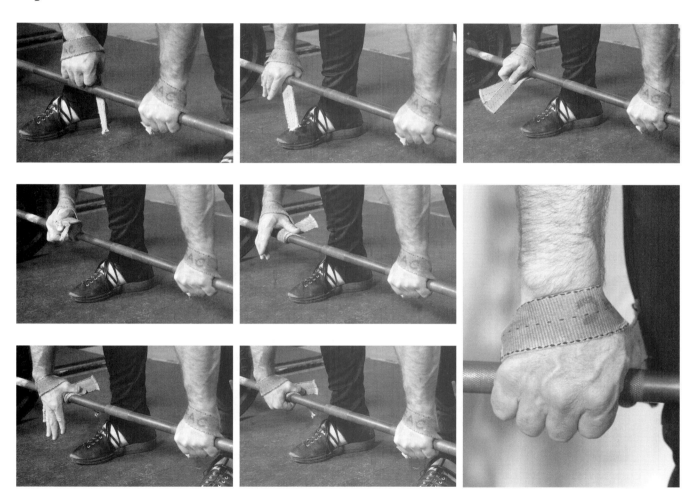

Figure 4-51. Using the straps is sometimes a challenge for novice lifters. Here's how it's done.

stay in adjustment on the bar.

The position of your belt in a deadlift might be slightly different from that used in the squat. For deadlifting, most people seem to prefer to wear the belt a little lower in the front and a little higher in the back than they do for squatting. In fact, some people might prefer a different belt altogether, a thinner, narrower one that allows the deadlift's start position to be assumed more easily. The bottom position of the squat is acquired after the descent under load, while the start position in the deadlift must be acquired unloaded; a tight belt helps the squat stay together, but for some people, a tight belt will interfere with squeezing into the start of a pull. A different, lighter belt may be necessary for deadlifting, and some people even prefer no belt at all for most pulling if it prevents a good lumbar set position. Big deadlifts have been pulled with no belt, and you may find this best for your situation.

A CAVEAT

Finally, the author was a moderately good deadlifter during his career in the sport and learned many valuable lessons about strength off the floor during this time. Among them is that not everybody needs to do heavy deadlifts. People with injured backs that are prone to re-injury, and people who cannot learn to perform the movement correctly, don't need to deadlift with maximum loads. It's better if you can, since functional back strength is best built with functional back work, and the heavier you pull, the stronger you'll get. But if you are not powerlifting, you don't have to do limit singles. From a training standpoint, there is little to be gained by doing 1-rep max deadlifts, and your 1RM can be inferred from a 5RM if obtaining this information is somehow necessary. That having been said, deadlifts are still the best way to develop useful back strength. Apply yourself to learning them correctly.

Figure 4-52. The deadlift.

THE BENCH PRESS

There are few gyms left in the world that don't have a pressing bench. For good reason: The bench press, since the 1950s, has become the most widely recognized resistance exercise movement in the world, the one exercise most representative in the public mind of barbell training, the exercise the vast majority of trainees are most likely to want to do, and the exercise most often asked about by most people if they are interested in how strong you are.

Many incredibly strong men have benched big weights, long before the advent of modern supportive shirts and even good benches. Men like Doug Hepburn, Pat Casey, Mel Hennessy, Don Reinhoudt, Jim Williams (who lifted in excess of 700 pounds in a thin, cheap, white T-shirt), and Ronnie Ray were strong back in the early days of powerlifting, although the weights they lifted would, sad to say, scarcely turn a head at a 21st-century national meet. Accomplished powerlifters of the 1980s – men like Larry Pacifico, the incredible Mike McDonald, George Hechter, John Kuc, Mike Bridges, Bill Kazmaier, Rickey Dale Crain, and the late, great Doug Young – were masters of the bench press, using all the tricks at their disposal to establish national and world records in the lift (Figure 5-1).

The modern version of the bench press, like the squat, depends on an additional piece of equipment other than the bar for its execution. Until the upright support bench came into widespread use in the 1950s, the lifter had to lie on the floor and pull the bar into position, or lie on a flat bench and pull the bar up from the floor, over the head, and into position over the chest. Controversy abounded as technique was evolving, with questions about the legitimacy of assistance in getting the bar into position, the use of a heave from the belly, and even the use of an arch in the lower back, causing debate among physical culturists all over the world. Nowadays, the bench-press bench – the upright-support bench, as opposed to the plain flat bench – is standard gym equipment, and only a few innovative thinkers in the powerlifting community bother with doing the exercise the old, harder, and probably better way. After all, the more involved the exercise, the more the exercise involves in terms of muscle, nerve, and control.

The dumbbell version of the exercise, which actually predates the barbell version due to its less specialized equipment requirements, involves a greater amount of instability, which is inherent in having two separate chunks of metal waving around in the air over your chest. This is especially true if the weights used are sufficiently heavy to challenge your ability to actually finish the set. Most trainees use dumbbell bench presses as a light assistance movement, and never appreciate how hard they are or how useful they can be at heavy weights. They are performed on a simple flat bench, and the lifter has to take the dumbbells out of the rack or off the floor, get into position on the flat bench, do the set, and then get off the bench with them after finishing it. These movements are as large a part of the exercise as is getting to look at your arms in the mirror. Because dumbbells are not tied together between the hands as a barbell is, dumbbell bench presses require more active, conscious control, are harder to do, and are

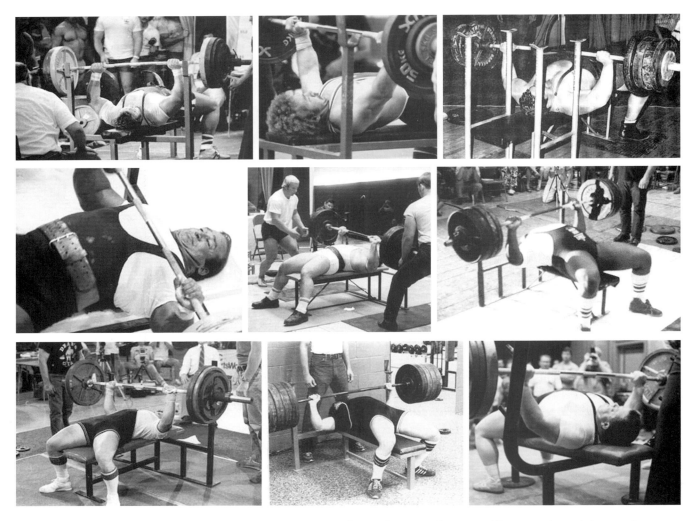

Figure 5-1. The bench press has a long, rich history. *Left to right, top to bottom:* Bill Kazmaier, Rickey Dale Crain, Pat Casey, Doug Young, Mel Hennessy, Jim Williams, Mike Bridges, Mike MacDonald, Ronnie Ray.

therefore less commonly done. The problem with dumbbell bench presses is that the equipment provides its own limitations in a progressively increasing program. Most dumbbell racks are not graduated in fine-enough increments due to the expense of having twice as many dumbbells as most gyms have the money or space for. Plate-loaded dumbbell handles that would permit such loading are not widely available, of sufficient quality that they are safe at heavy weights, or capable of being handled without a lot of help from two spotters. And with heavy weights, getting on and off the bench becomes such a large part of the task of completing the set that the logistics are a giant pain in the ass.

So, as good an exercise as the dumbbell bench may be, you will be bench pressing with a barbell, as

the weight of history and precedent demands. The bench press, or supine press (one occasionally sees old references to the "prone press" in badly edited sources), is a popular, useful exercise. It is arguably the best way to develop raw upper-body strength, and done correctly, it is a valuable addition to your strength and conditioning program.

The bench press actively trains the muscles of the anterior shoulder girdle and the triceps, as well as the forearm muscles, the upper back, and the lats. The primary movers are the pectoralis major and the anterior deltoid, which drive the bar up off the chest, and the triceps, which drive the elbow extension to lockout. The bigger posterior muscles – the trapezius, the rhomboideus, and other smaller

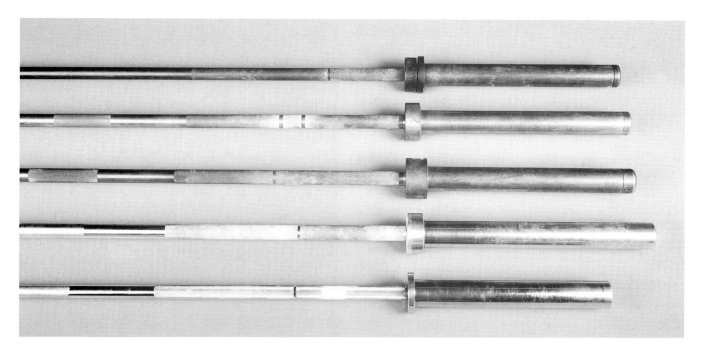

Figure 5-2. Bars for weight training can be obtained from several sources. "Power" bars are best for our purposes here because they are marked in ways that are the most useful for the exercises that constitute the bulk of this program. High-quality bars have uniform dimensions and similar mechanical characteristics, but there are differences that should be evaluated before you buy one. Subtle differences in diameter and tensile characteristics make some bars better for certain applications than others: whippier bars are better for cleans and presses, and stiffer bars are better for squats, benches, and deadlifts.

muscles along the cervical and thoracic spine – act isometrically to adduct the shoulder blades and keep the back stable against the bench. The pectoralis minor helps stabilize the rib cage into the arched position when the scapulae are anchored by the traps and rhomboids. The posterior rotator cuff muscles stabilize and prevent the rotation of the humerus during the movement. The lats, or latissimus dorsi muscles, rotate the rib cage up, arched relative to the lower back, thereby decreasing the distance the bar has to travel and adding to the stability of the position. They also act as a counter to the deltoids, preventing the elbows from adducting, or rising up toward the head, while the humerus is driving up out of the bottom, thus preventing the angle between the upper arm and torso from changing during the lower part of the range of motion. The muscles of the lower back, hips, and legs act as a bridge between the upper body and the ground, anchoring and stabilizing the chest and arms as they do the work of handling the bar. And the

neck muscles contract isometrically to stabilize the cervical spine – hopefully not while pressing too hard against the bench with the back of the head. Yes, bench pressing makes your neck grow, too, making new dress shirts inevitable. Since the bench press is a free-weight exercise, control of the bar is integral to the movement, and improvement in control is part of the benefit of doing it.

You will be using standard power bars and benches for the bench press. Standard power bars are widely available, and this configuration has proven itself as the most useful over the years for general-purpose gym use. It is probably the type that will be most available to you, at your gym or to buy for a reasonable price, Olympic weightlifting bars being quite a bit more expensive. The specifications are simple: the bar diameter should be 28 to 29 mm; the length is about 7 feet 2.5 inches; and the knurling should be adequate but not too sharp, and will extend in from the sleeves so that a 16.5-inch gap is left in the middle, with center knurling of 4.5 to 6 inches provided. The knurling will be scored with a ring at either end of the bar, with a distance of 32 inches between the marks, denoting the maximum legal grip width for competition. If standard power bars are not available, use what you have until better equipment can be obtained. If you have to use a non-standard bar, be familiar with its marking dimensions so that you can correctly apply the instructions for grip dimensions. Bars are absolutely the wrong place to save money, either when you buy one or when your gym does (Figure 5-2).

The benches should also conform to standard specs, although there is no standard configuration for constructing them. Standard specifications require the height of the bench surface to be 17 inches, and if this is too tall for short trainees, then blocks for the lifter's feet (or usually just barbell plates) will need to be provided. Uprights can be either fixed or adjustable, with a distance of about 45 inches between the uprights. Or you can use the power rack and a 17-inch flat bench for the bench press station (Figure 5-3). Most benches are provided with some type of vinyl upholstery, but auto seat fabric has proven itself over the years to last longer and provide better traction for the back during the lift. Benches – both upright support and flat benches – seem to have been the victim of manufacturing stupidity for the past several decades. A commercial gym should invest in standard competition bench press equipment, for safety as well as for training and competition consistency. Benches are a stupid place to save money, too.

Learning to Bench Press

When you're learning how to bench, it might be prudent to use a spotter if one is available. Spotting the bench press will be dealt with in detail later, but for our purposes in this early phase of learning, a spotter is there to keep the unracking and racking of the bar safe for the lifter. The leverage disadvantage of having the bar several inches behind the shoulders is not a problem at lighter weights, but as the load increases, it becomes one rather quickly.

Figure 5-3. Three ways to use equipment for the bench press. *Top to bottom*, The upright-support bench is preferred by most lifters, but the power rack offers adjustability and a better use of space and limited resources. It also allows you to safely train the bench press without a spotter.

With the right equipment, i.e., you are working inside a correctly set-up power rack, a spotter is not absolutely necessary. Even on an open bench, you are using very light weights during the learning phase, and you should not have enough weight on the bar to give a spotter anything to do. A bad spotter who will not stay out of your way while you train is actually a detriment and can quite often cause more problems for you than he can prevent. If you are just learning to bench and you're worried about your ability to handle the bar, you have too much weight on it. If a 45-pound bar is too heavy – as it might be in your particular circumstances – use a lighter bar. If you are concerned, use a spotter, but make sure to use an experienced, competent, patient individual who will not insist on "helping" you just for the sake of participating in your exercise program. If you are forced to use an inexperienced spotter, explain as thoroughly as possible the specifics of the job, described in detail at the end of this chapter.

As usual, start with an empty bar. ALWAYS start every lift with an empty bar, whether learning the lift for the first time or warming up for a personal record. Lie down on the bench with your eyes looking straight up. In this position, you should be far enough down ("down" always meaning toward the foot end of the bench) from the bar that when you look up, your eyes are focused on the down side of the bar (Figure 5-4). This means just a short distance, not several inches, which would increase the difficulty of getting the bar unracked. Your feet should be flat on the ground in a comfortable spacing comparable to the squat stance, with your shins approximately vertical. Your upper back

Figure 5-4. Eye position for the setup. The eyes look just past the bar, placing the body the correct distance down the bench.

Figure 5-5. Foot and leg position on the bench.

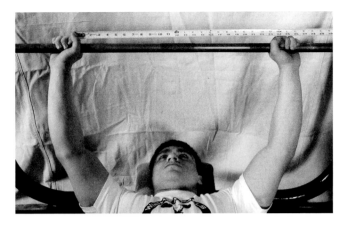

Figure 5-6 . Grip width for the bench press.

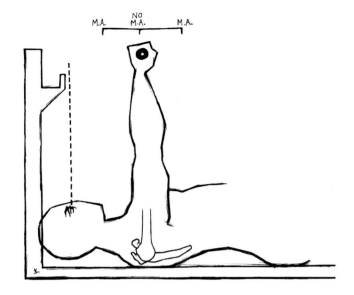

Figure 5-7. The bar is in balance when it is vertically aligned with the glenohumeral joints. Any horizontal distance between the bar and the balance point represents a moment arm that must be worked against. The distance between the rack and the start position is a significant moment arm at heavy weights, and the spotter's job is to help the lifter deal with this bad mechanical position. (*M.A.* = *moment arm*)

should be flat against the bench, with your lower back in an anatomically normal arched position – at first. We'll modify the back arch later.

After getting into position, take an overhand grip on the bar. Your grip should be somewhere between 22 and 24 inches, measured between the index fingers; the variation is based on differences in shoulder width. This grip width will produce a vertical forearm for most people when the bar is on the chest, a position that produces the most range of motion around the shoulder joint during the movement. The bar should rest on the heel of your palm (not up near the fingers), and directly over the bones of the forearm, so that power being transmitted up the arms and to the bar goes directly to the bar without being channeled through the wrists. Wrap your fingers around the bar AFTER you have set it correctly on the heels of your hands. This grip is best accomplished by pronating your hands, with a slight internal rotation of your arms.

You are now ready to take the bar out of the rack. Look directly up at the ceiling, above your position on the bench, and push up on the bar, locking out your elbows. With elbows locked, move the bar out to a position directly over the line of your shoulder joints – the *glenohumeral joints* – to place your arms in a perfectly vertical position relative to the joints and thus to the floor. Don't stop before you get the bar over your chest, because if you do, the bar will be over your chin or throat. Make sure the bar gets out to the place it needs to be, right over the joint. This is the place where the bar is in balance

at lockout, where there is no moment arm between the bar and the fulcrum that is the shoulder joint. Move the bar to this position quickly and without hesitation, with your elbows locked out the entire time. Your spotter can help you do this the first few times, just making sure the bar clears your face and neck and gets all the way out over your chest.

As the bar becomes stable in the lockout position, look at the very important picture directly overhead. You will be staring at the ceiling directly above the bar, and the ceiling with the bar in the foreground will comprise your entire field of vision. This picture is your reference for the path the bar will take as you move it down and up. You will see the bar against the ceiling in the lower half of your field of vision. Look at the bar's position relative to the features you see on the surface of the ceiling. Don't look at the bar; look at the ceiling and just *see* the bar. Move the bar a tiny bit. Notice that if the bar moves even a little, you can tell by the change it makes against the ceiling. The bar moves and the

Figure 5-8. View from the trainee's position on the bench. The position of the bar is referenced against the ceiling. Note the focus; the eyes look at the ceiling, not at the bar.

ceiling does not, and the ceiling is therefore your position reference for the bar.

Note carefully the position of the bar against the ceiling. You will lower the bar to your chest, touch the chest, and then drive the bar right back to exactly the same position. Stare at the place on the ceiling where the bar is to go. DO NOT look at the bar as it moves; do NOT follow the bar with your eyes, but just stare at the ceiling. You are going to make the bar go to that place every rep.

With the bar locked out over the shoulders, have your spotter touch your chest a few inches below (inferior to) the bar's vertical position, at about the middle of your sternum. Have him push hard enough that you can feel it after he takes the finger away. This tactile cue will quite effectively identify the point on your chest to touch the bar. If there is no spotter and you are benching alone inside a rack, unlock your elbows straight out to the sides and then allow them to drop towards your feet a little on the way down. Just a little. If you do this correctly, the net effect will be the same as the spotter's touch – the bar will contact your sternum a few inches below your clavicles, and therefore below

your shoulder joints. Note that the precise position the bar should contact the sternum will vary with the chest up position of the lifter on the bench, but the middle of the sternum, a few inches below the clavicles, is a good place to start. The goal here is to produce a bar path that is not vertical, for reasons which will be discussed in detail later.

With this in mind, look at the ceiling, unlock your elbows, lower the bar to the chest, touch it without stopping, and drive the bar back at the point on the ceiling your eyes have trapped. Try it for a set of five reps. You'll notice immediately that if your eyes don't move from their fixed position, the bar will go to the same place every rep.

This little eyeball trick works 90% of the time the first time it is used to produce a correct bench-press bar path. Even if you are "poorly coordinated," you should be able to do a fairly good bench press within a couple of sets by using this technique. "The groove," as the bar path is often referred to by bench pressers, is the first and most frustrating problem that novice trainees will experience because the tendency is to follow the bar with your eyes. By focusing your eyes on the ceiling, you can eliminate

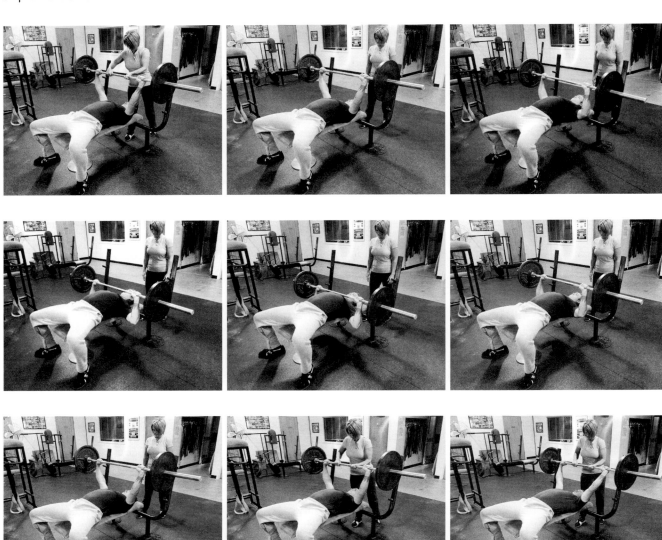

Figure 5-9. The bench press.

this problem the vast majority of the time. If the bar finds the groove automatically, as it does with this method, you can direct your attention to other aspects of the exercise that might be a problem.

The key to the whole method is staring at the fixed position and not at the moving bar. If you use a fixed reference point for the bar position, you can make the bar go to the same place – and therefore through the same path – each rep. If you follow the bar with your eyes, you have no way to direct the bar to the same place every time because you are looking at the thing you are moving and not at the place you want it to go. This is the same principle used to hit

a golf ball or a tennis ball: the implement moves to the target (the ball), and the target is the object of the fixed eye gaze. Granted, tennis balls move and golf balls don't (until they're hit), but the principle is the same. The brain coordinates the hands to take the implement – the club, racquet, pool cue, or bat, or the sword, sledgehammer, axe, or barbell – to the target, because the target is the reference for the eyes. When a tennis ball moves, the head and eyes move with it, rendering it a stationary point. Fortunately, most ceilings don't move in most weight rooms, so our task is easier than McEnroe's, but it is similar in that we are driving an object in our hands toward a stationary thing we are actively looking at. There are similarities between seemingly diverse activities, all of which involve movement directed by the eyes. Whether the object of the movement is stationary or in motion, the implement in the hands goes where the eye gaze is focused.

Do another set of five with the bar, reinforcing your eye position, and then rack the bar. This is done with locked elbows, after the last rep is finished, by moving the bar back to the uprights, touching them with the bar, and then setting it down in the hooks. Should you have a spotter, this movement back to the rack should be covered. For the next sets of five reps, add weight a little at a time – 10 pounds at a time for smaller kids and women, 20 or even 30 pounds for bigger trainees – until the bar speed begins to slow down and your form starts to change. Stay there for two more sets of five, and that is the first workout.

Common Problems Everyone Should Know How to Solve

Since the bench press is the most popular exercise in the weight room, lots of people do it. Since lots of people do it, lots of people teach it, and lots of extremely wrong ways to teach it have been developed over the years – things that make absolutely no mechanical sense, some of which are quite dangerous. The bench press is already the most dangerous exercise in the world due to the position of the body between the bar and bench, with no way to get the bar off of you by yourself in the event of an accident. Normally we let safety follow as the logical by-product of efficiency, but for the bench press, we'll pay extra attention to ways to avoid getting killed under the bar.

HANDS AND GRIP

The bar, being over the head, face, and neck during the bench press, presents some significant safety problems if certain common-sense precautions

Figure 5-10. *Left*, The thumbless grip vs. *right*, the thumbs-around grip. There are only a few ways to get badly hurt in the weight room, and using the thumbless grip is one of them. You can get the same position over the end of the arm with the thumbs-around grip, without the potential risk of dropping the bar on your face, throat, or chest.

are not observed. The subject of spotters and spotting will be dealt with in detail later, so these comments will involve things that *you* must do.

Maybe the biggest, dumbest, most common problem involving the hands is the use of the thumbless grip. **Except for the squat, there is no thumbless grip in barbell training.** Using a thumbless grip is absolutely the worst decision you can make with regard to safety, and it is detrimental to performance as well. Many lifters start with a thumbless grip in an attempt to get the bar over the very end of the arms, with the leverage off of the wrists, which is understandable. But doing this with a thumbless grip is unnecessary since the same position can be obtained with the thumbs hooked around the bar . The risk of having an unsecured bar over the face and throat is just too high. The grip is thumbless in the squat because the bar is not moving – you are. For the bench press, the thumbs secure the bar in your grip, and without your thumbs around the bar, it is merely balanced over the end of your arms.

The best spotter in the world cannot react quickly enough to save you from a dropped bar. The danger of this cannot truly be appreciated until one sees the effects of a dropped bar firsthand. In the United States every year, an average of eleven people are killed while training with weights, *essentially all of them under the bench press.* While this means that millions of lifters are doing perfectly safe bench presses, you still don't want to be one of the eleven who weren't. If you insist on using a thumbless grip on the bench, you need to do it at home so that when the ambulance comes (if anyone is there to call 911), it doesn't disrupt anyone else's training.

Another problem with the thumbless grip is that it diminishes lifting efficiency: what the hands cannot squeeze, the shoulders cannot drive as efficiently. This phenomenon can be observed when you're using large-diameter bars and fat-handled dumbbells: a 2-inch bar is about twice as hard to press as a standard 28.5mm (1 1/8 inch) bar. This difference is due to the inability of a person with a normal-size hand to effectively squeeze a fat bar with a good tight grip. Squeezing involves closing the thumb and fingers around the bar until effective pressure can be applied with the forearm muscles in isometric contraction, increasing the tightness of the muscles on the distal side of the elbow, making rebound out of the bottom more efficient, and increasing motor unit recruitment throughout the arms and upper body. (Distal is the end furthest from the center of the body, and proximal is the closest to it.) Some lifters like to think about leaving their fingerprints in the knurl of the bar to increase their squeeze. The thumbless grip is an excellent way to voluntarily reduce the lifter's ability to squeeze the bar. Try it yourself for demonstration purposes, with a light weight, please. Many big benches have been done with a thumbless grip, just like many big squats have been done with less-than-perfectly-efficient technique; some people get very good at doing things inefficiently. The point is that since the standard grip is safer *and* more effective, it should be used by everybody who has thumbs.

The thumbless grip is an attempt, as previously stated, to get the bar into a better position in the hands. The force generated by the shoulders and triceps is delivered to the bar through the bones of the forearms. The most efficient transmission of power to the bar would be directly from the heels of the palms to the bar, through the forearms positioned vertically, directly under the bar, so that no moment

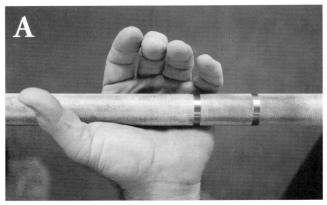

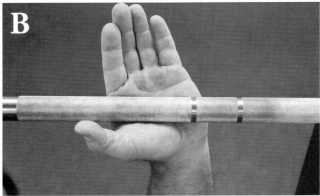

Figure 5-11. Most people will begin and end the grip process with the bar lying perpendicular to the line of the knuckles (A). The best position is achieved by rotating the hands into pronation (B), and then setting the grip (C). Note the position of the bar in relation to the hand.

arm exists between the wrists and the bar. Most people look at the bar, see the line of the bar in the air over their eyes, and then place their hands in a position that puts the knuckles in a parallel line with the bar. This position will produce a distance of 1–2 inches between the bar and the wrist – resulting in a lot of unnecessary leverage against the joint, and an inefficient force transmission configuration.

As discussed in the press chapter, the best way to position the grip efficiently is to set the grip width at the index finger and then rotate the hands into pronation by pointing the thumbs down toward the feet. This motion aligns the bar with the "radial longitudinal crease" and between the "thenar eminence" (the high spot adjacent to the thumb) and the medial palmar ("hypothenar") eminence on the other side (see Figure 3-10 page 83). Then, just lay your fingers down on the bar and squeeze the fingertips into the bar. When you take it out of the rack, the bar will be on the heels of your palms, directly over your forearm bones, as shown in Figure 5-11. This position hooks your thumbs around the bar and removes the wrists from the kinetic chain. Once your hands are in position, tighten your palms so that the bar is well supported and does not move during the rep. The thumbs do not interfere with this process at all. You don't need the bar down in your fingers, the same way you hold it in a deadlift, since gravity is not trying to pull it out of your fingers. In the bench press and press, the bar is in compression in your hands, not tension. Carrying your deadlift grip habits into the bench press and the press is just not productive.

It is common for the bar to shift back in your hand, toward the fingers, during the set, so that the bar ends up in a completely different position from where it started. This is the result of not maintaining a tight grip during the set. If the bar shifts much at all, it can change the lifting mechanics by altering the position of the load relative to the muscles driving it up, making a change in elbow or shoulder position during the lift likely. If the bar rolls back in the hands, it has also rolled back relative to the elbows and shoulders, and they have to adjust to maintain their drive. The bar should remain locked firmly in place during the set for efficiency and safety.

Grip width, within a certain range, is largely a matter of individual preference. Since you are trying to develop general upper-body strength, your form should be generalized, without too much emphasis on any one muscle group and with a lot of

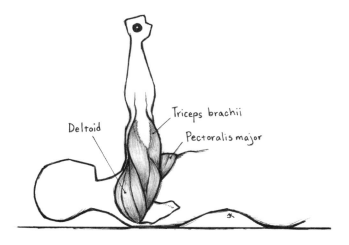

Figure 5-12. The major muscles involved in the bench press.

work for all of them. The greatest range of motion is obtained with a grip that places the forearms in a vertical position when the bar is on the chest. With a wider grip, the bar doesn't move as far and locks out before the triceps have done much work, so the pecs and delts end up doing more of what work gets done. But as long as the grip falls somewhere between 22 and 28 inches between index fingers, the purpose is served. This range allows enough leeway for people of all shoulder widths to find a grip they feel strongest with, while preserving the longer range of motion. Too much narrower a grip will, for most people, take pounds off the work set by placing the responsibility for most of the lockout on the comparatively smaller triceps, although most lifters can close-grip a fairly high percentage of their standard-grip bench press. A wider grip shortens the range of motion excessively and takes out too much tricep, as well as producing a longer moment arm between the hand and the shoulder joint. Heavier weights can be benched with a wide grip since the bar doesn't have to move as far (the legal width for powerlifting competition is 32 inches between index fingers).

But we are trying to make people strong by using the bench press, which isn't necessarily the same thing as making people bench a heavier weight. Most people will self-select a medium grip when they first do the exercise anyway. It feels more natural than a wide grip, which must be practiced

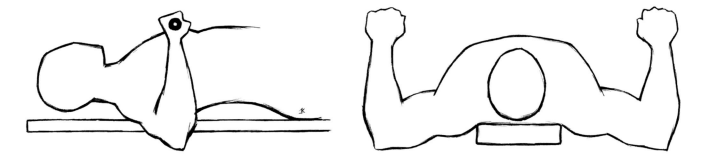

Figure 5-13. The forearm must be vertical from all angles to ensure optimum force transmission to the bar and to ensure that no rotational force is generated.

extensively before it will be productive. A medium grip gives all the muscles of the shoulder girdle a share of the work and produces the kind of overall shoulder and arm strength we want from the exercise.

ELBOWS

An understanding of elbow position is essential for lifting efficiency and, once again, safety. The elbow joint is at the distal end of the humerus, as it articulates with the radius and the ulna. The bony knob on the end of the ulna that most people think of as "the elbow" is the olecranon process, to which the triceps tendon is attached. The pecs and delts attach to the anterior side of the humerus up by the shoulder. Essentially, all the force being generated by the muscles involved in the bench press moves the elbow down and up, and the forearm parallel to the bar with elbow directly underneath the bar so that no moment force develops between the bar and the elbow. The action around the shoulder joint contributes to the movement of the elbow, but the shoulder doesn't – or at least shouldn't – change its position against the bench while the humerus is moving. Think of it as if the elbows move and the shoulders do not (even though this is not literally true).

The position of the humerus while it moves the bar is crucial to the success of the movement. This position is determined by the angle the humerus makes with the torso as it proceeds from the lockout position down to the chest and back, as seen from above. The bar starts at the lockout position directly over the shoulder joint. In this position, there is no moment arm between bar and pivot point – the bar is in balance, with no effort being expended to keep it there other than keeping the upper arms and the forearms locked in a straight column of support. At the bottom – on the chest – a humerus angle of 90 degrees to the torso, a position of complete "abduction," would have the upper arms at right angles to the bench, parallel to the bar, with the bar directly over the shoulder joints. If mechanical considerations were our only concern, this would be the ideal bottom position because it would produce a mechanically ideal bar path, with zero moment between bar and joint through the whole range of motion, and zero force to apply on any leverage between bar and shoulder.

But mechanical considerations are not our only concern. We need to be able to train the bench press without injuring our shoulders. Shoulder surgery is a GREAT BIG DEAL, I assure you. This makes anatomical considerations very important in an analysis of bench press mechanics.

The press is never a problem for shoulder health because when you are standing, the scapulas are free to rotate up and in toward the spine as you drive the bar up. This allows the scapular position to accommodate the humerus locked in line with the forearm, so that there is no impingement between the bony knobs on the lateral scapula – the acromion and coracoid processes – and the rotator cuff and bicep tendons. The scapula gets out of the way of the humerus because it can "float" into a position that doesn't hurt anything (Figure 3-5, page 78).

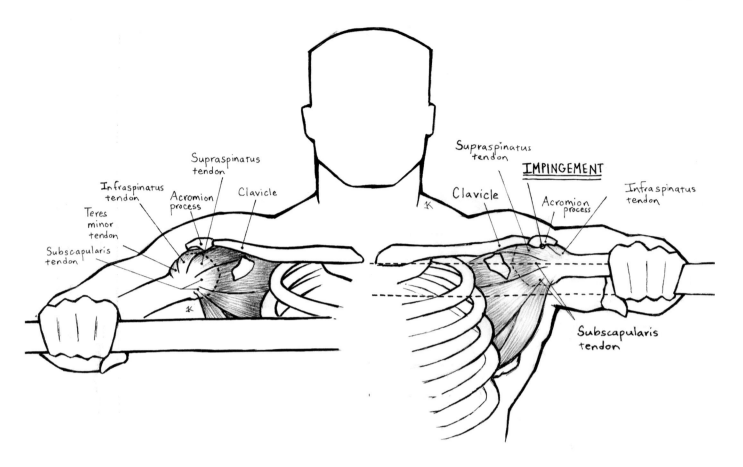

Figure 5-14. The bench press has the potential to cause shoulder impingement. *Right*, At 90 degrees of abduction, the humeral head can mash the rotator cuff tendon up against the acromioclavicular joint. *Left*, To avoid this problem, place your elbows down below parallel, with the glenohumeral joints at about 75 degrees of abduction.

In fact, the scapula is pulled out of the way by the trapezius muscle as the bar is shrugged into lockout.

In contrast, the bench press position traps the scapulas under the rib cage into a solid platform against the bench as the chest is shoved up and the back is arched. The scapulas are adducted – pinched together or retracted. They do not move if the position is assumed correctly, because they are functioning as the interface between the body and the bench. Therefore, they cannot accommodate the humerus if it approaches the bony processes. Since the scapula cannot adjust to accommodate the humerus, the humerus must accommodate the scapula by staying out of the way of the bony processes so that they don't saw a hole through the rotator cuff tendons.

The lifter keeps the scapulas out of the way by lowering the elbows, and thus the humerus, from 90 degrees of abduction to about 75 degrees. This shift allows the humerus to travel from lockout down to a position that permits the bar to touch the chest – the longest range of motion that can be made with a straight bar – and back to lockout without approaching a position that would impinge the shoulder. But as mentioned earlier, there are mechanical considerations.

The most mechanically efficient bar path would be one in which the bar traveled vertically down and up directly over the shoulder joints, with the elbows at 90 degrees of abduction. But since this would impinge the shoulders, we must tolerate some inefficiency in the form of a non-vertical bar

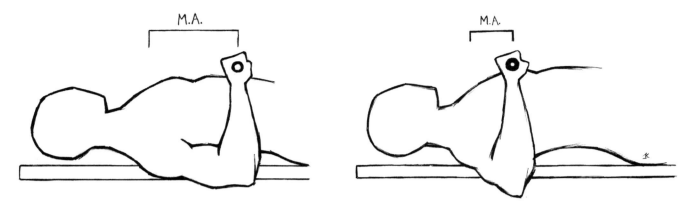

Figure 5-15. The upper arm angle determines the point where the bar will touch the chest. The lower the elbows, the lower the bar, and high elbows put the bar close to the throat. The moment arm is the distance between the bar and the shoulder joints, and it varies with the elbow position. (*M.A. = moment arm*)

path produced by the distance the bar travels down the chest as the elbows are lowered from 90 degrees of abduction. This non-vertical bar path creates a moment arm between the bar and the shoulder joints at the bottom of the movement; this moment arm is equivalent to the distance along the sagittal plane between the bar and the shoulder joints. The farther the elbows are allowed to drop out of abduction – i.e., the lower the bar is along the chest – the longer the moment arm is against the shoulder joints. The bar follows the elbows: if they rotate away from the ribs, the bar goes up the chest toward the throat, and if the elbows move toward the rib cage, the bar moves down toward the belly (Figure 5-15).

Your elbow position is therefore related to the bar position and to your individual anthropometry. For example, an experienced, proficient lifter with good upper back flexibility can arch his chest up high, thus allowing the bar a shorter trip down and up. This technique will have the bar touching lower on the chest, toward the bottom of the sternum, as the rib cage rotates up. For a person with less flexibility in the upper spine, this bar position on the chest would require the elbows to be at an angle of perhaps 45 degrees to the torso, about halfway between touching the rib cage and in line with the shoulders. But since our experienced, flexible lifter has his chest up higher, his shoulders are closer horizontally to the bottom of his sternum, when viewed from the side. This effect is due to the steeper

angle that his flexibility allows his upper back, and thus his chest, to attain. This steep chest angle allows his elbows to stay more in line with his shoulders than they would for a less flexible trainee.

More important, as the chest rotates up, the shoulder joint rotates into a position more in line with the bar on the chest when the humerus is in the preferred 75 degrees of abduction. This rotation returns some verticality to the bar path and some mechanical efficiency to the movement by reducing the distance – and thus the moment arm – between the bar and the shoulder joint (Figure 5-16).

The correct humeral angle can actually vary quite a bit among individual lifters, from 75 to perhaps 45 degrees depending on the flexibility of the upper back and the ability to produce a high arch. Some lifters use an elbow position where the humerus is essentially parallel to the torso, placing the bar quite a distance down the chest from the shoulders. This position produces an obviously very long moment arm between the bar and the shoulder, as well as a humeral angle that eliminates most of the pecs' function from the movement, reducing the muscle mass involved and the efficiency of the lift as an exercise for the whole upper body. This technique works well for powerlifters wearing a bench press shirt that does much of the work off the chest for the lifter, but for general strength training purposes, it is not useful.

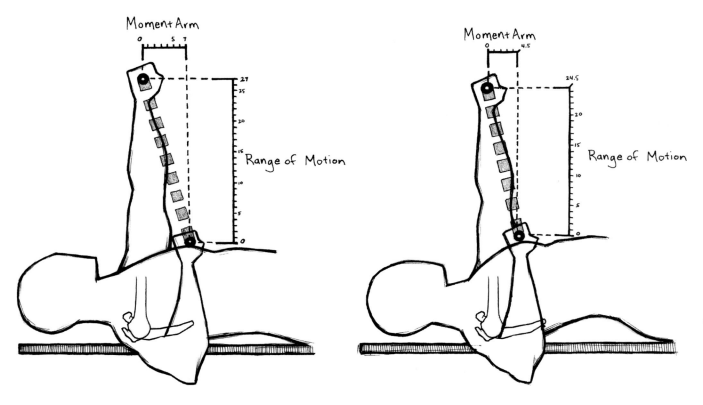

Figure 5-16. After lowering the bar down to the chest, you can recover the mechanical efficiency of a short moment arm by squeezing the chest up and rotating the shoulder joints back up under the bar. Doing this makes the bar path more vertical and shorter at the same time.

CHEST

The chest, for bench pressing purposes, is the anterior rib cage and the muscles attached to it. The main chest muscles – the pectoralis majors, or pecs – attach to the humerus at a long insertion point along the upper third of the bone. They wrap across the rib cage to a long origin along a line from the bottom of the sternum, up to the clavicle, and along the clavicle two-thirds of the way back to its distal end at the shoulder, with the muscle fibers fanning out in a broad angle. The frontal deltoids attach with the rest of the deltoid muscle at the deltoid tuberosity, a bump on the lateral aspect of the humerus, almost halfway down the shaft of the bone. The delts fan back into the shoulder and attach to the distal one-third of the clavicle in front and to the spine of the scapula in back. This wide angle of origin allows the pec and delt muscles to apply force to the humerus over a range of angles of

insertion, thus permitting a range of effective elbow positions in the bench press.

It is important to understand the relationship between the pectoralis major and anterior deltoid muscle attachments to the humerus and the angle of those attachments. Viewed from the horizontal (a cross-section of your chest perpendicular to your spine), the pec/delt attachments occur at an angle that varies with chest position. Refer to Figure 5-17. The higher the top of the chest – the highest point on the rib cage above the bench – the steeper the angle with which the pecs and delts attach to the humerus. The steeper the angle, the better, because of the increased mechanical efficiency of the contraction caused by the steeper angle of attack on the humerus. A lever system exhibits greater efficiency as the force gets closer to being perpendicular to the moment arm. So the higher the chest position above the arms, the better the pull the pecs and delts have on the arms. This effect is in addition to the mechanical

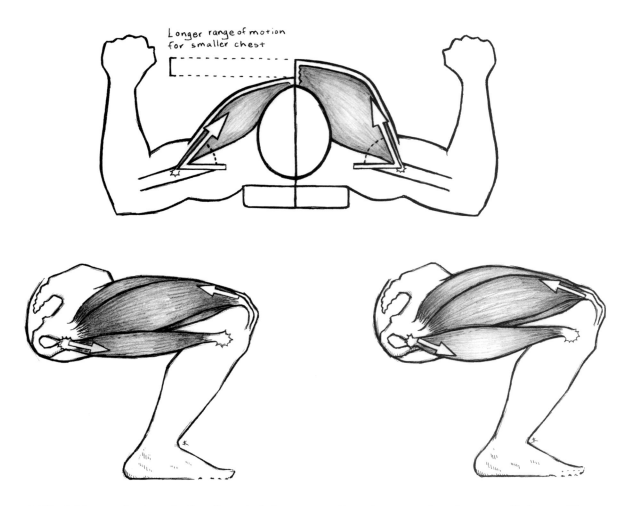

Figure 5-17. A bigger chest – whether from training or genetics – increases bench press efficiency. The increased steepness of the angle of attack of upper fibers of the pec and delt on the humerus increases the efficiency of the pull against the bone. This characteristic of levers explains one of the advantages to be obtained by increased bodyweight and is what is meant by the term "leverage." It applies throughout the barbell exercises.

improvement that the chest-up position produces in the previously discussed bar/shoulder relationship. The short version: keep your chest up high when you bench.

No discussion of the bench press would be complete without an explanation of the function of the lats in the movement. The latissimus dorsi muscles get implicated in a lot of bench pressing methods, but it is necessary to look at their actual function to assess their contribution to the movement. The lats have a very broad origin on the lower back, from T7 down across the thoracolumbar fascia to the iliac crest, covering the area of the entire lower back.

This broad origin turns into a large flat muscle belly that inserts by means of a thick, flat tendon on the *anterior* medial side of the humerus, parallel to the pec tendon insertion under the armpit. The action of the lat is thus the opposite of the pec's action – the lat pulls the humerus back while the pec pulls it forward. That's why chin-ups train the lats, and bench presses train the pecs.

But if this is the case, what function could the lats possibly have in the bench press? They can't make the bar go forward (up), because when they contract, they pull it backward (down). A case could be made for a large lat muscle belly providing a rebound surface for the tricep as it approaches the

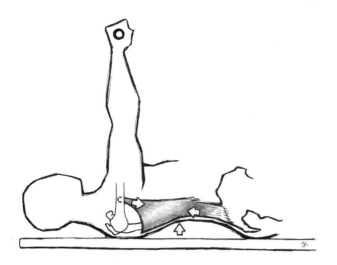

Figure 5-18. The latissimus dorsi and its contribution to the bench press. The lats cannot make the bar go up, but they are quite capable of reinforcing the chest-up position that is so important for mechanical efficiency.

bottom. But it is more logical that the contracted lat provides further reinforcement for the chest-up position, since a contracted lat would pull the lower back toward the shoulder, if permitted to do so, and would be aided by the other muscles that establish the arched position on the bench. The lats contribute to the bench press, but they don't do it by making the bar go up, because they can't. They just help keep the chest up, a very important function, as we have seen (Figure 5-18).

A common problem that could be considered chest-related is the failure to touch the chest with the bar at the bottom of every rep. Sometimes this is accidental, if you intend to touch but miss. If this is the case, you'll get it on the next rep, and the error will happen accidentally only the first couple of times you bench. But don't play games with the weight on the bar by failing to do a complete rep on purpose. It is, after all, easier to move a load a shorter distance than a longer distance, and when you cut it short, you are just lifting more weight at the expense of moving the bar through the whole range of motion. Work equals the force of gravity acting on the barbell multiplied by the vertical distance the barbell moves. If, over the course

of three months' training, the barbell doubles in weight but is traveling only half the distance it did on the first day of training, the work has stayed the same and you have wasted three months on training a partial ROM.

Sometimes a partial bench press may be done on purpose. There is a school of thought that justifies the use of less than a full range of motion by claiming that the pecs stop contributing to the movement when the humerus reaches a 90-degree angle with the forearm. (This same "analysis" requires an above-parallel squat because the quads supposedly stop contributing when the femur gets to 90 degrees with the tibia.) The problem with this model is that full-range-of-motion, multi-joint exercises are not supposed to isolate any one muscle. We use them precisely because they don't do that. We want these exercises to train lots of muscles through a long range of motion. We like it when some muscles are called into function as other muscles drop out of function, and when muscles change their function during an exercise. This is because we are training for strength, to increase the force we produce in a big, general *movement pattern*; we are not training a "favorite muscle." We are not concerned with our favorite muscles. We do not have favorite muscles.

The use of the full range of motion is therefore important for two very good reasons. First, it allows you to quantify the amount of work you do: if you hold the range of motion of an exercise constant, you are holding constant the distance variable in your work equation. Then, if the force you can exert on the load increases (if you lift more weight), you know that your work has increased for a given number of reps. You know you're moving the weight the same distance, and the weight is heavier, so you know you're stronger. You can therefore compare performances, both between lifters and between your own workouts over time. If you touch your chest with the bar every time you bench, progress – or lack thereof – can be assessed. This principle obviously applies to every exercise with a prescribed range of motion.

Second, full-range-of-motion exercises ensure that strength is developed in every position in which the joints can operate. Strength development is extremely specific: muscles get strong in the positions they are made to be strong in, and in precisely the way they are trained. And motion around a joint is usually composed of the functions of several muscles working together in changing relationships as the movement progresses. For instance, a quadriceps muscle worked through 30 degrees of its range of motion on a leg extension machine will adapt to this training by improving its ability to function in that 30 degrees of motion. The muscle will not get much stronger anywhere else in its range. And all the other muscles involved in a squat don't have a chance to get strong if it is performed through a short ROM, where only the quads work and the other muscles don't get called upon to do much. If we want to prepare an athlete to use his legs for a sport where he might be called upon to use them in a variety of positions, then he must train through a full range of motion in a way that strengthens the whole range. Any joint about which movement can occur will benefit from having its entire function improved. So, all the muscles that move a joint should be exercised, using a movement that calls into play as many of the muscles as is efficiently and safely possible.

The bench press, like the squat, benefits from a certain amount of rebound out of the bottom, using the stretch reflex phenomenon that is a feature of skeletal muscle (Figure 5-19). It takes practice and good timing to tighten up the bottom of the movement enough that you can get a correct rebound every rep, without actually bouncing the bar off your sternum and rib cage like an object on a trampoline. A competition bench press (theoretically at least) has no rebound due to the technical rules, which specify that the bar must cease its motion at the bottom before being driven up off the chest. A touch-and-go bench press allows you to lift more weight than a paused bench press. It must be said that a cheated bench, with a heave of the chest, a hard bounce off the pecs, and a bridge with the hips, allows more weight to be lifted than does a strict touch-and-go. Then why is a touch-and-go okay, but a bounce and a bridge are not? It is not always our objective, as noted earlier, to lift more weight,

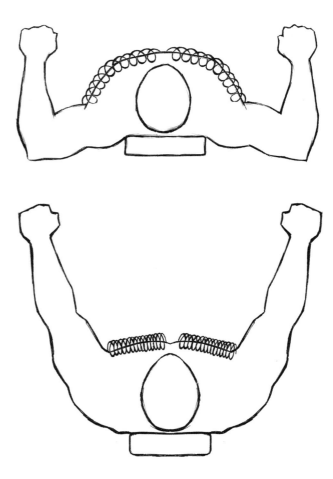

Figure 5-19. Several physiological and mechanical phenomena produce a rebound that makes for a stronger contraction. First, the viscoelastic nature of muscle makes it act like a spring – the longer you stretch it (up to a certain point), the more forceful the return. Second, there is an optimal sarcomeric length that results in the most force being generated by a contraction, and this optimal length is associated with a mild stretch. Last, the stretch reflex mediated by muscle spindles (intrafusal fibers) is activated by stretching and results in a more forceful contraction.

but the touch-and-go is easier to learn than a paused bench because the stretch reflex is such a natural movement; staying tight at the bottom during the pause is a skill that is difficult to master even for competitive powerlifters. The bounced, heaved, bridged, butt-in-the-air version of the bench press uses rib cage resilience and hip extension to aid in driving the bar up, taking work away from the targeted muscles. So a strict touch-and-go is a good compromise, letting you lift more weight but still providing lots of training for the pressing muscles.

You should be able to recognize excessive bounce and know when a correction needs to be made. For both the bench press and the squat, optimum bar speed occurs when the bar moves fast enough to efficiently elicit a stretch reflex and thus permit an efficient drive up. Bar speed is too slow when the descent produces fatigue, as it will if you deliberately lift submaximal loads very slowly. Bar speed is too fast when it actually adds momentum to the load on the bar on the way down, so that you must decelerate against both the weight on the bar and the effect of its excessive velocity on that load – where the effective load on the bar is actually heavier than the weight.

You bounce too much when the bar slams your chest hard enough to change your position with the impact and then slows down markedly a couple of inches up from your chest. This excessive bounce occurs because you allowed the downward velocity of the bar to increase in an attempt to increase mechanical rebound, so the initial upward velocity of the bar was due more to the physical rebound than to your active drive off the chest. This means you had to loosen your position to let the bar speed up as it dropped. If it's bad enough, the bar path will change after the rebound as your elbows shift position from the lack of tightness in your lats and delts. The whole messy thing is a result of a lack of tightness on the way down, and it can be remedied in a couple of ways.

One way to stay tight off the chest is to just barely touch it. You can't cheat the rep if you can't bounce the bar off your rib cage, and you can't bounce it if you just barely touch your chest. Think about touching just your shirt, not your chest, with the bar. Or you might imagine a piece of glass on your chest that you have to touch but cannot break.

Visualizing a light touch usually works, but it deals with symptoms. The best way to fix a bouncing problem is to address it at its root: by learning to be tight during the movement, and in a way that can be applied to other lifts as well. It is a way to conceptualize the lift so that tightness is built in and elastic energy can be stored in the

eccentric (negative) phase for use in the concentric drive up. The bench press, like the squat, consists of two movements: lowering the bar and raising the bar. Don't think about lowering the bar; just think about *driving it up*. As you lower the bar down to your chest, you should be thinking about driving up hard, not about the descent. Focus on *up* only. In an attempt to get ready for the upward drive, you will slow down the descent and be tighter as the bar approaches your chest, thus improving your rebound efficiency and minimizing rib cage bounce. By thinking about driving up while the bar is on the way down, you will have focused on the thing you are actually trying to do, at the best point in the movement to start the process. Lowering the bar is awfully easy, and if you think past that to the drive, you will slow your descent as you prepare to actively drive the bar up. This excellent technique works for any exercise with an initial eccentric component.

UPPER BACK

This important group of muscles has two functions. First, the upper back needs to be planted firmly against the bench and used as a platform to drive against while the arms drive the bar up. When this is done correctly, the shoulder blades will be adducted, or pulled together, to make a flat spot on the upper back to push against the bench itself. This stable platform is the anatomical surface against which the kinetic chain begins. Stated another way, when you bench press, you drive the bench and the bar apart – the bar moves and the bench doesn't, but you push against both (Figure 5-20). The upper back and shoulders push against the bench, and they need to be tight while doing so, just as the hands are tight against the bar. Second, the shoulders in their adducted position, and the upper back muscles as they contract and rotate or "tilt" the upper back into a chest-up position, push the rib cage up and hold the chest higher above the bench. This approach increases the mechanical efficiency of the pec/delt contraction by steepening the angle of attack on the humerus, as discussed earlier.

Keeping your back tight is sometimes a difficult thing to do, since so many other things are

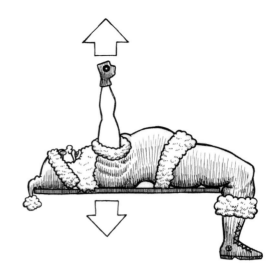

Figure 5-20. Just as we do when climbing a chimney (it still happens occasionally, really), when benching, we are in between and pushing against two opposing things. When we are benching, the bar moves and the bench does not.

going on at the same time. So it needs to be learned in such a way that it requires little active attention. Think about the "driving against the bench" model and why you need your chest up. Then sit on the bench in the same position you assume before lying down to take the bar. Before you lie down, imagine a hand touching you right between the shoulder blades, as illustrated in Figure 5-21, and imagine pinching the hand between your shoulder blades. This pinching will also cause you to raise your chest as your upper back tightens, further contributing to a good position. Now actively raise your chest, lifting it up as if to show someone your boobs (Again, sorry for the coarse analogy, but you now know exactly how to produce the contraction). This is the position you will take against the bench. Now lie down, take the bar out, and assume this position, making sure your shoulder blades are together and your chest is up high. Do a few reps, correcting your position before and after each one and focusing intently on the way it feels to do it correctly. This way, the position becomes embedded quickly and you can assume it without a lot of conscious thought or direction.

During the lift, minimal shoulder movement should occur. If the shoulders move much, something in the upper back has loosened and the chest has lost some of its "up" position. The thing that moves is the elbow. Now, it should be obvious that the humerus moves within the glenohumeral joint, so the shoulder movement referred to here is the forward shrug that novices often add to the end of the bench press before being coached. Some minimal scapular movement is unavoidable, particularly in a set of more than a couple of reps, but if it is excessive, it will compromise your

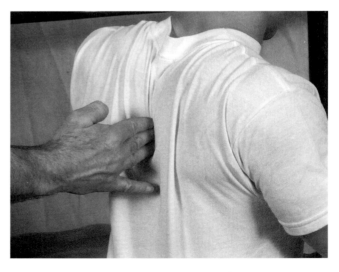

Figure 5-21. Retract the shoulder blades by thinking about pinching a hand between them. This effectively tightens the upper back for pushing against the bench.

Figure 5-22. Note the extra distance traveled by the bar when the shoulders are shrugged forward at lockout.

efficiency by adding to the distance the bar has to travel to lockout. This effect can be illustrated by examining what happens during a shoulder shrug and the distance it adds to the bar movement.

Lie on the bench and pull your shoulders back into full adduction, with your chest up in a good position and your back arched. Put your arms up with straight elbows in a position that simulates the start of the bench press. Note the position of your hands. Now shrug your shoulders up off the bench so that your shoulder blades come out of adduction, and note the difference in position. There will be a 4- to 6-inch difference in the distance from your hands to your chest from shrugged-back to shrugged-up. This is the extra distance you have to push the bar if you don't keep your shoulders back.

During a longer set (more than just a couple of reps), most inexperienced people will let their upper back deteriorate out of the shrugged position. If this happens, each rep is a little looser than the previous one and the bar must travel a little farther each time. At the end of a set of five, reset your shoulder blades and chest-up position. If you are

able to move them much at all, they have come out of position. Your goal is to be able to do all your reps without losing the set position.

NECK

The function of the neck muscles is to maintain the head's position and to protect the cervical spine during the loading of the chest and upper back as the bar comes down on the chest. The neck muscles therefore function isometrically to maintain position, in a role similar to that of the lower back muscles during the deadlift. But unlike the back muscles, the neck muscles should not transfer power along the neck to help with the lift. In other words, you do not use your neck to bench press. Do not push your head into the bench, even if you have been told that it will create a stronger rebound off the chest. It very well might, but this is an excellent way to injure your neck. You need to learn how to tighten up your neck without pushing on the bench with the back of your head. As a practical matter, this involves holding your head about a quarter-inch off the bench during the rep; think about touching the bench with your *hair* instead of with your head. If your head is held off the bench, your neck muscles are tight. It is tempting to use the neck to push the bench, as it adds contracted muscle and tightness to the upper back area, but it is too dangerous a habit to let become established in a novice lifter. If you become a competitive lifter and decide that pushing your head forcefully into the bench is enough help to your bench press to warrant the risk, fine. But save that for later, when you're in a better position to evaluate the cost/benefit situation.

Likewise, do not get in the habit of shifting your head so that your eyes can see one side of the bench uprights when you're racking the weight. Doing so requires that your fatigued neck rotate under a load, and this is just plain old dumb. You know where the rack is, and if your grip has been set correctly, your elbows are locked, and your spotter has been instructed even a tiny bit, the bar will get back into the rack just fine without your having to look at one side of the uprights.

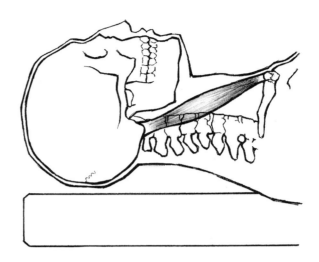

Figure 5-23. The preferred position of the neck and head during the bench press. Cervical injury can result from pressing the head into the bench under very heavy weights, and this position prevents the improper use of the neck muscles in this situation.

LOWER BACK, HIPS, AND LEGS

The bench press is an upper-body exercise, but since the lifter's feet are on the floor, everything between the feet and the upper body has the potential to be somewhat involved in the exercise. The lower back and the hips and legs are thus the connection between the ground and the upper back. Strictly speaking, the kinetic chain begins at the bar and ends at the upper-back/bench interface; the legs are not in the kinetic chain because the movement can be performed with a large percentage of 1RM with the feet up in the air. Since the movement itself is not dependent on the feet and legs, they are not part of the kinetic chain (*kinetic = movement, chain = components*), in the same way that the arms are not part of the kinetic chain of the squat. But the correctly utilized back, hip, and leg positions actually represent an important connection to the ground. In the same way the arms are a necessary connection to the bar in the squat, even though they're not an actual part of the kinetic chain, the legs do more than stabilize the lower body as the bar

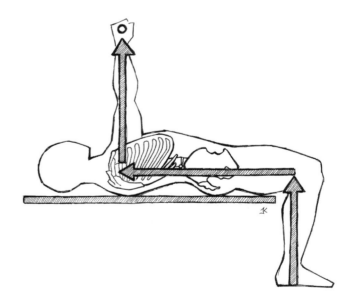

Figure 5-24. Force applied by the legs from the floor acts as a stabilizing force during the bench press and contributes to proper exercise posture.

Figure 5-25. Not the same thing as described in the previous figure. This is bridging, and it is a bad habit to acquire.

is moved through its path, although that is a major part of their function. Used correctly, the legs drive against the floor, transferring force horizontally along the bench through the hips into the arched back to reinforce the arch and keep the chest in its high position, established when the shoulders were pulled back. The legs and hips thus function as a brace for the chest and shoulders, giving the upper body a connection to the floor and allowing the lower body to contribute to the movement.

Before you have a chance to misinterpret, this is not the same thing as bridging or heaving the bar. That happens when the butt actually comes off the bench. Correct use of the legs and hips involves only the maintenance of chest and back position, with the force directed horizontally along the bench and not vertically up off of the bench. The descent of the bar tends to drive the elevated chest back down, taking arch out of the back if it is inadequately supported. The legs drive from the feet against the floor, back up along the bench, using a controlled isometric knee extension, with a slight hip extension produced by isometric contraction of the glutes and hamstrings. They actively counter the loss of arch in the back and chest height by reinforcing the arch from the floor.

But a common problem usually follows the realization that the legs are useful in the bench press.

Bridging – the intentional heaving of the hips clear of contact with the bench in order to meet the bar earlier – occurs as the lifter attempts to increase the chest height by using his lower body to steepen the angle of his upper back on the bench. Bridging takes work away from the target muscles by making the range of motion shorter. (The popular gym exercise known as the decline bench press takes advantage of this position of increased mechanical efficiency. Most people can decline more than they bench, thus the popularity.) Some purists believe that we are cheating when we arch the back at all, but this program seeks to use all reasonable means to increase strength on the bench press. Bridging is a good place to draw the line. Lifting the butt off the bench has got to be learned as *verboten* in the same way that use of the hands is in soccer. The temptation is always there, but if the correct habits are learned early, it will not usually be a problem.

The back arch is easy to learn. Assume your position on the bench, and imagine someone shoving a hand under your low back as you keep your butt in contact with the bench. Then imagine a clenched fist doing the same thing. Keep your lats in mind when you assume this position. Figure 5-26 provides a reference. Remember that you cannot raise your butt up off of the bench, so it's much better to learn to arch without cheating from the beginning. Make yourself do it correctly, and resist the temptation to bridge your butt up.

Figure 5-26. Learning to arch the lower back.

FEET

Your feet are your connection to the ground. If your foot slips during a heavy bench, the position supported by the lower body – your back arch and your chest-up position, everything you're using to push the bar – collapses. The feet must be in the correct position on the floor, and they must be positioned against the floor correctly.

Foot placement on the floor has two variables: width and placement relative to the hips. The feet need to be far enough apart to provide lateral stability for the hips and, through the tightness in the trunk muscles, the torso as it is planted on the bench. An excessively wide stance is seldom a problem, as it is uncomfortable and hard to maintain. A narrow stance does not guarantee disaster, and many competitive lifters prefer this position. In fact, for a competitive lifter, any stance that facilitates a legal bench press with optimum chest position is just fine. But a novice has enough to worry about with just learning to move the bar correctly, and a moderate-width stance presents fewer technical problems.

More of a problem is placing the feet up too far, back under the hips with the knees at an

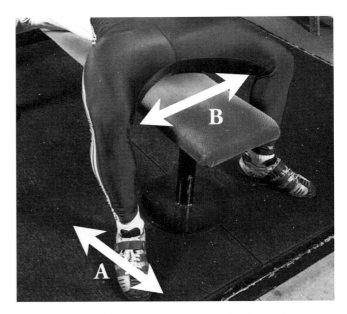

Figure 5-27. The main parameters for foot placement in the bench are up/down (A) and in/out (B).

acute angle. This position predisposes you to bridge your butt up in the air, and that is usually the reason people do it – if you have your feet too far up under your butt, and too close together with your heels up off the floor, you're going to bridge the heavy reps. A wider stance tends to moderate this effect. If the feet are up too far in a closer stance, the knee

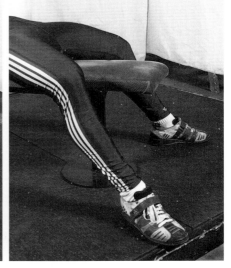

Figure 5-28. Correct positioning on the bench is important to learn. Place your ankles and knees first, and then position your hips as you lie down under the bar. *Left,* In a good position, the pelvis is flatter and the ankles and knees are positioned to drive against the floor and back up the bench to the shoulders. *Middle,* The bad position in the center is the perfect setup for a bridge. The entire foot should be in contact with the floor. *Right,* Likewise, too much knee extension provides a poor brace against the floor.

extension, being done from a more acute knee angle, tends to raise the hips. A more moderate knee angle generates force more parallel to the torso (Figure 5-28). Having the feet too far down, with the knees too straight, is commonly seen in novice lifters who have yet to learn how to use the hips and legs. This position makes it difficult to get enough "bite" against the floor to generate and maintain good tension in the upstream components (Figure 5-28). Your foot position should be set so that your shins are nearly vertical, give or take a few degrees either way, in both axes. This way, your knees are almost directly over your feet at any width, without any adduction of the femurs. This position allows for efficient use of your legs in reinforcing the arch, but doesn't create a predisposition to bridge.

This is not to say that everybody with their feet up under the hips will bridge. But most lifters who bridge do so from this position. A little wider foot position, particularly with the feet in full contact with the floor, will make it difficult to bridge because the slack has been taken out of the hips.

The proper position for the feet is flat against the floor so that the heels can be used as the base of the drive up the legs. As with most of the things in the weight room, your heels need to be nailed down to the floor. If you are up on your toes, you cannot use the force of knee extension nearly as efficiently as you can if your heels are planted, unless your feet are back under the hips. Flat feet are stickier feet, better connected to the ground through more surface area. A less-than-flat position represents a less-than-complete kinetic chain. Any rolling of the feet to either side during a rep implies that the knees have moved, the chain has loosened, or the floor connection has been interrupted. If you keep your heels down, driving off of them with flat feet, the problem goes away.

A bad problem when it occurs is an actual foot slip. It usually happens when the weight is very heavy and the floor connection is loaded heavily and therefore crucial. A foot slip results in a disruption and collapse of the lower-body support for the kinetic chain, and usually a missed rep or attempt, and any miss with a heavy bar can be dangerous. A foot slip is usually caused by conditions on the

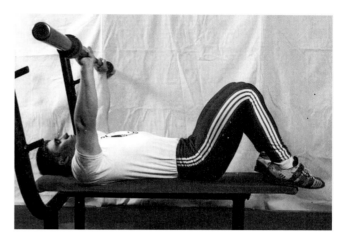

Figure 5-29. The knees-up position in the bench press is less stable than the conventional position and should not be used by novice lifters.

surface of the floor or the soles of the shoes, like the presence of baby powder (as is used on the legs in the deadlift in meets, or as an aid in putting on a tight squat suit) or just a dirty floor.

There are people – usually casual trainers, fitness enthusiasts, or retired powerlifters – who insist on benching with their feet up on the bench or even held up in the air (Figure 5-29). The effect of either position is to eliminate the use of the lower body during the movement and thus make the bench press less efficient than it would be with the brace against the floor. It is useful for a trainee with a lower-back injury that makes spinal extension painful, distracting, or otherwise contraindicated, but who still needs to bench. If you prefer to bench with your feet up, it might be due to lower back discomfort caused by a lack of lumbar flexibility; if the spinal ligaments are too tight to permit the degree of spinal extension that the normal bench position requires, stretching is in order. If your back is okay, you should be able to keep your feet down on the floor. Blocks or barbell plates can be used to add height to the floor for inflexible people until they stretch out or to accommodate shorter-legged trainees. The net effect of the use of the lower body is to increase the weight that can be lifted, so putting your feet up lowers the amount of weight lifted, but the exercise can still be done without it. The decision to do a feet-up bench should be made by a lifter who is cognizant of the benefits of training around

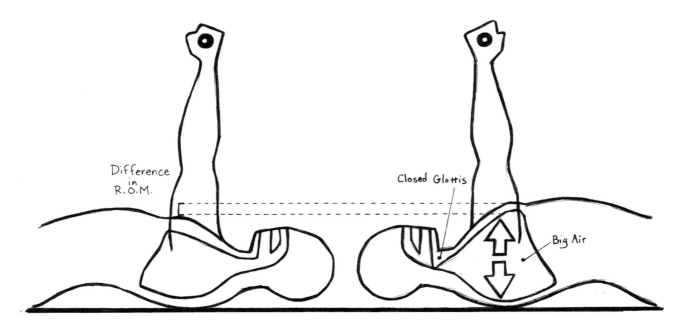

Figure 5-30. Inhalation at the top, with arms completely extended before the rep starts, allows for a more complete filling of the lungs, a better chest angle, and better stability.

injuries and the limitations inherent in doing it this way.

Breathing

As it is for all barbell exercises, air is support for the bench press. In the squat and deadlift, the Valsalva maneuver (as described in the Squat chapter) provides increased back support. In the bench press, it provides support for the chest. This support takes the form of increased tightness throughout the thoracic cavity due to the increase in pressure provided by the big, held breath. A tight rib cage allows for a more efficient transfer of power to the bar by the muscles attached to the rib cage when they contract. If the pec and delt origins on the external chest wall contract against a tight structure that does not move when they contract, then more of the force of that contraction can be transferred to the end of the kinetic chain that does move. When the rib cage is tight, less force gets absorbed, or dampened, by movement of the chest. This tightness, along with the support provided by the lower body connected to the ground, radically

increases efficiency in the bench press. Also, in the extended spinal position that the arch requires on the bench, the abs cannot tighten as effectively. They cannot therefore as effectively increase intra-abdominal pressure to contribute to the needed increase in intra-thoracic pressure, thus making the big breath the primary source of support for the chest.

The pattern of breathing during the bench press depends on the length of the set and the abilities of the lifter. Novices should take a breath before each rep, hold it during the rep, and exhale at lockout, using the very brief break between reps to make sure everything is positioned correctly. More experienced lifters may prefer to use one breath for the whole set. Any exhalation involves a certain amount of loosening of the chest to exhale and re-inhale, and some lifters may decide to stay tight and do the whole set in one breath if it is important and if they can hold their breath that long. Most people can manage only five reps this way before the discomfort from the hypoxia becomes too distracting. For a longer set, some quick breaths will be required.

Figure 5-31. On the final rep, it is common to push the bar back toward the rack before finishing the rep, instead of driving into a proper lockout over the chest. If you miss the last rep (and if you miss a rep, it will probably be the last one), where would you rather the bar come back down – on your chest or on your face? Get in the habit of finishing every rep correctly.

The breath has to be taken before the rep. If the breath is taken during the rep, the lungs will incompletely fill due to the loading of the rib cage by the now-contracted pecs. If the breath is taken at the top with locked elbows, the pecs are not pulling on the rib cage and a more complete inhalation can take place. Moreover, when the bar actually starts down, everything should be tight, from the floor to your fingernails, and this tightness will prevent you from taking a really big breath. If you can breathe during a rep, you're not tight enough.

No breath taken during the set will involve the complete exchange of the full tidal volume of your lungs. This takes too long, requires too much relaxation, and is unnecessary. Breathing during the set consists only of topping off the huge breath taken before the first rep, after a quick exhalation that might consist of only 10% of tidal volume. This short refresher of air is just enough to allow the set to be finished more comfortably. The fact that it amounts to so little air is the reason you might decide to forego it in favor of maintaining tightness, after you practice it.

Racking Errors

Taking the bar out of the rack and putting it back may seem like rather innocuous parts of the exercise, and most people give it no thought. Please be aware of the fact that any time a loaded bar is located above your face and throat, you have a potentially dangerous situation. The unracking and racking procedures must be done correctly from the beginning, because most of the danger involved in this most dangerous exercise in the weight room is associated with getting the bar in and out of the rack. So, in the interest of furthering safety in the weight room, here are The Rules:

1. **Do not use a thumbless grip on the bench press.** If the bar is not secure in your grip, it is not secure at all. A thumb around the bar by no means guarantees that you will never drop the bar, but a thumbless grip increases, by an order of magnitude, the likelihood that you *will* drop the bar.

2. Any time the bar is coming out of the rack or moving back into the rack, it will be over your throat and face. Therefore, **when the bar is moving into or out of the rack, your elbows must be locked.** This rule applies whether you are being spotted or not. The triceps should lock the elbows over the rack hooks so that the bones of the arm are in a straight line and the weight is being supported by the skeletal components instead of by the muscles when the bar moves over the head and neck. The first thing you do when unracking the bar is to lock your elbows before you move the bar into position. The last thing you do when racking the bar is to unlock your elbows after the bar touches the uprights.

3. **Start and finish every rep from the start position over your shoulder joints.** It is common to see novices stop the bar as it comes out of the rack short of the starting position, at a point over the throat, lower the first rep to the chest at an angle, and come

171

straight up to the correct position to start the second rep. Some people get in the habit of taking the bar down to the chest right out of the rack. But the bar should never start down before it is in place – if it does, there will be bar path problems due to the lack of an initial ceiling reference for position and the fact that the bar is going back to a different place than it started from. Both of these problems create the potential for killing yourself, so don't make either mistake. Only after the bar gets all the way to the start position and your eyes have found their place against the ceiling should the bar start down.

4. **Never shove the bar toward the rack before the rep is finished.** Many people do this on the last rep of a set, in a hurry to rack the bar. Always wait until the rep is locked out in the balanced start position before you move the bar back to the rack. If you're going to miss a rep and your spotter fails, it is preferable to have the bar come back down on your chest rather than on your face. If you don't make it to the rack with the bar, your bent elbows cannot support a heavy load over your face. This sloppy habit indicates a lack of patience, an unwillingness to take a few extra seconds to do things correctly and safely, and a lack of respect for heavy weights that can hurt you very badly in this position.

5. **If you are benching heavy by yourself, always bench inside a power rack.** You can set the pins at a level just barely below your chest so that if you miss a rep, you can lower the bar to the pins and escape safely. **If you do not have a power rack, do not bench heavy by yourself.** This is what kills more people with barbells every year than any other stupid thing people do with barbells. If you get trapped under a heavy bar, it can kill you. Really. It happens.

6. If you insist on not following rule #5, **at least have enough sense to NOT COLLAR THE**

BAR. If you secure the plates with collars, "for safety" like the poster in the weight room explains, and you get stuck under the bar by yourself, you cannot tilt the bar, slide the plates off, and get out from underneath it. Even the cost of wrecking the room by dumping the load on one side of the bar will be cheaper than your ass, which you'll admit is a higher price to pay.

7. **If your spotter has to take the bar, don't release your grip; help the spotter get the bar back in the rack.** Leaving the spotter with a heavy bar unsupported from below will get you both hurt – his back and your face. If your spotter is attentive enough to do his job correctly, be good enough to help get the bar back in the rack. Unless the spotter is very strong or the weight is very light, a loaded barbell any distance at all from his center of mass cannot be handled with arm strength. If you bail out of the rep and leave the spotter with what is most assuredly your problem, you will likely not get much help the next time you need it.

Spotters

In many gyms around the world, bench pressing is a team activity. The guy on the bench is "doing chest" while the guy standing over his head is working on his traps. It is truly amazing how much weight two guys working together like this can "bench press." It is not an exaggeration to say that the vast majority of big gym bench presses are exaggerations. If the spotter puts his hands on the bar during the first rep, and keeps them there for the rest of the set, then who has lifted what, and why?

There is a perfectly legitimate place in the weight room for spotters, but it is not in the middle of someone else's work set. Spotters should not be there to help with a set. The role of the spotter is to help get the bar out of the rack and into the start position over the shoulders by helping to overcome

Figure 5-32. The standard spotting position (A) allows for a quick and safe response to problems. But the proper role of the spotter must be understood. The spotter provides a measure of safety and confidence and can help through a sticking point on the last rep and ensure that the bar is racked safely (B)

the long moment arm between the rack and the shoulder joints. The problem with many spotters is that they create more problems than they solve. The bench press is actually a simple movement to learn correctly, and more people have problems with their spotters than they do with the exercise itself.

Spotters should be there for safety, when a question of safety exists. For everybody except rank novices, the first warm-up sets are not a safety concern and do not require spotters unless the spotter is also performing a coaching function. As the weight gets heavier, a spot becomes more necessary: some people need one on the last warm-up sets, and everybody should be spotted on the work sets because the weight is supposed to be heavy. Excessive caution and the insistence that every set be spotted for everybody is inefficient, unnecessary, and bothersome to other people in the gym who are trying to train. But if your gym contains mostly people who can't be bothered to help you when it is legitimately necessary, it could be a problem. Get a spot when you need to, and know when this is.

For the bench press, a competent center spot will suffice for all but the very heaviest attempts – the kind reserved for a meet, unless you're training at a national-level powerlifting gym. A good handoff is one of those rare commodities – there are more bad ones than good. A bad handoff interferes with the lifter's timing, balance, view of the ceiling,

and concentration by the spotter's attempting to participate in the rep. A good handoff spotter is experienced and appropriate with the timing and amount of bar contact, respectful of the mental requirements of the lifter, and, above all, conservative about when and how much to help.

The bench press spotter stands behind the head of the lifter, in the center of the bar (Figure 5-32). This position can be adjusted a little if necessary. The primary requirement of the position is that it is close enough for the spotter to grab the bar, but far enough back that after the handoff, the lifter has an unobstructed view of the ceiling. From this position, the spotter can do whatever might be necessary at the end of the set, from just watching the lifter finish the set, to securing the rack by following the bar as it meets the uprights, to taking the bar out of a sticking point.

If you actually get stuck during a rep, your spotter needs to be the one to decide that this has occurred, that he will take the bar, and how much of the weight to take when he does. The bar is stuck when it reaches a point of zero upward movement. This will shortly be followed by a deterioration in position as the bar begins to move down. Sometimes you'll be able to tell the spotter to take the bar, and sometimes you won't. Your spotter has to accurately evaluate the bar velocity, being certain not to take a bar that is still moving up, yet not failing to take it before it sticks for too long or goes back down too much or too fast.

After the spotter decides to take the bar, the amount of help provided will depend on the situation and a correct assessment of it. When someone is spotting an intermediate lifter with the last rep of the fifth set of five, the situation will warrant a different amount of help than in the case of an experienced lifter being spotted on a PR single, or a novice trainee doing the first heavy work set of his third workout. Each instance requires a different response in terms of how quickly to react, how closely to follow the bar, how much weight to take off, whether to help maintain bar velocity, and how fast and how hard to help rack the bar.

So, in the interest of fostering a constructive relationship between you and your spotter, here are The Rules for Spotters:

1. **At work-set weights, the spotter always watches every rep** and is ready to react to the lifter's situation. Complete riveted attention is not necessary for warm-up sets for which the spotter is not coaching a novice, but for heavy sets, when the weight has the potential to cause problems, the spotter must be watching the bar. A spotter who is looking around the room during a heavy set is *not spotting*.

2. This one is tough for many people because it seems to conflict with #1, so try to perceive the nuance: after the spotter hands the bar off to the lifter, **the spotter must *stay out of the way* until either the last rep is completed or the lifter *needs help*.** The lifter is looking at the ceiling, so "out of the way" means out of the lifter's sight picture of the ceiling and the bar. If you are the spotter, do not hover over the lifter and do not stick your hands anywhere near the bar, because doing so will distract the lifter, who is staring at the position reference on the ceiling. "Needs help" means that the lifter cannot complete the rep, indicated by the fact that the bar a) has actually stopped moving up for more than

1 or 2 seconds, b) has started to move back down, or c) has moved in a direction other than up, i.e., toward the face, toward the feet, or sideways.

3. If you are the spotter and you determine that the lifter needs help, take the bar with your hands and guide it back to the rack hooks. (The lifter should stay with you during this process, not releasing his grip on the bar.) But unless the lifter actually needs help – see rule #2 – **Do Not Touch The Bar.** This rule must be strictly obeyed because *any rep touched by anyone other than the lifter cannot be counted as a rep by the lifter.* This means that a set of 5 reps, the last one of which was "spotted," i.e., touched IN ANY WAY by the spotter, is officially a set of 4 reps. If you are the lifter, this rule keeps your rep count honest; without it, you have no way of knowing how much help you were given and therefore no way of honestly claiming to have done the rep unassisted.

If the numbers written down in your training log are not honest, you have absolutely no way to evaluate the results of your program. Since there is no point in lying to yourself about your workout, counting an assisted rep as yours is pointless in the long term. This principle obviously applies to all lifts that customarily require spotters. If you let your spotter help you on your work sets, you'll soon have absolutely no idea what you're really benching, and no idea if you're making progress.

4. This is worth repeating: **any rep touched by anybody other than the lifter does NOT BELONG TO THE LIFTER.** As a spotter, you are responsible for controlling your desire to participate in the set. Your job is to help if necessary, not to share the work and the glory. Stay away from the bar unless your help is actually needed; if you don't, the lifter has my permission to slap you for interfering with his potential personal record.

For both lifter and spotter, when racking the bar, make sure that you touch the uprights *first*. Don't try to set the bar down directly on the hooks. If you (the lifter) move the bar back with locked elbows until it touches the vertical part of the uprights, and then slide it down onto the hooks, you won't have to worry about whether it will stay in the rack. If the uprights are touched first, the bar will always be above the hooks. If straightening out your elbows got the bar clear of the hooks when you took it out, then locked elbows will ensure that it is high enough to get back over the hooks when you're racking it. (If your arms are short, you need to use a bench with adjustable uprights.) But if you try to set the bar down on the horizontal surface first, then you are not all the way back to the uprights as you try to set the bar down, and you will eventually miss the rack, usually one of the hooks on one side. This same advice applies to the squat for exactly the same reasons.

Certain circumstances might require the use of two spotters, as during the heavy attempts at a power meet, but normal weight-room conditions very seldom require more than one competent spotter. The problem with two spotters is the unalterable fact that two people cannot assist one lifter in a perfectly balanced way, especially when they must react quickly. The uneven loading that the lifter will inevitably experience is a potential source of injury. It is physically impossible for two people, even careful, experienced people, to pull upward with exactly the same amount of force on each side of a bar. They will therefore subject the lifter to uneven loading at exactly the time when that stress is most likely to cause an injury – during a rep that is too heavy to lift. This is true of both the squat and the bench press. The problem in the bench press is solved with the use of the single spotter, a perfectly reasonable way to spot for the vast majority of bench press workouts in which the weight on the bar has been correctly selected.

THE POWER CLEAN

The power clean cannot be done slowly. There is therefore no confusion over the nature of the exercise. In essence, it is a jump with the bar in the hands, after which the bar is caught on the shoulders. The power clean is used in sports conditioning because it trains explosion, and done correctly it is the best exercise for converting the strength obtained in the other exercises to power. Other, easier-to-learn exercises like the vertical jump require explosion, and plyometrics have recently come into fashion in strength and conditioning for this reason. But the clean and the snatch are unique in their ability to be incrementally loaded with an increasingly heavier weight, making it possible to develop a more powerful explosion in a simple programmed way. Since the nature of the vast majority of sports is explosive, involving the athlete's ability to accelerate his body or an object, the ability to accelerate is pivotal in sports performance. The power clean is our most important tool in this war against inertia.

In his famous book *The Strongest Shall Survive*, Bill Starr included the power clean in his "Big Three," with the comment that "If your program only allowed you to do one exercise, this would be the best." The power clean has always been used by weightlifters as an assistance exercise for the clean, the more complicated version of the lift. The term "clean" refers to a way to get the bar clear of the floor and up to the shoulders, without soiling the bar by touching the body on the way up, as required by the rules in place several decades ago. If this is accomplished in one movement, it is a clean; if it is done in two movements (if the bar stops on a belt or the chest on the way up), it is referred to as a "Continental," due apparently to the absence of a rule against it in mainland European contests at the time. In modern usage, the term "clean" refers to a full squat clean. It has not always been this way. The *split clean* – a style that used a forward/back split like that commonly used for the jerk in Olympic weightlifting – was the standard version until the 1960s, when the squat style began to be favored due to the heavier weights that could be lifted with this front-squat-based technique.

The term "power" as a qualifier in front of an exercise refers to an abbreviated version of a more

Figure 6-1. The power clean is a variation of the squat clean – usually referred to as the "clean" – used in Olympic weightlifting. Bill Starr cleans 435 at the 1969 Nationals.

complicated movement, the shorter version being harder to perform because the extra technique stuff is there to make it easier to lift more weight. A *power snatch* is a snatch without a squat or split, the use of which reduces the distance the bar must be pulled. The *power jerk* is a version of the last part of the clean and jerk, but in the power jerk, the feet do not split. Likewise, the *power clean* is the version of the clean without a split and without a front squat. The power clean therefore requires more "pull" in that the bar must travel higher as a result of the explosion, without moving the body to drop under the bar. As we'll see, the term is actually used correctly here as it pertains to the science of movement.

Any clean requires the lifter to pull the barbell up fast enough and high enough, by using power generated by the hips and legs, to catch it on the shoulders. After the feet break contact with the floor, force cannot be applied to the bar. This is because the force is generated by the components of the body that are operating between the load in the hands and the ground. When the feet break contact

Figure 6-2. The split clean was commonly used prior to the 1960s and is a useful competitive style for some lifters who lack sufficient flexibility to make the squat style advantageous. Rudolf Pflugfelder, Olympic and World Champion, using this style.

with the floor, the bar is moving up as fast as it is going to. It continues to travel upward due to the inertia it acquires during the active part of the pull. The faster the bar comes up, the higher it will go, because the faster it is moving, the more inertia it possesses. The heavier the weight, the harder this is to do. So the better a lifter is at accelerating the bar, the more inertia he can impart to the bar and the more weight he can clean.

As a corollary, a lifter can clean more weight if he can get better at getting under a bar not pulled as high. This is the purpose served by splitting and squatting: they both shorten the distance the bar has to be pulled by allowing the lifter to jump under the bar in a lower position. Since our purpose is sports conditioning – not cleaning heavy weights per se, but rather generating as much upward explosion as possible – we will use the power version of the lift.

A few authorities have taken the position that the squat clean is the superior version of the lift for most training purposes, arguing that going under the bar – when the front squat is taught as a part of the lift – translates into more foot movement and thus more athletic carryover. On this basis, a better case can be made for using the split clean. And a case can be made for the fact that the squat clean is easier on the knees because the hamstrings and adductors can help absorb the shock of the catch. A novice's knees are not yet this tender. But be aware that the front squat will interfere with your back squat form if you are learning both movements at the same time. The novice using this method will devote considerable time and energy to the task of unlearning a quadriceps-dominant squat, the result of poor prior instruction or no instruction at all. Incorporating a front squat into the clean will complicate the process without making the clean any more explosive – our primary objective in doing it, anyway.

The front squat and the back squat are radically different exercises, and while competitive Olympic weightlifters must learn and train the front squat, the back squat is far more important to general strength and conditioning. Even when used as a part of the clean, the front squat is best left to intermediate-level lifters to learn after good back squat technique has been nailed down by several months of training. This, in addition to the fact that a power clean is pulled to a higher position, is the reason that power cleans are the recommended explosive lift for novices.

The term *power* has a very specific meaning in the study of mechanics. *Work* is the amount of force applied to an object that makes it move a resulting distance, and this quantity expended per unit of time is *power*. Written as an equation, it is *(FD)/T = P*, where P is power, F is the force, D is the distance over which the force acts, and T is the time it takes to perform this work. When we're referring to the total amount of work done over a longer period of time – the duration of a set of five reps, for example – the proper term is *average power*. When the timeframe in question becomes very short, like the duration of a clean or snatch, the term used is *instantaneous power*. Physicists measure it in joules per second, or *watts*. In our discussion of the power clean and its application to explosive training and athletics, instantaneous power is what we are concerned with. It can be best understood as the ability to exert force rapidly – to display strength quickly.

More terms now: *Speed* is the rate of change in the position of an object. If the direction of the speed is specified, we refer to the *velocity* of the object – the bar moving *up* at 2 meters per second. *Acceleration* is the rate of change of velocity over time – the increase in velocity (or decrease, known as *deceleration*), or how fast the velocity is changing. *Force* is the influence that causes acceleration; for an object to accelerate, force must be applied to it. *Strength* is the physical ability to generate force against an external resistance. (It is difficult to define strength when it is applied isometrically, i.e., when the application of force causes no movement of an object outside the body, but rather stays within the physical system of the muscles and skeleton. Isometric force production is an important part of barbell training, but for purposes of defining strength, movement of the bar is our primary quantifying measurement.)

Power in the weight room is therefore the ability to generate force rapidly. A more familiar term for this might be "quickness," especially when applied to the movement of the body itself. For many sports, just being strong is not enough; you must also possess the ability to rapidly employ your strength so that you can accelerate better – both your own bodyweight and that of a physical opponent or a thrown implement. A strong man might very well be able to apply enough force to a very heavy weight to get it moving, but a *powerful* man can get it moving more quickly.

The vertical jump is a valuable diagnostic test for power. It directly measures an athlete's ability to generate force rapidly enough to accelerate his bodyweight off the ground, and it is a valuable assessment of genetic capacity. It is used by the NFL as part of their Combine test to predict this aspect of performance. Studies have shown that vertical jump performance is predictive of sports proficiency, that power clean performance is predictive of vertical jump performance, and that power clean performance is predictive of squat strength. Squat performance is predictive of squat jump performance, and squat jump performance is predictive of power clean performance. The power clean, by training the athlete's ability to move a heavy weight quickly, is the glue that cements the strength training program to sports performance.

One way to understand the concept of power in this specific situation is to compare performances in the power clean and the deadlift. As we have already seen, the deadlift is a straight pull off the floor, with the lifter standing up with the bar and the bar stopping at arms' length, whereas the power clean continues the pull on up through an explosive phase to a catch on the shoulders. A power clean has a bar path that is twice as long as the deadlift's, and it uses 50–75% of the load of a heavy deadlift. Since work is calculated by multiplying the amount of force used to overcome the weight of the bar by the vertical distance the bar travels, and since the bar is pulled perhaps six times faster in a power clean because it is half the weight of a deadlift, power outputs in a heavy clean might be five to seven times as high as in a deadlift. A deadlift can

Power Clean
*Timing & Synch
Recruitment Rate
Commitment
Explosion*

*Grind
Force Transmission
Neural Disinhibition
Recruitment Number
Positional Strength*

Deadlift

Figure 6-3. The power clean contributes to the deadlift, and the deadlift contributes to the power clean. The power clean teaches timing and athletic synchronization of complex multi-joint movements; it trains the commitment involved in getting under the bar, the all-or-none that is sometimes lacking in a deadlift attempt; it trains the rate of motor unit recruitment, thus improving neuromuscular efficiency; and it teaches explosion – the mental cue for highly efficient motor unit recruitment. The deadlift develops the concentric and isometric strength involved in holding the correct position through the slower parts of a heavy clean, and the ability to hold the back rigid during the explosive hip extension that makes for an efficient second pull; it increases the total number of motor units that can be recruited in a contraction; it teaches and enables "grind" – the patience necessary to maintain position through a long effort; it disinhibits the nervous system against heavier weights, so that heavy cleans feel light in contrast to heavy deadlifts; and it develops the good old-fashioned ability to produce force.

obviously be done with a heavier weight because it is a shorter movement with no inherent requirement to accelerate the bar – if you can just keep it moving up, however slowly, you can lock it out. Remember: there can be no slow power cleans because they will not rack on the shoulders, but a heavy deadlift might take 5–7 seconds to pull and it will still be a deadlift.

Here is one of the most important facts about training for strength, or power, or sports, or anything else: **it is always true that a man with a 500-pound deadlift will clean more than a man with a 200-pound deadlift.** At its very core, power is dependent upon strength: force production capacity that does not exist cannot be displayed, quickly or otherwise. However, between two men who both deadlift 500 pounds, the one moving it faster is producing more acceleration – more force over a shorter timeframe – and thus more power. This capacity is the ultimate difference between a strong man and a strong *athlete*. The power clean is an incrementally increasable way to develop this power.

A very strong powerlifter can deadlift two to three times the weight he can power clean –

because he probably doesn't train the clean at all. In the early days of powerlifting, most competitors had weightlifting experience or were coached by people who did. This being no longer the case, a powerlifter's power clean might be 40% of his deadlift. In contrast, an Olympic weightlifter might clean 85% of his deadlift. This difference is a direct result of genetics and training specificity. At the elite levels, all sports favor a certain type of genetic predisposition. The elite powerlifter is an athlete who is good at pulling heavy weights, and the elite weightlifter is good at pulling moderate weights fast. And weightlifters tend to train with lighter weights explosively, while powerlifters concentrate their efforts on the slower movements that allow the use of heavier weights. It is quite likely that a weightlifter who can deadlift only 450 pounds over a 385-pound clean has not trained with sufficiently heavy weights to develop his absolute strength. His clean would go up if he developed his absolute strength off the floor. There is no reason that a lifter with a 385 clean and a 450 deadlift can't get his deadlift stronger, unless he is happy with staying at a 385 clean. Or it could be that the powerlifter with a 600-pound deadlift and a 240-pound clean has neglected to develop his power off the floor. ("Powerlifting" is a bad choice of name for the sport; it should be "strengthlifting," but I predict that my suggestion will not be adopted anytime soon.) Both sports could benefit from more exposure to each other's training methods.

These examples illustrate a way to consider the relationship of absolute strength to power: you can think of the power clean as being done with a percentage of the deadlift. In other words, *explosive strength is displayed as a percentage of absolute strength.* The ratio between the two depends on training and genetics, and the vertical jump might be the indicator of the ratio. Training can improve the ratio to a certain extent, but genetics will limit this extent. What is certain is that as the ability to produce force increases, the potential to display that force as power goes up with it. The extent to which this is true at the extreme limits of performance is unclear, but for novice lifters, there is no question that the best way to make the clean stronger is to make the deadlift stronger.

If this is true, why train the power clean at all? For some people, this is a legitimate question. Older people with old-people's elbows, shoulders, and wrists may elect not to perform the exercise at all, as may very young trainees, people with poor athletic ability, older women, or people with osteoporosis, chronic knee tendinitis, or other problems that make the power clean more trouble than it is productive. But for most other people and all athletes, the power clean is the best way to increase the ability to explode – to display power – where this ability needs to be developed.

The Neuromuscular System

To understand the nature of power production by the human body, you need to understand the way the nervous system controls the muscles. A detailed discussion of the physiology of muscle contraction is outside the scope of this discussion, and can be found in *Practical Programming for Strength Training, Second Edition* (Aasgaard, 2009) and in many other sources. Very short version: The muscles

are composed of *muscle fibers;* these are controlled by the *motor neurons;* and the whole system of muscles plus the controlling nervous system is collectively referred to as the *neuromuscular system.* Each motor neuron controls many muscle fibers, and the term *motor unit* refers to one motor neuron and all the muscle fibers it innervates (supplies with nerve fibers). The contraction, or *firing,* of motor units by the neuromuscular system is called *recruitment.* It is considered to be an all-or-none phenomenon: the muscle fibers of the motor unit, when fired by a nervous impulse, come into contraction at 100% of their capacity to do so. This means that a submaximal muscle contraction is the result of a submaximal

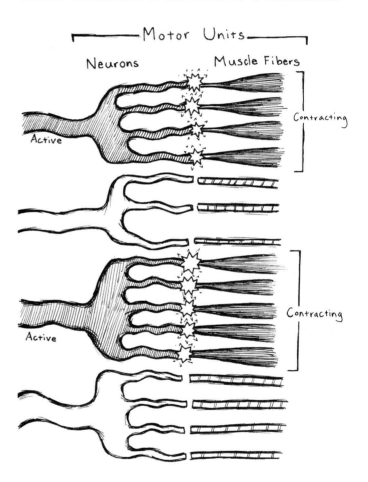

Figure 6-4. Motor unit recruitment is the total activity of varying numbers of motor units, all of which operate to the limits of their capacity when individually called into contraction. The recruited motor units are in full contraction, while the unrecruited motor units are not.

percentage of motor units being recruited. The greater the force production requirements of the task, the more motor units are recruited into contraction.

The ability to recruit motor units with great efficiency – i.e., recruit high numbers of them quickly when a task demands instantaneous high levels of force production – is largely controlled by the genetic endowment of the individual. This ability depends on the density of motor neuron populations within the muscles, the quality of the nerve tissue, the quality of the nervous system interface with the muscle fibers, the type of muscle fibers and their ratio within the muscles, and other factors. Some of these factors can adapt to the stress imposed by training, and some cannot. The vertical-jump test is a naked look at the quality of the neuromuscular system and is an indicator of the ultimate ability of an athlete to be explosive.

Exercises that require the body to explode into a high level of motor unit recruitment with heavy loads can develop the aspects of the neuromuscular system that are capable of adapting to the stress of the exercise. Athletes with a high vertical jump have the *potential* to be more explosive than athletes with a lower vertical jump. Likewise, athletes with lower verticals who work harder to develop their neuromuscular efficiency, compared to gifted athletes who sit on their asses, have the potential to be better athletes than their gifted counterparts. The power clean and other explosive exercises can develop this ability in an incrementally increasable fashion: more weight can be loaded on the bar each workout, and the increase can be precisely adjusted to match the lifter's ability to adapt, thus forcing the adaptation to occur. This process allows for the controlled and programmed development of explosive capacity and power.

Power, Force Production, and Velocity

Understanding power and its relationship to force production and velocity is essential to understanding how to effectively train this capacity and why the power clean works so well at doing

so. Figure 6-5 shows the velocity-power graph. The dashed line represents bar velocity – very high when the load is light, and slowing down to a stop as the load approaches maximum. The dashed line represents power production – the force displayed quickly.

Power is low on the left side of the graph, at very light weights, because light weights don't require much force to make them move fast. They move fast easily because the weight is light. Power is also low on the right side of the graph, where the weights get very heavy, because a very heavy weight is hard to move fast. Remember: power requires velocity. Power peaks in the range of 50–75% of 1RM, where a moderately heavy weight can still be moved relatively fast. The range represents differences in the nature of the various exercises, whether the exercise is primarily an upper-body or lower-body movement, and the skill, strength, experience, and sex of the individual athlete. (Women can typically use a higher percentage of 1RM explosively than men can.) This range (50–75% of 1RM) is also where the power clean usually falls as a percentage of the deadlift.

The popular Westside Dynamic Effort method, developed by Louie Simmons, trains power production by using weights in the range of 50–75% of max in the squat, bench press, and deadlift with an emphasis on maximum acceleration during the reps. Louie has essentially figured out a way to train the squat, bench, and deadlift as if they were Olympic lifts, by training them with weights that can be used at the velocity that produces maximum power.

A logical question, the converse of our earlier one, might be: why do we need to squat and deadlift to develop strength at slow speeds if we are training for power? Both types of training are necessary and each type contributes to the development of the other. Again, **a man with a 500-pound deadlift can clean more than a man with a 200-pound deadlift** because of the great difference in the ability to produce force. But between two men who both deadlift 500 pounds, the one moving it faster is producing more force, is therefore stronger, and is training in a way that teaches his muscles and nervous

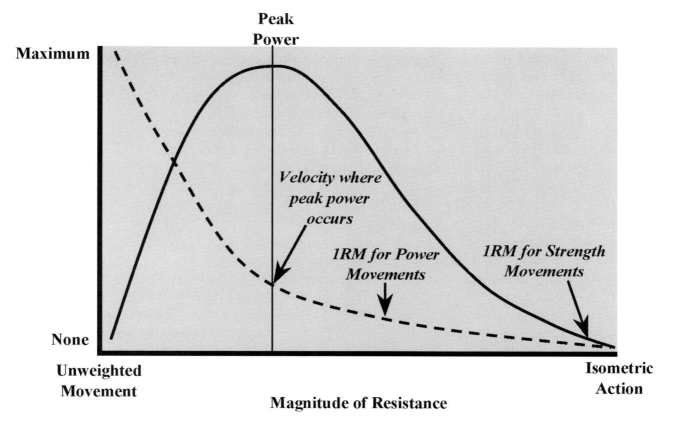

Figure 6-5. The velocity-power graph. The dashed line represents velocity, and the solid line represents power output. Peak power occurs at approximately 30% of maximal isometric force and 30% of maximal movement velocity. This would equate to 50–80% of 1RM, depending on the exercise. "Strength" movements are those that are limited by strength, such as the squat, press, deadlift, or similar exercises. "Power" movements are those limited by power output, such as the snatch, jerk, clean, or other similar exercises. From *Practical Programming for Strength Training, Second Edition*, 2009, The Aasgaard Company.

system to produce even more force. Training faster with a given weight requires more force production because acceleration requires force. And when the ability to produce force goes up, heavier weights can be lifted. This is why the power clean makes the deadlift go up and why the deadlift contributes to the power clean.

The weight that can be used for a heavy power clean, for most athletes, is the correct weight to use to improve force production. The weight is heavy enough to make the lifter pull hard, and by its very nature, the power clean cannot be done without explosion. Unless the bar is moving fast at the top, it will not even rack on the shoulders. The power clean's only drawback is that it is a technique-dependent exercise. Let's learn how to do it.

Learning the Power Clean

The power clean is best learned from the top of the pull, down. This means that you will first learn the technique of catching, or "racking," the bar on the shoulders, so the emphasis in your mind is on the rack position from the beginning. When you are learning the power clean, remember that speed becomes important at the top of the pull, not off the floor. The lower part of the pull, from the floor to the mid-thigh, gets the bar in the correct position for the explosive movement that racks the bar, and this lower part must be done correctly, not quickly, at least at first. From the middle of the pull on up, the movement must get faster, but this cannot be done correctly if the lift has not been started from

Figure 6-6. The basic stance for the clean is the same position used for a flat-footed vertical jump.

Figure 6-7. The difference in pulling stance (A), from which the clean begins, and the racking stance (B), essentially the same as the squat stance, the stable position the feet will reflexively seek after breaking contact with the ground.

the floor correctly. By learning the top of the power clean first, and worrying about getting it down to the floor later, you assign the correct priority to the most important part of the pull. After all, the first part of the power clean is essentially a deadlift, which you already know how to do. When you have learned the top of the pull, we will slide down, a little at a time, into a deadlift, making the transition from half a power clean to the whole thing.

The empty 20 kg (45 lb) bar will be correct for most people to comfortably learn the movement with, but some smaller kids and women might need a lighter bar, such as a 15 kg women's competition bar or an even lighter shop-built one. There is no point in adding weight to the bar at first, because you are learning the movement only. It doesn't make sense to learn this movement without a bar, as you do with the squat, because to do a clean, you need a bar to provide some resistance for the elbows to rotate around. A broomstick or a piece of PVC pipe is too light to have sufficient inertia to stay in place during the turn, and learning with PVC is an excellent way to introduce bad arm habits from the very beginning.

Foot position will be the same as for the deadlift, and similar to the stance for a flat-footed vertical jump or a standing broad jump: place your feet 8–12 inches apart, with your toes pointed slightly out. This is the stance that allows you to apply maximum power to the ground and begins

the process of convincing you that the power clean is really a jump. You will have to reset your stance before each rep, because after the jump, your feet will land in what is essentially a squat stance.

Now that you have the correct stance and an empty bar of the right weight, you will learn the hang position, the rack position, and the jumping position, in that order.

LEARNING THE HANG, RACK, AND JUMPING POSITIONS

First, the position at the top of the pull, with the bar in the hands at arms' length and with straight elbows, straight knees, and chest up, is referred to as the **hang position** (Figure 6-8). Get into the hang position by taking the EMPTY bar

Figure 6-8. The hang position. Note the straight elbows, internally rotated, and that the lifter's chest is up, eyes are looking slightly down, and feet are in the pulling stance.

off the floor with a correct grip and deadlifting it. The correct grip for most people will be about 2–3 inches wider on each side than the grip they use for the deadlift. The power-clean grip is wide enough to let the lifter's elbows freely rotate up into the rack position, to be described shortly, and will obviously vary with shoulder width. Later, we will learn the hook grip, but for now, a normal thumbs-around, or *double-overhand*, grip will be fine. Your eyes will be looking at a spot on the floor about 12–15 feet in

front of you, just as in the deadlift.

In the hang position, your arms will be internally rotated, placed in that position with the same motion used to pronate the grip. This movement is used in the hang position to start the process of learning to keep the elbows straight, one of the most important, and apparently one of the hardest, things to learn about the clean. Get in the habit early of snapping the elbows into this position every time to begin the process of the clean.

Figure 6-9. In the hang position, your reminder for straight elbows will be rotating them internally. Make sure they stay in this position anytime the bar hangs in the hands.

Figure 6-10. The rack position, with chest up and elbows pointed forward.

The next step is to get the bar onto the shoulders. From the hang position, with the correct-width grip, get the bar up onto your shoulders, any way you want to right now. It should sit right on top of the frontal deltoids (the meaty part of the front of the shoulders), well away from the sternum and collarbones. This position is referred to as the **rack position** (Figure 6-10). The key to this position is the elbows: they must be up very high, pointed straight forward, with the humerus as nearly parallel to the floor as possible. Some people will have trouble getting into this position due to flexibility problems. A grip width adjustment usually fixes this, especially if the forearms are longer than the upper arms. Widen the grip a little at a time until the position is better. If your elbows are up high enough, the bar will clear the bony parts and sit comfortably on the bellies of the deltoid muscles. The bar should not be sitting in the hands, and the hands are not supporting any of the weight. The weight is resting on your shoulders, and your hands are trapping it in position between your arms and shoulders, just like they do in the squat. This position is secure and pain-free to the extent that you will never in your entire life clean a weight that will be too heavy to hold like this. It is imperative that you understand that this is where the bar goes and not anywhere

else – not sitting on your chest, and not just carried in your hands. You must not stop with your elbows pointing at the floor (Figure 6-11).

Lower the bar by dropping it down the chest and catching it at the hang position. This means that you do not reverse-upright-row or reverse-curl the bar down to the hang position – you actually *drop the bar and catch it.* Some people actually let it slip from their grip before they figure this out. Just catch the bar at the hang, with no attempt

Figure 6-11. The incorrect elbow position places the elbows directly under the bar and places the weight of the bar on the arms and wrists instead of on the shoulders.

at all to lower it with the arms. This step teaches two important things. First, the bar path in a clean must be as close to vertical as possible for physical efficiency, and when you drop the bar down from the rack position close to your chest, you are practicing the vertical bar path on the way down that you will use on the way up. If you un-curl the bar to put it down, you are pushing it away from the vertical balance line; dropping the bar close to the chest keeps it directly above the mid-foot. Second, the arms do not interact with the weight during a clean – what makes the bar go up is the jump, not your arms performing an upright row (perhaps the most unfortunate exercise ever invented, for several reasons). If you learn immediately that the arms do not either raise OR lower the bar, you will help solve the arm-pull problem before it has a chance to develop. And when you practice this way, you double the amount of bar path practice you can get when you clean. So we'll start the process from the first rep. Just drop it and catch it.

Get back in the hang position, and then unlock your knees and your hips. Do this by sticking your butt back as you bend your knees. Let the bar slide down your thighs to a position somewhere in the middle of your thighs. This position we will call the **jumping position** because it is the same position you would drop into to perform a vertical jump (Figure 6-13). Your elbows will be straight and internally rotated, just as in the hang position; your arms will be vertical; and your knees and hips will be unlocked. The bar will not be too far down the thighs; it will be at about the middle of the thighs – possibly higher if your arms are short or lower if you have long arms – and *in contact with the skin, actually touching the thighs.*

This last point is very important, so much so that the jumping position can be thought of as *both* the knees-and-hips-unlocked position and the place where the bar touches the thighs. You find this place by positioning your hips and legs to jump. It is always the last place you should feel the bar until you catch it on your shoulders, and **if you don't feel the bar on your thighs when you clean, it is wrong**.

Figure 6-12. The cure for incorrect elbow position. To fix the problem of lifting your elbows after an incorrect rack, you can lift them (or have them lifted) repeatedly enough that initially catching the bar in the correct position becomes reflexive.

This point cannot be emphasized enough: the bar being in contact with your thighs means that it's in the proper place in balance over the mid-foot, and that you are in the correct place to jump. Make it your policy to touch your thighs each time you clean.

Now, from the jumping position, *with straight elbows*, jump straight up in the air with the bar hanging from your arms. Don't bend your elbows. Concentrate on the fact that you are jumping and leaving the ground. Jump as high as you can, enough that you have to fully extend your knees and hips to do it. Focus on your jump the first few times, and then focus on keeping your elbows extended. It will be normal at this point to shift your feet from the stance used for pulling into a stable position for catching the bar in the rack position. For most people, this **racking stance** will approximate the squat stance because it will be familiar from squatting, and because the bent knees are used to absorb the weight of the dropping body and barbell best distribute the load to the ground in this position. Don't worry about the stance at

Figure 6-13. The jumping position. Note the position of the bar in contact with the thighs. In all cleans, the bar must touch this place on the thighs before the jump occurs.

this point unless your feet move laterally wider than your squat stance.

Think hard about not bending your elbows as the bar slides down your thighs to the jumping position. Many people will try to bend their elbows instead of letting the bar slide, but don't you be that person. If you find that you're bending your elbows anyway, use your triceps to lock the elbows in hard extension, and think about this for a few more jumps.

Once the act of jumping with the bar in your hands and with your elbows straight is firmly embedded, jump and catch the bar on your shoulders in the rack position. Catch it in the same place you had it before, with your elbows up. The bar should stop on your shoulders, not in your hands. Slam your elbows up into the rack position from the top of the jump – go from elbows-straight directly to slammed-forward. Aim your shoulders at the bar and jam them into it without thinking about raising your elbows, as if there is no step between straight elbows and the rack position.

Jumping is the key. The power clean is not an arms movement, at all, and if you first learn that a jump with straight arms is the core of the movement, you will never learn to arm-pull the bar. The jump generates the upward movement of the bar, and later, when your form is good, you will think of the jump as an explosion at the top of the pull. For now, just jump and slam the bar onto the shoulders. Each time, be sure that 1) you start from the jumping position with the bar touching the thighs and your elbows straight, 2) you actually jump, and 3) you rack the bar with your elbows up high. Check the position of the bar as it passes your chest: it should be close enough that it touches your shirt.

During this process, you will find that your hands get tired, so rest them as needed. Check your eye gaze direction, too – on the floor 12–15 feet in front of you, not straight down and not up at the ceiling – because this important detail can get lost in the process. It is not productive to let fatigue interfere with concentration and good form. Take the time necessary to go through this critical process properly.

Figure 6-14. The three basic positions in the power clean: the hang position, the jumping position, and the rack position.

When you are consistently producing a good jump and rack, you are essentially doing the "clean" part of the power clean. The remaining task is to get the bar from the position it would occupy loaded on the floor, up to the place on the thighs where the jump starts. This part is nothing more than tacking a deadlift onto the movement. It can be made more complicated than this, but it is not productive to do so. The process of tacking the deadlift on starts at the top and proceeds stepwise down to the floor. We will do it in three pieces.

With the bar close, elbows straight, and arms rotated in, slide the bar down to the jumping position and then do the jump and catch. This is the first step, and you've already done it several times now.

The second step is to lower the bar to a point just below the bottom of the kneecaps. Unlock your knees, shove your hips back, and slide the bar down to a point just below the bottom of the patellas, in the middle of the patellar tendon, above the top of the tibias. Slide the bar down by driving your hips back, driving your shoulders forward, and keeping your knees just a little unlocked. The bar never loses contact with the thighs on the way down, and you might need to think about pushing it back into your thighs so that it doesn't lose contact. The weight will be over the mid-foot with your shoulders out in front of the bar, again with *straight elbows*. It is tempting to unlock the elbows as the bar slides down the thighs – perhaps the tendency is to "cock the spring" on the way down before the jump? – but force them to stay straight. Your chest should stay up and your low back should stay locked in position.

From this position just below the patellas, slowly slide the bar back up to the jumping position, jump, and catch the bar in the rack position. The jump will happen when the bar reaches the place on the thighs that you will now recognize as the jumping position. When it reaches this spot, the slow slide turns into a jump without any pause; it will be as though the bar has touched a trigger that trips the jump into an explosion without any hesitation at the point of firing. During the entire movement, the bar must stay on the thighs, touching the actual surface of the legs as it moves down and up, until the jump. The elbows must remain straight during this sliding along the thighs; they do not bend until after the jump.

The second step is the hardest one because it is the transition between the two phases of the pull: the deadlift part and the clean part. It is the step that causes the most trouble because the clean is just a jump and a catch, and the deadlift involves nothing more than pulling the bar straight up at arms' length. This transition phase will be where you make the common mistakes that occur in a power clean: the elbows will bend before you jump, or you will slow down or stop the pull before you jump and catch. Maybe you'll do both. Keep your elbows straight by maintaining your internal rotation and screaming at yourself "Elbows straight!" and maintain your pulling speed until you "trip the trigger" at the jumping position. Be sure to WAIT until the bar touches the jumping position to jump.

After you do this movement from just below the knees a few times, we'll introduce the third step of the movement. From the hang position, lower the bar down past your knees to the mid-shin. This is the position the bar will occupy against your leg when the bar is on the floor and loaded with plates. Slide the bar down the same way as before, by shoving your hips back and your shoulders forward, keeping the bar against your thighs, and now against your shins as well, all the way down. As the bar passes your knees, let them bend a little to drop you into what is actually the starting position of the deadlift. Make sure the bar is low enough, actually in the position it will be in with plates on the bar – the tendency here

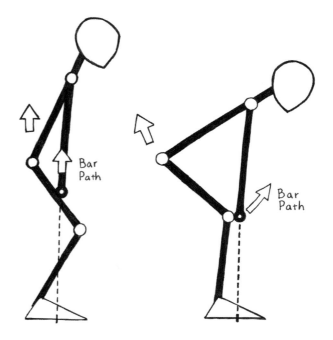

Figure 6-15. If you hit the jumping position correctly, the bar rises in an efficient vertical path. If you are impatient and fail to wait until the bar gets up to the jumping position, i.e. if you jump from too low on the thighs, the bar will travel forward. This occurs because the back angle has not become sufficiently vertical to allow the force of the jump to be directed vertically.

is to fail to get low enough. From there, slowly drag the bar up the shins, past the knees, to the jumping position, and then jump and catch the bar in the rack position. Don't try to pull the bar from the bottom up the legs any faster than a slow deadlift right now – there will be time for that later. Right now, concentrate on keeping straight elbows and

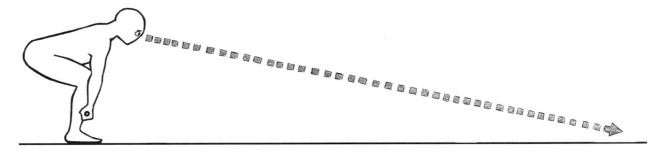

Figure 6-16. Eye gaze direction should be precisely controlled. It facilitates balance and a safe position for the cervical vertebrae during the pull.

waiting until the bar gets to the jumping position. The instant the bar touches the jumping position, the jump is triggered, and not before.

This phase of the pull is where impatience rears its ugly head. Most people will be anxious to clean the bar, and one of two things will happen: the bar speed will increase beyond a manageable speed; or the jump will happen too early – that is, it will happen too low on the thighs, before the jumping position is actually reached. If the bar is moving too fast at this stage in the learning process, bar path problems will arise. It will be hard to keep the bar in contact with the legs, and therefore in balance over the mid-foot. Move the bar slowly now so that you can correctly move it fast later. And if the jump occurs too early, the bar will travel forward instead of straight up. This error will cause you to jump forward as you catch the bar in the rack position; your feet will move forward instead of staying in their same horizontal position. Since jumping forward is inefficient, don't pull early. Wait patiently until the bar touches the jumping position and then explode into the clean. Incorrect eye gaze direction can contribute to problems here, so check it repeatedly. Do a few reps from this depth with the empty bar.

ADDING WEIGHT TO THE BAR

When the movement is correct from the jumping position, from below the knees, and from the mid-shin, you're ready for the next phase of the teaching method. Load the bar with regulation-diameter plates that are light enough to clean from the top – not so heavy that there is any problem with the weight at all, but heavy enough that the bar is perceptibly loaded. For most guys in a well-equipped gym, this will be the bar and 10 kg bumper plates. Kids and women will need lighter plastic training plates. You will now repeat the learning sequence from the top down. Deadlift the bar to the hang position, drop down to the jumping position, and jump and catch the bar in the rack position. At this point, you will see the whole purpose of this exercise: the bar is now heavier, so what do you have to do? *You jump harder.* This is why we clean.

After you clean the bar from the jumping position, drop down to below the kneecaps and clean it from there. Again, the bar never leaves the skin during the slide down and back up, and it leaves the thighs as it touches the jumping position, not one centimeter or tenth of a second sooner, and with no hesitation when it gets there. After this, drop down and touch the floor with the plates and immediately start back up the shins to the jumping position without losing tightness at the floor. This clean will be your first official full power clean. Do this succession of positions without a lot of repetition at each level, so that you start learning to make each rep count. If I were coaching you, I'd let you do only one rep at each position. After you finish this process, set the bar down, set up a correct deadlift with your clean grip, deadlift it off the floor, and clean it. Do a couple reps from the floor like this. If you are wearing weightlifting shoes with higher heels, remember to get back off of your toes before you start the pull.

At this point, unless there is a timing problem or some other reason to repeat a step, all your subsequent power cleans will be from the floor. The progression from the top down serves to emphasize the jumping aspect of the movement, and once this is understood and mastered, the full pull should be used. Understood and mastered means that:

1. During the pull from the floor, the bar never leaves the skin of your legs.

2. Your elbows stay straight until after the jump.

3. The jump does not start until the bar gets to the jumping position.

4. The bar lands on your shoulders with your elbows pointed forward; it does not land in the hands.

5. Right now, the speed happens at the jump, not from the floor.

As it feels better, the pull will increase in speed from the floor, but for now, think *slow and correct* from the floor and *fast* at the jump. Again, make sure your eyes are forward and slightly down. An incorrect gaze direction makes a correct clean much more difficult, and a sloppy clean can sometimes be repaired with this simple change.

Note that from the point at which the knees unlock at the top, they do not move forward any more as the bar is lowered to the knees, and that from just below the knees on down, they do move forward. In other words, the hips lower the bar to the knees, and the knees lower the bar to the floor. Coming back up is the exact opposite movement – straighten your knees until the bar clears them, and then return to the jumping position by dragging the bar up your thighs as you extend your hips.

USING THE HOOK GRIP

Within a couple of workouts, when the movement is good enough for you to worry about peripheral matters, start using the hook grip (Figure 6-17). The hook grip is critical in enabling heavy weights to be used. It should not be considered optional. The hook grip should be learned before much weight is being handled in the lift. The hook grip consists simply of laying the middle finger on top of the thumbnail as you wrap your hands around the bar, and letting the bar settle into the bottom of the "hook" made by the fingers. This grip allows the bar to rest in the bend in the fingers during the pull, not up high in the tight fist. The friction between the thumbnail and the middle finger provides the grip security, enabling the forearm muscles that would otherwise squeeze the grip tight to relax. This relaxing enables the elbows to rotate faster when the bar is being racked. Most people will release the hook as they rack the bar, due to a lack of flexibility in the wrist. You will need to reset the hook for each rep.

After the hook grip is adopted and the mechanics of the movement are sound, the pull from the floor can "mature" into a more efficient movement. At first, the model is *slow to the jumping position, and then fast at the jump.* As the pull becomes more comfortable and the correct movement pattern is more embedded, the model becomes *the higher the*

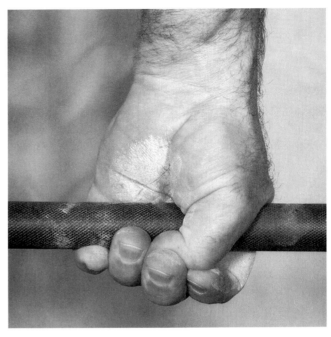

Figure 6-17. The hook grip. Note that the middle finger catches the thumbnail. The friction of the finger against the thumb is amplified by the weight of the bar squeezing the grip components together, and it makes for a much more secure grip than grip strength alone can produce. The hook grip also allows the bar to ride slightly lower in the hands than does a standard grip, thus effectively lengthening the arms just a little.

bar, the faster it moves. This model provides for the acceleration needed to rack heavy weights. Start the bar off the floor from the mid-foot, and then start pulling it faster as it comes up. The objective is to be pulling it as fast as possible as it touches the thighs. Since the bar speed begins to drop immediately after the jump, the momentum you impart to the bar before this point is all it will ever have.

Concentration is required to provide the explosion necessary for a heavy clean, and this starts during the warm-up sets. The bar should be slamming into the rack with light weights, and you should be visualizing the bar moving past your chest like a blur. This phase of the pull is where you will learn how explosive an athlete you can be. Proper focus on this acceleration teaches explosion that carries over into athletics. The barbell is a marvelous concentrator of focus because there are no other factors to distract your attention – no opponents to

Figure 6-18. The power clean.

hit you, no ball to catch or hit, no field of play to deal with. There is only the bar and your ability to pull faster than you did last time, and thus to clean heavier weights.

A FEW NOTES ON THIS TEACHING METHOD

Several things about this method make it an efficient way to quickly learn what is usually regarded as a complicated skill. It is possible to build into a teaching progression several movement details which – although usually regarded as necessary to enumerate and teach – can happen reflexively within the movement if they are embedded in the larger pattern. The *shrug* is usually coached in most power-clean teaching methods; notice that this is the first use of the word in this chapter. The shrug is a reflexive action that occurs as a result of jumping with the loaded bar in the hands. In an attempt to protect the shoulders from the load in the hands, which would otherwise pull the scapulas down as the body goes up, the traps fire into a concentric contraction. This shrug has been taking place since you started jumping with the bar, but it has demanded none of your attention. Later, you can focus on the shrug to help you rack very heavy weights, but right now, it's already in the movement without your having to think about it. This method allows you to focus on developing the correct straight elbow position, jumping high, and keeping the bar close – the more important things for a novice learning the clean.

Another movement considered important for an efficient clean is the "double knee bend" or the "second pull." Figure 6-18 illustrates the sequence of the power clean. Note the knee position in the first five frames: as the knees extend in the initial pull from the floor, the shins become vertical, placing the knees back far enough to allow the bar to come up in its vertical path. After the bar clears the knees and as it slides up the thighs, the knees will come forward a little to a position under the bar as the hips extend. This motion puts the back in a more vertical position to facilitate the jump with the bar hanging from the arms. Then the jump occurs, and the knees and hips extend explosively. So the knees actually extend twice – once off the floor and again at the top during the jump – allowing the quadriceps to contribute twice to the upward movement of the bar. Olympic weightlifting coaches refer to this movement as the "second pull," although "second push" (against the floor) might be more descriptive. This movement will occur as a natural physical consequence of your getting into the jumping position and of having the bar touch the thighs as you jump. When you heed the reminder to touch your thighs with the bar at the jumping position, you are re-bending your knees to do it. So instead of thinking about a sequence of events sometimes considered too complicated to even try to teach, you accomplished this double knee bend by merely touching your thighs with the bar. The more steps that are built into the method that require no conscious direction, the more time you have left to focus on the foundation of the movement – jumping and catching the bar.

Correcting Problems

The power clean is simply a deadlift that accelerates into a jump, after which the bar is caught on the shoulders. The things that make for a good deadlift must also occur in a correct pull from the floor. At the mid-thigh, the jump occurs, and for the barbell to fly up to the rack position with optimum efficiency, the bar path must be as vertical as possible and directly plumb to the balance point over the mid-foot. The elbows do not bend until after the jump has occurred. And since the whole purpose of the exercise is power production, the movement must be done explosively.

STANCE AND GRIP

Stance is chosen to maximize the force that can be applied to the floor, while the grip is chosen to maximize racking efficiency (Figure 6-19). The stance should be the same as that used in the deadlift. Your feet should be in the stance used for a flat-footed vertical jump, for the same reason. We are going to rapidly transfer force to the floor, and this stance, heels 8–12 inches apart, is the best for this purpose. Toes will be pointed out for the same

Figure 6-19. The stance and grip for the power clean.

reasons they were in the deadlift: femur and torso clearance and the involvement of more adductor and external rotator muscle mass. Some very tall individuals with wide hips and shoulders will need a stance wider than this, but not many and not much wider. If wider hips seem to make a much wider stance necessary, try using a wider toe angle first to see if it produces the needed accommodation. Too wide a stance dilutes the ability to jump, as is easily demonstrated by vertical jumps with different stance widths.

The bar will be in position right over the middle of the foot, as in the deadlift. All major standing barbell exercises depend on this position for balance and for force transfer to the floor. Lining up the stance with the bar forward over the ball of the foot creates a situation that will have to be corrected after the bar leaves the floor, because the bar wants to ride the vertical line over the mid-foot. If the bar doesn't leave the ground from this position, you will have to expend some energy to get it back there, or the bar will be forward of the balance point all the way up. And if it is forward on the way up, you will need a backward pull at the top to get the bar onto your shoulders. Most lifters who chronically pull with a backward curve in the bottom of the bar path cause this to occur by using a stance that is too far from the bar, or by dropping their hips and thus pushing the knees, shins, and bar forward. If the most efficient bar path is a straight vertical line, using a start position that enables this to happen

close to the body makes for the most efficient pull. Keep the bar close and don't drop your hips.

The hook grip is recommended for power cleans as soon as the movement is comfortable, as noted earlier. When using it, start with the warm-up sets and use it all the way up to the work sets to desensitize your thumbs to the pressure. Very heavy deadlifts – 800+ pounds – have been pulled with a hook grip, so power clean loads will not be a problem. Athletic tape may help if the discomfort is distracting or if many accumulated workouts tear up the skin of the thumbs.

People with longer forearms might need to use a wider grip because the proportions produced by a long forearm and a short humerus make a high elbow position impossible with a closer grip. The bar must rest on the shoulders in the rack position so that heavy weights can be used; if the forearms are too long, the bar will rest in the hands because the elbows cannot come up enough to let the bar down onto the deltoids (Figure 6-20). The only way to functionally alter these proportions is to widen the grip spacing to create a "shorter" forearm, in the same way that the snatch grip or the sumo stance shortens the functional length of their relevant segments. Some people with exceptionally weird proportions may find the clean impossible to rack. If this is the case, a lifetime of stretching will not make the clean any more possible, and these people might need to learn the power snatch as a replacement explosive exercise.

Figure 6-20. Long forearms may make the clean very hard to rack without a wide grip. People with very long forearms might not be able to use the exercise.

OFF THE FLOOR

We have discussed the mechanics of the pull off the floor in great detail in the Deadlift section of this book. All of that material necessarily applies to the power clean because the relationship of the human musculoskeletal system with the barbell as it comes off the floor *does not vary with the subsequent height of the pull*. The vast majority of the Olympic weightlifting literature that deals with the clean and the snatch advises that the bar be pulled from the floor from a position forward of the mid-foot, and advises that the resulting backward or horizontal bar path off the floor is not only efficient but also desirable. This reasoning is an example of *phenomenology*, "a theory which expresses mathematically the results of observed phenomena without paying detailed attention to their fundamental significance" (*Concise Dictionary of Physics*, Oxford: Pergamon Press, 1978, p. 248). We are not really interested in pulling from the floor in a manner that is demonstrably inefficient just because some very strong elite weightlifters have been observed doing it this way – an argument that is based on description rather than analysis. The limitations of mechanical efficiency apply less stringently to stronger lifters than to less-gifted lifters who have a smaller margin of error in which to display their abilities.

This is especially true when it is not necessary to pull the bar in a curved path – the human body can quite easily conform itself to the realities of gravity and mechanics and pull the barbell up in a straight vertical path. In fact, when this happens, the top part of the pull increases in efficiency along with the bottom part, as we shall see. It is important to be as efficient off the floor as possible. Most problems that develop at the top part of the pull can be traced to an incorrect starting position and the resulting bad initial pull off the floor.

The path the bar makes through space from the start position to the rack position is a major factor in diagnosing the efficiency of the lift, because it describes the interaction of the lifter with the bar. Observe the bar path by looking at the end of the bar from a position at right angles to the lifter, with your eyes looking straight down the bar. Imagine that the end of the bar traces a line in the air during the lift; this line is the bar path, and it is very important to develop your ability to form an image of this line. Watch other lifters do the movement, and learn to translate the image formed of the bar path to your perception of the bar as it moves up from the floor to the rack position.

There are several advanced movement-analysis instruments that record and interpret bar path information, but none is as immediately useful in real time as the experienced eye of a coach. The power clean is a complicated movement, and of all the lifts presented in this program, it benefits the most from the input of an experienced coach.

An ideal bar path is illustrated in Figure 6-21. If the correct position over the middle of the foot and the correct back angle are established, the bar comes off the floor in a vertical path as the knees straighten out, and the back angle will be constant for at least the first few inches of the pull. The bar follows an essentially vertical path until it reaches the jumping position, after which it curves slightly away as the lifter's elbows begin to rotate under the bar. At the top, the bar path will make a little hook as the bar comes back and down onto the shoulders in the rack position. Individual body segment lengths and girths may vary among lifters, but this general bar path will be observed in every correct power clean.

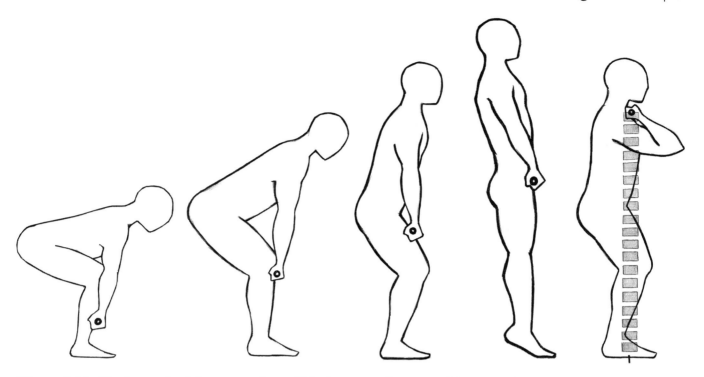

Figure 6-21. The bar path of the power clean. If the bar starts from a position over the middle of the foot, the bar should travel in an essentially vertical path until the jump occurs at mid-thigh. This ideal vertical path will be altered if the start position is forward of the mid-foot.

Let's review the angles involved in the pull and see what varying them does to the bar path. The knee angle, hip angle, and back angle are the same for the power clean's pull off the floor as for the deadlift. The correct starting position facilitates an efficient pull. For example, when the knee angle is too closed, as when your knees are too far forward, your back angle will be too vertical, placing your shoulders behind the bar and your hips too low. Two possibilities exist for the next action on the bar, and in neither of them can the bar come up in a straight line (Figure 6-23).

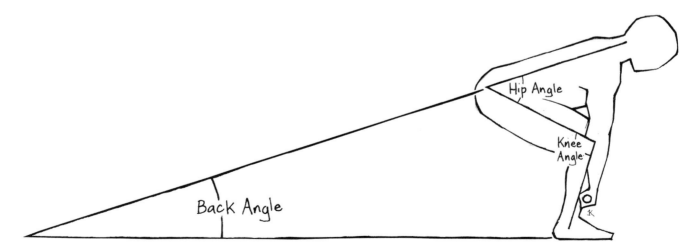

Figure 6-22. The angles for analyzing the power clean are the same as for the deadlift or any pull from the floor: the hip, knee, and back angles.

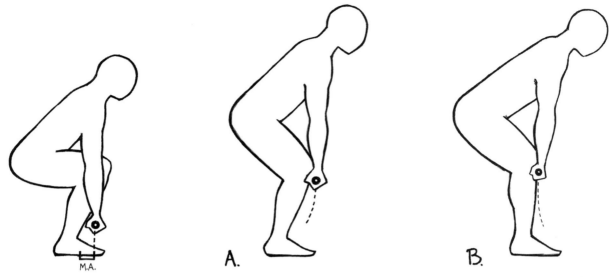

Figure 6-23. Bar path errors caused by the knees-forward/hips-down start position. (A) The bar goes forward around the knees, usually only at light weights. (B) The bar comes back toward the mid-foot, having been pushed too far forward by the knees. Neither bar path is vertical off the floor. (*M.A. = moment arm*)

First, the bar can move forward to get around the knees. This usually occurs only with lighter weights. Pulled forward around the knees this way, the bar will be too far out in front – off-balance forward – as it approaches the jumping position, and the lifter will have to either pull it back in or follow it forward by leaning into the bar or jumping forward at the rack position. Second, the bar can move back toward the mid-foot as it comes off the floor. This is what usually happens with a heavy clean. The pull starts, balance is off forward with the weight on the toes, so the bar gets pulled back into balance over the mid-foot. The knee angle opens and the back angle becomes more horizontal as the bar curves back into balance during the first part of the pull, below the knees. A common complication of this position error is that the back angle overshoots equilibrium with the pull, becoming more horizontal than it should. This angle throws the shoulders too far forward and causes the bar to follow the shoulders, again making the bar run forward of the mid-foot balance point. Better lifters can stabilize their back angle before it becomes too horizontal, but they won't need to if the bar comes off the floor in an efficient vertical path in balance over the mid-foot. The correct starting position facilitates this balanced vertical bar path.

You correct both errors (letting the bar move forward or backward) by raising your hips and pulling the bar back into your shins, thus putting the bar in the correct line of pull before it leaves the floor. You might need to think about keeping your weight back on your heels, especially if you are wearing weightlifting shoes with higher heels. Shoes are an important piece of personal equipment, but if they throw you into a forward position before you start the pull, they will create more problems than they solve. Remember to get back off of your toes and onto your mid-foot before you start the pull.

So, one extreme occurs when the knee angle is too closed, the back angle is too vertical, the shoulders are behind the bar, and the hips are too low. The other extreme occurs when the knee angle is too open, the hip angle is too closed, and the back is nearly parallel to the floor. This set of angles (much less commonly observed due to the tendency of most people to start with their hips too low) presents a different problem. Here, the quadriceps muscles of the thighs have essentially been removed from the lift, since their job of extending the knees has already been done before the bar leaves the floor. If the knees extend before the bar moves, the quads contribute nothing to the first part of the lift. Again,

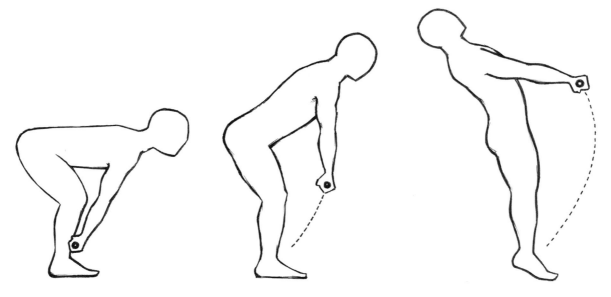

Figure 6-24. The hips-too-high starting position. Even with the bar in the correct place over the mid-foot, the shoulders will be too far in front of the bar. This position causes the bar to swing away forward to the normal pulling configuration, where the humerus is stable at 90 degrees to the lats, leaving the bar out in front.

a starting position problem contributes to problems higher in the pull. The back is nearly parallel to the floor, and this position places the shoulders out in front of the bar. When the bar leaves the floor, it swings forward to get in position under the scapulas, leaving it forward of the mid-foot. If the pull is rescued from this mistake, then when the bar gets to the jumping position, the knees are still too straight and the back angle too horizontal for the

lifter to jump efficiently, because jumping requires a balance between knee extension and hip extension that produces a vertical bar path. If the lifter's back is too horizontal, then as the hip angle opens, the bar swings away from the body, in a "loop," a classic error in which the bar goes out instead of up. This is just one way to loop the pull in a clean or snatch. Catching a looped clean requires jumping forward, which obviously kills your pulling efficiency. You can

Figure 6-25. A simple correction for a too-forward starting position (A) is getting your weight back over your mid-foot by shifting the weight back off the forefoot and toes (B).

Figure 6-26. Preparing to squeeze the bar off of the floor (A) versus preparing to jerk the bar off of the floor (B). The bent elbows and incorrect back angle ruin the pulling mechanics, and the jerk that follows as the slack comes out of the elbows worsens the situation (C).

easily correct the problem by adjusting your starting position: lower your hips, squeeze your chest up, and keep the bar against your shins as you pull.

The point here is that a vertical bar path off the floor reduces the amount of variation in the bar path higher up in the clean. Using a start position that produces a vertical bar path off the floor every time makes for a more easily reproducible pull at the top, because the bar enters the second pull from a position of balance over the mid-foot every time. The correct starting position reduces errors and allows the lifter to focus on explosion instead of on bar path and technique problems, as well as making the pull more mechanically efficient.

These examples represent the extreme variations in starting errors, and define a gradient that will be observed throughout people of differing anthropometry, skill, and talent. Most starting position errors will lie somewhere along this continuum. It is very difficult for the lifter himself to detect the subtle variations in starting position by feel. Even elite weightlifters experience "form creep," in which a good starting position erodes into a bad one over several workouts. The use of a video camera (if one is available), so you can see the relevant angles, or the eyes of an experienced coach are extremely helpful for holding your clean technique together.

These next comments are possibly the most important to understand in the whole discussion of the pull from the floor. Remember from the last part of the teaching method that the bar accelerates from the bottom to the top, getting faster as it gets higher. This means that the bar starts off the floor slow and gets faster as it comes up. The entire purpose of the lower half of the pull, the deadlift part, is to deliver the bar into the jumping position so that it can be accelerated. It is far more important for the pull from the floor to be *correct* than for it to be *fast*, especially at first. Remember this: the bar must be pulled **correctly** at the bottom and **fast** at the top. Pull the bar slowly and correctly off the floor, then fast and close at the top. The off-the-floor errors mentioned above usually occur when you get in a hurry and either rush through your start position or get impatient and jerk the bar off the floor. If you jerk the bar off the floor, you jerk yourself out of position. If you're out of position, you can't hit the jump. So *squeeze* the bar off the floor. The bar always leaves the floor more slowly than it moves up the shins and past the knees.

Any position error that is caused by being in a hurry off the floor will be magnified on the way up, as described earlier. Since the movement is so fast, there is no time to correct the error. But if the bar comes off the floor slowly, your proprioceptive skills – your ability to sense your position in space – have time to make the small corrections that might be needed to put the bar back in the right place before it begins moving so fast that a correction is impossible. Control of the bar position is the whole point of coming off the floor slowly, so that you can enter the jumping position correctly every time.

Jerking the bar off the floor is a common problem for people not using this method of learning the power clean. From the starting position, many people bend their elbows a little and then jerk the slack out of their arms in an attempt to get the bar moving rapidly as it leaves the floor. This jerk is often accompanied by a passive knee extension and a shift to a horizontal back angle. This error must be identified and dealt with the first time it happens. Pay close attention to the sounds you hear as you start the pull: if the plates and bar rattle, you have jerked it. Several things work to fix this. Think about "squeezing" the bar off the floor. Or think about "long straight arms." Or just "slow off the floor."

Make sure that your eyes are looking forward enough and not straight down, since eyes-down is often associated with hips-up. The correct eye gaze direction – 12–15 feet ahead on the floor – makes a correct floor pull much easier. Your perception of back angle is affected by the positional feedback you get from the stationary reference point you are staring at on the floor ahead of you. This eye-gaze point on the floor gives you real-time "telemetry" info that makes balancing much easier. Many poorly positioned starts have been corrected quickly and easily by a cue about the eyes.

THROUGH THE MIDDLE

The part of the pull that encompasses the transition from the basic floor pull – essentially a deadlift – into the actual clean part of the power clean has the potential to cause the most form problems. Errors that start on the floor get magnified in this range, and there is plenty of potential here to start brand new ones. Let's examine some general principles of force transmission and see how they apply to the power clean.

It has been mentioned several times, to the extent that you're probably sick of hearing it, that the elbows must stay straight until the jump occurs. The earlier advice to internally rotate the arms as a reminder to keep them straight was given for this reason. You should know not to bend the arms early, since you have learned this in the deadlift, and the lower part of the power clean is a

Figure 6-27. Bent elbows just absolutely suck. They are one of the most persistent, hardest to correct, and most detrimental of bad habits that a lifter can acquire. Make it a priority to learn and keep perfectly straight elbows.

deadlift. So another reminder: the function of the arms is to transmit the pulling power generated by the hips and legs to the bar. Power is transmitted most efficiently down a non-elastic medium, like a chain, as opposed to a medium that stretches, like a spring. A chain transmits all the power from one end to the other, while a spring absorbs some of the force as it stretches. When the bar is pulled from the floor with bent arms, the bent elbow is essentially a deformable component, a thing that can straighten out, thus creating the potential for some of the pulling force to be diverted from the bar. Little variances in the degree of elbow bend result in a slightly variable amount of force transfer to the bar and in an unpredictable bar path. The best clean is a highly reproducible clean – exactly the same each time, with each rep a perfect example of lifting efficiency. If the bar path varies with each clean, bent elbows are often the problem. And once elbows are bent, they cannot be straightened out during the pull; that would require the forearm, biceps, and brachialis to relax, which they will be

Figure 6-28. The spine during the pull should be in absolute thoracic and lumbar extension. Any softness in the chest-up position or lower-back arch reduces the effectiveness of the back as the transmitter of force from the hips and legs to the shoulder blades and on down to the bar.

reluctant to do even if there were time for you to think about it and do it.

Your elbows might bend because you are trying to curl or upright-row the bar with your arms. Your elbows can rotate very fast – blindingly fast, in fact – if the muscles of your arms are relaxed and provide no resistance to the rotation. The very second you tighten the forearms, biceps, and triceps as you attempt to use these muscles to move the bar, you slow the movement down. After you rack the bar, this tightness causes the elbows to stop at the point where these muscles reach the end of their range of motion in contraction, which leaves the elbows pointing down and the bar sitting on your sternum. (This is another good reason to use the hook grip. The hook makes for a secure grip without the need to squeeze the bar with the fingers, thus contracting the forearm muscles.)

The same force transmission analysis can be applied to the low back. The back is the transmission attached to the hips/legs engine, and force generated against the ground travels up the back, across the scapulas, and down the arms to the bar. If the low back is not locked in hard, absolute extension, it is not as tight as it could be. A round back is a deformable component in the same way that bent elbows are, and it will result in the same unpredictable bar path that is the inevitable consequence of unpredictable force transfer. If form problems are occurring without any set pattern, this might indicate that your low back is not as tight as it could be. Both straight elbows and a solid back position are the basic mechanical requirements of a technically perfect clean.

As the bar approaches the jumping position, the most important part of the movement occurs. If you are correctly pulling the bar, it is accelerating as it moves up the shins, sliding up your skin or your sweats. As it gets to the middle of the thighs, the trigger trips as the bar touches the jumping position, and you try to jump off the ground with the bar. The reaction with the ground during this explosion produces the impulse that imparts momentum to the bar. The knees, hips, and ankles extend simultaneously, with the knees and hips being the primary contributors to force production. But it is important to understand that the acceleration of the load starts BEFORE the jump actually occurs, and this acceleration results in peak velocity at the jump.

The leverage produced by the moment arm of the back can be thought of in two ways. (Remember that the moment arm along the back is the *horizontal distance* between the load and the hips, not the length of the back itself.) The pessimist will view the load hanging from the arms as moment force against the hips that would be better configured as a shorter moment arm with a more vertical back angle in order to take the "load" off the hips and low back. The effective lifter will see the moment arm of the back as a tool with which to accelerate the barbell more effectively. The same way a pitcher throws a ball by *using* the moment arm provided by the length of his forearm (no one would argue that a short arm is an advantage to a pitcher), the lifter accelerates the bar through the middle of the pull by *using* the length of the moment arm along the back

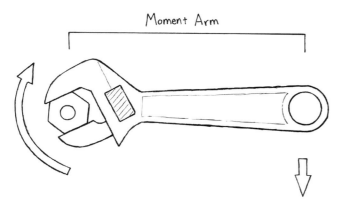

Figure 6-29. The important mechanical concept of the moment arm, as illustrated by the wrench and bolt.

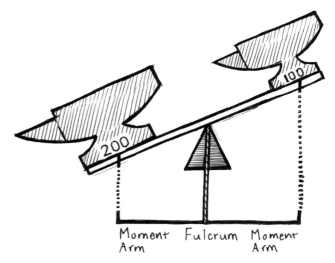

Figure 6-30. The Class 1 lever.

as a tool. Back strength makes this possible and is one of the ways the deadlift is useful for heavy cleans.

The wrench analogy was used to illustrate the concept of moment force, with the bar on the shoulders being the force that turns the bolt, the back being the wrench handle, and the hips being the bolt. But in this specific application, the force gets directed from the hips to the bar, and the moment arm is the tool used to command the bar to move

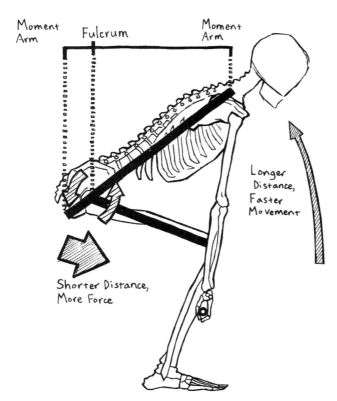

Figure 6-31. The human hip, a Class 1 lever.

faster with the force generated by the muscles that open the hip angle. When we squat, the muscles of the hips and back are used to *resist the rotation* that could be produced by the loaded bar on the way down. But when we clean, we are using the muscles of the hips and back to *produce the rotation* along the back that is required to accelerate the bar upward.

Remember that the human hip is a Class 1 lever. The back and the pelvis form the rigid segment; the hip joints are the fulcrum; the hamstrings, glutes, and adductors of the posterior chain are the force pulling down behind the hips; and the load in your hands is the force pulling down in front of the hips (Figure 6-31). Because our muscles can only contract a small percentage of their length, our skeletal levers must multiply this distance if we're going to move anything efficiently. This amplification of muscle contractile distance comes at the expense of greater force production. If you are strong enough that the force generated by the posterior chain is high enough, the short segment behind the hip joint – the ischium of the pelvis – can lever up the long segment, and *the length of the back multiplies the velocity of the hip rotation.* **The short side moving a short distance with enough force can make the long side accelerate its load over a long distance.** This acceleration starts during the middle of the pull, as the bar approaches the knees, when the back angle changes to make the moment arm between the bar and the hips much shorter. This change in

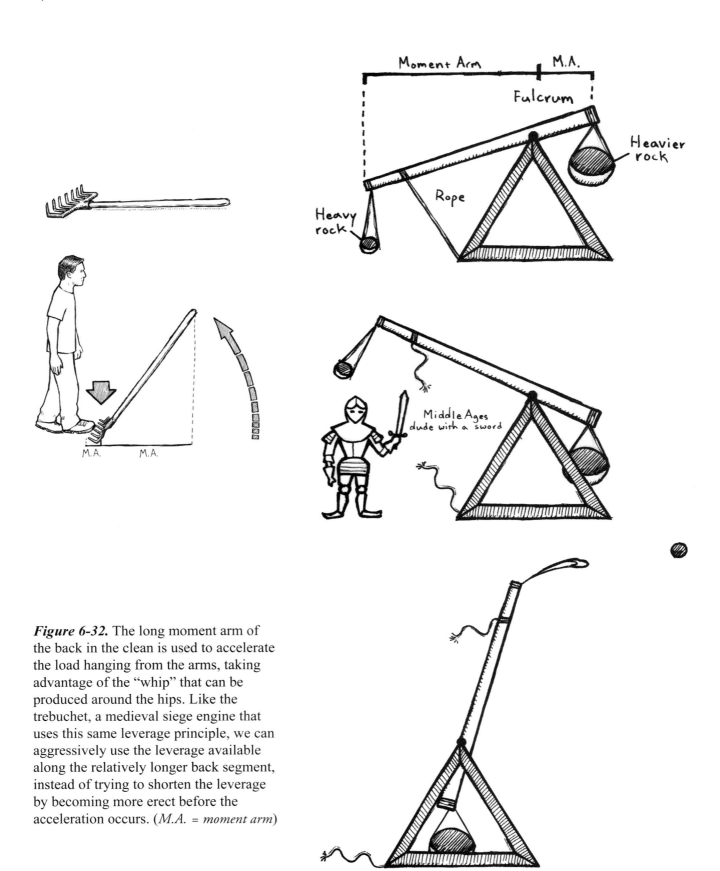

Figure 6-32. The long moment arm of the back in the clean is used to accelerate the load hanging from the arms, taking advantage of the "whip" that can be produced around the hips. Like the trebuchet, a medieval siege engine that uses this same leverage principle, we can aggressively use the leverage available along the relatively longer back segment, instead of trying to shorten the leverage by becoming more erect before the acceleration occurs. (*M.A. = moment arm*)

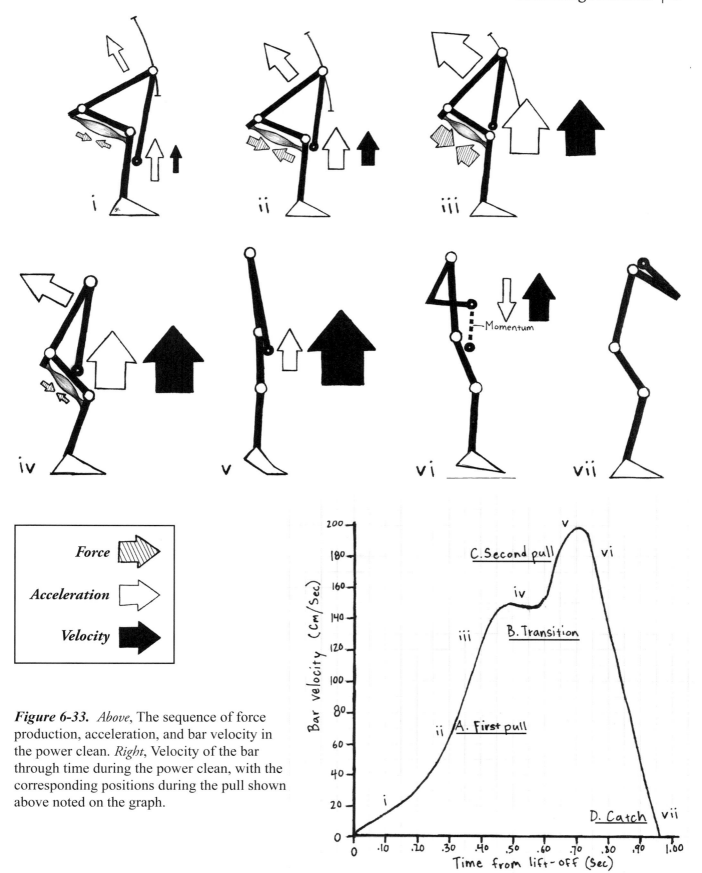

Force [arrow]

Acceleration [arrow]

Velocity [arrow]

Figure 6-33. *Above,* The sequence of force production, acceleration, and bar velocity in the power clean. *Right,* Velocity of the bar through time during the power clean, with the corresponding positions during the pull shown above noted on the graph.

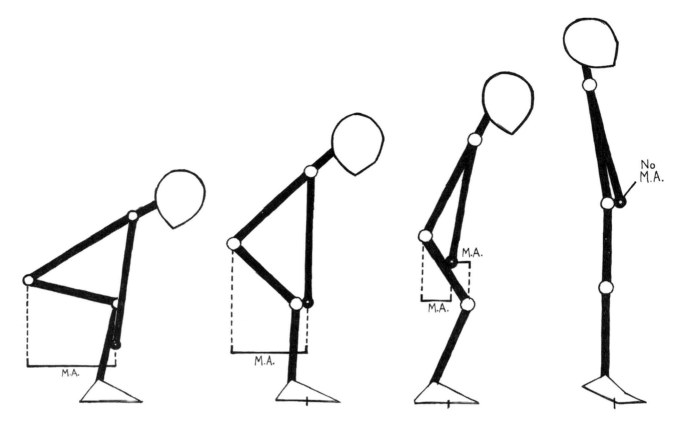

Figure 6-34. The change in moment arm length between the bar and the hips and the bar and the knees during the pull. As the knees rebend, the moment arm along the femur becomes a function of the knee extensors. (*M.A.* = *moment arm*)

angle whips the back through perhaps 60 degrees of angle in a fraction of a second, making the bar accelerate along with it.

As the angle of the back becomes more vertical, faster, the angular velocity – the rate at which the angle described by the plane of the back changes around the axis of the hips – increases. As this occurs, the linear velocity of the bar hanging from the arms increases as well. The bar hanging at the end of the arms increases its velocity with the angular acceleration of the back angle, just like the ball thrown from a forearm whipping through the angle it makes when the upper arm accelerates into internal rotation. A looping bar path would take further advantage of this phenomenon as the bar whipped away from the body. Indeed, this is one of the reasons that a lifter loops the bar – the speed of the bar increases if it is allowed to follow the arc of the changing angle. But the bar has to be kept

close to the body, in a vertical path, or inefficient horizontal motion is introduced. We do this with the lats, by changing the arm angle to maintain the vertical bar path, keeping the bar close to the body even as the back whips through its angle to become more upright into the jump. If the lats fail to do their job of keeping the bar close, the lifter has to lay back with the upper body to counter the forward bar travel; *pulling* is vertical, *swinging* is horizontal.

And it is here that the analogy to the jump we have used to facilitate learning the clean actually breaks down – a little. The "whip" through the middle of the pull – using the moment arm along the back – is what actually starts the acceleration of the load, and this occurs well below the knees, not at the top as in a vertical jump for height. The knees re-bend as the bar passes them to allow the quadriceps to extend the knees a second time, but this occurs during the process of building velocity from the acceleration which started lower in the pull. Velocity builds during the whole acceleration phase, from the floor to the top of the pull, not just at the top. But during this shift from hips to knees it is typical that the increase in velocity slows, giving many people the impression that the only fast part of the pull is the top. The drop in bar velocity is due to the sudden reduction in work being done on the bar as the shift occurs – for a brief instant to acquire a better position to continue the pull, you are moving your body instead of the bar (Figure 6-34).

As the hip angle opens, the hip extensors' ability to accelerate the load along both the back and the femur diminishes as the moment arm from the hip shortens. The hips lose their ability to effective operate the "tool" we're using to accelerate the bar, and to continue to increase the bar velocity we have to re-configure the levers. The knees re-bend and create leverage against the bar from the knee backwards, now powered by the quadriceps and adding to the velocity acquired during the middle of the pull. This "second pull" makes use of the fact that the moment arm along the femurs can be operated by both the knee and the hip extensors. So in some sense, it is still a jump – "jumping" keeps the bar from swinging into a loop. (The deadlift does not make use of this shift in leverage because the slow velocity at which a heavy deadlift is pulled will not allow a further loss of bar speed without actually stopping the pull and creating an illegal "hitch.")

If this re-bend is excessive, as it will be if you try to stand up too vertically too soon, it will greatly reduce your ability to use the angular acceleration of the back through the middle of the pull. Excessive knee flexion slacks the hamstrings distally, removing much of their contractile potential from the pull and removing the posterior chain from the most critical part of the pull. A deliberate attempt to shorten the moment arm between bar and hips by coming into a vertical position before acceleration reveals a misunderstanding of the leverage system used in the clean. By keeping your shoulders out over the bar, you enable your back to whip the load up quickly. So the acceleration of the pull actually starts before the place we earlier identified as the jumping position. As the back loses its horizontal

Figure 6-35. It is important that the bar be in contact with the thighs. At this point in the pull the back angle has become quite vertical and the knees have shifted into position to finish the extension. The bar must move from this position upward with as explosive and vertical a line over the mid-foot as possible, and peak power directed correctly upward cannot be developed at this critical position if the bar is forward of the thigh.

angle, the knees shift into position to continue the acceleration of the bar through to the top of the pull. This is why you can clean more from the floor than from the hang position.

So there are actually two periods of acceleration during the clean pull: the first through the middle of the pull as the back angle whips from more horizontal to more vertical, and the second after the knees re-bend to allow the knee extensors to add to the bar velocity. If the first phase is performed correctly, there will be little loss of velocity as the second phase begins. This entails the proper understanding of the acceleration function of the first part of the pull.

The bar needs to be in contact with your legs during this phase, touching the skin all the way up, as you maintain straight elbows. The path is vertical because the knees and hips extend in a coordinated way that results in the load's moving up in a straight line, with as little forward or backward deviation (seen as horizontal movement in the bar path) as possible. During this section of the pull, forward movement of the bar is usually due to an incorrect start, as previously discussed. Starting errors are magnified as the bar goes up. If the bar feels like it is too far forward – if it is not touching your thighs all the way up – check your starting position again. Your hips may be too low, the bar may be too far forward, or you may need to think about using your lats to actively push the bar back into your legs on the way up.

One way to ensure that the middle of the pull is finished correctly every time is to establish a marker for its successful execution. If you actively try to touch the same place high on your thighs with the bar during each rep, and develop the ability to feel the contact point and control it, you will gain a large measure of conscious control over the finish of the power clean. Bar contact on the thighs is necessary for correctly meeting the jumping position, and if you use that contact as a cue, you are much more likely to perform the clean correctly. Using this bar contact as a cue can also increase the speed of the clean because the bar will be hitting the thighs harder and you will be using more extension power to cause that contact. You can also use this contact as a diagnostic tool, clothing permitting, by looking at your thighs to see where the red mark from the bar contact is. You can identify pulling errors by seeing where the mark is on the thighs in relation to where it should be for the most efficient finish.

AT THE TOP

After the bar has been pulled up past the knees from the correct starting position, it should assume an essentially vertical path until it reaches the jumping position. During this phase, the bar must remain over the mid-foot for the most efficient power production to occur. As you jump, and your feet break contact with the floor so you can drop under the bar for the rack, force stops being applied

to the bar. The bar path can deviate from vertical at this point because force is no longer being produced, and the racking phase happens after the bar has stopped its upward acceleration. Some deviation will occur at the top due to the actions that occur while the elbows rotate up into the rack position, and as long as the deviation is not excessive, it will not be a problem. If it is excessive – more than a couple of inches – something happened on the way up that caused the deviation.

All cleans and snatches involve the shrugging of the shoulders, as video analysis will show. The shrug is a concentric trapezius contraction that protects the bony anatomy of the shoulders during the upward explosion and adds force to the pull at

Figure 6-36. The finished pull results from the hips and knees coming into full extension, with the traps having shrugged and the momentum causing a rise up into plantar flexion. Any completed pull will go through this position at the top.

Figure 6-37. An exaggerated layback indicates an attempt to use the lifter's bodymass to manipulate the horizontal position of a bar that is too far forward of the mid-foot. Refer to the diagram in Figure 4-24, page 120.

the top. The scapulas are suspended from the spine by the traps and related musculature; they hang from the muscles of the upper back, and their only bony attachment is at the arms and collarbones. If you didn't shrug as you jumped up with the heavy bar in your hands, your scapulas would be explosively compressed down onto your rib cage by the upward force of the spine in the jump. The traps' contraction is an involuntary reflex: it occurs as a consequence of having the bar in your hands as you jump, and this is why we don't need to talk about it during the early part of learning the clean. But later, after the weight gets heavier as you get stronger, the shrug becomes an important cue for completing the upward explosion against the load.

The shrug occurs as you jump with a slightly backwards-directed movement. Shrugging on a bar in front of you has to be a little backwards-directed so that the shrug does not pull your body forward. This keeps the system's center of mass over the mid-

foot during the last part of the pull. Because the hips have extended very hard and pushed the bar slightly away, and because the elbows must rotate under the bar for you to rack it on your shoulders, the bar path at this point may deviate forward a little from the vertical. The point immediately before this deviation is actually where peak power is produced. This deviation is a technique issue if it occurs before the jump, in which case it adversely affects power production.

As the bar comes up high enough that your elbows must unlock, they begin to rotate up into the rack position. The clean is finished as the elbows complete their rotation by coming to a position pointing forward. During this rotation, the elbows NEVER rise above the level of the shoulders – in fact, they never even approach the level of the shoulders until the bar is racked. After you have stopped applying force to the bar, at the end of the jump, your elbows unlock and rise a short distance to the point where they are in flexion, and then they start forward into the rack. **The elbows bend only after the force generated against the floor stops.** Nothing slows a clean down more than an attempt to row the elbows up high and lift the bar with the arms.

There is a bodybuilding exercise known as the *upright row*, in which the bar is raised to the chin with a narrow double-overhand grip. Most people have embedded deep in their brains a little bundle of brain material that tells them that all things must be lifted with the arms, especially if these things are going to be lifted above the waist. And embedded in your mind is a picture of a bodybuilder doing an upright row. It is a slow movement that uses the arms and deltoids, and though it bears a superficial resemblance to the clean, it has absolutely nothing to do with our explosive power clean. After the bar leaves the jumping position, no thought whatsoever should be given to the arms. None. The clean is a jump with the bar in the hands, after which the elbows are jammed *forward* to catch the bar on the shoulders. It should be as though there is no elbow activity at all during this phase; the bar rises up in response to the jump, and then the elbows jam forward and the shoulders jam into the bar.

After the bar leaves the jumping position, it must stay close to the chest so that it doesn't have to travel very far back to get into the rack position. If the bar heads away from the body between the jump and the rack, in the trajectory that is referred to as a "loop," the distance between the bar and the shoulders has to be closed. You will have to do this either by pulling the bar back in to the shoulders (possible with light weights) or, more likely, by jumping forward to meet the bar. Neither of these motions is efficient; any amount of force that directs the bar anywhere other than straight up to the shoulders is wasted, because that force can be used more productively.

You correct a loop by first determining why the bar is going forward. If the jump starts early, i.e., if you hit the jumping position too low on the thighs, the bar will loop forward due to a back angle that is not vertical enough. If the bar is to go straight up, your back must be vertical enough that most of the hip extension is already over before you jump; otherwise, the remaining hip extension will swing the bar away into a loop (Figure 6-38). You determine this fault by observing where on the thighs the bar is when the jump occurs. Immediately after the clean, pull your sweats down (discreetly) and look for the faint red line on the thighs where the bar touched; the line will be visible for several seconds after the contact. Or you can chalk the bar to make this mark more visible on the sweats themselves (Figure 6-39). If you have a jumping position that starts consistently too low on the thighs, think about waiting longer or touching higher before you jump.

If the loop occurs because you are forward on your toes during the lower pull off the floor, your heels will be "soft" against the floor and your knees will be forward as the bar passes them. In this case, the bar loops because it is headed forward from the ground up, as the bar path will show on your video or to your coach (Figure 6-40). Get back off of your toes and onto the mid-foot to start the pull, and make sure you keep your heels down until you jump with the bar well up on the thighs.

If you somehow manage to loop the bar from the correct jumping position, you may be

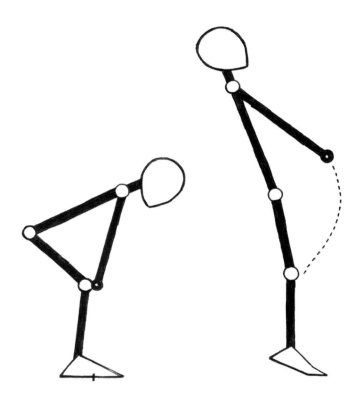

Figure 6-38. If the jump starts early, i.e., the bar is too low on the thighs, the bar swings away forward. This happens due to the back angle: the finish of the pull depends on the rigid back's angular velocity, generated by hip extension, and if the back is not sufficiently vertical, the force of the jump will be directed along a non-vertical path.

"banging" it away from you, off of the thighs. This rather uncommon problem is caused by not jumping up, the movement that makes the bar climb straight up the body. This error would occur as the result of an incorrect understanding of the movement: the perception that the clean "swings" into position on the shoulders, propelled by a bounce off the thighs. Our teaching method for the power clean makes a mistake like this almost impossible, but bad habits imported from previous instruction are often in evidence. The emphasis on the jump and the correct use of the arms keeps the bar close to the body on the way through the top part of the pull. You can think about shrugging the bar at this point if you need to, or you can make the bar touch your shirt on the way up. Keep the bar close enough to you that you feel it on the way up as it passes your chest, and you will have shrugged it.

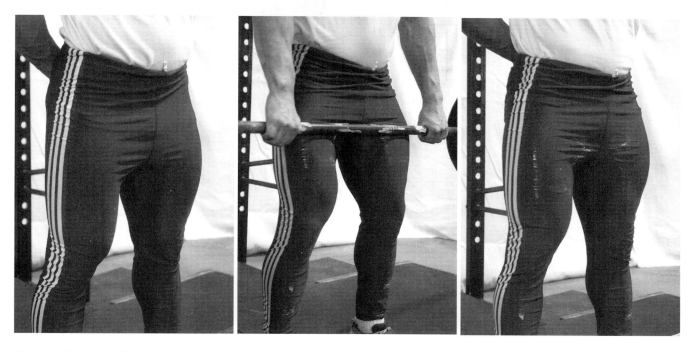

Figure 6-39. Chalk is a handy tool for many jobs in the weight room. In this case, it lets you identify and gauge the contact of the bar against the thighs at the jumping position.

Figure 6-40. A trajectory error originating below the knees. This error occurs when the start position is especially bad, with the heels "soft" – not planted firmly - against the floor, the knees forward, and the bar forward of the mid-foot.

Figure 6- 41. Touching the shirt on the way up keeps the bar closer to the ideal vertical bar path. Thinking about getting it there can unconsciously correct the pulling errors that led to the problem: the bar cannot swing away forward when you are pulling toward the shirt, and the hips and knees cannot get in a position to swing the bar away if you are doing what it takes to keep it close from the start of the pull. This is NOT the same thing as using the arms to raise the bar up to the shirt – an upright row, the most useless exercise in the world.

Actually, if you try to touch your shirt on the way up, this will usually correct the errors made at the bottom. This is an excellent example of "correction displacement," in which sufficient attention focused on correcting an error later in a sequence of movements unconsciously causes the correction of the initial problem earlier in the sequence. If you manage to touch your shirt with the bar before you rack it, you will have to get back on your heels to do it, since the shirt is more back toward the heels than forward toward the toes. This correction displacement trick comes in handy many times in the weight room and throughout athletics.

A "finished pull" is characterized by a position common to both the clean and the snatch. The hips and knees are in full extension; the feet are in "plantar flexion" (up on the toes); the traps have pulled the shoulders up into a shrug; the head is in the normal position relative to the neck, with the chin perhaps slightly up but the neck not in overextension; the elbows are not yet unlocked; and there is a slight backward lean (see Figure 6-36, above). This position will be attained if all the power of the hip and knee extension has been milked out of

the pull. It is common to fail to fully extend the hips and knees, leaving untapped the most mechanically powerful position at the end of the range of motion. The cue to "Finish the pull!" echoes through training halls all over the world as coaches encourage their athletes to get all possible power out of the jump.

Despite the fact that the fully extended top position has the lifter up on his toes, active ankle extension is not really a huge contributor to the explosion. The calf muscles do contract and produce force, but the momentum of the knee and hip extension is what actually carries you up onto your toes at the top of the pull. Some coaches have had success with adding some calf raises into the program, and this may work by making the lifter aware of this component of the finished position. A cue like "Toes!" may be a useful reminder to finish the pull by making you aware of the completed finished position. But an active attempt to perform a hard plantar flexion will not add much to most lifter's clean.

As noted before, power production stops when the feet break contact with the floor, and this occurs as the process of catching the bar in the rack

Figure 6-42. The transition between the pull and the rack happens very quickly. Immediately after the final acceleration is imparted to the bar, the direction of the body's movement changes from up to down as the rack position is assumed. The instant that force stops being applied to the bar and gravity ceases to be overcome by the pull, the weight decelerates, goes to zero upward velocity, and starts back down, and the rack must occur before the bar falls too far. Some downward bar movement is inevitable, but it must be minimized before the acceleration of gravity results in high downward momentum that will be more difficult to control.

position begins. As soon as the feet move out of the pulling stance, you have stopped pushing the floor. If you hadn't, your feet could not move. The full extension of the knees and hips is the last piece of the act of pulling the bar, and after this final position is attained, the process is over. Even if heavy weights could be rowed by the arms after the pull – and they can't – the result of the drop in pulling force would result in a drop in bar speed. The reality is that the upward momentum of the bar quite rapidly approaches zero, at which point the bar will begin falling. You have to catch it in the rack position before this happens, so you'd better hurry. The faster your feet move from the stance used for pulling into the stance used for catching, the less time the bar has to decelerate.

It is natural to move the feet from the pulling-stance width to a position approximately equal to the width used in the squat. This will happen naturally without your having to think

about it, like several other things we've discussed. It is an artifact of having jumped, of the feet having actually left the ground and landed. The feet move laterally outward a little so that the knees and hips can absorb the shock of the landing. This lateral movement is reflexive and useful. Jumping forward is not. Usually caused by a bar path error, jumping forward wastes time and energy that could more efficiently be used to make the bar travel up. Jumping to an excessive width is also unproductive; excessive width takes excessive time to cover, which means that time better spent finishing the pull was used to perform the excessive lateral split.

THE RACK POSITION

After the elbows rotate up and jam into position, pointing forward, the bar is said to be in the rack position, or "racked." The upward rotation of the elbows causes the deltoids to come into a

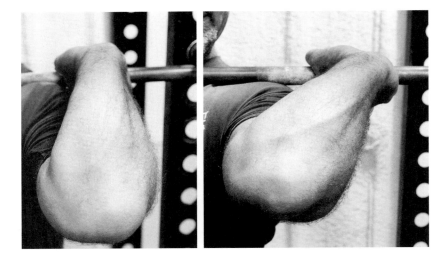

Figure 6-43. *Right*, The rack position, with arms rotated such that the forearms and upper arms are beside each other, as opposed to stacked (*left*).

contracted position that raises them higher than the chest, permitting the bar to sit comfortably clear of the sternum. At this point, most lifters will have relaxed the grip somewhat, and some will have released the hook grip. It is okay to release the hook, or even to let the last two fingers drop off the bar if it facilitates a good rack position. It is not okay to completely let go of the bar, although this does occur with some very inflexible lifters. The most important factor in the rack position is the elbow position and its effect on the deltoids, making a place for the bar to sit.

This is actually the position of the bar for a correct front squat. The correct rack position is the one that allows the most weight to be supported on the deltoids. In the correct position, the bar sits on the contracted deltoid muscle bellies. The delts

hold the elbows up high, keeping the weight off the sternum. The rib cage is held up by tension in the upper back musculature, the shoulders are elevated by the traps, and the entire trunk is held rigid in isometric contraction and further supported by the Valsalva maneuver. In this position, you can easily support as much weight as you can clean.

When you rack the bar, the best position for the forearms relative to the upper arms is one where the humerus is externally rotated. This means that the forearm is really beside the humerus, as opposed to stacked on top of it (Figure 6-43). It is helpful to think about lifting the elbows up *and in toward the middle*. In this position, the bar is lying on more muscle mass, and the elbows can finish their rotation in a higher position than they can if the bones of the forearm and the humerus are merely stacked

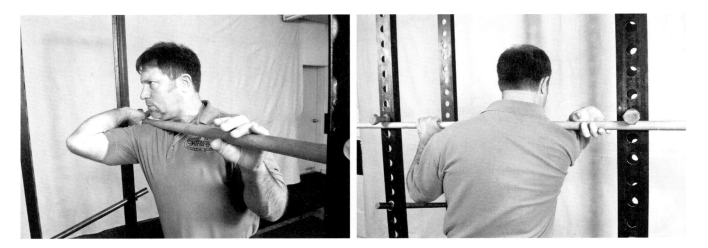

Figure 6-44. This stretch in the power rack enables the training of racking-specific flexibility.

on top of each other. This external rotation upon racking the bar proceeds from the internally rotated position of the elbows that you used to reinforce the straight-elbow position when learning the clean. The process of externally rotating the arms happens in the transition from the jump to the rack and adds to the "snap" that the movement should display.

Many people will catch the bar with their elbows pointing at the floor. This error is due to a misunderstanding of the concept of the rack position, a lack of flexibility, or a grip that is too narrow for the length of the forearms. A sufficiently flexible trainee using a grip suitable for his anthropometry should be physically able to get his elbows into the correct position, although he may be reluctant to do so for various reasons. If you rack the bar incorrectly a few times and feel it bump your sternum because your elbows were down and the deltoids were not up enough, you may become gun-shy and try to hold the bar up with your hands, exacerbating the problem. Rack the bar once and then move your elbows up into position, very high so that the bar comes up off of the sternum. In this way you can feel where your elbows should be. If you can't do this, you need to stretch, or adjust your grip to a width that facilitates the position.

Many times, a lack of wrist and tricep flexibility prevents the quick, complete rotation needed to rack the bar. Wrist flexibility is the more obvious of the two, but tight triceps may also prevent the elbows from coming up high enough to permit a good deltoid contraction. To extend your range of motion, you can stretch your wrists and triceps, using the bar or a stick in the rack (Figure 6-44).

If your flexibility is not sufficient to permit the full rotation of the elbows into a good rack, the fingers under the bar are the expendable part of the chain. After the pull has stopped, their function as the last element of force transfer to the bar is over. This concept is sometimes the source of confusion; the hands do not hold up the bar, and they stop being critical to the clean after the elbow rotation starts. So the fingers can do what they want to as you rack the bar. They can hang on, or they can release to the extent that only the index, middle, and ring fingers are in contact with the bar.

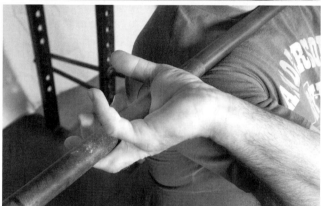

Figure 6-45. Under ideal circumstances, the best grip for the rack position is with four fingers under the bar (*top*). Flexibility limitations may make it necessary to use fewer fingers, but the most important consideration is elbow position. Do what is necessary to get the elbows up.

If your flexibility is sufficient but you still cannot rack the bar quickly, you might just be reluctant to let go of the bar enough to permit the elbows to come up. All you need is a little relaxation of the hands and a willingness to quickly rotate all the way up into position a couple of times to see how it feels to do it right. Several mental tricks can help with racking speed. Imagine slamming your elbows into the hands of your coach. Sometimes it helps to aim your shoulders at the bar, or to hit the bar with your shoulders, like you're trying to strike a blow even as the elbows come up. The crucial concept here is that the bar is not racked until the elbows point forward, and stopping the elbow rotation before it reaches this position is not acceptable.

At the same time the bar racks, the feet stomp the floor. Since the feet must break contact with the floor if a jump occurs, they must set back down on the floor, and thinking about stomping is a way to make this happen explosively – like everything about the top of the clean needs to be. This foot movement causes everything happening simultaneously with it to synchronize better. It feels better when the feet stomp and the bar racks at exactly the same time, and your body will time the rack to coincide with the stomp. And if the stomp is fast, it pulls the rack along faster with it. The simultaneity of the two events is fairly automatic, and not too many people will stomp out of phase with the rack because it just feels too weird. So the stomp actually sharpens the timing of the racking movement. A certain amount of knee bend, necessary to cushion the catching of the weight, will accompany the stomp. Catching the weight with perfectly straight knees is not desirable and actually doesn't occur very often since it also feels too weird. The stomp thus makes the movement faster, while cushioning the catch.

The feet will stomp into a position that's approximately the same as the squat stance, as mentioned earlier. In practice, this should mean a couple of inches per side wider. Some people will shift their feet out to a position wider, and perhaps much wider, than a squat stance. This is an attempt to drop lower under the bar, in lieu of pulling it high enough. You don't get a good stomp going this wide because the angle is not conducive to stomping and the distance covered is so great that it takes too long. Stomping is quick; lateral splitting is not. Correct this error by stomping into your correct starting position footprints several times

Figure 6-46. A lateral split is very common among novices and high school athletes who have never been corrected. It is often associated with other racking technique problems, such as bad elbow position and leaning back. It is corrected by giving the feet a job to do: stomp your feet back into your footprints or just a little wider.

without the bar, and then focus on this foot position during the clean with a lighter weight that you can rack properly. Stubborn cases may have to actually attempt to stomp into the pulling-stance footprints, or even narrower, in order to get enough correction to eliminate the lateral split. A lateral split is a bad thing to choose as a habit: it is dangerous, hard to control, and ineffective. The purpose of the power clean is to pull the bar as fast and as high as possible. We don't want to make it easier to get under the bar; we want to pull the bar higher. And if we were going to make it easier to get under the bar, we would use the standard squat or the split version of the clean, not some weird bastardized mutation thereof.

Another stomping error involves pulling the heels up very high in the back and slamming them back into the platform, as if to merely make noise.

From the side it looks like a knee flexion, certainly not an efficient part of a well-finished pull. This is called a "donkey kick," and it takes so much time to perform at exactly the wrong time that it can ruin the last 10-20% of the pull. Anything that takes away from pulling the bar as high as possible diminishes the ability to clean heavy weights. The donkey kick is a misinterpretation of what the feet do at the end of the pull; it will not be a problem for you if you learned the clean using our method. It is corrected by a conscious focus on finishing high on the toes.

After you rack the bar, recover into a fully upright stance with your elbows still in the rack position. Don't develop the habit of putting the bar down before you have fully recovered and you have established control of the bar in the final position. If you're in a big hurry to put the bar down after you rack it, you might soon find that you've gotten in a big hurry to rack it and start racking it wrong. Disaster follows close on the heels of such things. Finish each clean correctly.

Power cleans are not like squats or deadlifts, movements that can be ground out to a bone-on-bone finish through perseverance and hard work. Even if a deadlift is a little out of position, you can lock it out by just pulling harder if you're strong enough. The movement is slower and there is time to fix minor form problems before the pull is over. The clean takes less than a second to do, and if it is not right, it doesn't rack. Cleans can be racked only if all the contributing factors are there: strength, power, and technique. Since the clean is a much more mechanically complicated movement, it is more sensitive to each contributing factor than the slow movements are. This fact is evidenced by the experience common to all lifters, who find that 100 kg is good for many attempts but 105 *just will not rack*. Finishing the pull collates all the factors involved in the pull, and causes them all to come together at the right time to contribute to racking the weight. The slow movements rely on *absolute strength* – the simple ability to generate force in the correct position – at their limit capacity, while the quick lifts utilize the ability to apply maximum power at exactly the right time, in exactly the right

place. These are two distinct skills, producing different types of training stress, and resulting in two different types of adaptation. Recognizing this difference between the slow lifts and the explosive lifts is fundamental to your understanding of barbell training.

AFTER THE RACK

After the clean is racked and recovered, the bar must be dropped safely, without destroying you or your equipment. The method used here will depend on the equipment. If a platform and bumper plates are available, as they should be, the bar can be dropped from the rack position in a controlled manner. Care should be taken to prevent the bar from bouncing away from where it is dropped; you do this by keeping the bar level on the way down. While the bar is dropping, your hands should not leave it until just before it gets to the floor. Bars that are released at the top and allowed to free-fall are much more likely to bounce unevenly than bars that are tended to as they drop. Free-falling bars are also

Figure 6-47. Bumper plates are designed to make the explosive lifts safer for the lifter and easier on the bar and platform; they absorb the shock of the drop so that the bar can be lowered by dropping rather than through the use of an eccentric effort, as was necessary before the invention of the equipment. But bumper plates must be used correctly so that the bounce can be controlled. As a general rule, don't let go of the bar until it is just above the floor.

much more likely to get bent by the "whip" that occurs as the bar contacts the floor unevenly and the shear force of the deceleration propagates down the length of the shaft. Even an expensive bar can be warped this way.

If bumper plates are not available, the task becomes harder. The bar must be released from the rack and caught at the hang, and then lowered to the floor, to prevent damage to the barbell and the floor. This is actually the way all cleans and snatches were dropped before bumper plates were widely available, so it can be done, believe it or not. But it can be tricky, since it really hurts to actually drop the bar right on the thighs. You have to release the bar but retain enough grip on it to be able to slow it down before it hits your thighs. It is decelerated with the traps, using a movement that is the opposite of the shrug used during the jump. The bar needs to stop here under control before being lowered on down to the floor. And if metal plates are used, it would be prudent to use rubber mats to protect the floor. But really, get some bumper plates. They are important enough to consider necessary.

The Power Snatch

Although it has the reputation for great technical complexity and for being difficult to both learn and coach, the power snatch is not any more complicated than the power clean. The power snatch also is a jump with the barbell in the hands and a catch in the rack position. It's just that the rack position is overhead in the hands, in balance directly above the shoulder joints, instead of on the shoulders. The power snatch also obeys the laws of balance, force transfer, and leverage. It has a longer range of motion than the power clean, and a longer distance to travel after the force stops being applied to the bar, so it has to be done with both lighter weight and more speed through the jump. But it can often be done by people who cannot rack a clean for various reasons, and the lighter weights used make it a viable option for some training programs. Don't be afraid of the power snatch – it's just not that big a deal to learn, and it is useful enough that all lifters should know how to do it.

The most noticeable feature of the power snatch is the grip – it is wide, sometimes, for some tall, long-armed people, as wide as the bar permits. This would be a sleeve-to-sleeve grip. The width is needed to reduce the bar path's distance; just as in a clean, the application of force to the bar stops after the jump, and since the bar has to fly up under the momentum imparted to it before the loss of foot contact, it would be best if the distance the bar had to travel unpowered could be reduced. The wide grip allows a savings of 5–6 inches over the distance of the pull, although it alters the start position on the ground. A wide grip produces the functional equivalent of short arms, making the lifter's back angle more horizontal in the starting position. You

Figure 6-48. The difference in back angle in the two pulls, resulting from the change in grip width.

Figure 6-49. The power snatch.

may need to compensate for this angle by pointing your toes and knees out a little more to provide more clearance between the thighs for the belly.

The snatch, upon superficial inspection, looks like it is accomplished by using the arms to lift the bar overhead. Perhaps the wide grip fools the uninformed eye – the clean seems easier to understand as a pull. But the movement must be appreciated as a jump with the barbell in the hands, followed by a catch overhead, made possible by a drop into position that straightens out the arms. The bar is not lifted into place with the arms, and it is not swung into place through an arc-shaped bar path. The jump carries the bar up in an essentially vertical line if it is done efficiently, just like every other barbell exercise performed while standing on the floor.

The power snatch – frequently the hang version done from what we call the jumping position – is a favorite exercise of post–high school strength coaches because it is a long movement, it requires some athletic ability, and it is explosive. In fact, the highest power outputs ever recorded in human movement are generated at the second-pull position of the snatch. It can be done by bigger guys who can't rack a clean, it's no more difficult to learn than a power clean, and if you know how to do it already, you'll impress the right people in the college weight room. But it is done with lighter weights, so it doesn't have the potential to cause the same level of adaptation as the clean does. The power snatch

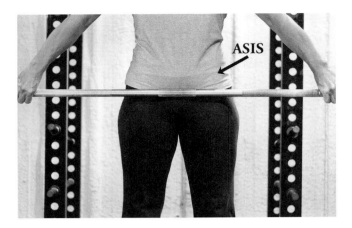

Figure 6-50. Grip width places the bar above the pubis and below the ASIS (the hip pointer).

is frequently looped, it requires enough shoulder flexibility to make an effective shrug in the lockout position over the shoulders, and its longer bar path provides more time to screw up, so it presents perhaps more technical challenges than the does power clean.

The power snatch uses essentially the same teaching method as the power clean, and it takes about the same amount of time to learn. Again, we learn the movement from the top down, perfecting the jump and the catch in the rack position, and then tacking the deadlift onto the front of the movement off the floor.

So, we'll start the same way, with the empty bar in the hands at the top of the pull. This will be

Figure 6-51. The grip at the proper width will leave the hand at an angle that minimizes the contact between the ring and little fingers and the bar. The hook is the primary holding mechanism in the snatch.

Figure 6-52. The hang position.

the **hang position**, just as in the clean. The hang position will be the default position for holding the bar between reps while you're learning to perform the movement. Again, a PVC pipe or a broomstick is too light to learn to pull anything with, and you need to have the right equipment if you want to lift weights. Women really should consider the smaller-diameter 15 kg bar if snatching is in the program; their usually smaller hands have a hard enough time making a grip at the angle at which they meet the bar in a snatch. For men, any 20 kg bar will do for right now. It is true that Olympic weightlifting bars are better for the snatch and the clean and jerk at heavy weights, but for novices learning the movement, most any bar will work well enough.

The snatch grip has been described by many authors as being derived from some percentage of arm length, with measurements taken and the bar marked. The reality of the situation is that everybody will adjust the grip to a position that works for them, no matter how much precision was used in originally determining the grip. And what works will be determined by where the bar strikes you as you jump. If your grip is too narrow, you lose the advantage of using a wide grip (duh), and if it's too wide, you hit yourself in the hip pointers. So the optimal grip will place the bar somewhere between the anterior superior iliac spine (ASIS) and the pubis for everybody (Figure 6-50). The best way

to set the grip is to stand up with the bar and slide your hands out wide (and obviously overhand) to a point near the sleeves where the bar rests against your lower belly, just below your hip pointers and just above your pubis. This placement gives you a range of a couple of inches on your belly, and about an inch either way at the hands. When in doubt, go wider, since the point is to shorten the bar travel. After setting your grip, refer to the bar markings and spot your position so that you can duplicate it quickly and precisely every time.

Go ahead and use the hook grip you learned earlier in the clean. This grip width will result in a rather acutely angled hand position on the bar, so that the thumb, index finger, and middle fingers do most of the gripping, with little contribution from the ring finger and little finger. This angle makes the use of the hook grip more important for the snatch because fewer fingers must do most of the work of holding the bar. You already know how to make the hook from doing it for the clean, so you should not have a problem adding it now. Chalk is important, too, and any gym that lets you snatch shouldn't have too big a problem with a little judiciously applied $MgCO_3$.

Once your grip is set, note the position of the bar against your belly. It should be in contact with the skin when you are standing erect, with chest up, elbows straight and internally rotated,

Figure 6-53. The rack position in the power snatch. The bar is supported overhead by the shrugged traps, which support the scapulas and thus the arms.

knees and hips extended, and eyes looking forward and slightly down at the same point 15 feet away on the floor. Your stance right now will be the standard pulling stance used for the clean and the deadlift: heels 8–12 inches apart and toes pointed slightly out. We'll modify the stance later.

The internally rotated elbows are important. They are your reminder to keep your arms perfectly straight during the pull. When you set your grip, set your arms into position by rotating them the way you would if you were standing with your palms facing the floor, and then pointing your thumbs down at the ground. Later, when you rack the bar at the top, the racking motion will involve rotating the arms externally, the opposite direction. This rotation provides much of the "snap" that is characteristic of racking a snatch.

The next position is the **rack position**. The snatch racks overhead, just like the top position of

Figure 6-54. The correct grip (A) will hold the hook in place with the palm of the hand facing up. Attempting to hold the bar in the web of the thumb (B) prevents the load from being correctly supported by the arms and places the elbows in a potentially dangerous internally rotated position.

Figure 6-55. The bar in balance overhead will be vertically aligned with the glenohumeral joint. Any distance forward or behind this point will be a moment arm that will have to be handled.

the press but with a wider grip. The bar is in balance when it is directly over the shoulder joints, since that is the point at which no moment arm exists between the load and the point of rotation. The rack position has nothing to do with your head or your neck, especially considering the fact that your neck can move around quite a bit under the racked bar. In this position, the bar, the shoulder, and the mid-

foot will be vertically aligned, something that is very important when the weight gets heavy.

Get the bar in position over your head with your snatch grip any way you have to, and don't let go of your hook. Your arms must be perfectly straight. They will go from internally rotated in the hang position, to externally rotated overhead. If you point the palms of your hands directly at the ceiling,

Figure 6-56. The change in position from the hang to the rack is one of internal vs. external rotation. This change is what enables the vertical bar path through the top of the pull.

you will produce this position. Holding onto the hook prevents the bar from rolling back into the fingers to make a long moment arm between the bar and the wrists. Some leverage is inevitable, but the hook keeps it from getting excessive.

After the bar is in position overhead, make sure it is in balance over the shoulder joints. Push the bar back a little to feel the posterior extent of your balance; then bring it forward until you feel the weight start to pull the bar forward. The balance point is right in the middle, where the rotation force on the shoulders is neutral. For most people, this position will be a little behind where they think it should be, especially if they have been told to keep the bar over the top of their head. During this process, the elbows remain perfectly straight.

Once the balance point has been identified, the final part of the rack position is added. Shrug your shoulders up, like you are reaching for the ceiling with the palms of your hands. Shrugging the traps in the rack position recognizes their anatomical role as the main supporters of the scapulas, and thus the bar. Think of it as though the delts and triceps are holding the arms straight and the traps are holding the bar up. The shrug also allows the rack position to be met with a solid base of upper-body support; instead of just holding up the bar with your arms, you'll be supporting it with the strongest muscles in your upper back. Remember that your palms are pointing at the ceiling, your elbows are perfectly straight, and your eyes are looking forward and slightly down.

Lowering the bar from the rack position correctly at first is an important way to teach yourself more about the bar path in the snatch, starting from the very beginning. Just as we did in the clean, we'll start practicing a close, vertical bar path from the very beginning, preparing early for what comes later. Barbells are in balance when they are directly over the mid-foot, so when you lower the bar from the rack position, keep it there: unlock your wrists and let the bar fall straight down past your face and chest, and then catch it at the hang position. Wrists were the last things to extend on the way up, and they are the first things to unlock as you drop the bar back down. As it falls straight down, in balance over the mid-foot even with the light weight of the empty bar, you begin the process of learning that **arms do not power the snatch**. They don't lower the bar, either – the bar falls and you catch it. Don't try to slow it down with your rowing muscles, but rather just cushion the fall with bent knees and hips. Aim for your nose the first couple of times to learn how close the bar can actually stay on the way down. Make it touch your shirt after it falls past your face – not by slowing the bar down with your arms but by keeping it close from the top as it falls. It helps here to actually think about the mid-foot and the slot directly over it in the air that you drop the bar into. You will still have your hook grip, so you won't lose the bar as it hits the hang position. Practice this a few times.

The next position is the **jumping position**, just like the clean again but with one important difference. In the clean, the bar leaves the thighs at this last point of contact somewhere in the mid-thigh, where the knees and hips have unlocked, the bar is touching the skin, and your elbows are straight; the jumping position is both the knees/hips-unlocked position *and* the point on the thigh where this occurs. In the snatch, the jumping position is just the knees/hips-unlocked position because the bar will slide up to touch the belly with straight elbows before it leaves the body. **The jumping position for the snatch is the belly – the same as its hang position – not the thigh like the clean.**

Unlock your knees and hips, just like you do for a vertical jump or standing broad jump. As you do this, slide the bar down the thighs, never letting it leave contact with the skin. It is common to bend mostly the knees here, which will leave the shoulders behind the bar. The involvement of *both hips and knees* in the jump is critical, since two joints extending explosively generate more power than just one. If both joints are unlocked, the shoulders will end up directly over the bar with it this far up the thighs. (The shoulders go forward of the bar, into the standard pulling position, when the bar gets lower.) The elbows are still straight and internally rotated, eyes are looking forward and slightly down,

Figure 6-57. The jump and the rack.

and feet are in the pulling stance.

From this position of contact on the thighs, slide the bar up to the belly and jump as high as possible. This should be a smooth motion that accelerates as the bar slides up. Before it leaves the body on the way up, the bar touches the same place on the belly that it did in the hang position. As you leave the ground, make sure your elbows are straight and that you're jumping as high as you can, high enough that you have to fully extend the knees and hips to do it. A good jump will leave the toes pointed at the floor, not because you performed a calf-raise as a part of the explosion but because the explosive extension carried you up onto your toes. This knee

Figure 6-58. The 3 teaching positions: hang, jump, rack.

and hip extension is what makes the bar touch your belly, so make sure the touch occurs. Don't worry about the elbows the first few times – just jump high with straight elbows.

When your jump with straight elbows is working, jump and catch the bar in the rack position. Keep the bar close to your chest on the way up, and let the elbows bend **after the jump** to facilitate this. If you bend your elbows before the jump, you will dilute the power being transmitted down the arms to the bar (remember towing the car with a chain vs. a spring?), and the tight biceps will slow down the rotation that must occur to rack the bar. If you try to keep the elbows straight *after* the jump, the bar will swing away forward into a loop. So you must eventually bend your elbows, along with your wrists, but not until after you jump. If you just think about catching the bar in the rack position, your elbows and wrists will perform in the correct order.

The elbows snap from internal rotation to external rotation as the elbows and wrists unlock after the jump and then relock in the rack. This unlocking after the jump permits the bar to fly up past the chest and face, staying close to vertical over the mid-foot. The unlocking of the two joints allows the arms to behave like the links in a chain that connects the shoulders to the bar. The jump provides the power that elevates the bar and propels it up with enough momentum to carry it through the unpowered part of the pull to the rack position.

The arms merely connect the back to the bar to transmit this power; they generate none of their own.

The final part of the snatch is the **drop** that straightens out the wrists and elbows at the top. As you feel yourself rise to your toes as a consequence of the jump, and the bar flies up past your chest and face, drop under the bar. This drop is a bending of the knees and hips again, perhaps back to the same position from which you jumped. This time they just unlock, to permit you to catch the bar with straight elbows in a cushioned position. It is the drop that finally straightens the elbows and wrists as your hips and back move down – not your muscles pulling the bar up into this final position (an assistance exercise, by the way, known as a "muscle snatch").

The drop provides the final snap that permits the external rotation of the arms into the rack position, and the speed of the last 10% of the snatch depends on your commitment to drop under the bar and catch it with straight arms. The movement should be fast enough to cause the bar to audibly rattle as you rack it – make it slam into position as you drop. To make the movement quick and sharp, you might want to think about "stabbing" your hands up into the bar as you drop. Practice this a few times, and then set the bar down to rest your hands.

Remember to lower the bar by unlocking your wrists first and catching the bar as it falls past

Figure 6-59. The below-the-knees position, on the way down to the floor.

Figure 6-60. The mid-shin position, where the bar would be loaded with plates on the floor.

your chest. You do not un-press a snatch any more than you use a press to raise the bar into the rack position. If you have pressed it into position, then the wrists have extended before the elbows, the jump was not the force that carried the bar up, the drop has not explosively rotated and straightened the elbows and wrists, and the movement has been very slow. Many people have been allowed to raise the bar the final few inches with the wrists already turned over, and their mental picture of the movement is consequently quite incorrect. And it won't matter how fast you can do it wrong – if you lose the last piece of jumping explosion by trying to turn the bar over early to press it with a snatch grip, you lose the power from the last part of the jump and you lose the speed from the drop. Unlocking the wrists first to lower the bar from the beginning stops this problem before it starts.

Once you're catching the bar in the rack position with a drop and a snap of the elbows and wrists, you're doing the basic snatch movement. The next part will again involve getting the bar from the floor up to the jumping position, and again the deadlift is the most efficient physical model of a pull from the floor. We'll start at the top. From the hang position, slide the bar down into the jumping position, slide it up as you jump, and catch it in the rack position a couple of times. Then slide the bar down to the position just below your kneecaps, below the joints but not much below the very top

of your shins. Slide the bar up slowly until it reaches the mid-thighs, and then accelerate it up and jump, making sure to touch the belly and to keep straight elbows when you jump. Do not stop at the mid-thigh position – treat it like a "trigger" for the acceleration, just as you do in the clean, so there is no pause in the pull. Rack the bar, unrack it, and repeat the snatch from this position a couple more times. Set the bar down if you need to between these steps; the snatch can be hard on the hands.

The mistake you're going to make here will be letting the bar lose contact with the thighs, either just above the knees or at the mid-thigh. If you get in a hurry and lose patience with the pull, the usual result is an early jump, well below the correct level. This inevitably carries the bar, and you, forward. Or you might think that the bar actually leaves the thighs at the jumping position, but this is a misunderstanding of the motion. Drag the bar up in contact with the skin, never leaving the thighs. The bar must be in skin contact until it leaves your belly for an efficient vertical bar path. Take your time, and remember that fast happens at the top, not at the bottom or even in the middle, at first.

The next position will be at the mid-shin, where the bar would be if it were loaded with plates on the ground. This position will challenge your ability get into a good, mechanically correct deadlift – with shoulders in front of the bar and the back in hard extension – because of the width of the grip. Compensate for this more horizontal back angle by making sure your knees are out enough. **Most people will touch the inside of their elbows with the outside of their knees if they are correctly set up,** with contact similar to the deadlift start position. This knees-out position gets the thighs out of the way of the belly, and makes the more-horizontal back angle easier to use. Make this a feature of the start position from this point forward: reach out with your knees to touch your elbows before you squeeze up into the pull. Toes-out enough makes knees-out much easier, so adjust your stance now if your feet haven't already sorted this out for themselves. From this position, *slowly* pull the bar up the shins as the knees extend, then past the knees, and up to the mid-thigh, staying in contact with the skin for the whole pull. When the bar gets to mid-thigh, accelerate into the jump and rack the bar.

Most people tend to pull the snatch too fast off the floor. Even after the movement has been learned correctly, the tendency will be to hurry through the "floor pull," the first part of the pull from the floor. Make up your mind now that the first part will be slow and correct, and that the explosion starts only after the bar is in the higher part of the pull.

At this point, you are doing a full power snatch. Rest a second, and put some light plates on the bar. The power snatch is best practiced with light plates at first, especially if you are not already pretty strong. "Light" may mean lighter than the commonly available 10 kg bumper plates. If this is the case, they will need to be obtained. They tend to be expensive, and their lack of availability may be a deciding factor in using the power snatch for trainees who cannot easily manage a 40 kg load. If they are available, use them; they make the process

of learning to jump with heavier loads much more seamless than does an abrupt jump from 20 kg to 40 kg. Too big a jump here often results in an arm pull and a complete breakdown in the careful progression we have detailed. Go up slowly and convince yourself that the snatch is a jump with straight elbows that ends with a drop, not a panic-stricken retreat into a wide-grip upright row.

When the snatch is up to 40 kg on the bar loaded with bumper plates, most people drop the bar from overhead to the platform in one movement, letting the rubber do its job. Before the invention and widespread availability of bumper plates, snatches had to be lowered eccentrically. This requirement added another dimension to the workout that was probably beneficial, if less fun. If you have the luxury of bumper plates, learn to use them correctly. Drop them from overhead while precisely controlling the drop by not letting go of the bar until it is close to the floor. Make sure that the plates land evenly if at all possible; an uneven drop can bend even the best bars. It is fashionable in some circles to drop empty bars from overhead or to let go of a dropped bar from overhead. These circles can go somewhere else to train, because equipment is expensive and the gym must be respected as a place where you control your immature urges to call attention to yourself.

The power snatch is best trained with doubles – sets of two reps – or singles. The pull is long, it is sensitive to fatigue, and sets of, say, five reps will cause you to start making mistakes that would not happen were you not fatigued. High-rep sets will very quickly have you practicing sloppy snatches. If your workouts entail more incorrect reps than correct ones, you will get highly proficient at doing them wrong. So limit yourself to two-rep sets, and accumulate workload by doing multiple sets instead of doing too many reps per set.

USEFUL ASSISTANCE EXERCISES

The squat, bench press, deadlift, press, and clean form the basis of any successful, well-designed training program. But there are other exercises that can assist these five and improve certain aspects of their performance.

There are, quite literally, thousands of exercises that can be done in a well-equipped gym. Bill Pearl, in his classic text *Keys to the Inner Universe,* includes cursory descriptions of 1621 exercises. Not all of these exercises are useful for strength training purposes, though, because few of them actually contribute to the performance of the core barbell exercises.

This point is important for a couple of reasons. Your training priorities, which should depend on your advancement as an athlete, should involve strength, power, or mass. No matter how long you train, or how strong, explosive, or big you get, your training will always be tied to the performance of these basic movements or their derivatives. The fact that resources – time, recovery, the patience of family and friends – are always in shorter supply than we'd like makes the efficiency with which your goals are accomplished an important consideration. The best assistance exercises are those that directly contribute to the performance of the basic movements that produce the most benefit.

Not that the basic movements need much help. They are complete exercises in and of themselves, since they all involve lots of muscles moving lots of joints in anatomically normal, functionally useful ways. But after a certain period of time, usually several months after serious training begins, the stimulation provided by the execution of the basic exercises alone is not enough to produce sufficient stress to cause further adaptation. This change is due not to any deficiency in the basic exercises but to the trainee's ability to successfully adapt to the stress these exercises provide. A natural result of training is that progress slows down after progress has been made, and progress is why we train. These topics are discussed at great length in *Practical Programming for Strength Training, Second Edition.*

For example, an excellent assistance exercise for the bench press and the press is the chin-up. Chin-ups add enough work to the triceps, forearms, and upper back that the contribution of these muscle groups to the bench press is reinforced for the trainee who needs a little extra work. And this work is done using another multi-joint functional exercise. In fact, chin-ups are so useful that they are included in the program from very early on as the only non-barbell component of the program. A less efficient way to accomplish the task would be to add a triceps isolation movement like cable triceps extensions, a machine-based movement that, when done with what is usually considered strict form, leaves out the lats, upper back, forearms, posterior deltoids, biceps, and grip strength. Since the bench press uses all these muscles, why lose the opportunity to train them all together at the same time with another multi-joint exercise? Chin-ups work better as an assistance movement, as do heavy lying triceps extensions, an exercise that actually is more beneficial when performed with what would conventionally be interpreted as less-than-strict form.

Before we get started, let's discuss adding exercises to your program. Anytime a new movement is introduced, be conservative with the weight you use the first time you do the exercise. This is a lesson you will learn the hard way eventually, but it's better to learn it now. Anytime you try a new exercise, you will be working with a movement pattern or a piece of equipment that you have not used before. Even if you are using a partial range of motion from a familiar exercise, you have not used that piece of the movement by itself before. You have previously used it in the context of the whole movement, and working it separately is a different mechanical task than the whole movement – it is sufficiently different that you have chosen to do it that way instead of the other way. You are not adapted to the new exercise, and as a result it will make you sore, perhaps very sore. This soreness may be due to the simple fact that you are doing a different number of reps with the assistance exercise than you use for the parent movement. A rep range to which you are not adapted will make you sore, too.

But a brand new movement pattern has the potential to go beyond simple soreness. It is one thing for unadapted muscles to get sore, and quite another thing for unadapted joints to get sore. Sore joints usually mean inflammation, if not outright structural damage. Sore muscles mean inflammation, too, but muscle bellies are vascular – supplied with lots of vessels and capillaries that carry blood to help them heal quickly – whereas joints are not. Joint soreness is a much more serious matter than muscular soreness or even muscular injury. Joint problems can persist for years, while muscle belly injuries will heal in a matter of days or weeks. And lots of sore joints start on the day you try something new with as much weight or as many reps as you can do with it.

This is not to suggest that you be a weenie. It is to suggest that you be intelligent and prudent with new exercises so that you don't end up being an *involuntary* weenie later. This point is especially important if you are an older trainee. Start a new exercise with a good warm-up, and only go up as heavy or to as many reps as you would consider being equivalent to a moderately heavy warm-up set, leaving something on the bar for next time. This way, there can be a next time soon enough that you can proceed to make progress on the new exercise, instead of having to wait for something to heal.

Assistance exercises fall into three categories. These exercises 1) strengthen a part of a movement, as with a partial deadlift (either a rack pull or a halting deadlift); 2) are variations on the basic exercise, as with a stiff-legged deadlift; or 3) are ancillary exercises, which strengthen a portion of the muscle mass involved in the movement in a way that the basic exercise does not, as with the chin-up. All assistance exercises of value can be assigned to one of these three categories.

Partial Movements

The deadlift, as mentioned earlier, can be a brutally hard exercise. When done with very heavy weights, as a very strong trainee would use, deadlifts can become very hard to recover from during the period of time called for in the program. A limit set of five in excess of 500 pounds might require a week or more for adequate recovery for the next workout, and in the meantime squats have suffered as well. When your deadlift gets strong enough that heavy sets of five create more stress than you can easily recover from within the timeframe of your training, it becomes useful to alternate two assistance exercises instead of the deadlift. *Halting deadlifts* come from the floor up to the top of the kneecaps and cover the bottom part of the movement, and *rack pulls* are done from below the knees up to full lockout at the top. The combination of the two covers the entire pull, while producing less recovery demand than the full movement.

Halting deadlifts

The halting deadlift (Figure 7-1) is done with a double-overhand grip and from the same

Figure 7-1. *Left to right,* The bottom, middle, and top positions of the halting deadlift.

stance as the deadlift. Like deadlifts, haltings are pulled from a dead stop. A brief review of pulling mechanics might be useful here; refer to Chapter 4 if necessary. The knee extensors move the load up from the floor; the hamstrings and glutes maintain the back angle while this happens; the hips then extend; and the spinal erectors keep the spine rigid in extension so the transfer of force from the knees and hips to the bar can occur efficiently. The traps and rhomboids transfer this force to the scapulas, from which the arms hang, and the lats keep the arms back so that the load stays in position over the mid-foot during the trip from the floor to the top of the knees and back down.

Take a normal deadlift stance and a double-overhand grip of the same width as for a deadlift. Lift your chest and lock your back into extension, using the normal deadlift setup discussed in Chapter 4. In a deadlift, the back angle will start to become more vertical as the bar approaches the tibial tuberosity, the enlarged bump at the top of the shin, a few inches below the patella. Haltings are a little different in that you actively try to hold the back angle constant as the bar passes this point, so that the back gets worked harder through what would be the middle of the full deadlift. Try to keep your shoulders in front of the bar until it crosses the patellas. The back angle will probably change before the bar gets to the patellas, but your job is to deliver as much work to the erectors and lats as possible by

staying out over the bar as long as you can. This extra back work is one of the reasons for the exercise. The amazing part of this exercise is how much work the lats get while doing their job of holding the weight in position over the mid-foot.

Drag the bar up your shins until the patellas are just cleared, and then set it down. Don't worry about setting it down slowly, since the work on a halting is supposed to be mostly concentric. Remember: you're starting each rep from a dead stop. Bill Starr would tell you to hold the bar at the top position for a second before setting it down, and doing so adds greatly to the effort required of the back muscles and lats. It is very helpful to think about 1) pushing the floor with your feet, 2) pulling the bar back into your shins as it comes up, and 3) keeping your shoulders out over the bar for as long as you can pull it that way. Breathing is the same as for the deadlift; take a big breath before you pull, and hold it until you set the bar back down. Start with 135 pounds and take reasonable jumps up to your work-set weight.

You will not do haltings in the same workout as the deadlift, so you will not be warm when you start them, as you might be with a smaller-muscle-group assistance exercise done after the core movement. Haltings should be warmed up just like deadlifts. Haltings seem to respond well to higher reps, but due to their shorter range of motion, work sets of, say, eight reps will use heavier weights than

Figure 7-2. *Left to right*, The start, middle, and finish of the rack pull.

a deadlift work set of five will, and possibly as high as 85% of 1RM. At this load, one work set is plenty.

Breathing takes place at the bottom, and is the biggest problem during the exercise due to the bent-over position; the last reps of a long set are no fun when you're out of air, and you can't really get a good breath in the start position. The grip is a straight double-overhand, or clean, grip, as mentioned earlier. Supinating one hand for a heavy single deadlift is a necessary evil in a meet, but multiple reps with one shoulder in internal rotation and the other in external rotation produce an asymmetric shoulder stress that some people do not tolerate well. Haltings are very good for developing the grip, since you won't be using your 1RM deadlift weight for them, and the double-overhand grip is harder than the alternate grip, so use the halting as a grip exercise, too. If you get strong enough that your grip strength is exceeded, then you can either use straps or switch your alternate grip, changing the supine hand each rep. This change is a little trouble, and straps are fine if your grip is otherwise strong enough, i.e., you don't normally have any trouble hanging onto heavy deadlifts.

Pay attention to keeping the bar against your shins on the way up – this is the lats' job. Haltings can be thought of as "pushing the bar away from the floor with the feet" at the bottom, and almost as a row at the top as the bar breaks over the knees.

RACK PULLS

Rack pulls are the other half of this pair (Figure 7-2). They are done from inside the power rack, from level pins set at a point somewhere below the knees. How far below the knees the pins are set determines the amount of overlap that the halting and the rack pull have with each other. Just below the patellas is probably not enough, while down to mid-shin defeats the purpose of dividing the whole pull into two movements. Three or four inches below the joint line is about right, just below the tibial tuberosity. The point of the halting deadlift is to work the initial drive off the floor, which depends heavily on the quads for the drive and on the hamstrings to anchor the back angle. The rack pull should use as little quadriceps drive as possible, with the main emphasis on hip extension – working the hamstrings and glutes, and above all, keeping a flat back while this happens. With hip extension as the primary point of the exercise, rack pulls are obviously also done from a dead stop.

Your stance for the rack pull will be the same width as for the deadlift, but with your shins more vertical than they'd be in the start position off the floor. The bar should be in the position it would be in were it deadlifted to that height off the floor – bar over mid-foot and in contact with the shins, just barely below the knees. Your shoulders should be in front of the bar, and it is very important that they stay there until the bar is well up your thighs; in this respect, both haltings and rack pulls differ from deadlifts, which allow the natural change in back angle to occur when the bar is below the knees. Your back must be locked hard in both lumbar and thoracic extension – the chest is up, and the lower back is arched but not overextended – a normal anatomical position of extension, the position described for the squat and deadlift and for all barbell pulls. It is easier to get in this position when the bar is higher up the shins because less hamstring tension is pulling on the pelvis/lumbar lock at this point. As with the halting deadlift, the rack pull is performed with a double overhand grip, usually with straps due to the heavy weights used.

From the starting position, drag the bar up your thighs, keeping it in constant contact with the skin, with your shoulders out over the bar, your chest up, and your knees held in position with no forward movement. When the bar is high enough up the thighs that you cannot keep your shoulders forward, extend your hips forcefully – "shoot the hips" is a good cue for this movement. The finish position is the same as for a deadlift, with shoulders back, chest up, knees and hips straight, and eyes focused on the floor about 12-15 feet ahead. No exaggerated shrug is necessary or useful; the hips are shoved forward into extension with the chest held up, and this is all that needs to be done at the top. Breathing is also the same as for the deadlift, with a big breath taken and held before each rep. Sets of five work well for rack pulls. The weights that can be used are quite heavy, due to the shorter range of motion, and it is

not uncommon to do a 5RM rack pull with very close to 1RM deadlift weight. Again, they should be warmed up with the same progression as for a deadlift.

As simple as this movement sounds, it is very easy to do wrong. Most people will allow their knees to come forward as soon as the bar passes them, making the back angle more vertical and dragging the bar back up the thighs along an angle – and supporting some of the weight on the thighs – instead of keeping the bar path vertical. This knee shift is illegal in the deadlift in a powerlifting meet, since the bar will actually go down a little, and it is referred to as a "hitch." Your body wants to do this for the same reason the second pull on a clean works: you get a second opportunity to use the quads to straighten out the knees if you re-bend them. But unlike a clean, the rack pull is specifically used to strengthen the hamstrings, and they must be made to do their job as intended to pull the hips into extension while the back stays flat. It is important to stay out over the bar, keep the knees back, keep the bar on the legs, and extend the hips only after the bar is well up the thighs.

BARBELL SHRUGS

The *barbell shrug* is a type of rack pull that starts up above the knees, at about the point where the hips shoot forward at the very top of the deadlift. Barbell shrugs can be done with very heavy weights, 100 pounds over your PR deadlift or more, due to their very short range of motion and good leverage position. In fact, to be effective, barbell shrugs must be done very heavy. But they are an advanced exercise, and not everybody should do them. The fact that they are done so heavy means that a novice lifter unadapted to heavy weights, in terms of bone density, joint integrity, and motor control, can become very injured very quickly even when doing them correctly. An impatient friend of the author broke the spinous process off of C6 doing these prematurely. Barbell shrugs (Figure 7-3) are best left for competitive lifters who have trained for at least a couple of years, and there is no real reason

Figure 7-3. The barbell shrug.

for athletes who are not powerlifters or weightlifters to do them at all. They are included here for the sake of completeness, lest anyone think that they do not exist.

If you are sure you're ready, set your rack pins at mid-thigh and load the bar inside the rack to 135 pounds. A shrug is done like the top part of a power clean, and the best warm-up for a shrug is racking the bar on the shoulders with 135 from this high position. This warm-up establishes the correct movement pattern for the subsequent heavier sets and weeds out the novices: if you cannot easily hang-clean 135 from a dead stop on the pins, you have no business doing heavy shrugs. After a couple of sets of five at 135, add another big plate and try to clean it for five. If you can, good; if you can't, you have shrugged it. The mechanics of the movement should be the same as the second pull of the clean, the heavier weight limiting your ability to rack the bar on your shoulders but with the rest of the movement intact. As the weight goes up, the bar will travel less and less, until for the last warm-up and the work set, the elbows do not even unlock and only the hips, knees, and shoulders move.

The point of this heavy load is to make the trapezius muscles finish what the hips and legs have started. The key to the movement is the snap that must be used to make the traps work at the top. The bar will start up slowly from the pins, and you will have your chest up, your low back locked

VERY tightly, and your elbows straight; then you will shrug your shoulders back explosively, as if to touch the top of your traps to the back of your skull. Now, this does not mean that the head moves back – it means that the traps shrug back and up, not forward toward the ears. Do not try to hold the position at the top. For each rep, catch the bar in the finish position of the deadlift and lower it back to the pins. Don't let the bar fall from the shrug back onto the pins without catching it at the hang; this is an excellent way to hurt your back or hips very badly. Each rep starts at and is returned to the pins; this requirement distinguishes a proper barbell shrug from incorrect versions in which all reps start from the hang and there is no explosive movement. The start from the pins, using hip and leg drive to propel the bar up into the trap shrug, is what allows the enormous weights to be used and causes it to be such an effective exercise.

Heavy shrugs make the traps grow; there is no doubt about it. At lighter weights, done with sets of five at the 1RM deadlift weight, they are good for cleans, and at heavier weights, they prepare the traps for the top of the deadlift and prepare the brain for the feel of very heavy weight. The heavier sets will always be done with straps, due to the snap that *must be present* at the top when the traps shrug the bar. One work set after warm-ups is enough; sets across are extremely stressful due to the heavy skeletal loading involved in supporting this much weight, even for the brief time it takes to complete a rep. Likewise, barbell shrugs should be used conservatively in the schedule, maybe once every two weeks in the appropriately designed program.

Notes about the power rack. The rack pull and the barbell shrug obviously depend on the power rack, and its design is critical for these and all the other exercises in this program that can be done in one. A good rack should not be too expensive, and some of the simplest designs are actually the best. The rack should have a floor – it should not be merely *on* the floor, with you standing on something that is not also holding the rack down. A heavy plywood floor inside the rack and attached to the frame ensures that the weight of you *and* the loaded bar is always acting to stabilize the rack, so that when you set the bar back down on the pins, the rack does not move. Your position between the uprights will be determined by the depth of the rack (the distance between the front and back uprights).

Shallow racks are a pain in the ass, and if the dimensions are wrong, the rack can be very hard to use. It should be deep enough to squat inside of, with some play front to back not being a problem. Drift during the set will occur no matter how careful you are, and if the uprights are so close together that you keep bumping them when you move a little, the quality of the set will suffer. If the rack is too deep, the pins will have too much "bounce" because the long span between front and back uprights requires longer, and therefore springier, pins. Having the bar bouncing around on the pins is also disruptive during the set. The rack pictured in Figure 7-2 is 22 inches deep.

If the rack is not wide enough, it can make loading the bar a problem. A narrow rack will allow an unevenly loaded bar – which they all are while being loaded – to tip. This, and the fact that a narrow rack is potentially very hard on the hands when you're racking the squat, makes 48–49 inches outside to outside a very handy width for a power rack. The holes in the uprights should be on 3-inch centers or closer. This spacing allows for fine enough adjustments in height that it is useful for all exercises inside the rack, as well as for squatting and pressing outside the rack. (For more details about racks, and the plans for building your own, see the Equipment section of the Programming chapter.)

PARTIAL SQUATS AND PRESSES

These same principles – using different versions of the parent exercise or portions of its range of motion as assistance exercises, which we lump together under the term "partials" – can be applied to squats and presses. Squats and presses, however, respond differently due to the fundamentally different nature of the exercises. The deadlift starts from the floor without a stretch reflex, distinguishing it from a squat in more ways than just the location of the bar. The hip and knee angles in the squat are already more acute than at the start of the deadlift, and this longer range of motion is a terribly critical distinction between the two, since the added ROM just happens to be in the most mechanically disadvantageous part. The only thing that mitigates this mechanically hard position is the stretch-reflex rebound out of the bottom provided by the hamstrings, glutes, and adductors. Squats that start from a dead stop, removing the help provided by the stretch reflex, are quite useful when performed from different positions: just below parallel, well below parallel, and just above parallel. The pause makes the drive up very, very hard; a below-parallel paused box squat done for five reps might be only 50–60% of your 1RM. If you strengthen the squat at these positions from a dead stop, the explosion you must generate to start up from the bottom without the benefit of the bounce makes for a stronger squat when the bounce is added back in.

Paused squats. Paused squats can be done in two ways: off a box or in the power rack. The box squat is an old training method that has worked effectively for several generations of lifters. The box is set up on the platform and behind the lifter, another step back from the regular foot position for safety in backing up to the box. The box can be an actual box, built of wood or metal, a plyometric jump box, or a stack of bumper plates. The height should be variable, the box should not slip against the platform or your

Figure 7-4. Box squats done with stacked bumper plates. Use what you have, as long as it is sturdy.

butt, and it must be hell for stout. The stance is generally the same as for the squat, perhaps a little wider to allow the adductors to stretch a little more and increase their contribution from the dead stop.

Take the bar out of the rack and step carefully back to a position that allows a firm contact with the box as your hips reach back at the bottom. This distance may vary with the box, but in general your heels will be parallel to the front edge of the box; if you are using stacked bumper plates, their radius will allow your heels to be a little behind the front of the plates. The squat itself will be an exaggeration of the correct form, with lots of attention paid to getting the hips back, the knees out to the sides, and enough forward lean to stay in balance with this extreme hips-back position. This exaggeration is needed because you're going to stop dead, with no rebound, and then drive your hips up from the pause below parallel. The difference in stance reflects

the need to tighten up the bottom position for an exaggerated hip drive without a rebound.

As you approach the box, slow down so that you don't slap it with your butt. The purpose here is to load the box carefully to avoid compressing your back. Pause for a second or two and drive the hips straight up hard. Do not exhale at the bottom. Air is support, and if ever in your life you need support, it will be at the bottom of a box squat. This exercise can be used for varying numbers of reps and sets, depending on the effect desired. The box can be varied in height from several inches below parallel to an inch or two, *no more*, above parallel. The deep versions use lighter weights, as mentioned earlier, and the high-box version can be done with weights greatly exceeding a 1RM squat. (This alone should indicate how important it is to squat below parallel; high squats are much easier to do with lots more weight because they are not a full-range-of-motion exercise, and yes, a couple of inches does make this much difference.)

A version of this exercise known as the "rocking box squat" (developed at Westside Barbell in Culver City, California, in the 1960s) has the weight leaving the feet briefly as you rock back slightly and then coming back onto the feet before you drive your hips up hard off the box. But keep this in mind: box squats are an advanced exercise with a huge potential for injury if done by inexperienced or physically unprepared trainees. The risk of spinal compression between the box and the bar is very high, and high school coaches *should* know better than to allow it. Please do not do them if you are not prepared, and this statement most definitely constitutes a disclaimer.

Partial squats inside the rack. The other way to do partial squats is inside the power rack with the pins set at a height that produces the desired depth when the bar on your back touches the pins at the bottom. There are, fascinatingly enough, two ways to do these. The easy way is to set the pins at the desired depth, set up the hooks inside the rack, take the bar out of the hooks, squat down to a dead stop on the pins, and then come up. This method permits you to get tight and store some elastic energy on the way down to the bottom even without a bounce, preserving the effects of the eccentric and concentric order of things. The hard way is to load the bar on the pins at the desired bottom position, squat down under it and get in position to squat at the bottom, and then squat the bar up from what is most assuredly a *very* dead stop. This method is really a challenge at the lower reaches of depth and is hard with even light weights. As with box squats, they get easy at rack heights much above parallel, with so much quadriceps and so little posterior muscle involved that they become good only for producing sore knees.

Bouncing the bar off of the pins substitutes for the rebound that your hamstrings and adductors should be providing, thus defeating the purpose of doing the exercise in the rack. The bar should be lowered to the pins, fully stopped, and then driven up. The dead stop from the pins provides the same

Figure 7-5. Two ways to do squats in the rack. *Top,* The top start allows the eccentric contraction to assist the concentric phase even in the absence of a stretch reflex, and it can be used with much heavier weights. *Bottom,* The bottom start, with the bar resting on the rack pins, requires that the concentric contraction be started from a dead stop in the hardest position of the movement, greatly increasing the difficulty and decreasing the weight that can be used.

opportunity to work initial explosion out of the hole that box squats do, without the risk of any spinal entrapment compression. It is easier to get tighter at the bottom if you have had the whole trip down to the box or the pins to do it; it is hard to get in an efficient position to squat if you have to do it while wadded up at the bottom, unable to stretch down into the bottom from the correct position assumed at the top. There are advantages and disadvantages to each method, but by the time you're ready to

Figure 7-6. Pressing from different positions within the range of motion inside the rack.

do partial squats, you'll have a feel for which one will work best for you. Just remember: **this type of squat training is not for novice trainees.**

Notice that these options do not include a half-squat, which would be done from approximately the hip and knee angles seen at the start of the deadlift. The half-squat is an arbitrary position to start or stop in since there is no anatomical reason to do so. The full squat works because the hamstrings and adductors achieve full stretch at this depth, but nothing good occurs at half-squat depth. The positions from which the squat can be trained with useful assistance exercises are all very close to the positions of the full range of motion. Training from the bottom up to the middle and then going back down is useful, as are all the variations that work up from the bottom with a pause to kill the rebound. (The top half of the squat is very easy if the bottom is strong, since the top half is the mechanically easy part; conversely, training the top will not strengthen the bottom.) But unlike splitting up the deadlift, it is not very productive to divide the squat into an upper and a lower component and then train each one separately. The top does not need the work, half-squats are hard on the knees, and the bottom is the hard part of the squat, anyway; in contrast, there

is no easy part of a deadlift, and both halves of it can successfully be worked separately.

Partial presses and bench presses. The press, like the deadlift, starts from a dead stop, at least for the first rep of a set and for a 1RM. Partial presses from different pin heights in the rack can be very useful assistance exercises. Dead-stop explosion can be worked from every position the rack permits to be set and loaded – from eyeball level, to lockout, to overhead support work starting from locked-out elbows. The bench press can be worked the same way as the squat inside the rack, with the dead-stop assistance versions adding to the effectiveness of the rebound when the regular bench movement is resumed.

For presses, set the pins at the desired position, from chin level (just off the shoulders) on up, even as high as slightly below lockout, and press the bar off the pins with your standard press grip, keeping the bar close to your face with good elbow position and your chest up. Before it leaves the pins, tighten up against the bar, taking all the slack out of your elbows and shoulders before you try to make the bar move up. *Make sure you preserve the critical movement of the torso under the bar.* The higher the pins, the heavier the weight can be. The heavier the

Figure 7-7. Rack bench presses allow for the use of heavier weights at different heights above the chest. They must be respected for the amount of stress they can produce if overused.

weight, the greater the instability at the top, the harder it becomes to prevent excessive layback, and the more stress the shoulders and abs will receive. A belt is a very good idea here.

Resist the temptation to do lots of sets with weights heavier than you can press, especially the first time you try this. Pin positions in the middle of the movement – where most people get stuck, the point at about the top of the forehead where the transition from delts to triceps is trying to occur – are good places to apply this kind of work. And as a general rule, any partial exercise is quite useful when applied to the sticking points in its parent movement, and most of the partial exercises were developed specifically for this purpose. Reps can vary from sets of 3 to 10, but don't get carried away with the volume. Sets across from a dead stop will beat your shoulders up, so pick a weight, do it for the number of reps you want to use, and then adjust the weight in your next workout if you picked it wrong.

The bench press can be used the same way, with the bar loaded on pins set at the desired height above the chest. Carefully center the flat bench so that it accommodates the correct position under the bar, with your head on the bench and your chest and elbows in the same place under the bar and in the same position they would be in had you pressed the bar off your chest to this level. As with the press,

take all the slack out of your elbows and shoulders before you push the bar up off the pins; this is important for correct mechanical execution and to prevent excessive dynamic shock to the tendon insertions on your humerus. Sets of five work well for both presses and bench presses, but again, just use one heavy set. These are very stressful, and you will develop pec insertion tendinitis if you do too much work on partial exercises that allow the use of heavy weights. Shoulders are easier to injure and more susceptible to overuse than knees and hips are, and dead-stop exercises with heavy weights tend to inflame the attachments pretty badly if they are used too often or at excessive volume. But if you don't get carried away by the glamour of the heavier weights that are possible because of the shorter range of motion, partial benches can make you very strong.

You can also start either pressing movement from the lockout position at the top by setting the hooks inside the rack at this height, unracking the bar and then lowering it to the pins, pausing, and driving back up, as with the rack squat. And as with the squat, a bounce off the pins defeats the purpose of the exercise; its value lies in the fact that it allows sticking points to be worked from a dead stop. You must control the pause to prevent the bar from getting out of position on the pins. This version of the press is not commonly used, but it could be. More common is the *board press*, which uses varying thicknesses of lumber laid directly on the chest to make up the spacing for the partial. It was developed to strengthen the top of the movement after the use of the bench-press shirt (which helps the lifter get the bar off the chest) became commonplace in competitions. The board press does not require a power rack, but does require the assistance of a spotter for the placement and removal of the board.

Many versions of all these exercises have been developed by many people over the years and used with varying degrees of success. The key is good form, an understanding of the function and desired result of the exercise, and the judicious use of loading.

So it appears that for all the basic exercises – the ones that normally use a stretch reflex as well as the ones that start from a dead stop – partial movements from a dead stop are useful. For the deadlift and the press, they mimic the mechanics of the parent movement by training the dead-stop start from different positions within the range of motion. For the squat and the touch-and-go bench press, they make you generate all the upward motion without the help from a stretch reflex. Either way, they are beneficial.

But partial movements are not substitutes for the parent exercises. The full movement is the primary work, and the partial versions function as assistance work. If they were capable of replacing their parent exercises, they would have already. The full movement, by definition, involves muscles and neuromuscular details that the partial movement does not; the partial movement is therefore inferior to the whole parent exercise in its ability to improve performance. Even the deadlift is better than its partial derivatives; there are technical aspects to the deadlift that need to be practiced, and only experienced lifters should substitute haltings and rack pulls for the bigger, harder movement. For all these partial exercises that allow the use of heavier weights or harder positions, the point is to apply more or more-specific stress than the parent exercise can produce. They must be used sparingly, under appropriate circumstances, by trainees experienced enough to understand how and why.

Squat Variations

There are a couple of variations of the basic barbell squat that should be discussed. Front squats and high-bar, or Olympic, squats are commonly used assistance exercises. They are not pieces of the back squat, but rather alternative versions of the parent movement that can be used as a substitute if need be. Opinions differ, and in the interest of full disclosure, they are described here.

OLYMPIC SQUATS

The Olympic squat is preferred by many coaches over the low-bar position described in this book. This could be because it requires no coaching: the high-bar position, on top of the traps, is what a trainee will self-select unless made to do otherwise, and the knees-forward position at the bottom is what happens in the absence of the intentional recruitment of the posterior chain. If you tell a kid to "Go over to the rack and do some squats, I'm busy here teaching the highly technical, and might I add more rewarding to coach, snatch and clean and jerk" – in other words, if you have him squat without teaching him how to do it – he will do a high-bar squat. Coaches dealing with lots of trainees may prefer to just let them carry the bar high, thus relegating the question of bar position to an insignificant issue in the grand scheme of things.

The high-bar position is easier to get in for people with inflexible shoulders, and some older trainees with chronic shoulder problems have no choice but to squat this way; for them, it is obviously better than not squatting at all. Shoulder flexibility this bad sometimes improves, but sometimes, especially for older trainees, it doesn't improve much at all, especially if it is due to bony changes within the joint capsule. We've already discussed the reasons for preferring the low-bar position, so here we'll assume that the high-bar position is the alternate version and that there is a compelling reason for using it.

The high-bar position requires that more attention be paid to keeping the chest up, which depends on upper back strength. The closer to

Figure 7-8. Three views of the front squat. Note the very steep back angle and the position of the bar over the mid-foot.

vertical the back is, the smaller the effects of the longer back segment. This more upright position is also required if the squat is to stay in balance, since any squat is in balance only when the bar is over the middle of the feet. But the more upright the back and the more closed the knee angle, the less the hamstrings are involved in the movement, since the hips are already extended and the knees are more flexed. **The farther forward the knees are, the less involved the hips are.** All these position requirements and leverage disadvantages make it necessary to use lighter loads in the Olympic squat than in the low-bar version. If you decide that the high-bar version might be useful, then use it as your standard squat and focus on the upright chest position. Hip drive will be greatly diminished, so it will not be useful as a cue.

FRONT SQUATS

The front squat is a completely separate exercise (Figure 7-8), for a couple of very important reasons. It varies enough from the squat that it should not be used by novices still trying to learn that movement. The front squat uses a different movement model than the squat, in that the hips are not the emphasis when the lifter is thinking about how to do it – the knees and the chest are the keys to the front squat. The differences in the two movements are entirely due to the bar position (Figure 7-9). Any squat that is in balance will keep the bar over the mid-foot, while it is in the resting position at the top and as it travels down and up through the whole range of motion of the exercise. The low-bar squat will thus be done with a back angle of somewhere between 30 and 50 degrees, depending on individual anthropometry, to permit the bar's vertical position over the feet. But in the front squat, since the bar sits on the anterior deltoids, with the elbows up and the hands trapping the bar in place, the back angle must be nearly vertical to keep the bar over the mid-foot and prevent it from falling off the shoulders. Front squats are missed when the weight is too heavy to squat or too heavy for the back to stay upright enough for the lifter to hold the bar in place. In either instance, the bar falls away forward.

And since the back must stay nearly vertical, the knees and hips must facilitate this: from the earliest part of the movement in a front squat, the knees track forward (and out) and the hips stay under the bar. This combination places the tibias in a much more horizontal position than in a squat, and this position significantly changes the mechanics around the knees and ankles, as well as the hips and lower back.

The position of the bar determines the best way to drive up out of the bottom. The low-bar squat uses a forceful, deliberate initial hip drive. The idea is to drive the butt straight up out of the bottom, which more effectively makes the glutes, hamstrings, and adductors contract. This hip drive is possible because the bar is low enough to place the lifter's back at an angle which permits it; driving the butt up with the bar on the back just requires that the chest be maintained in position, preserving the back angle.

Hip drive does not work for the front squat. When the back is at a more horizontal angle, the hips present a "surface" – the top of the glutes, the sacrum, and the lowest part of the lower back – that a coach can touch with the hand and identify to the trainee. The coach can place his hand on this area and tell the trainee to "push it up," a tactile cue that greatly improves the efficiency of the contraction of the muscles that produce the movement. The front squat has the hips directly under the bar, or as nearly so as possible – a position which presents no surface for cueing. The column of the torso stops at the chest and shoulders, and these, along with the elbows, are the surfaces that get cued. A focus on the chest, shoulders, and elbows – driving them up, even as you lower the bar – preserves the vertical position that is so critical to finishing a heavy front squat. This focus is in stark contrast to the squat's, both in position and in the way the movement is visualized. The differences are great enough that they should not get confused, but they quite often do, and for this reason the front squat is best left alone until the squat's movement pattern is thoroughly embedded.

Since the front squat has such radically different form, you might expect that it should produce a different result than the squat. It does, for the back, hips, and legs. The vertical back position of the front squat seems like it would result in a more direct compressional load on the spine than the squat's more horizontal angle would produce. This is partially true. The lower back is in a nearly vertical position, but the upper back has a much tougher job because the load it is holding up is farther away, forward. The bar in a back squat, low-bar or high-

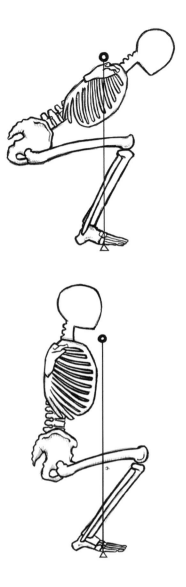

Figure 7-9. The relationship between bar position for the two types of squats and the resulting back, knee, and hip angles.

bar, sits right on top of the muscles that are holding it up. The front squat places the bar all the way across the depth of the chest, which in a bigger guy might be 12 or more inches. This distance is a moment arm that presents a mechanical challenge to the muscles that maintain thoracic extension (it is very common for lifters to get pretty sore between the shoulder blades when first starting the exercise). And since the bar is forward of the hips, too, there's also a moment arm against the hips, although probably not as long as in a squat, and certainly under a lighter load. So while the lower back is vertically positioned,

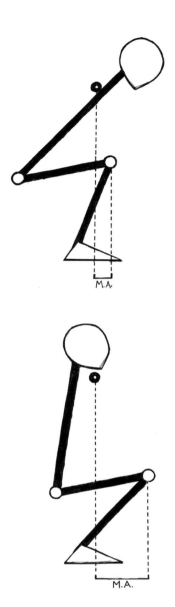

When you front-squat, don't worry about your back; worry about your knees. To facilitate the vertical back, they have to track forward so that the hips can stay directly under the bar. This means that the shins will be much more horizontal at the bottom of the front squat, with a closed knee angle, dorsiflexed ankles, and a lot more moment force operating along the tibias than there is in a squat. For most people, these factors will mean contact between calf muscles and hamstrings at the bottom, and sometimes a rather dynamic loading of the Achilles tendons and quadriceps. For some people, this closed knee angle will create enough "wedging" on the posterior knee cartilage that it can produce instability and injury, a situation that essentially *never* happens in a properly performed low-bar squat. For everybody, the job of opening the knee angle through a much greater ROM, with muscles working against more moment force because of a more horizontal shin, is much harder.

Since the front squat places the knees so much farther forward than they are at the bottom of the squat, the hamstrings are not nearly as involved in the hip extension. In the front squat, the vertical back and pelvic position and the acute angle of the tibias place the hamstrings in a position where the origin and insertion points are closer together, so the muscle bellies are shortened. If the hamstrings are already contracted, they cannot contract much more and thus cannot contribute much to hip extension. The hamstrings' role in the front squat is to maintain the vertical back angle, and their already contracted position prevents them from contracting much further.

But the hips must still extend, so the glutes and adductors end up doing most of the job without the help of the hamstrings. The knees-forward, vertical-back position puts the quads in a position to do most of the work, since most of the angle to open will be the knee angle. Three of the four quadriceps cross only the knee joint, so any exercise that extends the knee will involve most of the quads every time. The difference in the front squat is that very noticeable glute soreness is usually the result the first few times you do it.

Figure 7-10. The knee position in the front squat, necessitated by the vertical back position, produces a moment arm along the tibias, a phenomenon that is not significant in the squat. (*M.A. = moment arm*)

your thoracic erector muscles have a lot of work to do. What actually happens is a gradual shift from compression to moment, from low back to upper back, so things are not as simple as they may seem. The load on the lumbar spine in the front squat is friendlier (because it will be lighter) as long as the upper erectors can maintain position, and for this reason, many people find front squats to be easier on the low back. But this also means that the front squat is a less effective back exercise than the squat.

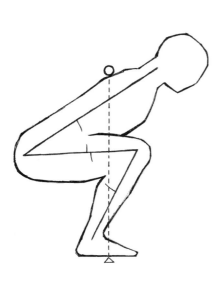

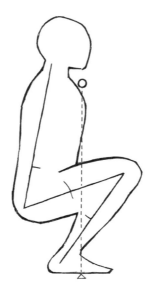

Figure 7-11. The differences in the squat and the front squat are determined by the position of the bar. The resulting angles and their effects on the biomechanics of the movements are responsible for the different training effects of the two exercises.

So the primary difference between the squat and the front squat is one of degree in terms of the amount of involvement from the contributing muscle groups. The knees-forward position increases the moment force on the tibias, making the mechanics of knee extension less efficient. At the same time, the contribution of the hips is diminished by the vertical back position. The net effect is that you cannot front-squat as much weight as you can squat in the low-bar position. And the primary reason for the difference is the position in which the system is in balance – the bar in both cases must be over the middle of the foot, and the resulting correct back angle is the one that keeps it there.

Learning the front squat is best done from the power rack or squat stand. The bar is set at the same position as for a back squat, the level of the mid-sternum. The grip is a very important component of the front squat, more so than in the back squat. The grip must allow your elbows to come up high enough that your shoulders can support the load while your back remains vertical during the movement. The grip width will depend largely on individual flexibility, and it will vary between trainees and during the individual trainee's career as flexibility is acquired through stretching or lost due to injury. In general, the less flexibility a trainee exhibits, the wider the grip will need to

Figure 7-12. Differences in forearm length relative to the upper arm affect elbow position in the front squat and the clean. *Left,* An extreme example of forearm disproportion. Long forearms shove the elbows down lower. This can be compensated for by widening the grip, *middle and right.*

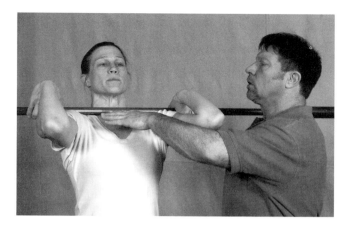

Figure 7-13. The cue for lifting the chest. The hand is the target.

be. And some people have long forearms relative to their humerus length and find it hard to elevate the elbows with what would otherwise be a normal grip width. Adjust your grip width as needed so that you can raise your elbows high enough to support the bar. And if you cannot assume a position with at least some fingers on the bar with the load on your deltoids after stretching and adequate shoulder/elbow/wrist warm-up, you might not be able to front-squat productively.

Take the weight of the bar onto your shoulders, with elbows in the elevated position, shoulders tight, and chest up, before you unrack the bar. The weight sits on the meat of the deltoids, and if your elbows are not in the up position before the weight is unracked, they'll never completely get there. Your chest must also be up in a position that reinforces the shoulders, and you place it there with the upper back muscles. Maintain this position by lifting both your elbows and your chest as high as possible, from the time you unrack the bar until you finish the last rep. To cue this movement, think of touching a hand held above your sternum.

Take the bar out of the rack and step back a couple of steps to clear the hooks. (When the bar is loaded, preferably with bumper plates, a miss will be dropped forward and no spotters will be involved, so your distance from the rack must be sufficient that the bar can fall without hitting anything but the floor.) Your stance will be essentially the same as for the back squat: heels at shoulder width and

toes out at about 30 degrees. After assuming the stance, lift your chest and elbows, take a big breath to support this position, and squat. The vertical position of the back is retained on the way down by forcing the knees forward and out, keeping the chest and elbows up, and possibly even thinking about leaning back slightly. The bottom of the front squat is quite easy to feel because some contact between the calves and the hamstrings will occur.

There is no pause at the bottom, and the ascent starts with an upward drive of the chest, not the elbows. Elbows stay up, and the chest is driven up, since merely raising the elbows will not positively affect the upper spine – the whole point of the "chest up" cue. As the chest is driven up, the hips rise vertically underneath it, maintaining the

Figure 7-14. An upright torso for the front squat is necessary, and this is one way to visualize the situation.

vertical position and keeping the bar on the delts so that it doesn't roll forward and down. The elbows-up position traps the bar between the fingers and the neck, but the weight is on the delts, not on the hands. At no time during the movement is the back relaxed, at either the bottom or the top; the spine must be consciously squeezed tight and held in position vertically, more of a challenge in the front squat due to the bar's position in front of the neck and the consequently greater leverage against the upper back.

The differences in bar position and hamstring function between the front and back squats necessitate a different set of cues for each version. The back squat depends on hip drive, and it is cued at the sacrum, as mentioned previously. The chest and elbows are the focal points for attention in the front squat. "Big air" is critical to chest position, as is the strength of the upper part of the spinal erectors, which get sore when this position is trained hard the first few times. Thinking about leaning back on the way down may produce a feel for the position if it does not interfere with balance; most people can grasp this concept without falling backwards.

Some people have proportions that make the front squat difficult. A short torso with long legs is a bad combination for good front squat form, and little can be done about this. In extreme cases, it may be best not to perform the exercise if correct form cannot be maintained due to an anthropometric problem that cannot be solved (Figure 7-15).

Front squats are usually done in sets of three, due to the greater sensitivity of the exercise to form deterioration. Volume is accumulated with multiple sets across.

Breath control is terribly critical in the front squat. More leverage against the upper back – the result of the increased distance of the bar from the spine – results in more rotational force that must be countered. The support provided by increased intrathoracic pressure is often the difference between holding a heavy last rep in place and dropping it on the floor. A big breath keeps the chest up, the shoulders up, and the elbows up by tightening the

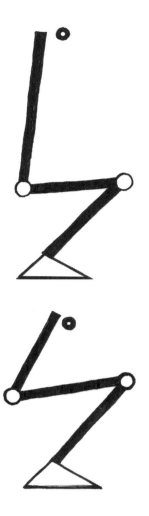

Figure 7-15. Anthropometry affects the lifter's ability to assume an efficient position in the front squat, as it does with all barbell exercises. The front squat suffers from a short torso and long legs.

entire upper body. You will need a new breath at the top of each rep, maybe just a top-off of the previous breath so that you maintain tightness.

As mentioned previously, a missed front squat will fall away forward off the shoulders. This is unavoidable because if you are training hard, you will eventually miss a front squat, so you might as well prepare for it by practicing it occasionally during warm-ups. And unless you are used to getting away from the bar as it falls – putting enough distance between you and the bar that it won't hit you on the way down – you might drop it on your knees or lower thighs. This potentially painful error is usually prevented by most people's sense of self-preservation,

Figure 7-16. The California front squat. This position is not advised.

but it is prudent to have at least practiced missing the front squat a few times.

One of the problems associated with front squats is related to bar placement. If the throat is squeezed too hard by a bar racked too far back on the shoulders, the result can be a blackout. It is caused by the occlusion of the carotid arteries from the pressure of the bar. This is dangerous because of the fall that will occur if you allow yourself to pass completely out before doing something about it (the blackout itself is harmless). If you feel your perception start to change – and you'll know it when it happens – either rack the bar while you can, or drop it safely on the platform and take a knee so that you don't have as far to fall if the blackout continues to develop. An uncontrolled blackout can cause severe head injuries if you hit the racks, the bar, or the plates on the way down. To repeat: the blackout itself is harmless and is corrected by moving the bar away from the throat a little. Once the buzz diminishes, you can resume the set with no trouble as long as you have made the correction. But if you manage to black out once, you will find that you're more prone to it for the rest of that workout, so be careful when correcting the rack position.

One more thing: There is a version of the front squat, referred to around here as the *California*

front squat, in which the lifter's arms are crossed in front, with the right hand on the left shoulder and vice versa. This form involves less upper body flexibility than does the standard hand position, and proportionately less security on the shoulders. It is not as safe at heavy weights, and since we train with heavy weights, we don't use it.

The standard position is derived from the clean, the movement typically preceding the front squat in Olympic weightlifting, in which the bar is trapped against the shoulders by the upraised elbows jamming the hands and the bar *back* into the rack position. The crossed-arms position relies entirely on the elbow position and completely loses the stability provided by the hands. Doing front squats this way is tantamount to just holding your hands out in front of you with the bar balanced on the delts. And if you need to drop the bar in the event of a miss, the crossed-arms position makes the drop awkward and hard to control. There is an argument to be made for cleaning everything you're going to front-squat, and California front squats contribute to the argument.

Bench Press Variations

The bench press is such a popular exercise that it's no surprise there are lots of variations of the basic version. Selectorized bench press machines that control the bar path have long been a feature of multi-station machines; bars have been developed that allow the weight to travel past the top of the chest, down to where the elbows aren't supposed to go; machines have been invented that allow each side to work independently of the other (like dumbbells, only much more expensive); the pec-deck takes the triceps out of the exercise. None of these variations are particularly helpful advances in exercise technology. The bench press is a valuable exercise because it couples heavy potential load with the motor-control aspects of barbell training, and these devices remove much of this benefit. The most valuable variations preserve the benefits while allowing different aspects of the movement that might need additional work to receive it. They are of

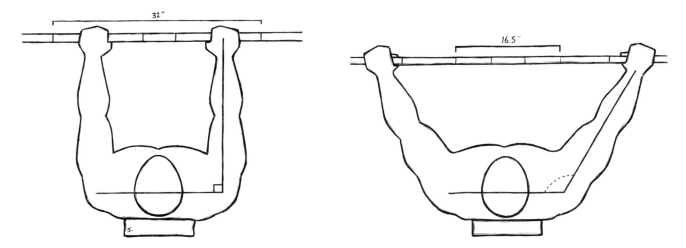

Figure 7-17. A comparison of the start positions of the close-grip and wide-grip bench presses. The distance the bar travels is at maximum when the lifter's arms are vertical in the lockout position.

two types: variations in the grip width and variations in the angle of the shoulder during the press.

VARIATIONS IN GRIP WIDTH

The grip can be either wider or narrower than standard. The narrower the grip, the more inclined toward the middle the forearms are at the bottom, the sooner the elbows stop traveling down as the bar touches the chest, and therefore the shorter the range of motion around the shoulder, even though the bar travels farther at the top. The less angle the humerus covers as it travels down, the less work the chest muscles do; the more angle the elbows open up, the more work the triceps do (Figure 7-17). A medium grip – with the forearms vertical at the bottom – uses the longest range of elbow motion, and a very wide grip involves a shorter range of bar *and* elbow motion because the bar touches the chest before the elbows can travel down very far. With a wide grip, the triceps extend the elbows over a shorter angle, and the pecs and delts end up doing more of what work gets done. So, bar travel is at maximum when the arms are vertical at lockout, and elbow travel is at maximum when the forearms are vertical at the bottom. It is for this reason that wide-grip benches have the reputation for being a chest exercise. More weight can be benched due to the shorter range of motion, and that is done without as much help

from the triceps, so the chest gets most of the work.

The close-grip version is not really just a triceps exercise, though it seems to have that reputation. The large elbow angle the triceps opens provides more stimulation for that muscle group; the pecs and the delts are performing the same function – adducting the humerus – but over a different range of motion, since the humerus is more vertical at lockout but not as deep at the bottom with the closer grip. Less weight can usually be done close-grip than with the standard grip due to the decreased contribution of the pecs and delts out of the bottom, but not much less. Compared with the wide grip, the narrow grip is much harder in terms of total weight that can be used, due to the range of motion and less pec and delt involvement, while the wide-grip bench is a shorter movement that produces less work and permits heavier weights to be used. It omits some of the triceps work while relying much more on pecs and delts. The close-grip version uses lots of triceps, uses the pecs and delts less, and is harder. If your primary interest is in moving the heaviest weight, as a powerlifter needs to do, the widest grip legal for the meet is the one to use. If your interest is in the greatest amount of muscle stressed to cause an adaptation, a medium grip is the most useful. And if you need to get more triceps work, a close grip is useful for that.

The greatest effect comes from the closest

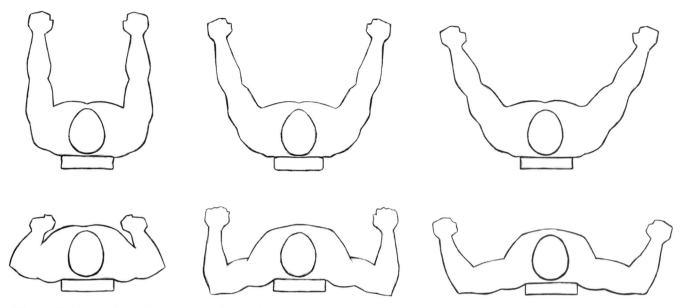

Figure 7-18. *Right to left*, A comparison of the top and bottom positions of the close-grip, standard-grip, and wide-grip bench presses. The deepest range of motion around the shoulder joint occurs with the grip that allows the forearms to be vertical at the bottom. Any other forearm alignment causes the bar to touch the chest before the full range of motion is reached.

grip you can tolerate, and this will be controlled by your wrist flexibility. On a standard power bar, the knurl has a gap of between 16 and 17 inches, so the edge of the knurl makes a good place to start. After a bench press workout, take about 50% of your 1RM out of the rack with a grip set so that your index fingers are on the lines formed by the edges of the knurl. The exercise is performed the same way as the standard bench press, with the same breathing, back setup, foot position, and chest position. Rack the set, wait a little, and do another set with the grip one finger-width narrower on each side. Continue to narrow each set of five by one finger-width until your wrists begin to complain at the bottom, and then widen back out by one finger-width. You might have to widen your grip a little as the weight goes up, because what doesn't hurt with light weights may very well be painful at heavier weights.

Close-grips are usually used at higher reps, but this is merely tradition, and there is no reason that they must be done this way. Since they use a lighter weight than the standard bench press, they can be done after a bench workout, or they can be used as a light-day exercise on a separate day. Care must be taken to hold the bar very tightly; the wrist position makes for a less secure grip than the conventional grip provides, and it has been known to fail on the way up when the wrists twitch inconveniently. Close-grips are also famous for reaching failure rather suddenly, with the last completed rep giving little indication that the next one will get stuck on the way up. As a general rule, exercises that depend on less muscle mass or fewer muscle groups tend to fail more abruptly in their bar path than do exercises that use more muscles.

VARIATIONS IN ANGLE

The other way to usefully vary the bench press involves the angle at which the humerus approaches the chest, controlled by the angle of the bench on which the exercise is performed. The back angle thus determines the quality and quantity of pectoral and deltoid involvement in the press. There are two variations from horizontal: the decline, in which the shoulders are lower than the hips; and the incline, in which the shoulders are higher than the hips.

The decline press is a rather useless exercise because the angle of the back in the decline position

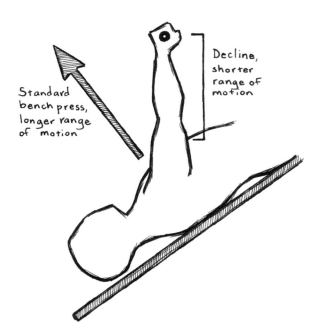

Figure 7-19. A comparison of the ranges of motion of the bench press and the decline bench press.

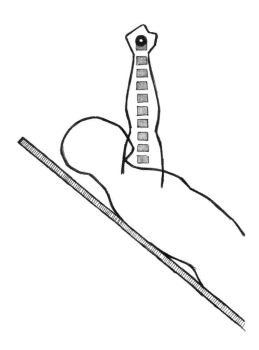

Figure 7-20. The position of the bar in the incline bench press, directly over a point just below the point where the collarbones meet the sternum. The bar will be very close to the chin on the way down.

shortens the distance the bar can travel, decreasing the amount of work done by decreasing the range of motion. By decreasing the difficulty, the decline press increases the weight that can be used in the exercise, which in turn leads to inflated perceptions of one's ability – it is essentially masturbation, much like that which is possible with a 30-degree leg press or a half-squat. The decline press gets recommended for its effects on the "lower pecs," but dips perform this function much more effectively, while involving more muscle mass, more balance and coordination, and more nervous system activity, as discussed later. Declines are dangerous because if their point of contact on the lower sternum gets missed, the next stop is the throat. Couple this problem with a heavy weight and a lousy spotter, and you might have a really, really bad "chest" workout.

The incline bench press, however, can be a useful variation. If you are doing both bench presses and presses, then everything that the incline bench press accomplishes is redundant; there is no aspect of shoulder and chest work that these two exercises do not more than adequately cover. "Upper pecs" are quite thoroughly involved in the press, and the bench press uses the whole muscle belly, so there is no need to try to isolate this portion of the chest

musculature. But many sports involve the use of the arms at an angle somewhere above 90 degrees from the torso, and some people believe that this angle should be specifically targeted for resistance training. The incline bench press does this, albeit at the cost of the body's being supported at this angle while the work is being done, something that never occurs during the sports in question (see the discussion of this in Chapter 3).

But limitations are what make them "assistance" exercises – if they were perfect, they'd be major exercises and have their own chapters. The incline is useful in some cases, as long as it's done correctly; but it is easy to cheat, and pointless when cheated. Most commonly, the effects of the angle of incline are negated when the trainee raises his hips up off of the incline bench, thus making his torso more horizontal. If a horizontal bench press is what you want to do, just do the bench press. Indeed, this is a good reason to just bench press and press. When doing inclines, people often allow their greed to overwhelm their sense of honesty, and they try to lift too much weight for the limitations of the inclined position, thereby causing their hips to bridge just to get the last rep back in the rack. The incline is an assistance exercise – don't use so much weight that it has to be cheated, because this defeats the purpose of doing it. Keep your butt on the bench.

Most incline benches are made to be adjustable so that the incline can be varied according to individual preference. They are made with support uprights for the bar, like a bench press bench, and the supports are also adjustable to enable the bar to be unracked at a position that matches the angle of the bench. (Fixed-position incline benches are available from some manufacturers, with neither the angle nor the uprights adjustable.) The incline bench also has a seat built into the frame so that trainees can maintain a secure position without their feet becoming too critical to the lift. It would actually be better if the feet were more involved, since this would extend some, although not all, aspects of the kinetic chain down to the floor. You occasionally find very old benches built this way, with a foot plate at ninety degrees to the bench angle at the floor, but they are not the industry standard now.

When doing the exercise, select a back angle of between 30 and 45 degrees from vertical. Flatter angles are too similar to the bench press, and steeper angles are too similar to the press, with the disadvantage of having the back angle held immobile in a position that is very hard on the shoulders. One reason the press might be a better choice is that the stress of a tough rep can be accommodated by the natural adjustment of the back position, whereas the incline bench nails you into a fixed position that might exceed the capacity of the fatigued shoulders.

The uprights should support the bar at a height that allows the lifter to take it out, complete the reps, and rack it with a minimum of elbow extension but no danger of missing the racks. This means that the uprights should be set as high as possible so that the lifter's elbows are nearly straight, and so that when they are straightened, the bar clears the hooks by a couple of inches. If the supports are too low, too much work has to be done getting the bar out, and more important, too much work will have to be done getting it back in the rack at a time when lots of control might not be possible. The easiest rack position will vary with your bench, and

Figure 7-21. A useful type of incline support bench.

finding it will involve some trial and error.

Most of the differences between the incline and the bench press are positional. The two are basically executed the same way. The chest is up, the back is tight, the drive is to the point of focus on the ceiling, the feet are planted to connect firmly with the floor, and "big air" supports the chest. The position of the shoulders and back against the bench, the elbow position, the eye gaze direction, breath control, grip, and foot position are all the same for the incline as they are for the bench press, while the differences are related to the angle. The shoulders are squeezed together for a tight position, and the back is arched into a brace between the seat and the point of contact on the shoulders. The elbows stay directly under the bar for the whole movement; they control the bar path as they do for a bench press. The eyes focus on the stationary reference of the ceiling; they do not follow the bar. The breath

Figure 7-22. The incline bench press. Note the vertical bar path and the position of the bar over the clavicles.

is held during each rep, with breathing occurring between reps at the top. The grip is the same as that used for the bench, with the thumb around the bar, which rests on the heel of the palm. The feet are firmly planted against the floor as a brace for the position against the bench. The bar path will be straight, but instead of touching the mid-sternum, the bar will touch right under the chin, just below the sternoclavicular articulation (the point where the collarbones and the sternum meet). The range of motion, through an almost perfectly vertical bar path, is slightly longer than for a flat bench press. The elbows' position directly under the bar will place the point of contact on the chest, at a place that is even with the shoulder joints. The humeral angle – which does not approach 90 degrees of abduction – does not produce any shoulder impingement, as the bench press does.

The starting position, at lockout over the chest, will be the point where the bar is in balance directly above the shoulder joints and where the locked-out arms are vertical, just as in the bench press. But because of the angle, the distance between the rack and the start position is much shorter for the incline, so the bar is actually much easier to unrack and re-rack than it is for the bench press. For this reason, the experienced lifter might find that a spotter is less important for the incline, although this statement should not be construed as permission to be stupid.

If the incline is to be spotted, the equipment must be compatible. Most good benches have a spotter platform built into the frame. This allows the spotter to be sufficiently above the lifter such that if a problem occurs, the spotter can safely pull the bar up from a position of good leverage close to the bar. A spotter standing on the floor cannot be depended on to help, and if heavy weights are to be used, the equipment must allow for correct spotter position. Likewise, if you feel as though two spotters are necessary for the weight you're doing, you should either use a lighter weight or do a different exercise, because two spotters cannot safely spot an incline, and heavy 1RM attempts on the incline bench press demonstrate a poor understanding of the purpose of assistance exercises.

Figure 7-23. The great Nicu Vlad: the importer, as legend has it, of the Romanian deadlift. Vlad was pretty damn strong.

Deadlift Variations

We'll discuss four main variations here: the RDL, the SLDL, deadlifting from blocks, and the goodmorning (both flat-backed and round-backed).

ROMANIAN DEADLIFTS

Once upon a time, as legend has it, the incredible Romanian weightlifter Nicu Vlad visited the U.S. Olympic Training Center. Vlad was strong, probably as strong as any human being has ever been at a bodyweight of 220 pounds; word on the street has it that he front-squatted 700 pounds for a double. So when Vlad performed an exercise that no one had seen before, it quite naturally got a lot of attention from people not as strong as he was. The exercise involved taking the bar out of the rack from the hang position, stepping back to clear the rack, and then lowering the bar down to the mid-shins and raising it back to the hang position. This movement looked like a deadlift, but one that started at the top instead of the bottom, so naturally it had to have a new name. The term "Romanian deadlift" has been applied to it since then, although its name translated from the Romanian is probably something different (if it even has a Romanian name; the exercise has been developed since that day entirely in the USA and may simply have been Vlad's way of dealing with unfamiliar equipment). It is referred to by the initials "RDL."

The RDL has two important characteristics that distinguish it from its parent exercise. The first is that it uses very little quadriceps because the knees start off nearly straight – unlocked, but not very – and pretty much stay that way, so the quads don't have an opportunity to actively extend the knees during the movement. The RDL is specifically intended as a hip extension exercise, and the quads are not supposed to be involved except to isometrically anchor the knee angle from the anterior. All the work that occurs through the bottom of the range of motion and that would normally be shared between knee extensors and hip extensors is done only by the glutes and the hamstrings. The lower back muscles keep the lumbar spine locked in line with the pelvis. The hamstrings, acting at their attachments on the ischial tuberosities, cause rotation around the hip joints when they pull the bottom of the pelvis and the back of the knees together, making the hamstrings and glutes the prime movers during the exercise.

But more important is the difference in the fundamental nature of the two movements. The deadlift starts with a concentric contraction as the bar is pulled from the floor, and the eccentric phase is not really emphasized because the lift is essentially over after it is locked out at the top. In contrast, the RDL is like the squat in that the movement starts with an eccentric contraction, the "negative," which precedes the concentric. The bar starts from a position of knee and hip extension, the bar is lowered down into flexion, and a stretch reflex initiates the concentric contraction back into extension.

Any concentric contraction is stronger when it is preceded by this stretch reflex, due to increased efficiency in motor unit recruitment and to the

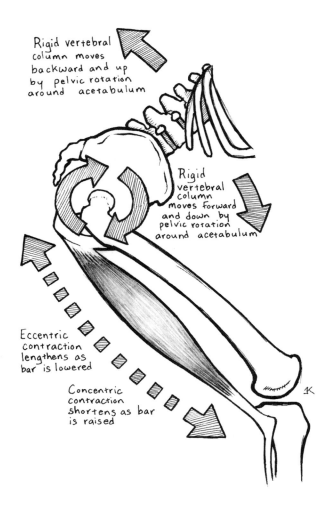

Figure 7-24. The function of the hamstrings in the RDL is essentially all hip extension, both eccentric and concentric.

ability of the elastic components of the muscles and connective tissues to store elastic energy developed during the eccentric lengthening of the muscle bellies. A jump is the best example of this principle; every time a jump of any kind is performed, it is preceded by a short drop of the hips and knees that creates a stretch reflex in the muscles about to contract for the jump. It takes a great effort of will to jump without this drop – it is such a normal part of human movement that it is very difficult to exclude. The stretch reflex also explains why bouncing the second through fifth reps of a set of five deadlifts off the floor is so popular. The majority of weight room exercises can be "cheated" with the use of a cleverly applied or exaggerated stretch reflex. I myself have "curled" 205 in this way.

Figure 7-25. The Romanian deadlift.

But for the RDL – and the squat, the bench, the jerk, and maybe the press, depending on how it's done – the stretch reflex is not cheating but is an inherent part of the movement. The bounce out of the bottom of the RDL enables rather heavy weights to be used in the exercise despite the fact that the quads have been excluded from helping with the movement. RDLs take advantage of the stretch reflex just to the extent that it affects the hip extensors.

The RDL starts in the rack with pins set at a position a little lower than the level of the hands in the hang position. This rack position allows for an easy, safe return to the rack in the event of a slipping grip that might lower the bar before you rack it. With a clean-width grip, take the bar out of the rack and step back just far enough to clear the pins. Assume the same stance you use for a deadlift,

with heels 8–12 inches apart, toes pointed slightly out. Raise your chest, and focus your eyes on a point on the floor about 10 feet in front of you.

The whole point of the RDL is that the back stays locked in extension while the hip extensors work. Unlock your knees so that a little tension comes into the quads, but no more than enough to lower the bar an inch or two down the thighs. Very little knee-angle change should occur, although the knee position over the feet will change slightly. This position will place your knees above a point about halfway between the toes and the instep. Lift your chest up and arch your low back into a tight lock, trying to maintain this position for the whole movement. Start the bar down your thighs by shoving your hips back, allowing your hips to come into flexion with the bar never leaving the skin of the legs. At the same time, push your shoulders

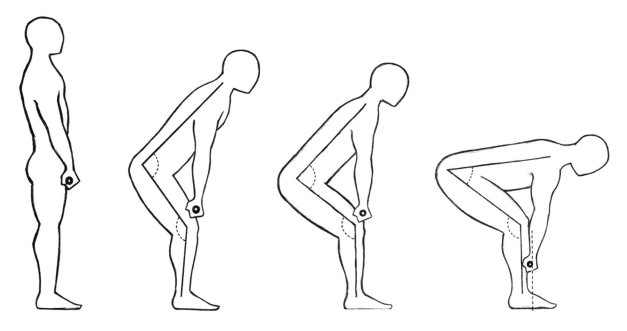

Figure 7-26. The progression from top to bottom in the RDL. Note that the hip-angle change is predominantly responsible for the ROM of the exercise.

forward, out in front of the bar, to the familiar pulling position. As the bar approaches your knees, shove them back, too, shifting the shins into a vertical position. Drop the bar down past your knees, keeping it in close contact with the shins, and go *as low as possible without unlocking your lower back*. Stop just before your back begins to unlock – a position you will identify on the first few reps – and start back up. The stretch at the bottom should help change the direction of the bar without any pause. On the way up, keep the bar in contact with your legs and keep your chest and back locked in position. Breathe at the top, taking a big breath for every rep.

The emphasis on driving everything back is very important; the use of the hips instead of the knees is what engages the hip extensors and excludes the quads. It helps to think about the weight shifting back to the heels, the knees moving back, the bar being shoved back to stay in contact with the legs, and the butt moving back; in fact, everything moves back except the shoulders, which slide forward, out over the bar. The shins must come to vertical before the bar reaches the knees, and the knees must never move forward at all after the initial unlocking. Any forward knee movement puts the quads in a position

to contribute to the movement by extending the knees on the way back up, canceling out the desired hip-extension effect.

The most common error will be the knees-forward problem. You will be tempted to relax the tension on your knees at the bottom; the hamstring tension builds all the way down and is not relieved until the muscles are shortened, either by having done the work of extending the hips at the top or by your relaxing your knees forward at the bottom. If you shorten the hamstrings by allowing the knees to drop forward – thus flexing the knees and causing the two ends of the hamstrings to come together, taking the tension off from the bottom – then the quads will do the work that the hamstrings should have done when they extend the knees during the recovery to the top.

Remember from the discussion of pulling mechanics in the Deadlift chapter that the shoulders stay in front of the bar. This means that the arms are inclined back from the shoulders at a slight angle, with the lats pulling back on the humerus to keep the bar over the mid-foot. The lower the bar goes down your legs without your knees bending, the more angle your arms must assume to keep the bar over the mid-foot, and the more work the lats must do to maintain this position. At a very low position on the shins, this angle becomes quite extreme, contributing to the difficulty involved in doing a strict RDL very far below the knees. In fact, if you touch the floor at the bottom of an RDL, you are probably doing it with a fairly light weight.

Also common is the failure to hold the back rigid in absolute extension. One of the main benefits of the RDL is the isometric work it provides for the erectors, as they hold the spine rigid while the hamstrings extend the hips. This back position is rather hard to hold, and the lifter needs a lot of concentration to keep the chest up and the low back arched with no looseness, while sliding the hips back, the knees back, the bar back, the heels down, and the shoulders forward. For a slow exercise, the RDL is technically difficult because it is very easy to do wrong. If the back rounds or the knees come forward, less work is being done by the targeted muscle groups and the movement feels easier. But done correctly, with the back locked into rigid extension and no knee extension involved, the RDL is perhaps the best assistance exercise for deadlifts and cleans because it works the very things that cause heavy deadlifts to be missed.

The best cues for good form on the RDL are "chest up," "arch the back," and "knees back," with an occasional reminder to keep the weight off the toes. The chest cue will remind you to keep the thoracic spine in extension, while arching the back usually gets interpreted by most people as a low-back cue. The knee cue keeps the quads out of the movement, but it can also cause the bar to fall away from the legs, and you might need to cue the lats by thinking "push the bar back."

When you're doing heavy RDLs, use a double-overhand grip. The shoulder asymmetry that results from an alternate grip is not desirable for this exercise, and the lats cannot effectively pull the bar back into the legs if you are using a supine hand on one side. The weights that will be used for heavy RDLs are not really heavy relative to the deadlift, with most people being able to use between 65% and 75% of their 1RM deadlift for the exercise, so using a plain old double-overhand grip will not usually be a problem. Use a hook grip or straps if your grip strength is insufficient, which it should not be at 65–75% of 1RM, but both your hands must be in the prone position. Being an assistance exercise, RDLs are done in the range of 5–10 reps.

STIFF-LEGGED DEADLIFTS

The stiff-legged deadlift (or SLDL) is possibly a more familiar exercise in most gyms, as a result of the fact that many people do the deadlift wrong and it ends up looking this way accidentally. The SLDL is essentially an RDL off of the floor — without the stretch reflex but with the higher hips, more horizontal back angle, and more vertical shins of the RDL. Since the SLDL starts on the floor, it

Figure 7-27. The conventional deadlift start position (*left*) and the stiff-legged deadlift start position (*right*).

Figure 7-28. The stiff-legged deadlift.

involves a longer range of motion than does the RDL, which is supposed to stop at the point where the low back unlocks due to limitations in hamstring extensibility. Most people can't do a strict RDL all the way down to the floor with the bar loaded with 17-inch plates, so you will have to do the SLDL with enough knee bend to allow your back to get into a good position to start. The amount of knee bend will obviously depend on individual flexibility. The point of the exercise is stiff legs – knees extended as much as possible and hips higher than in a deadlift, with the low back flat in the start position – so use as little knee bend as possible.

Take your regular deadlift stance, with the bar directly over the mid-foot. Use the regular double-overhand clean grip, for the same reasons mentioned above for the RDL. Unlock your knees and set them in position hard, as straight as your flexibility permits. Raise your chest, take a big breath, and pull. The SLDL is essentially a deadlift

done according to the five steps outlined on page 107, but without Step 3, the dropping-the-shins-forward-to-the-bar part. This means that the bar leaves the floor from over the mid-foot but is still in the air while in front of the shins. When the bar is just above your knees, it comes onto your legs, and the pull is then locked out like a regular deadlift at the top. Again, each rep is replaced on the floor, reset, and pulled from a stop; it is a deadlift, not an RDL, and *each rep starts from a dead stop*.

Both SLDLs and RDLs are versatile exercises and can be applied to your training in many ways. They can be done in a variety of rep ranges, depending upon the desired effect. When they're used as a substitute for the deadlift on a light day, sets of five work well; in fact, SLDLs and RDLs can be used for sets across, unlike the deadlift, since they do not produce the stress that the full heavy movement is known for. For back-off work following deadlifts, they can be used for sets of 8–10 reps to accumulate extra volume. And high-rep sets of 20 RDLs can be an interesting addition to your training.

Despite the fact that both the RDL and the SLDL can produce extreme hamstring soreness in the short term that can interfere with the normal range of motion of the knees, both exercises provide an excellent way to increase the extensibility of the hamstrings over time. They are excellent stretches and are often used with light weights as warm-ups for the deadlift and the squat.

DEADLIFTING FROM BLOCKS

Another variation on the deadlift is to do the exercise while standing on blocks. By adding their height to the range of motion, the blocks increase

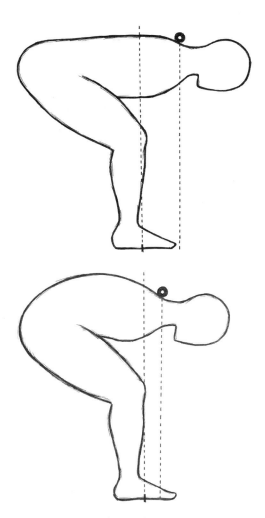

Figure 7-29. Two versions of the goodmorning.

the amount of work done (you can get the same effect by using plates with a smaller than 17-inch diameter). The blocks also add more knee extension – and therefore more quadriceps – to the exercise. Because the bar is farther away from lockout, the lifter needs more knee and hip flexion to assume the start position at the bottom, and the more acute angles require more hamstring extensibility for the lifter to assume the start position with an extended lumbar spine. These requirements make it more difficult for inflexible people to get in a correct start position, so not everybody can do this exercise. Be aware that for obvious reasons, a deadlift on blocks is an even more stressful movement than the full deadlift, so treat it with respect. No sets across with max weights, because deadlifts on blocks are an assistance exercise; use them at sub-max loads to accumulate work and to make the deadlift easier off the floor.

GOODMORNINGS

The goodmorning is sometimes thought of as a squat variation since the bar is taken out of the rack, as in a squat, and carried on the traps. But since the goodmorning functions as a back and hamstring exercise, with no more knee extension than an RDL, and with lots of elements of pulling mechanics in the movement of the bar, a case can be made for considering it a deadlift variation. Goodmornings get their name from the rather tenuous similarity between their appearance and that of a subordinate individual greeting his superiors in the a.m. They are an old weight room exercise, largely unused today, but they are worthy of consideration as a way to strengthen your pull.

In a goodmorning, the bar sits on top of the traps, as it does in a high-bar squat. Basically, you perform a goodmorning by bending over with the bar on your neck until your torso gets to parallel with the ground or lower and then returning to an upright position. The movement is similar to that of the Romanian deadlift in that the whole thing is essentially a hip extension that begins with an eccentric contraction – think of it as an RDL with the bar on your neck.

Figure 7-30. The flat-backed version of the goodmorning.

In the RDL, as with a pull, the bar stays over the middle of the foot, with a vertical bar path; in the goodmorning, the bar makes an arc as it is lowered. The arc occurs because the distance from the bar to the hips along the back is usually longer than the distance from the hips to the unlocked knees, and when the bar is lowered, it travels forward (Figure 7-29). This arc produces the intentional departure of the bar from a position of balance above the mid-foot, thus creating a moment arm between the bar and the balance point and using that as an aspect of the resistance in the exercise, as a heavy barbell curl does. As the weight gets heavier – and as the resulting center of mass of the lifter/barbell system gets closer to the bar – the bar path moves closer to the mid-foot.

There are two ways to do goodmornings: flat-backed and round-backed. The flat-backed goodmorning places the hips a little farther back at

the bottom of the movement than they are at the bottom of the RDL (since the bar is on top of the traps instead of hanging below the scapulas), even though the bar is in front of the toes. The round-backed version allows both the bar and the hips to stay closer to the mid-foot balance point. The difference is in the effective length of the back – the flexed spine is effectively "shorter" than the spine in rigid extension – and thus the two movements differ in the length of the moment arm they create between bar and hips.

Flat-backed goodmornings are the most like the RDL. The knees are unlocked, the chest is up, the low back is arched, and the bar is on the traps, with the hands pulling it down into the neck to keep it from rolling or sliding up at the bottom. (It is important to stabilize the bar against your neck and keep it from sliding, especially when you're using a bar with a center knurl; it will most assuredly dig a ditch in your neck if it moves.) The movement basically consists of sliding your hips back to lower the bar down as far as hamstring flexibility permits before your low back rounds. The idea is to keep the back in extension the whole trip down and up, and the parallels to the RDL should be clear. Your flexibility will determine your depth, and the goodmorning improves hamstring length; there is not a much better stretch than a strict flat-backed goodmorning.

The round-backed goodmorning is a completely different exercise. We have many times described the efficient and safe back position as "normal anatomical position" – thoracic and lumbar extension. This position is the best way to load the intervertebral discs and the most efficient way for force to be transmitted along the torso. But there are many situations, either at work or in many sports, where lifting must take place under circumstances that prevent an ideal extended-spine position, and it makes sense for post-novice lifters to train for this eventuality. Strongman competitions, for example, involve stone lifting, where a large stone that cannot be placed in a position that allows the competitor's spine to be extended must be lifted off the ground to an upright position. The trip from the ground to hip and knee lockout has to be done with the back in flexion. Or a situation may arise "in the field" that requires you to lift an object – perhaps a fellow soldier in 85 pounds of kit – whose shape has no respect for your finely developed sense of correct kinematics.

If spinal flexion is the position that must be used, the big held breath is the mechanism that must stabilize it. The intervertebral discs are best positioned to bear a compressive load when they conform to their normal resting geometry. But lifting a load from the ground is not primarily compressive until the final stages of the pull, when the back becomes erect. Moment forces with a rotational or shear component are the primary stresses on the back as the load comes off the ground. If the spine is in flexion and its rigidity in flexion can be maintained, the submaximal loads normally encountered in

Figure 7-31. Round-backed lifting trains the back for situations where perfect lifting mechanics are not possible. Stone lifting is a good example of this.

a field situation can be safely handled, especially by a strong lifter used to handling much heavier weights. The same Valsalva maneuver used in all barbell exercises provides stability and protection for the spine in the less-than-optimal positions often encountered outside the gym.

Some round-backed lifting prepares you for this inevitable situation, and when planned and executed on your terms instead of the universe's, it can be made a productive adjunct to normal pulling and back work. The round-backed goodmorning deliberately employs less-than-optimum spinal mechanics in order to strengthen the back against the inevitable occurrence of bad mechanics during a fatigued deadlift attempt or a normal day at work. It is a relatively safe way to introduce this position in the context of a controllable, increasable barbell exercise.

Round-backed goodmornings are probably better than round-backed deadlifts because of the tendency to use lighter, safer weights for them and because of the lack of interference with the correct movement pattern in a lift that is already prone to errors. But since round-backed movements would have to be considered advanced exercises, and therefore not really indicated for inexperienced lifters, the advantages of round-backed goodmornings over round-backed deadlifts

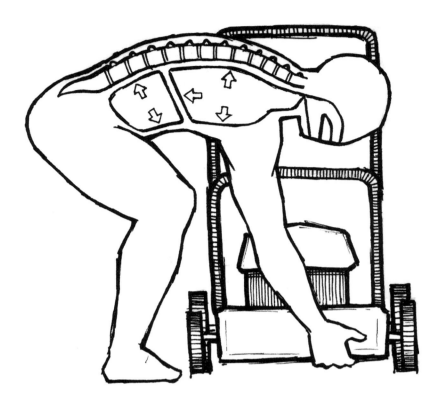

Figure 7-32. Handling an awkward object will not be so much a matter of the heavy weight, because heavy weights cannot be handled from a position of bad mechanics. The issue will be spinal stability in the awkward position. For a flexed spinal position where the mechanics cannot be improved, the best protection for the spine is a solid Valsalva maneuver.

are not really germane; advanced lifters should have no trouble separating two styles of deadlifting from each other. The important points are that round-backed lifting is not always bad, because it is inevitable, and that goodmornings done this way are a good introduction to this aspect of conditioning for sports and for life.

Take the bar out of the rack as you would for a flat-backed goodmorning, take a big breath, and start down by dropping your hips back. Immediately drop your chest, rolling it down toward your knees. It is usually possible to go lower than the flat-backed form permits, since adequate hamstring flexibility to maintain lumbar extension is not the limiting factor in this version. Maintain the flexed back position all the way down and back up, using your air to support the curve. Come back up by first lifting your back and then shoving your hips forward, and finally by raising your chest to coincide with the return

to the starting position. As with flat-backed GMs, higher-rep sets of 8 to 10 work well. Round-backed goodmornings are an optional, advanced exercise. No one's feelings will be hurt if you don't do them at all, but if you use them, do them right, and light.

The goodmorning allows for more direct stress on the hip extensors. But you must remember that this weight is sitting *on your neck*. Any work done by the hip extensors must be transmitted along the spine, and the leverage against the smaller cervical and upper thoracic vertebrae will be very high. Be careful about using lots of weight and generating high velocities; the goodmorning is an assistance exercise, not a primary lift, and it must be respected for both its usefulness and its potential for injury. The smartest of the strongest men in the world never use more than 225 pounds for the goodmorning, and since it is an assistance exercise, they use sets of 8 to 10 reps. Done correctly, goodmornings make the back stronger; done incorrectly, they can

Figure 7-33. The round-backed goodmorning.

make the back injured. Use good judgment when deciding how much weight to use. There will never be a reason to use more than 35% of your squat for sets of 8–10, and there is no reason to do them at all until 35% of your squat is 95 pounds.

Press Variations

Two main variations here: the behind-the-neck press and the push press.

BEHIND-THE-NECK PRESSES

The first thing that usually comes to mind when people think of different ways to press overhead is the behind-the-neck version, along with its close relative, the Bradford Press, which involves changing the bar position from front to back during the press. When the bar is behind the neck, the shoulders are put in a position that is not particularly advantageous under a heavy load. This position is right at the edge of the shoulder's range of motion and puts a lot of stress on the ligaments that hold the shoulder together.

The shoulder (or glenohumeral) joint is formed by the articulation of three bones: the clavicle or "collarbone," the scapula, and the humerus. The head of the humerus is the ball, and the *glenoid fossa* of the scapula is the socket of this ball-and-socket joint. The glenoid is a rather stingy little cup, not a nice deep socket like the acetabulum of the pelvis, and it depends much more on ligamentous and tendinous support for its integrity than the hip does. The net effect of this arrangement is a joint that is less stable at the edge of its range of motion than might be desired. The behind-the-neck press places the humeral head in just about the worst position it can assume under a load. If this exercise is to be used in a program safely, it has to be done with such light weights that it becomes almost a waste of time if strength is the goal. It has been done with heavy weight by big strong men, but none of them got that way with this exercise.

Push presses

A better exercise is the push press. It is more than just cheating the press with your legs. The push press uses momentum generated by the hips and knees to start the bar up, and then uses the shoulders and triceps to go to lockout, as in a normal press. The movement begins with a stretch reflex, where the knees and hips unlock, you drop down a little,

and then you drive back up – the extensors lengthen a little and then immediately contract forcefully into lockout. This sharp extension provides enough drive to get the bar off the shoulders and started on its way up. It is not really a "push" so much as it is a bounce, since the knees and hips do not unlock and then stop in the unlocked position. It is exactly as though you are trying to bounce the bar up off of your shoulders by using your hips and legs.

This bounce requires that the bar be resting on the meat of the deltoids when this upward force gets there. If the bar is being held in the hands – resting on the palms or fingers instead of seated firmly on the shoulders – then the force of the bounce gets absorbed in the elbows and wrists instead of being transmitted to the bar. This may mean that the grip

Figure 7-34. The push press.

Figure 7-35. The tendency to dip to the toes instead of staying flat-footed introduces a forward component into the upward motion. You can control this motion by thinking about keeping the weight on your heels during the dip. A balanced dip distributes the stress evenly between the hips and the knees.

for a push press is a power-clean grip, wider than you use for a press, since longer forearms make the bar harder to set on the delts with a standard press grip. The solid connection between the bar and the shoulders allows the full effects of the hip and leg drive to carry the bar on up. A full breath before each rep braces the torso and makes the push more solid.

More weight can be lifted with a push press than with our press technique in chapter three, and certainly more than with a strict press, and for this reason, a heavy set of presses might get finished with a push press or two. A better approach is to keep the two exercises as separate as possible in your mind, choosing your work weights carefully enough that a set of five presses does not turn into a set of two presses and a triple push press. After finishing your last set of presses, you might add extra work in the form of two heavier sets of push presses. Or better yet, you could use push presses as a completely separate exercise on a different day, either after bench presses or as their own primary upper-body exercise.

In addition to the same problems that affect the press, the push press has its own problems that derive from the involvement of the knees and hips. The most common error is the tendency to dip

forward onto the toes during the push. The bounce must come from the whole foot, not from the toes, or the lifter/barbell system gets displaced forward. If the dip has a forward component, the motion of down-and-forward turns into up-and-forward, instead of straight down and straight up. You will then have to "chase" the bar as it goes forward on the way up, diluting your shoulder drive. Correct this error by making sure your dip is to your mid-foot, and if you are dipping forward, the easiest way to ensure a straight dip is to raise your big toes inside your shoes before each rep. Your weight will shift back toward your heels, and once you get used to the way this feels, the problem will stop without your having to cue the big toes for each rep. This is a handy trick to learn, especially if you have entertained the possibility of any Olympic weightlifting; the dip that precedes the split jerk is essentially the same as the push-press dip, and if you correct it now, it will not be a problem later.

Push presses can be hard on the knees, believe it or not. The knee extensor tendons are subjected to some rather high forces during heavy push presses, and this is especially true if you are dipping to your toes. Stay out of your knees as much as possible to minimize the abuse. Knee wraps may help, but good form helps the most.

Just so you won't think they've been forgotten, assistance exercises for the power clean fall squarely in the bailiwick of Olympic weightlifting and are outside the scope of this book. Those of you who are interested are encouraged to contact a competent weightlifting coach and develop a relationship with the sport. There is no better way to use barbells to train for power production.

Ancillary Exercises

Not every assistance exercise necessarily duplicates a portion of a parent movement. There is no chin-up-like motion in any of the five major lifts, yet chins are a terribly useful exercise for lifters at all stages of training advancement. Chin-ups are multi-joint, they involve the movement of the whole body, they work many muscle groups, and they depend on a complete range of motion and correct execution for their quality – all characteristics of the major exercises. In contrast, it is difficult to do a wrist curl wrong, and really, who cares if you do? Good ancillary exercises contribute to functional movement the same way the major lifts do: they work several joints at one time through a range of motion that, when made stronger, contributes to performance in sports and work.

Ancillary exercises have traditionally been performed for higher reps than the core lifts are. This is not necessarily a hard-and-fast rule; some of these movements are very valuable as strength exercises in and of themselves. Some lend themselves better to this than others: weighted chin-ups and dips are quite useful at lower reps and heavy weights, whereas heavy weighted back extensions can be rather hard on the knees. Each exercise has its own specific applications and fits into each individual trainee's program in different ways.

CHIN-UPS AND PULL-UPS

Possibly the oldest resistance exercise known to the human race is the pull-up. Arboreal primates use this movement in the process of locomotion, and ever since we've been standing on the ground, it's been difficult to resist the temptation of grabbing a branch overhead and putting our chins up over it. And you should be strong enough to do that; the pull-up is not only a good exercise but also a very good indicator of upper-body strength. If you can't do very many chin-ups, your press and bench

Figure 7-36. The chin-up (*left pair*) uses a supine grip, and the pull-up (*right pair*), done in the power rack, uses a prone grip.

press will increase as you get stronger on this very important exercise. And that is why it is the only ancillary exercise included in the novice program.

Chin-ups and pull-ups are most famous for their effects on the latissimus dorsi muscles (the "lats"), but they are equally important for the other muscles of the upper back – the rhomboidius, the teres major, the serratus groups, and the rotator cuff muscles, as well as the forearms and hands. Chin-ups even work the pecs a little, if done from a diligent dead hang, and abs, if enough reps are used to get them fatigued.

In this book, the term "pull-up" refers to the version of the exercise with the hands prone, while "chin-up" or just "chin" refers to the version done with supine hands. The major and significant difference between the two is the biceps' involvement in the chin-up and the lack of it in the pull-up. The addition of the biceps makes chin-ups a little easier than pull-ups, as well as adding the aesthetic elements of arm work to the movement. Pull-ups are harder, and they probably emphasize lat involvement more since the absence of the biceps means that something else must do its work. Because of the pronation, pull-ups also might aggravate the elbows for a lifter who is not very flexible. The prone grip shortens the distance between grip and shoulders; the supine grip tends to increase this distance if you don't pay attention to keeping it close (Figure 7-37, right). So the pull-up might seem easier for some people if they stay too far away from the bar on chin-ups. Once your strength permits, you can add weights to strict chins and pull-ups for increased workloads. The more your trunk moves, the more trunk muscles are involved, and this is why abs can get sore. But any version of the chin-up or pull-up, where the whole body moves, is better than the machine version of the exercise, the "lat pulldown," in which only the arms move.

Chin-ups are a better introductory exercise than pull-ups, and perhaps a better exercise altogether because they involve more muscle mass. We'll use a bar set at slightly above the level of the up-reached fingertips while we're standing flat on the floor. When you are hanging from this level, your toes should just touch the floor. This is, of course, an

Figure 7-37. A correct chin-up starts with straight elbows and ends with the chin well over the bar, as high as possible. An incorrect chin-up displays an incomplete range of motion, starting with bent arms (*left*) or ending under the bar (*right*).

ideal height, and your equipment may be lower or higher. The crossbar at the top of a power rack works well, as might a bar set high in the rack pins. If you are fortunate enough to train in a gym enlightened enough to have provided chin bars, enjoy them, for they are not common. A bar that is 1¼ inches in diameter feels the best in most hands, unless they are unusually small. But it is not hard to make do, and most training facilities will have a place for the innovative trainee to chin.

In the chin-up grip, your palms are facing you, about shoulder width apart. Grip width can vary several inches depending on elbow flexibility; the more easily the hands can supinate, the wider the grip can be. The wider grip increases supination and biceps involvement. The wider the grip is, the greater the external rotation of the humerus is. The closer the grip is, the more internally rotated the humerus, the more abducted the scapulas, and the less involved the scapula retractors and posterior delts are. Grip width may not be a practical variable to manipulate due to the joint stress it causes at the extremes of wide and narrow, but since grip width affects the way the shoulders interact with the load, some shoulder injuries can be affected by grip width. A shoulder-width grip is good for our purposes and

Figure 7-38. The jumping chin-up, used to strengthen the lifter for a complete chin-up later.

presents no problems for most people. Chalk makes for a better grip and fewer calluses, and using it is a necessary. A knurled or rough bar destroys the hands and therefore adversely affects the rest of your training.

The movement itself is obviously simple: take your grip, and pull your elbows "down," which results in your leaving the ground. Each rep starts from a full stretch at the bottom, with elbows straight and scapulas stretched up, and is complete when your chin clears the bar. A more honest approach might be to touch your chest to the bar, but we'll count the rep if your chin clears the bar with your face forward, and your head not back. Try to stay as close to the bar as possible. The Gold Standard rep is done from a dead hang, with a slight pause at the fully stretched-out bottom. It is terribly common to see partial chins, which should be called "foreheads" or "nose-ups" and are usually accompanied by less-than-straight elbows at the bottom. For a high-rep set, you can use a stretch reflex at the bottom as long as the bottom is actually The Bottom. In this case, breathing will consist of a *quick* breath at the top of each rep. For a higher-rep set to failure (maybe 12 or more reps), you'll find that the first two-thirds to three-fourths of the set will be rebounded, and the last reps will be done from a dead hang as you take a couple of breaths between reps at the bottom. The same rules apply to pull-ups, if you decide to do them.

Cutting the rep short at either the top or the bottom is as bad as squatting high: the primary benefit of the exercise lies at the ends of the movement. The bottom stretches out the lats, and

the first shrug of the stretched-up scapulas down is all lats and upper back muscles. The finish at the top is biceps and triceps, and a completed rep means you have moved your body a constant, measurable distance through space. Each rep is therefore the same, and your effort becomes quantifiable, not just a flailing-around in the air.

But what if you can't do a complete chin-up? Lower the bar a little (or raise the floor, possibly an easier thing to do, artificially) and use a jump to get the movement started until you're strong enough to do it strict (Figure 7-38). Be sure to lower yourself under control to get the most out of the negative, and always use *only* as much jump as necessary. Or you can use resistance bands in the rack until you are strong enough to do the movement with only a jump. The ability to do an honest chin-up may be beyond some novices at a heavier bodyweight, and if you cannot do a good strict rep at all, it will

Figure 7-39. Chin-ups assisted by the use of resistance bands in your handy-dandy power rack.

Figure 7-40. The kipping pull-up.

be best to wait until your lats and arms are stronger from deadlifts and presses or until your bodyfat comes down enough to permit you to handle your bodyweight effectively on the bar.

Kipping chin-ups and pull-ups are gymnastic derivatives of the jumping version. The kipping version uses the momentum of a slight swing preceding the pull, when the swing is converted into an upward roll of the hips, translating the swing energy into upward movement. The kip distributes the movement over more muscle mass, using the abs, hip flexors, and lower back in addition to the lats and arms, so that more muscle mass is used in the exercise and more reps can be done. Strict chins and pull-ups concentrate the effort on less muscle mass and work it harder.

Kipping chin-ups and pull-ups have proven themselves to be useless as a way to strengthen the strict versions of the movement, and in the absence of enough strength to do the strict versions, they have proven to be dangerous for shoulder health. Resist the temptation to jump on any bandwagon that encourages short-term gratification at the expense of long-term progress. Many people who can do 15 kipping reps cannot do 2 dead-hangs, and have made *no progress* on their dead-hangs since they started cheating the movement with the kip. If you want to use kipping pull-ups or chin-ups in a conditioning workout, make sure your shoulders and arms are strong enough to do 8–10 strict reps first so that you don't hurt yourself chasing a meaningless

number. If you cut this important corner, shoulder surgery may be the only reward you receive.

Weighted chins and pull-ups are an excellent source of heavy non-pressing work for the upper body. Plates are suspended from a chain on a belt, or a dumbbell can be held in the feet if not much weight is used. A good rule of thumb is that when you can do 12–15 bodyweight reps, it is probably time to start doing some of the work weighted, possibly alternating higher-rep bodyweight workouts with lower-rep weighted workouts. Several sets across are appropriate for chins and pull-ups, either weighted, unweighted, or assisted. And many people have made steady linear progress by microloading their chins the same way they program the bench press and press, adding 1.5–2 pounds to three sets of five reps every workout. Try them all and see what works best for you.

Dips

The parallel-bar dip is a movement borrowed from gymnastics. It consists of supporting yourself by the arms, between and above two parallel bars, lowering your body down, and then driving it back up. The dip is a good substitute for the bench press if it cannot be done for some reason, and is far superior to the decline bench press, which there is no good reason to do. If the "lower pecs" and triceps are the object of your desire – the apple of your eye, as it were – then dips are your exercise. They are better than the decline because, like any

Figure 7-41. "Parallel-bar" dips, performed on an angled dip station. Note that the bottom of the movement drops the shoulders below the elbows.

good exercise, they involve the movement of lots of your muscles, besides the lower pecs and triceps. In this case, dips involve the movement of your entire body; they are like pushups in this respect. They are better than pushups because they can be weighted – and thus incrementally increased in load – and performed alone, whereas pushups cannot be weighted conveniently even with two people involved.

The quality of an exercise increases with the involvement of more muscles, more joints, and more central nervous system activity needed to control them. The more of the body involved in an exercise, the more of these criteria are met. When the whole body moves, a more nearly ideal state is achieved, with lots of muscles and nerves controlling lots of joints, and the central nervous system keeping track of lots of different pieces of the body doing many different things, hopefully correctly. By this logic, pushups are better than bench presses since pushups involve the movement and control of the entire body. But they are very difficult to do weighted, especially alone, because of the problems with loading the human body in this position. Were it possible, a good weighted pushup device would be in use today.

It has long been assumed that the bench press has solved that problem, when in fact it hasn't. The only thing moving in the bench press is the arms, so in this particular way the bench is to the pushup

what the lat pulldown is to the pull-up. But the bench does allow the same approximate movement to be loaded, and has allowed many people to increase their pushup numbers without high-rep pushups. Without adding weight, a fit person will find it difficult to train a pressing motion moving in the anterior direction without using very high reps, which are seldom appropriate for most training goals. Dips address both problems, allowing heavy weights to be used while the entire body moves during an upper-body exercise.

Unweighted dips are harder than pushups because the whole body is moving, not just the part that isn't supported by the feet. And for the more advanced trainee, dips are very easy to use weighted, either by hanging plates or other objects from a belt or by holding a dumbbell between the feet (an option which works well only for light weights). The anterior aspect of the movement is provided by the slightly inclined torso position, a function of the fact that the forearms stay vertical during the whole movement. If the body's mass is to be evenly distributed relative to the position of the hands on the bars – i.e., half of the mass in front of the hands and half of it behind the hands – then the body will have to assume an inclined position during the movement. There is enough angle to provide for a tremendous amount of pec involvement, using primarily the lower part of the muscle belly. And since the arms are operating downward relative to the upper body, the lats are also involved in the adduction of the humerus, adding even more muscle mass to the exercise.

Heavy weights can be used in this exercise, and many powerlifters have used it to maintain bench strength while an injury heals, one that the bench aggravates but that dips do not. Dips can be used unweighted for high reps or weighted, just like the bench would be trained, as a progressively loaded lift. The whole-body effects are felt more as weight increases, with very heavy efforts producing fatigue throughout the trunk and arms.

Dips are best done on a set of dip bars, a station designed for this purpose; most modern gyms do not have a set of parallel bars as might be found in a gymnastics studio or, previously, most gyms. Dip-station bars are usually 24–26 inches wide, and the most comfortable ones are made out of 1¼- or 1½-inch pipe or bar stock. They are between 48 and 54 inches high, tall enough to allow the trainee's feet to completely clear the ground at the bottom of the dip. They really, really need to be stable, either attached to a wall or built with enough base that any possible amount of wobble during the movement will not tip the bars. A non-parallel station, with the bars at a 30-degree angle, allows for a variety of grip widths that can more closely approximate the press, bench press, or jerk grip without adversely affecting the neutral hand orientation. But in a pinch (or a motel room), two chairs can serve as a dip station if they are stable when turned back to back.

To perform dips, select your grip and jump up into position on the bars, with your elbows locked and chest up. Take a big breath and hold it; start down by unlocking your elbows and leaning forward a little; and continue down until your shoulders are below your elbows. This position is easily identified by someone watching you; the humerus at the shoulder will dip below parallel. This criterion ensures a complete range of motion, plus a good stretch for the pecs. It also provides a way to judge the completeness of the rep — a way to quantify the work and compare performances between two people, thus serving the same purpose that the below-parallel criterion does in the squat. Drive your body up out of the bottom stretched

Figure 7-42. The dip station, shown above and in the previous figure, that permits a variety of grip widths.

position until your elbows are locked out, raising your chest into position directly above your hands on the bar. Exhale at the top after finishing the rep, and when you need a breath, be sure to take it only when you're locked out at the top. Don't exhale during the rep; the pressure provides rib cage support that is important for effective control of the body while it is moving.

The two most common errors in performing dips involve the completeness of the movement. Most people, when not being yelled at about it, will cut the depth off above parallel. They do this because it is easier to do a partial dip than a full dip, just as it's easier to do a partial squat than a full squat. A partial dip does not carry the injury potential that a partial squat does. But partial dips are not as valuable as deep dips for the same reason that half-squats are less than adequate: they work less muscle mass. If you go to the trouble of loading a dip belt to do the exercise weighted, and then

Figure 7-43. Dips can be done between two chairs if other equipment is not available or if you are traveling.

cheat the depth, you are just wasting training time and kidding yourself about how strong you are, just like when you cheat any other exercise. Do your dips deep, with a lighter weight if necessary, so you don't miss the actual benefit.

The other problem is a failure to lock out the elbows at the top between reps. This is not the heinous crime that cutting off the depth is, because it is usually unintentional. Tired triceps don't always know they are not completely contracted. The chest-up position at the finish helps cue the elbow lockout because it pulls the mass of the upper part of the torso behind the hands so that the triceps can extend the elbows against a more evenly distributed load.

And gentlemen, when you're doing weighted dips with a chain and a belt, be sure to arrange the

chain and plates in such a way as to minimize the chance of damage to the important structures that are in unfortunate proximity, in the event of a loss of control or a swinging plate.

Ring dips are best left to gymnasts or other people at lighter bodyweights who are not training primarily for strength. Ring dips are a dangerous movement for your shoulders, and weighted ring dips are foolish for anybody; it doesn't take very much lateral movement of the rings to place the shoulder joints in a position of such instability that it cannot be controlled. The shoulders can easily be impinged during a dip because the load is driving the humerus and AC joint together, and the addition of lateral moment force to the configuration has resulted in many avoidable surgical repairs to many rotator

Figure 7-44. Dips done in a power rack, making use of equipment that's already in the gym.

Figure 7-45. Weighted dips, done with a dip belt and plates.

cuffs (see Figure 3-7, page 80). Do your shoulders a favor, and just do your dips on bars.

BARBELL ROWS

First, **barbell rows are not a substitute for power cleans.** If you use them for this purpose, you have decided to omit a more important exercise in favor of an assistance exercise, an easier movement that does not provide most of the benefits of the more important basic exercise. I say this because of the prevalence of this substitution since the second edition of this book was published. Power cleans are one of the primary constituents of the program, and barbell rows – useful as they may be to intermediate lifters – are not.

Now that this is out of the way, let's get one more thing out of the way. Most people associate rows with machines that place you in a position to do them; cable rows or the machine version of the T-bar rows are the most common. But the most valuable rowing exercise is the one that makes you assume the position and maintain it throughout the set. This way, you get the benefits of both moving the bar through the rowing motion and doing the stability work needed to hold your back in the right position to do the rowing motion. As with all beneficial barbell training, the more work you have to do during the exercise, the better the exercise. So let's learn how to do a proper barbell row.

Barbell rows start on the floor and end on the floor, each and every rep. The bar does not hang from the arms between reps. Each rep is separated by a breath and a reset of the lower back. Starting from the floor enables the hamstrings and glutes to help get the bar moving, so that the lats and scapula retractors can finish a heavier weight than they could from a dead hang in the arms. Done this way, the exercise works not only the lats, upper back, and arms – the muscles typically associated with rowing – but the low back and hip extensors as well.

When you are rowing from the floor, the most critical factor in technique is the position of the lower back. The lumbar spine must be held in extension, just like it is in a deadlift and for exactly the same reason. A major difference between rows and deadlifts is the fact that in rows, the back angle changes as the bar comes off the floor; the knees are already extended and are not really involved much, so the hip extensors contribute to the initial pull from the floor by raising the chest using the locked back, transmitting this force to the bar. The finish occurs as the elbows bend and slam the bar into the lower rib cage area. The bar will leave the floor from a position directly below the scapulas, just as in a deadlift; but in a barbell row, unlike a deadlift, the back angle will never become vertical, and will not rise much higher than the shoulders at about 15–20 degrees above horizontal.

Approach the bar with a deadlift stance, maybe not quite as close; light weights can be pulled

Figure 7-46. The barbell row. Each rep starts and stops on the floor.

in a curved bar path to the belly as you warm up, but as the weight gets heavier, standard pulling mechanics will prevail and the bar will operate vertically over the mid-foot, as it does in all heavy pulling exercises. As weight is added, the bar will adjust itself to the correct position over the foot, whether you want it to or not. The grip width can vary quite a bit, but a grip that's about the same as the bench-press width is perhaps the best place to start. With heavier weights, you can use a hook grip or straps. Your eyes should be fixed on the floor a few feet in front of you. Don't look straight down, but don't try to look straight forward, either, because doing so will extend your neck too much.

Take a big breath, raise the bar from the floor with straight elbows to get it moving, and continue bringing it up by bending your elbows and slamming the bar into the upper part of your belly. This movement leads with the elbows, and you should think about slamming your elbows into the ceiling. The most important part of the technique of the barbell row is the back position: the spine must be locked into extension, with the chest up and the lower back arched, the whole time the bar is moving. After the bar contacts your belly, lower the bar back

to the floor, exhale and take a new breath, and reset your back before each rep. Don't attempt to hold the bar against your belly at the top or lower the bar too slowly; the barbell row is like the deadlift in that the work is intended to be mainly concentric. Since heavier weights will essentially be dropped, you'll want to use bumper plates for rowing, or use rubber mats under your standard iron plates.

The row requires that the bar be started off the floor with a hip extension, not a knee extension. With light weights, you can perform rows with just your arms, but as you approach work-set weights, hip extension becomes more important. Your knees will be almost straight, just slightly unlocked, with your hips higher than they would be in a deadlift before the bar moves up – the same position used to start a stiff-legged deadlift – so that there is little chance the quads can be used. The movement starts with your arms straight and with your chest coming up, raising your back angle slightly as the bar leaves the floor – a movement performed with the hamstrings and glutes acting on the rigid back, which is held in isometric contraction by the erectors. This initial hip extension starts the weight up, and your elbows catch the momentum and carry the bar on up with a shoulder extension and scapula retraction. The lats, triceps, biceps, forearm muscles, posterior deltoids, and smaller muscles around the shoulder blades are the prime movers here. The trunk muscles that stabilize the spine enable the trunk to act as a rigid platform, against which the force can be generated. The hamstrings and glutes, after their initial action off the ground, act to anchor the pelvis, and therefore the lower back, during the final rowing motion generated by the upper body. As is so often the case in complex human movement, muscles change actions during the course of the activity, starting off with one function and ending with another, and the function of the hip extensors during the barbell row is a good example of this shift.

Rows are not useful at weights so heavy that form is hard to maintain. The finish position, when the bar touches the belly, is controlled by some of the same factors that limit a clean, in that a weight that can be rowed correctly may be only 15 pounds lighter than a weight that cannot be rowed at all. A row that is not finished will not engage the range of motion that is unique to the exercise, and thus might as well be called a "partial SLDL." For this reason, sets of five or more reps are used, since weights that can be rowed for only a triple probably cannot be done correctly anyway. As with any ancillary exercise, it is much better to get good reps with a lighter weight for sets of 5, 8, or 10 and do several across than to lose the benefit of the exercise with a weight that is too heavy.

The first few reps will use only a slight – maybe less than 10 degrees – amount of hip extension, but as the set progresses and the upper body becomes fatigued, more hip extension gets thrown in to get the reps finished. Be sure to continue doing rows and not deadlifts. Your back should never get much above horizontal, and if your chest comes up too high on the last reps, the bar is hitting too low, the range of motion for the target muscles has shortened, and the weight is therefore too heavy.

As the weight gets heavy, there will be a pronounced tendency to allow your chest to drop down to meet the bar, completing the rep from the top down instead of from the bottom up. When

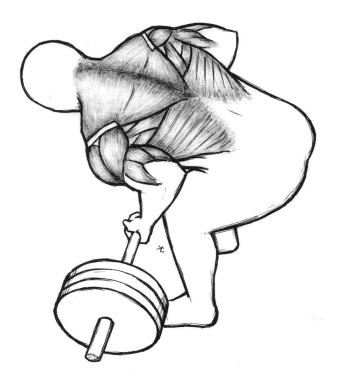

Figure 7-47. Seen from above, the supine-grip barbell row has the lats working across the back where the fibers of the muscle bellies are roughly parallel to the bar.

this chest drop becomes excessive, the weight is too heavy. And "excessive" is a rather subjective concept here. Someone might decide that no chest drop is allowable, in which case heavy weights cannot be used in the exercise. Or someone might decide that as long as the chest can be touched with the bar, the rep counts. This degree of variability is one of the things that distinguish an ancillary exercise from a primary exercise: if a large degree of variability is inherent in the performance of an exercise, it cannot be judged effectively or quantified objectively. For this reason, the barbell row makes a very good ancillary exercise but a very poor contest lift.

A variation on the standard barbell row is to supinate the grip, thus adding more biceps to the exercise. This reverse-grip row is irritating to the elbows in inflexible people; the rather extreme degree of external rotation of the humerus, combined with the completely supine hand, is irritating to the forearm muscles' insertion points on the elbows when they are flexed with a heavy weight, even though this rotation is usually tolerated well for chin-ups. The reverse-grip row can produce tennis or golfer's elbow very quickly, so if you decide to try this version of the movement, start with light weights and cautiously work up to your heavier sets the first time or two. And use a narrower grip than you would for the prone-grip version to minimize the grip position problems.

BACK EXTENSIONS AND GLUTE/HAM RAISES

There are a couple of ancillary exercises that require special equipment but are useful enough to make it worth locating. The Roman chair is an old piece of gym equipment that can be found in one form or another in most training facilities. It was developed in the late 1800s by the famous physical culturist Professor Louis "Attila" Durlacher from a device known as a "Roman column" that served a similar function. The Roman chair is a very basic bench (a bench has no parts that move during an exercise; a machine does) that supports the trainee's shins or feet from the top while supporting the thighs from below, thus allowing the trainee to be in a horizontal position, supported by his legs. You can use the Roman chair while facing up for abdominal work or while facing down for back work.

Ab workouts done on this bench are called *Roman chair sit-ups*, after the device. The back exercise has been for many years referred to as a "hyperextension," although that term specifically refers to a position that most joints don't like to be placed in, so the exercise is therefore preferably termed simply a "back extension." You may hear "hyperextension" used for the exercise from time to time, but it is losing its place as more people become familiar with biomechanical terminology.

The back extension is a very good way to directly work the spinal erectors using both concentric and eccentric contractions. The normal function of the trunk muscles is stabilization of the spine, using an isometric contraction that allows little or no relative movement of the vertebrae. But

Figure 7-48. The supine grip sometimes used for the barbell row. This lifter also uses the hook grip.

the trunk muscles can be strengthened by the active motion of the spine during this exercise, which functions like a reverse sit-up; the erectors extend the spine from a flexed position over a broad range of motion. The fact that the spine is extended in a position parallel to the floor is a function of the simultaneous hip extension, which the glutes (all of them, the maximus, medius, and minimus), hamstrings, and adductors perform in coordination with the spinal extension.

You perform the back extension by assuming a face-down position in a Roman chair, with the middle of your thighs on the front pad, the back of your legs (just below the calves and just above the heels, right on the Achilles tendon) jammed up into the foot pad or roller pad, and your body held parallel to the floor. Keep your knees very

Figure 7-49. A simple type of Roman chair.

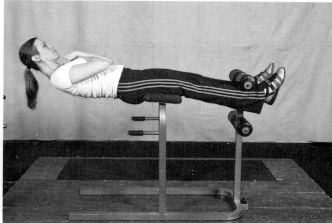

Figure 7-50. Back extensions (*left*) and Roman chair sit-ups (*right*).

slightly unlocked but not bent, with just a little tension from the hamstrings protecting the knees from hyperextension. The movement is an eccentric spinal extension – just let your chest drop down toward the upright of the bench, until your torso is perpendicular to the floor – and then an concentric spinal extension, raising the chest, followed by a hip extension, which kicks in the glutes and hamstrings to finish the exercise with the torso parallel to the floor. It is important to lead up with the chest, making it draw the back into extension – a full arch at the top of the movement. It works the spinal erectors, the glutes, and the upper hamstring function.

The glute/ham bench is a modified Roman chair that allows the back extension to be carried on up into a bodyweight "leg curl" in an exercise called a *glute/ham raise*. Glute/ham benches are becoming more popular as more people figure out the utility of the glute/ham raise. In the finish position of the glute/ham raise, your torso is vertical. This exercise thus includes all the elements of the back extension but with lots and *lots* more hamstring involvement. The modification that allows this added movement is a plate welded onto the frame right behind the foot roller (Figure 7-51). This plate gives the feet a place to push against, allowing a knee flexion to occur which carries the torso and thighs on up to the

Figure 7-51. A glute/ham bench, a modified adjustable Roman chair with toe plates for the full-range-of-motion exercise.

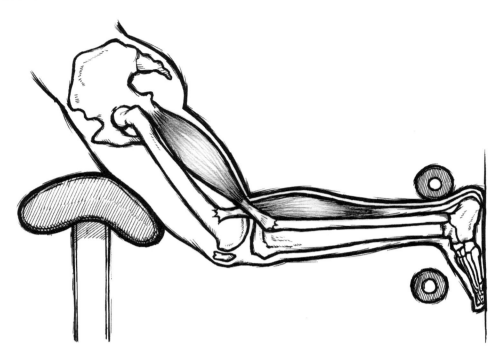

Figure 7-52. The glute/ham raise is essentially a back extension followed immediately by a bodyweight leg curl. The knee flexion can be completed because the feet are blocked by the plate, enabling the calf muscles to contribute their proximal function to knee flexion. Without the plate, you won't be able to fully flex the knees and reach an upright position, as shown in Figure 7-53.

vertical position. The hamstrings can do this with the plate against the feet because they have the help of the gastrocnemius, which cannot contribute to knee flexion unless its proximal function is facilitated by having its distal function blocked against the plate.

Muscles that cross two joints can affect movement around either joint. The *proximal function* is that which is performed by the joint closest to the center of the body, and the *distal function* is performed on the other end of the bone, the one farthest away. Most of the joints in the body are moved by muscles that also attach across another joint. The hamstrings are perhaps the most classic example because they both extend the hips and flex the knees – the glute/ham raise causes them to do both. The gastroc is another example of this type of muscle; it attaches to the calcaneus, or heel bone, by the Achilles tendon, and attaches to the lateral and medial epicondyles of the femur, behind the knee, as it splits into right and left heads. The gastroc both extends the ankle (an action referred to as "plantar flexion" in this particular instance) and flexes the knee. The other major calf muscle, the soleus, shares

the Achilles tendon with the gastroc but attaches proximally to the tibia and therefore does not cross the knee.

The glute/ham bench takes advantage of this anatomy and gives the feet a surface to push against. The weight of the body out in front of the forward pad traps the heels against the roller, allowing the body to be levered up, while the tension of the calves holds the feet against the plate. The plate blocks the ankle extension so that the contraction of the gastrocs is transmitted to the femoral insertions, causing the knees to flex. The glute/ham raise is essentially a back extension until the torso is parallel to the ground, where the hips have extended as well as the spine. Then the feet push the plate, and the knee flexion adds to the upward momentum generated by the back extension, carrying the torso on up to a vertical position, with the knees flexed at 90 degrees, the back and hips in extension, and the chest up.

The glutes engage more strongly here than they do in a simple back extension. They help generate momentum through the transition

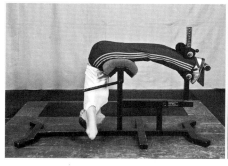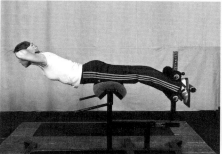

Figure 7-53. The glute/ham raise.

between the back extension and the knee flexion. Depending on the individual, the glutes might not be particularly perceptible as they work in the exercise. The trainee might not feel the glutes much because of the huge contribution of the hamstrings working over a much longer range of motion, and because the glutes contract very efficiently over a shorter distance, since their origin and insertion points are not that far apart. The poorer the conditioning of the athlete, especially with regard to the squat, the more noticeable the glutes will be in this exercise. And the poorer the conditioning, the less likely the trainee will actually be able to do an entire set of 10, or even a complete rep. Glute/ham raises are hard at first, but get easier very quickly as the movement pattern and the trainee's associated neuromuscular efficiency improve.

The movement is performed in essentially the same way as a back extension until the spine reaches the full arched position, which must occur in a coordinated fashion or the timing will be off. The knees then kick in to finish raising the chest up all the way to vertical. The best cue for this is the chest: think about raising your chest up fast and hard, and the hamstrings, calves, and glutes will do their job at the right time. The hands are held either crossed on the chest, the easier way, or with fingers locked behind the head, the harder way because more mass is farther away from the hips. Glute/hams like to be done at higher reps; 10 to 15 for three to five sets works best.

In this exercise, you are lifting the part of your body that is in front of the pad with muscles located behind the pad, and the more mass there is in front of the pad, the harder the job is to do. Most glute/ham benches are adjustable between the front and back pads for this reason, and the difficulty of the movement can be adjusted accordingly. Set the front pad back far enough to ensure that your crotch clears the pad, for rather obvious reasons, and to make the exercise hard enough for you to get enough work out of it. But be careful about setting the back pad so far forward that the front pad is too close to your knees. This position does increase the difficulty, but it also dramatically increases the amount of shear force on the knees, which are, after all, only held together by the cruciate ligaments, the capsular ligaments, and muscular tension. More-advanced lifters can carry weight behind the neck or on the chest to increase the work if necessary. *It is much better to add load with weight than with leverage in this exercise.*

When your thighs slide or roll down the pads, you have allowed allow your knees to bend before you have completed the back extension. Remember: anytime the knees bend, the hamstrings shorten. If you allow this to happen before you finish the back-extension phase of the movement, then 1) you have contracted the hamstrings without making them do any actual work, since they haven't contributed to the lifting up of the torso, and 2) you have placed them in a position of partial contraction, where they cannot contribute a full contraction to the exercise after the back-extension phase has finished. **Don't let your knees slide down from the thigh pad before your chest is up and your hips are extended.** This is the most common error people make, and it ruins the effect of the exercise. And for the same reason, do not do glute/ham raises on a bench constructed with rollers for the front pad.

When you first start doing them, glute/ham raises may be very hard. Typically, an untrained person cannot do a complete rep all the way up to vertical. This is fine; just come up as high as you can for each rep of the set, even though that height will deteriorate as the set goes on. The exercise gets easier very fast, as mentioned before, primarily because you learn how to do it more efficiently very quickly. Within six or seven workouts, most people can perform at least one complete rep. When you can do several sets all the way up, add load after a warm-up set by holding a plate to your chest or a bar behind your neck.

A good definition of "functional exercise" is a normal human movement that can be performed under a scalable, increasable load. By this definition, neither back extensions of any type nor sit-ups are functional exercises. Some people have trouble with them, taking the form of chronic back pain or a tendency to get repeated small back injuries. The normal function of all the muscles surrounding the spine is spinal stabilization, and the squat, press, and all pulling exercises provide plenty of work for these muscles by challenging their function along with those of the prime movers of the exercise. If you are an older lifter with a degree of the normal spinal degeneration that accompanies advancing age, you might decide that eccentric and concentric back work and flexion-based abdominal work cause more problems than they correct. If you are continually plagued with lower-back injuries, try eliminating all exercises involving spinal flexion and extension for a few weeks and see what happens to the injury frequency. Your abs and back muscles will remain strong from doing their primary jobs under the bar, and you'll stop having injury problems that interfere with your training.

CURLS

Since you're going to do them anyway, we might as well discuss the right way to do curls. Curls are performed to train the biceps, a muscle that commands an inordinate amount of attention from far too many people. But that is the nature of

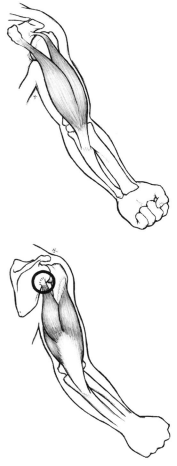

Figure 7-54. Both the biceps (*top*) and the triceps (*bottom*) muscles cross the elbow and shoulder joints, causing movement around both.

things, and who are we to question so fundamental a matter? Effective curls require an awareness of the biceps anatomy and a willingness to diverge from the conventional wisdom regarding technique.

The biceps muscle is one of the many muscles of the body that crosses two joints. (Technically, this muscle is the *biceps brachii*, or "arm" biceps, which is distinct from the *biceps femoris*, one of the hamstring muscles.) Like its partner the triceps, the biceps crosses both the elbow and shoulder joints, and therefore causes movement to occur around both joints. The chin-up uses a combination of elbow flexion and shoulder extension. But so does the pull-up, the difference being the prone versus supine grip. The elbow flexion during the pull-up is performed without much biceps involvement, while the biceps are heavily involved in the chin-up.

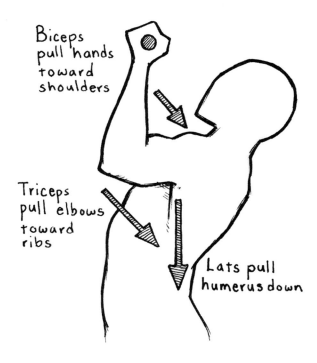

Biceps
pull hands
toward
shoulders

Triceps
pull elbows
toward
ribs

Lats pull
humerus down

Figure 7-55. Chin-ups are an example of an exercise involving elbow flexion (a function of the distal biceps and forearm) and shoulder extension (a function of the lats and proximal triceps).

This difference is due to the anatomy of the elbow. The distal end of the biceps attaches to the radius – the shorter of the two forearm bones – at a point called the *radial tuberosity*, located on the posterior and medial aspects of the radius when the forearm is pronated (the palm is facing back). "Supination" is the term given to the position in which the hand is rotated forward and the palm is up, and the palm-up position of the hand is referred to as "supine." The forearm supinates when the biceps attachment on the radius rotates inward and upward as the muscle shortens. In fact, if the biceps are in full contraction, the hand is supine. The pull-up, performed with a prone grip, utilizes very little biceps – and therefore proportionately more triceps and lats – while the chin-up uses lots of biceps. The elbow-flexion part of the pull-up is accomplished by the other elbow flexors: the brachialis, the brachioradialis, and some of the smaller forearm muscles.

The biceps also performs the movement known as shoulder flexion. Anatomical movement descriptions can sometimes be arbitrary, and flexion in the shoulder joint is defined as the forward and upward movement of the humerus. The biceps contributes to this movement because the proximal attachments (yes, there are two, thus the name *bi*ceps) are located on the anterior (forward) side of the scapula, the main bone of the shoulder joint. Because the tendon attachments cross the joint, the muscle moves the joint, and shoulder flexion is therefore a biceps function.

Elbow flexion, along with shoulder extension, is used whenever anything is grasped and pulled in toward the body. This is why chin-ups and pull-ups are such functional exercises: they duplicate this very normal motion under a load (Figure 7-55). In fact, elbow flexion is normally accompanied by shoulder extension; this is the way the arm is designed to work. And this is why elbow flexion with an immobile shoulder requires special equipment: the preacher curl was invented for the purpose of providing a way to work the biceps in isolation. The isolation of a single muscle group that moves a single joint seldom contributes significantly to other, more complex movements which include that muscle group. Remember that our definition of "functional exercise" is a normal human movement that can be performed under a scalable, increasable load. By this definition, no exercise that requires a machine or specific device to perform it can be a functional exercise (we're not including the barbell or power rack in the "specific device" category here, since we can't limit our training to the use of sticks and rocks). And if a muscle is isolated in an exercise, its tendon attachments are, too; this fact has a bearing on the injury-causing potential of these types of exercises.

Examples of shoulder flexion are harder to find, since raising things overhead is generally accomplished with a prone hand and a pressing motion that relies primarily on the deltoids and triceps. Shoulder flexion with a supine forearm pretty much exclusively occurs during exercise. But since the biceps do perform this function, it should be incorporated into biceps training so that this function gets worked – curls should involve shoulder flexion because they can. Barbell curls

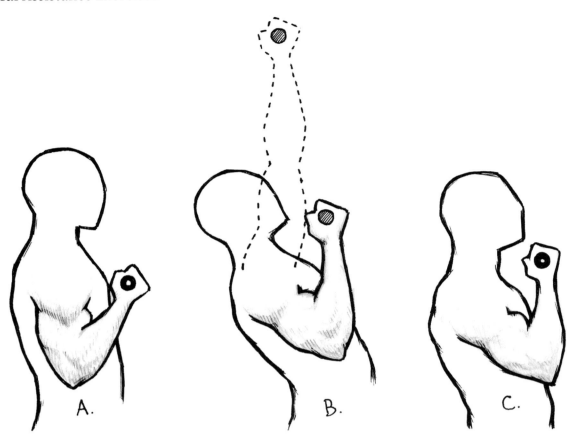

Figure 7-56. Three ways to work the biceps. (A) Elbow flexion in isolation: a strict curl. (B) Shoulder extension with elbow flexion: a chin-up. (C) Elbow flexion with shoulder flexion: a barbell curl as described in this book.

allow for both elbow flexion and shoulder flexion, they utilize a normal function of the arms, and they do not require specialized equipment (again, the bar being considered non-specialized). So barbell curls could be considered a functional exercise in the strict sense of the definition.

There are as many ways to do curls as there are muscle-magazine authors. If you're going to spend time doing all these variations, you have missed the point of this book. Let's assume that you haven't, and that you want the best way to work the most biceps in the least time. That way is the barbell curl, done with a standard Olympic bar. It is performed standing (since it cannot be performed seated), and it is best done out of a rack set at the same height that it would be for the press.

Approach the bar with a supine grip, with the width varying between somewhat closer than shoulder width and several inches wider. The wider the grip, the greater the degree of supination that will be required to maintain that grip; the greater the supination, the more the biceps will be contracted at full flexion. Depending on individual flexibility, a grip just wider than the shoulders will allow the full effects of the exercise to be expressed (this will be about the same grip used for the chin-up, for the same reasons).

This version of the barbell curl starts at the top, with your elbows in full flexion, as opposed to the more common method of starting at the bottom with extended elbows. When the bar is lowered to full extension and then raised back into flexion without a pause at the bottom, the biceps get the benefit of utilizing a stretch reflex to contract harder, thereby allowing the use of more weight. Breathing is done only at the top, with none of the supportive pressure released at the bottom. The elbows are kept against the rib cage and start from a position in front of the bar.

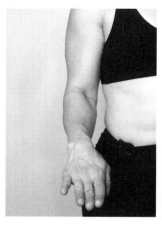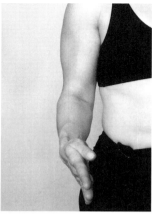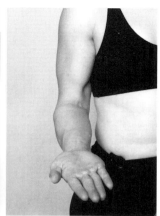

Figure 7-57. The effect of forearm supination on biceps contraction. The biceps brachii is the primary supinator of the forearm, and the biceps is not in complete contraction unless the forearm is fully supinated.

The barbell curl, like the goodmorning, intentionally uses a bar path that deviates from the mid-foot balance point. You lower the weight eccentrically in an arc, away from your body. In doing so, you create moment arms – between the bar and your elbows, between the bar and your shoulders, and between the bar and the mid-foot – so that you are intentionally manipulating the mechanics of the system to create the resistance. Keep your elbows against your ribs, in front of the mid-axial line that separates front from back. As your elbows get almost straight at the bottom of the curl, they slide back into a position behind this line. The elbows never straighten completely, because doing so would mean that tension is off the biceps, but they get close. Some tension is needed to initiate the concentric flexion that comprises the essence of the movement, and perfectly straight elbows make this very hard and inefficient.

Start the upward phase of the curl by sliding your elbows forward as you move the bar in the same arc that it moved in on the way down. Elbows stay against the ribs the whole way up; this keeps the hands in supination by maintaining the supine position of the forearm. A good cue for this position is to think about pushing the medial pad of the palm – the part just above the wrist and on the little-finger side of the hand – into the bar, as if this were the only part of the hand in contact with the bar. You will need to keep your wrists in a neutral position, neither flexed nor extended but in a position that keeps the metacarpal bones of the hand in line with the forearm. Drive the bar back up to the starting position, keeping your hands supine

and your elbows on your ribs. During this upward phase, your elbows will move forward to return to their position in front of the bar, producing shoulder flexion in addition to elbow flexion. It is common to see the elbows leave the rib cage and assume a position in line with, or even outside, the hands on the bar. This error involves the deltoids in the movement and reduces the biceps' involvement. Keep your elbows close to your ribs and make them slide forward on the way up.

During the curl, it will be very difficult to maintain a perfectly upright posture if you use any weight at all. The lifter/barbell system must balance over the middle of the foot, which means that as the bar moves forward through its arc, the

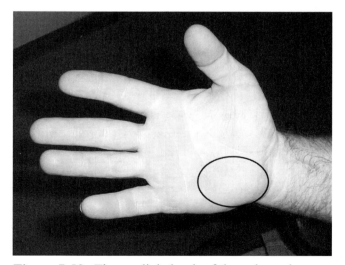

Figure 7-58. The medial chunk of the palm – the "hypothenar eminence" (see Figure 3-10) – is the key to ensuring maximum supination during a curl. Push the bar up while thinking about using this part of the hand.

Figure 7-59. The barbell curl. Note the starting position at the top with the elbows in flexion.

body must balance the mass of the bar by leaning back. The heavier the weight, the more the lean. It is neither necessary, desirable, nor possible to try to stay strictly upright during a heavy barbell curl. If you are training for strength, you must use heavier weights, and you will find that the physics of placing a heavy bar in front and your body in back cannot be circumvented. Do not flex or extend your knees at all, or let an excessive amount of upward movement out of the bottom be initiated by the hips instead of the elbows. "Excessive" is a judgment call – once again we see why some exercises are "ancillary." Cheat curls are a legitimate exercise, depending on what you want out of the movement. If a heavy weight is started with a little hip extension and finished with a substantial amount of unassisted elbow and shoulder flexion, the cheat curl is probably legit. But if you start it with your hips and knees and then dive

under the bar to receive it in full elbow flexion, you are doing a reverse-grip clean, defeating the purpose of the exercise, risking several injuries, and inviting the criticism of more experienced, disciplined lifters.

TRICEPS EXERCISES

Most of the triceps work that gets done in gyms all over the world is performed on some type of cable device. In most cases, the common "triceps pressdown" is the exercise of choice, being the one most frequently seen in magazines and exercise books, and being the easiest to do while looking in the mirror. But the simple pressdown only works the distal triceps function – elbow extension – and ignores the fact that the triceps crosses both the shoulder and the elbow and therefore has a proximal function as well. Shoulder extension is the proximal

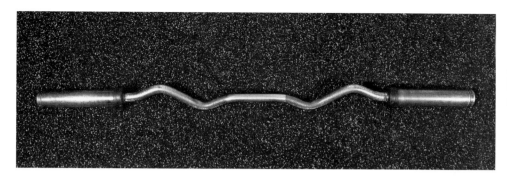

Figure 7-60. The EZ Curl Bar, used for lying triceps extensions.

function, and the most efficient triceps exercises incorporate both functions. Cable pressdowns can be done in this manner, but they have an interesting limitation: as you get stronger, you will eventually be able to use enough weight that your feet cannot stay on the floor.

There is a better triceps exercise, one that is so effective at building lockout strength for the bench press that Larry Pacifico called it "the fourth powerlift." It is the *lying triceps extension* (LTE), done on a flat bench in a supine position with heavy weights. Done correctly, it is safe, brutally hard, and very effective for general upper-body strength with an emphasis on the triceps. Done the way many foolish people do it – as a "skullcrusher" – it loses much of its effectiveness and safety.

The preferred equipment for the LTE is the EZ Curl bar, a cambered bar intended for doing curls as an alternative to using a straight bar. The EZ

Curl bar was invented back in the early 1970s by some poor bastard who probably didn't make a dime off of the thing. It apparently ended up with one of the big magazine publishers who also happened to sell equipment and who started marketing it as his own device. Typical situation.

The problem is that the EZ Curl bar doesn't work nearly as well for curls and for recruiting biceps contraction as a straight bar does. As we discussed earlier, the degree of supination of the forearm and hand directly affects the amount of biceps in contraction. The EZ Curl bar does in fact take the stress of supination off of the wrists and elbows, but it does so at the expense of a good biceps contraction. The camber of the bar is specifically intended to decrease the supination of the forearm, and anything less than full supination results in a less-than-complete biceps contraction.

Figure 7-61. The effect of supination on biceps contraction, and the main reason that the EZ Curl bar is best left for triceps work.

Figure 7-62. The lying triceps extension.

But the EZ Curl bar works perfectly for the lying triceps extension. The triceps is composed of three bundles of muscles, which originate on the humerus and the scapula and share a common insertion point on the olecranon process of the elbow. (The lateral and medial heads of the triceps originate on the humerus; the long head originates on the scapula.) The angle of the hand on the bar makes no difference in the quality of the triceps contraction. The more prone grip afforded by the EZ Curl bar is more comfortable for this exercise and does not reduce its effectiveness.

The thing that distinguishes the LTE from other triceps exercises is the inclusion of the proximal function of the triceps, where the design of the movement produces shoulder extension, using the long head of the muscle, as well as elbow extension. It also includes the lats, some pec, costal muscle, and abdominal involvement, and the forearms. This exercise dramatically increases the number of other muscles activated and is the first choice when you are adding a triceps assistance exercise to your program.

The LTE, like the bench press, requires a spotter at heavy weights. Take a position on the bench, with the top of your head just past the edge of the pad. Receive the bar from the spotter, who has deadlifted it into position, handed it to you, and

stepped back out of the way. The EZ Curl bar has three angles in the middle; take your grip on the inside-most angle with your hands prone (palms facing up), and the middle bend in the bar facing down. Your elbows will be pointed down the bench in external rotation, and the bar will be locked out over your shoulder joints, as in a bench press. Your chest should be up, butt in contact with the bench, feet in a stable position on the floor, and eyes looking at the ceiling for the whole rep (Figure 7-62).

Unlock your elbows while keeping your upper arms vertical, letting the bar arc backward behind your head and toward the floor. When your elbows get to about 90 degrees, let your shoulders rotate back to drop the bar down just above your head, touching your hair, down to about the level of the bench. This motion will stretch your triceps, deltoids, and lats, and when the bar is just below the level of the back of your head, let the stretch turn the rep around and start back up. Pull the bar back up with your elbows, and as they approach the top, extend them to lock out the bar in the start position.

Keep the bar as close to the top of your head as possible while stretching down to the bench, and lead up with the stretch reflex, like you're throwing the bar at the ceiling and using your elbows to start the throw. The stretch reflex adds a lot of range of motion – and power, if you move explosively – to the movement, making the LTE much more useful than the standard "skullcrusher." If you keep your elbows too straight and let the bar go back too far away from the top of your head, you lose some of the ROM around the elbows. A big breath at the top inflates the chest and makes the stretch reflex at the bottom more effective. When the LTE is done in this way, both shoulder extension and elbow extension are used, and more triceps mass is stressed over a longer ROM. Do sets of 10–15 reps with this exercise.

Barbell Training: There's Just No Substitute

There are lots of useless assistance exercises which contribute nothing to the performance of the major exercises or of sports activities, and which might do worse than merely waste time. Exercises that use only one joint, and that usually require machines to do, are non-functional in the sense that they do not follow a normal human movement pattern. They also quite often predispose the joint to overuse injuries, and the vast majority of weight room injuries are produced by these exercises. This is true not only by default, since it is obvious that in a world where most people only use machines, most of the injuries will occur on machines. Isolation exercises cause tendinitis because human joints are not designed to be subjected to the stress of movements in which all of the shock, moment force, tension, and compression are exclusively applied to one joint. There is no movement that can be performed outside the modern health club that involves only the quadriceps; the only way to isolate the quads is to do an exercise on a machine designed for that purpose. This is a function that hundreds of millions of years of vertebrate evolution did not anticipate. The knee is the home of many muscles, all of which have developed while working at the same time. Any exercise that deviates from the function for which the joint is designed contributes very little to the function of that joint and is a potential source of problems.

Exercise machines have made several people a lot of money, and while there's absolutely nothing wrong with that, they have been a very large diversion from more productive forms of training. The pendulum swings, and barbell training is once again being recognized as the superior form of exercise. Glad we could help.

PROGRAMMING

It is May 15, and you decide that this year you are going to get a suntan – a glorious, beautiful, tropical suntan. So you decide to go out in the back yard (to spare the neighbors and innocent passersby) to lay out at lunchtime and catch a ray or two. You lie on your back for 15 minutes and flip over to lie on your belly for 15 minutes. Then you get up, come in and eat lunch, and go back to work. That night, your skin is a little pink, so the next day you just eat lunch, but the following day you're back outside for your 15-minutes-per-side sunbath. You are faithful to your schedule, spending 30 minutes outside every day that week, because that's the kind of disciplined, determined person you are. At the end of the week, you have turned a more pleasant shade of brown and, heartened by your results, resolve to maintain your schedule for the rest of the month. So, here is the critical question: what color is your skin at the end of the month?

If you ask a hundred people this question, ninety-five will tell you that it will be really, really dark. But in fact it will be exactly the same color it was at the end of the first week. Why would it be any darker? Your skin adapts to the stress of the sun exposure by becoming dark enough to prevent itself from burning again. That's the ONLY reason it gets dark, and it adapts exactly and specifically to the stress that burned it. Your skin does not "know" that you want it to get darker; it only "knows" what the sun tells it, and the sun only talked to it for 15 minutes. It can't get any darker than the 15 minutes makes it get, because the 15 minutes is what it is

adapting to. If you just got darker every time you were exposed to the sun, we'd all be black, especially those of us who live in a sunny area, since we all get out of the car and walk into the house or work several times a day. The skin adapts not to total accumulated exposure but to the *longest* exposure – the hardest exposure. If you want your skin to get darker, you have to stay out longer in order to give the skin more *stress* than it has already adapted to. The widespread failure to comprehend this pivotal aspect of adaptation is why so few people actually understand exercise programming.

Exercise follows exactly the same principle as getting a tan – a stress is imposed on the body and it adapts to the stress, but only if the stress is designed properly. You wouldn't lay out for 2 minutes and assume that it would make you brown, because 2 minutes isn't enough stress to cause an adaptation. Likewise, only a stupid kid lays out for an hour on each side the first day, because the stress is so overwhelmingly damaging that it cannot be recovered from in a constructive way. Lots and lots of people come into the gym and bench 225 every Monday and Friday for years, never even attempting to increase the weight, sets, reps, speed, or pace between sets. Some people don't care, but some are genuinely puzzled that their bench doesn't go up, even though they have not asked it to. And some people bench press once every three or four weeks, or maybe even more rarely than that, using some arbitrary number like their own bodyweight for 10 reps, then 9, then 8, 7, 6, 5, 4, 3, 2, and finally 1 rep, and wonder why their bench doesn't go up, and also wonder why they're so damned sore all the time.

Your bench press strength doesn't adapt to the total number of times you've been to the gym to bench or to your sincerest hope that it will get stronger. It adapts to the stress imposed on it by the work done with the barbell. Furthermore, it adapts to *exactly* the kind of stress imposed on it. If you do sets of 20, you get good at doing 20s. If you do heavy singles, you get better at doing those. But singles and 20s are very different; the muscles and nervous system function differently when doing these two things, and they require two different sets of physiological capacities, and thus cause the body to adapt differently. The adaptation occurs in response to the stress, and *specifically* to that stress, because the stress is what causes the adaptation. This is why calluses form where the bar rubs on the hand, and not on the other parts of the hand, or on your face, or all over your body. It can obviously be no other way.

Furthermore, the stress must be capable of being recovered from. Unlike the 2 hours of sun the first day or the 55 bench reps once a month, the stress must be appropriate for the trainee receiving it. If the stress is so overwhelming that you cannot recover from it in time to apply more of it in a timeframe which permits accumulated adaptation, it is useless as a beneficial tool that drives progress.

An awareness of this central organizing principle of physiology as it applies to physical activity is essential to program design. **Exercise and training are two different things.** *Exercise* is physical activity for its own sake, a workout done for the effect it produces today, during the workout or right after you're through. *Training* is physical activity done with a longer-term goal in mind, the constituent workouts of which are specifically designed to achieve that goal. If a program of physical activity is not designed to get you stronger or faster or better conditioned by producing a specific stress to which a specific desirable adaptation can occur, you don't get to call it training. It is just exercise. For most people, exercise is perfectly adequate – it's certainly better than sitting on your ass.

But for athletes, an improvement in strength provides more improvement in performance than any other adaptation does, especially if the athlete is not already very strong. Strength is the basis of athletic ability. If you are a good athlete, you are stronger than a less-good athlete at the same level of skill. If you want to be a better athlete, you get stronger. If you are already very strong, you need to devote most of your attention to the development of other aspects of performance. But there is a very high likelihood that you are not that strong, since most people are not. You may think you're very strong, but really, you know you could get stronger, don't you? Sure you do. You may have convinced everybody else that you're strong enough; you may even be convinced of this yourself. Your coach may have told you so, too. This deception is not productive, though, because if you can get stronger, you should do so, and a lack of strength may be why you're not performing as well as you know you should be. If your progress is stuck, and has been for a while, get stronger and see what happens. And for a strength training program to actually work, you must do something that requires that you be stronger to get it done, and this requirement must be inherent in the program design.

The less experienced the athlete, the simpler the program should be, and the more advanced the athlete, the more complex the program must be. We are going to take advantage of a phenomenon I have called the "Novice Effect." Simply described, this is what happens when a previously untrained person begins to lift weights – he gets stronger very quickly at first, and then improves less and less rapidly as he gets stronger and stronger. It is nothing more than the commonly observed principle of diminishing returns, applied to adaptive physiology. Rank novices are not strong enough to tax themselves beyond their ability to recover, because they are so thoroughly unadapted to stress; they have made almost no progress on the road to the fulfillment of their athletic potential, and almost anything they do that is not heinous abuse will cause an adaptation.

When an untrained person starts an exercise program, he gets stronger. He always does,

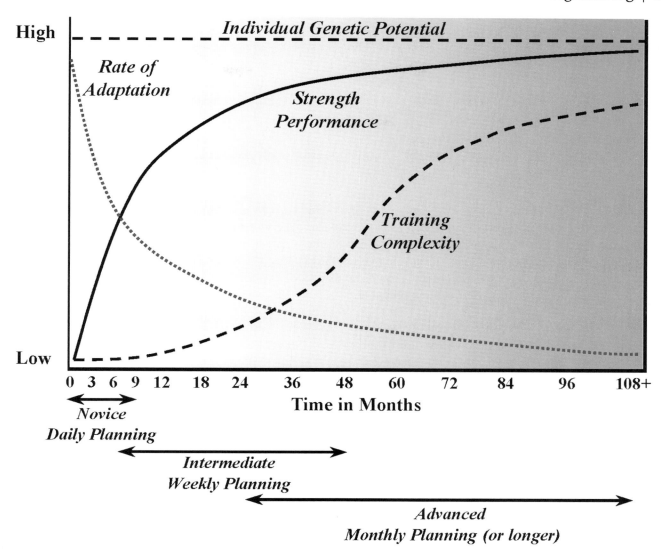

High — Individual Genetic Potential

Rate of Adaptation

Strength Performance

Training Complexity

Low

0 3 6 9 12 18 24 36 48 60 72 84 96 108+

Time in Months

Novice Daily Planning

Intermediate Weekly Planning

Advanced Monthly Planning (or longer)

Figure 8-1. The generalized relationship between performance improvement and training complexity relative to time. Note that the rate of adaptation to training slows over a training career.

no matter what the program is. He gets stronger because anything he does that is physically harder than what he's been doing constitutes a stress to which he is not adapted, and adaptation will thus occur if he provides for recovery. And this stress will always produce more strength, because that is the most basic physical adaptation to any physical stress that requires the body to produce force. For a rank novice trainee, riding a bicycle will make his bench press increase – for a short time. This does not mean that cycling is a good program for the bench press; it just means that for an utterly unadapted person, the cycling served as an adaptive stimulus. The problem with cycling for a novice bench-presser is

that it rapidly loses its ability to act as an efficient enough *systemic* force-production stress to continue driving improvement on the bench, since it does not produce a force-production stress *specific* to the bench press.

The thing that differentiates a good program from a less-good program is its ability to continue stimulating the desired adaptation. So, by definition, a program that requires a regular increase in some aspect of its stress is an effective program for a novice, and one that doesn't is less effective. For a novice, any program is better than no program at all, so all programs work with varying degrees of efficiency. This is why everybody thinks *their*

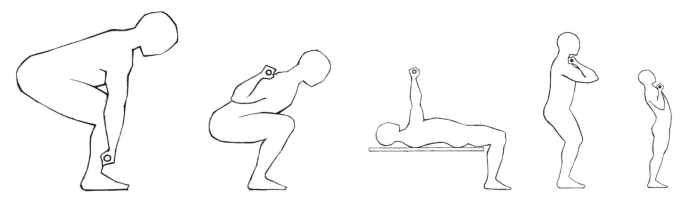

Figure 8-2. In order from left to right, strongest to weakest, the continuum of potential strength gains for the basic barbell exercises for the early part of the typical trainee's career. The deadlift, squat, bench press, and press actively involve decreasing amounts of muscle mass. Other factors affect the power clean; although it involves a large amount of muscle mass, the technical requirements of the lift place it somewhere between the bench press and the press in strength and improvement potential.

program works, and why you'll always find perfectly honest testimonials for every new exercise program on TV or the Internet. But nothing works as well as moderately increasing some loading parameter each time, for as long as an adaptation to the increase continues to occur, because it is specifically designed to produce both stress and adaptation.

And since the best way to produce athletic improvement in novices is to increase strength, a program that increases total-body strength in a linear fashion is the best one for a novice athlete to use if he is to improve his performance the most in the shortest time possible. It seems rather apparent that there can be only one efficient way to program barbell training for a novice, and that is to apply a linear increase in force-production stress while using basic exercises that work the whole body. If applied in a way that can be supported by adequate recovery from the stress in a timeframe that efficiently produces progress, this approach *always* produces a linear increase in strength because it takes advantage of the most basic rule of biology: organisms adapt to their environment if the stress causes an adaptation and if the stress is not overwhelming in its magnitude.

Rank novices can be trained close to the limit of their ability every time they train, precisely because that ability is at such a low level relative to their genetic potential. As a result of this relatively

hard training, novices get strong very quickly. (Novices can recover from relatively hard training because they are weak, and the training is not really that hard in absolute terms.) *Weak people can obviously get stronger faster than strong people can.* But that changes rapidly, and as you progress through your training career, your program should get more and more complicated as a result of the changing nature of your adaptive response. The intermediate trainee has advanced to the point where the stress required for change is high enough that when that stress is applied in consecutive workouts, it exceeds the trainee's capacity for recovery within that period of time. Intermediate trainees are capable of training hard enough that some allowances for active recovery must be incorporated into the training program, but progress still comes faster for these athletes when they are challenged often by maximum efforts. Advanced athletes are working at levels close enough to their genetic potential that great care should be taken to ensure enough variability in the intensity and volume that overtraining does not become a problem. These principles are illustrated in Figure 8-1 and are discussed at length in *Practical Programming for Strength Training, Second Edition* (The Aasgaard Company, 2009).

So, as a general rule, you need to try to add weight to the work sets of the exercise every time you train, until you can't do this anymore. This is the basic tenet of "progressive resistance training," and setting up the program this way is what makes it different from exercise. For as long as possible, make sure that you lift a little more weight each time. Everyone can do this for a while, and some can do it for longer than others, depending on individual genetic capability, diet, and rest. If you are challenged, you will adapt, and if you are not, you won't. Training makes the challenge a scheduled event instead of an accident of mood or whim, and certainly not a random occurrence within an exercise program.

Before you even get through the door of the weight room, you should already know every single thing you will do while you are there, the order in which you will do it, how much weight you will do it with, and how to determine the next workout based on what you do today. No one should ever arrive to train not knowing exactly what to do. Wandering around the gym, deciding what looks fun, doing it until the fun stops, and then doing something else is not training. Each training session must have a definite achievable goal, usually an increase over the previous workout in the amount of weight lifted, or another definable objective based on the person's training history.

Strength in each exercise will progress differently, due to differences in the amount of muscle mass involved and in the sensitivity of the movement to technique problems. The more muscle mass involved in an exercise, the faster the exercise can get strong and the stronger it has the potential to be. The deadlift, for instance, improves rather quickly for most people, faster than any of the other lifts, due to its limited range of motion around the hips and knees and the fact that so many muscles are involved in the lift. In contrast, the press goes up rather slowly due to the smaller muscles of the shoulder girdle, while the shorter kinetic chain of the bench press allows it to progress faster than the press.

In a trained athlete, the deadlift will be stronger than the squat, the squat stronger than the bench press, the bench press and the power clean close to each other (with the bench usually a little stronger), and the press lighter than the other four. This distribution holds for the majority of athletes and is predictive of what should happen. For example, if you bench more than you deadlift, something is out of whack. You may have a grip problem, an injury, or a motivational discontinuity, e.g., a strong dislike for the deadlift. In any case, this situation should be addressed lest a strength imbalance cause problems for other lifts. The differences in the nature of the lifts must be considered in all aspects of their use in the weight room.

Learning the Lifts

Learn the squat first because it is the most important exercise in the program and its skills are critical to all the other movements. When you begin this program, if you have been taught the movement incorrectly, you will have to unlearn it (the worst-case scenario); if you have never been shown the movement, it will be easier to learn because you won't have incorrect motor pathways to fix (the best-case scenario). It is much harder to correct an embedded movement pattern than it is to learn a new one, as any sports coach will attest. The problem is particularly evident in the weight room, where correct technique is the essence of everything we do, and a stubborn form problem resulting from prior incorrect instruction can be costly in terms of time and slowed progress.

Assuming that you have time to learn more than one exercise the first day (and you should arrange things so that you do), the next exercise will be the press. The squat has fatigued the lower body, and the press gives it an opportunity to rest while another skill is introduced. The press is usually easy to learn because of the absence of preconceived notions acquired from pictures in the muscle magazines or from helpful buddies. Since the press is relatively unfamiliar to most people these days, it makes a good first-day upper-body exercise, grabbing your attention so that you know we're actually doing something different in the weight room this time around.

The deadlift will be the last thing to learn the first day. The deadlift is where you learn to set the lower back, and doing this at the conclusion of the first day, after the squat, will solidify the concept of back position and make it more understandable to your body and your mind. The mechanics of the correct pull from the floor are crucial to the clean, and the deadlift serves as the best introduction to the idea that pulling from the floor is not complicated. If the squat that first day has been difficult or has taken a long time, or if you are older or very deconditioned, the first deadlift workout might just be an introduction with light weight, and no attempt to go to a heavy work set. Going light prevents excessive soreness after the first session, which would definitely compromise the second one. The next deadlift workout can be heavier, and the target weight more easily and accurately determined, after you have recovered from the first squat workout.

You will learn the other two lifts at the next workout, provided that you encountered no major problems. Start the second workout with the squat, and then learn the bench press. Your shoulders and arms may be tired from the press, but this will have little effect on the bench press, a stronger movement anyway. The bench press provides the same break for the lower body between exercises that the press does, and you will need this break because you will be power cleaning next.

The power clean, being the most technically challenging of the exercises, should be introduced last, and only after the deadlift is correct off the floor. If that occurs in the first workout, you can learn the clean in the second workout. If you need more time to correct the deadlift, take it. Introducing the power clean too early will produce problems, since the bottom part of the movement depends on the deadlift's being fairly automatic.

WORKOUT ORDER

For novices, and in fact for most advanced trainees, a very simple approach to training should be taken. Effective workouts need not be long, complicated affairs. Many people are under the impression that progress in the weight room means learning more ways to curl, the basic one or two not being sufficient. But progress means more *strength*, not more exercises; the variable we manipulate is load, not exercise selection. You do not need to do many different exercises to get strong – you need to get strong on a very few important exercises, movements that train the whole body as a system, not as a collection of separate body parts. The problem with the programs advocated by all the national exercise organizations is that they fail to recognize this basic principle: the body best adapts *as a whole organism* to stress applied to the whole organism. The more stress that can be applied to *as much of the body at one time* as possible, the more effective and productive the adaptation will be.

For a rank novice, the simplest of workouts is in order. This short program can be followed for the first few workouts:

A	**B**
Squat	Squat
Press	Bench Press
Deadlift	Deadlift

The two workouts alternate across the MWF schedule for the first couple of weeks, until the freshness of the deadlift has worn off a little and after the quick initial gains establish the deadlift well ahead of the squat. At this point the power clean is introduced:

A	**B**
Squat	Squat
Press	Bench Press
Deadlift	Power Clean

After the first couple of weeks, you squat every workout and alternate the bench press and press, and the deadlift and power clean. This schedule is for three days per week, allowing a two-day rest at the end of the week. It will mean that one week you press and deadlift twice, and the next week you bench and power clean twice. Do the exercises in the listed order, with squats first, the upper-body movement second, and the pulling movement third. This sequence allows the squat to get everything warm for the next exercise (it does this well); then the upper-body exercise allows the legs and back to rest and recover for the pulling movement to be done next.

For most people, and for quite some time, this schedule will work well. After two or three more weeks, chin-ups can be added as the only really useful assistance exercise at this point in the program. You might decide to add three sets of chins after your power cleans, and stay with this program for as many months as possible. Or, back extensions or glute/ham raises can be added in place of pulling every workout, dropping the deadlift frequency to every fifth workout, alternated with power cleans. This might be necessary if recovery is becoming a problem, as it might be for an older trainee, a female trainee, or someone who just refuses to eat and sleep enough. Now the program looks like this:

A	**B**
Squat	Squat
Press	Bench Press
Deadlift/Power Clean	Back Extensions
	Chin-ups/Pull-ups

This makes the next two weeks look like this:

Week 1

Monday	**Wednesday**	**Friday**
Squat	Squat	Squat
Bench Press	Press	Bench Press
Back Extensions	Deadlift	Back Extensions
Chin-ups		Chin-ups

Week 2

Monday	**Wednesday**	**Friday**
Squat	Squat	Squat
Press	Bench Press	Press
Power Clean	Back Extensions	Deadlift
	Chin-ups	

Any supplemental exercises other than chin-ups should be chosen *very carefully* so as not to interfere with progress on these five crucial movements. Remember: if progress is being made on the primary exercises, you are getting stronger and your objective is being accomplished. If in doubt, leave it out. Ha.

After you progress beyond the novice phase, you can still use this workout, with very few additions. The variety is introduced into the programming of each lift, and variations are made in the workload. Even for more advanced trainees, it is unnecessary to add lots of different exercises to the workout, as the purpose is always served when strength levels increase on the basic lifts. Any assistance exercises that are added must be kept in their proper perspective; they are there to help you get stronger in the basic lifts, not as an end in themselves. The press and the bench press, for example, will always be more important than arm work, and if curls and triceps exercises interfere with your recovery from pressing or benching, instead of adding to your strength in these lifts, they are being misused.

Most Olympic weightlifting coaches will use a workout order that places faster movements before slower movements, so that the explosive lifts – the snatch, the clean and jerk, and their variations – are performed before the strength exercises, like the squat and the pressing movements. This order makes sense if the competitive lifts are the emphasis of the program, even though some of the most competitive nations in Olympic weightlifting don't always do it this way. Our program uses the power clean as the explosive movement, but since none of the exercises in this novice program are approached as competitive lifts, doing the power clean as the last exercise in the workout is more productive for strength development because it leaves the emphasis on the squat. Doing the squat first provides a superior warm-up for all the subsequent movements, and doing the squat while you're fresh grants it the attention it deserves as the most important exercise in the program.

WARM-UP SETS

Warm-ups serve two very important purposes. First, warm-ups actually make the soft tissue – the muscles and tendons, and the ligaments that comprise the joints – warmer. General warm-up exercises increase the temperature in the soft tissue and mobilize the synovial fluid in the joints. These exercises include walking fast or jogging, riding an exercise bike (a better method, due to the greater range of motion the knees are exposed to during the exercise, better preparing them for the squat), or using a rowing machine (the best method, due to its range of motion and the full involvement of the back and arms as well as the legs). Specific warm-ups, like the empty-bar sets of the barbell exercise itself, also serve to warm, mobilize, and stretch the specific tissues involved in that particular movement. This step is important for injury prevention, since it is more difficult to injure a warm body than a cold one.

The elevation of tissue temperature is very important and requires that several variables be kept in mind. The temperature of the training facility should be considered as a factor in this phase of warm-up. A cold room interferes with effective warm-up, while a hot room aids it. Winter months and summer months produce different warm-up requirements for most athletes, who will usually arrive at training feeling different in August than they do in January. A healing injury needs extra warm-up for the affected tissues. And the age of the trainee affects warm-up requirements as well. Younger people are less sensitive to a lack of warm-up than adults are, and the older the adult, the more time is needed for pre-workout preparation.

The second function of warm-ups is especially important in barbell training: it allows you to practice the movement before the weight gets heavy. Light warm-up sets, done first with the empty bar and then progressively heavier until the work sets are loaded, prepare the movement pattern itself so that when the weight gets heavy, you can focus your attention on pushing hard instead of worrying about how to push. The *motor pathway* – the neuromuscular adaptation to a complicated movement pattern – must be prepared every time it is used, whether you're throwing a baseball or doing a squat. The more familiar the movement pattern, the less critical this aspect of warm-up becomes, but for a novice it is always very important. The warm-up sets prepare the motor pathway at the same time that they prepare the tissues for the upcoming heavier work. While you are doing the first sets, you

can address and fix form errors so that during your work sets, you can focus more on driving the load and less on maintaining correct form.

It is foolishness to neglect warm-ups. Many government school programs, in an attempt to implement a strength program without allotting sufficient time to do it, omit most of this crucial part of the workout. The coach in charge of a program that does this commits **malpractice**. Please heed the following rather strong statement: if your schedule does not allow time for proper warm-up, *it does not allow time for training at all*. It is better to omit strength training from your program than to suffer the inevitable injuries that will result from lack of warm-up. Yes, warm-ups are that critical.

Warm-ups will vary with the lift being warmed up. If the room is cold, an initial warm-up on a rower or exercise bike might be useful to raise overall body temperature; if the room is warm, this will probably not be necessary. The squat, by its nature a total-body movement and being the first exercise of the workout, serves quite well as its own warm-up. It should be carefully and thoroughly prepared with a couple of empty-bar sets, and then as many as five sets between those and the work sets. The next upper-body movement will benefit from this preparation and, in the absence of an injury, can be warmed up adequately with only three or four sets. The deadlift will be warm from the squat, provided that the pressing hasn't taken so long that you have gotten cold. The power clean, being a more complex movement, will require more warm-up for technique purposes. Assistance exercises, if they are done, will be done last with already warm muscles and joints, and will require only one or two warm-up sets.

Any area that is injured will require additional warming up. If the injured area does not respond to the warm-up sets by starting to feel much better after you do two or three sets with the empty bar, you will have to decide whether to continue with light sets or wait until the area has healed better.

First, some terminology clarification. A *work set* is the heaviest weight to be done in a given workout, the sets that actually produce the stress

Squat	Weight	Reps	Sets
	45	5	2
	95	5	1
	135	3	1
	185	2	1
Work sets	225	5	3

Bench Press	Weight	Reps	Sets
	45	5	2
	85	5	1
	125	3	1
	155	2	1
Work sets	175	5	3

Deadlift	Weight	Reps	Sets
	135	5	2
	185	5	1
	225	3	1
	275	2	1
Work sets	315	5	1

Press	Weight	Reps	Sets
	45	5	2
	75	5	1
	95	3	1
	115	2	1
Work sets	135	5	3

Power Clean	Weight	Reps	Sets
	45	5	2
	75	5	1
	95	3	1
	115	2	1
Work sets	135	3	5

Table 8-1. Example distributions of warm-up sets and work sets.

which causes the adaptation. *Warm-ups* are the lighter sets done before the work sets. "Sets across" refers to multiple work sets done with the same weight. The work sets are the ones that provide the training effect; they are the sets that make strength

go up, since they are the heaviest – for novices, the weight you haven't done before. The warm-up sets serve only to prepare the lifter for the work sets; they should never interfere with the work sets. So plan your warm-up sets with this principle in mind. The last warm-up set should never be so heavy that it interferes with the work sets, but it must be heavy enough to allow you to feel some actual weight before you do the work sets. It might consist of only one or two reps even though the work sets will be five or more reps. For instance, if the work sets are to be 225 x 5 x 3 (three sets of five reps at 225 pounds), then 215 x 5 (five reps at 215) would not be an efficient choice for a last warm-up; a better choice would be 205 x 2, or even 195 x 1, depending on your preference, skill, and experience. Since the focus is on completing all the reps of the work sets, the warm-ups must be chosen to save gas for the heavier sets, while still being heavy enough that the first work set is not a shock.

As an example of the importance of proper warm-up, let's examine the effects of a bad warm-up carried to the extreme. There is an old workout, known as "The Pyramid," still floating around weight rooms and gyms all over the world. For the bench press, this workout would go something like 135 x 10, 155 x 8, 175 x 6, 185 x 5, 195 x 4, 205 x 3, 215 x 2, and 225 x 1. By the time you finish the last set, you might feel like you've had a pretty good workout. The problem is that you have done 6390 pounds of work before getting to the last set at 225, so your chances of ever increasing this last single are slim. By the time you reach what should be a work set, you are all used up, since all of your warm-up sets have essentially been work sets, too. The warm-ups didn't prepare you to increase your work sets, so you will never lift any more weight than you did the last time you did this workout, and you are therefore quite thoroughly stuck. If the warm-up sets fatigue you instead of prepare you, they are not warm-ups and your strength cannot increase.

As a general rule, it is best to start with an empty bar ("45" lb/20 kg), determine the work set or sets, and then divide the difference between 45 pounds and the work-set weight into even increments. Some examples are provided in Table 8-1. Most people will need to select three to five warm-up sets, depending on the work-set weight; extremely heavy weights may require more increments for the trainee to get warm so that the jumps are not too big. If additional warm-up is desirable (as with a cold room, older trainees, or injured lifters), multiple sets can be done with the empty bar and the first loaded set. This approach provides the benefits of the warm-up without causing fatigue from doing too much work at heavier weight before the work sets.

As the warm-ups progress from the empty bar up through heavier weights, the time between the sets should increase a little. As a general rule, the time between sets should be sufficient for you to recover from the previous set, so that fatigue from the prior set does not limit the one you are about to do. The heavier the set, the longer the break should be. This type of training requires that all of the reps of each work set be completed, because the program is based on lifting more weight each workout, not on completing each workout or each exercise faster. A strength training program is designed to make you stronger, i.e., able to exert more force and lift more weight. Some training programs used in bodybuilding rely on the accumulated fatigue produced by short breaks between sets, and these programs specifically increase muscular endurance. Although endurance increases as a function of strength, it is not a parameter specifically targeted by our program at the novice level. You will benefit more by lifting heavier weights, through the efficient timing of sets to allow for recovery, than by trying to decrease the time between the sets and thereby allowing fatigue to limit your ability to exert maximum force.

The time between sets will vary, in a couple of ways, with the conditioning level of the athlete. Rank novices are not typically strong enough to fatigue themselves very much, and they can go fairly quickly, just a minute or two, between sets, since they are not lifting much weight anyway. The first two or three sets can be done as fast as the bar can be loaded, especially if two or more people are training together. More advanced trainees need more time, perhaps 5 minutes, between the last warm-ups and the work sets. If they're doing sets across, very strong lifters may need 10 minutes or more between work sets.

WORK SETS

The number of work sets to be done after the warm-ups will vary with the exercise and the individual. The squat benefits from sets across (three sets for novice trainees), as does the bench press and the press. The deadlift is hard enough, and is usually done after a lot of squatting, and one heavy set is usually sufficient, with more tending to overtrain most people. The power clean can be done with more sets across, since the weight is lighter relative to the squat and deadlift, and the limiting factors are technique and explosive power, not absolute strength.

Multiple work sets cause the body to adapt to a larger volume of work, an adaptation that comes in handy for those training for sports performance. One school of thought holds that one work set, if done at a high enough intensity, is sufficient to stimulate muscular growth. For novices, several problems with this approach immediately present themselves. First, inexperienced trainees do not yet know how to produce maximum intensity under the bar, and they will not know how for quite some time. Second, if they don't know how to work at a very high intensity, more than one set will be needed to accumulate sufficient stress to cause an adaptation to occur – one set will not provide enough. Third and most important, one intense set adapts the body to work hard for one intense set, since exercise, as we know, is specific. It is true that strength is the most general athletic adaptation, and the more force you can produce, the better. But for a novice trainee, the context in which strength is produced is quite important, and for the same reasons we don't train novices with 1RM work, we don't use 2–5RM-level efforts either (to be discussed immediately below). Except for sumo wrestling and a couple of others, sports do not usually involve one isolated, relatively brief intense effort, but generally involve repeated bouts of work. And one single set at very high intensity is not the best way to build force-production capacity if you lack the experience to effectively produce enough force in one low-volume set. A sets-across routine more closely mimics the effort usually involved in sports and more effectively allows the trainee to learn to work hard, and therefore produces a more useful adaptation.

In fact, one of the most effective strategies for intermediates is to do the squat, bench, and press for five sets across of five reps, once a week as one of the three workouts, increasing the weight used by very small manageable amounts each week.

The easiest way to stop your progress between workouts is to fail to finish all the reps of all the prescribed work sets. And the easiest way to make this happen is to fail to rest long enough between work sets to allow fatigue from the previous set to dissipate before you start the next set. If fatigue accumulates as the work sets progress, the predictable outcome will be that instead of 5-5-5 reps, you will do 5-4-3 when 5-5-5 was actually possible had you waited long enough between sets. This is the most common error made by novice trainees: the confusion of strength training with conditioning work. The program requires that you increase weight every workout for as long as possible, and if you fail to complete all the reps of all the work sets, you cannot increase the weight in your next workout. Make sure you give yourself enough time to complete your reps. If the weight is actually too heavy – because you took too big a jump or you have not recovered from the previous workout – then your programming must change. But impatience is a poor reason to allow progress to come to a halt.

How many reps should a work set consist of? It depends on the adaptation desired. Five reps is a good number for most purposes, but an understanding of the reasons for this is essential so that special circumstances can be accommodated correctly.

When you're trying to understand the nature of any given set of variables, it is often helpful to start with the extremes, the limits of which can reveal things about the stuff in the middle. In this case, let's compare a one-rep max, or 1RM, squat to a 20RM squat and look at the different

physiological requirements for doing each set. Credit for this explanation goes to Glenn Pendlay, from a conversation that yielded perhaps the most useful model of adaptation to exercise ever developed.

The single most important contributing factor to the successful heavy one-rep attempt is the ability of the muscles involved to produce force. The heavier the weight, the more force required to move it, as should be obvious. The one-rep set doesn't take very long to do, so muscular endurance is not a factor, and neither is cardiovascular capacity, for the same reason. Even a bone-on-bone limit attempt doesn't take more than a few seconds. The only thing the muscles must do is produce sufficient force to overcome the weight on the bar as it moves through the range of motion of the lift one time. So, in response to 1RM training, the body adapts by getting better at producing high amounts of force, one rep at a time. It does this by adjusting the components of the system that produce the force: the nervous system, the neuromuscular system, and the muscles themselves, specifically the components of the muscle that actually produce the contraction.

There are other adaptations that are secondary to the main ones, but they all involve helping the body perform a brief, intense effort. Psychological adaptations enable the lifter to overcome his fear of a heavy weight. The heart adapts by getting better at working with a huge load on the back, and the blood vessels adapt by becoming capable of responding to the demands of increased peak blood pressure. The tendons thicken to better transmit force, and the ligaments thicken and tighten to hold the joints together under the load. The skin under the bar gets thicker, the eyeballs get used to bugging out, and new words are learned that express the emotions accompanying success or failure with a new PR squat. But the primary adaptation is increased force production.

On the other hand, a heavy set of 20 reps is an entirely different experience, one of the most demanding in sports conditioning. A set of 20 squats can usually be done with a weight previously assumed to be a 10RM, given the correct mental preparation and a certain suicidal desire to either grow or die. The demands of a 20RM, and therefore

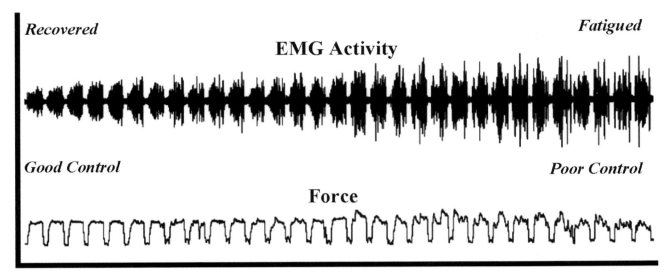

Figure 8-3. Sets of 5 reps are optimal for learning barbell exercises. It is apparent from electromyography (EMG, a recording of neuromuscular electrical activity, top) and force plate data (a measure of muscular force generated, bottom) that there is a progressive loss of motor coordination as reps increase. In reps 1–5, the muscle is firing in a coordinated manner, with tight, uniform EMG waves and consistent force production. By reps 10–14, there is a loss of motor coordination, with erratic EMG wave and force continuity. By reps 25–29, EMG activity is highly random and force production has deteriorated. Using more than 5 reps per set during the learning phase of a new exercise will usually make correct technique harder to reproduce and master. Note that the peak level of force production is the same on rep 1 and rep 20, although control has begun to degrade; a 20-rep set is not really "heavy," but it sure is long and hard.

the adaptation to it, are completely different. A 20RM is done with about 80% of the weight of a 1RM, and even the last rep is not really heavy, in terms of the amount of force necessary to squat it. The hard part of a set of 20 is that the last 5 reps are done in a state resembling a hellish nightmare: making yourself squat another rep with the pain from the falling muscle pH, an inability to catch your breath, and the inability of your heart to beat any faster than it already is. The demands of a 20RM involve continued muscle contraction under circumstances of increasing oxygen debt and metabolic depletion.

In response to this type of stress, the body gets better at responding to the high metabolic demand that is created. Systemic adaptations are primarily cardiovascular in nature, since the main source of stress involves managing blood flow and oxygen supply during and after the set. The heart gets better at pumping blood under a load, the vessels expand and become more numerous, and the lungs get better at oxygenating the blood – although not in the same way that a runner's lungs do. The main muscular adaptations are those that support local metabolism during the effort. Glycolytic capacity increases. The contractile part of the muscle tissue gets better at working under the acidic conditions produced by the stress of the long work set. Psychologically, 20RM work is very hard, due to the pain, and lifters who are good at it develop the ability to displace themselves from the situation during the set. Or they just get very tough.

It is essential to understand that the 1RM work does not produce the conditioning stress that the 20RM work does, and that the long set of 20 reps is not heavy in the same way that the 1RM is. They are both hard, but for different reasons. Because they are so completely different, they cause the body to adapt in two completely different ways. These extremes represent a continuum, with

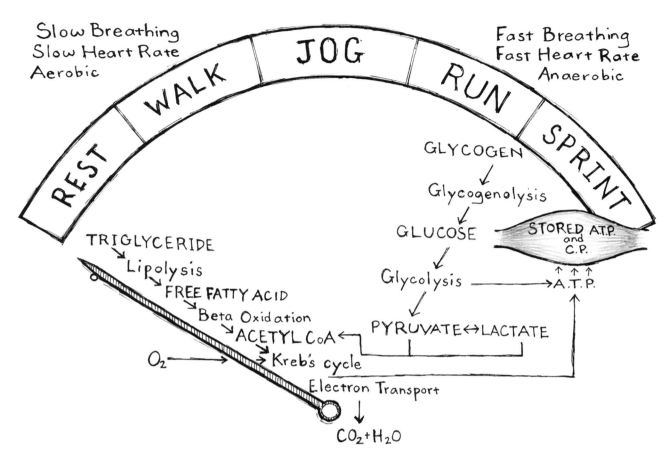

Figure 8-4. The metabolic speedometer. How hard and how long we exercise directly affects which metabolic pathways our bodies primarily use to fuel the activity. All physical activity lies along a continuum, from rest to all-out maximal effort. All activities are powered by the ATP already present in the muscle, and all bioenergetic activity acts to replenish these stores. Low-intensity exercise depends on cardiopulmonary delivery and muscular uptake of oxygen, the ready availability of which enables the body to use aerobic pathways and fatty acids as substrate. These aerobic processes take place inside the mitochondria within the muscle cells. As activity levels and energy requirements increase, the ability of oxidative metabolism to meet the increased demand for ATP is exceeded. Weight training and other forms of high-intensity training exist at the anaerobic end of the continuum, using substrate that does not require added O_2. The diagram above represents the relationships between the energy substrates and the metabolic pathways in which they are used in different types of exercise. With the exception of short-duration all-out maximal efforts, no activity uses only one metabolic pathway, so the illustration above represents a sliding scale of continually increasing intensity of activity.

a heavy set of 3 more closely resembling 1RM in its adaptation, and a set of 10 sharing more of the characteristics of a 20RM. Sets of five reps are a very effective compromise for the novice, and even for the advanced lifter more interested in strength than in muscular endurance. They allow enough weight to be used that force production must increase, but they are not so heavy that the cardiovascular component is completely absent from the exercise.

Sets of five may be the most useful rep range you will use over your entire training career, and as long as you lift weights, sets of five will be important.

PROGRESSION

The effective training of novices takes advantage of the fact that untrained people get strong very quickly at first, and this effect tapers off over time until advanced trainees, who are already strong, gain more strength only by carefully manipulating all training variables. Novices can and should increase the weight of the work sets every workout until this is no longer possible. In fact, novices get strong as fast as the workout makes them, and what was hard last time is not hard today. They can adapt so quickly that the concept of "maximum intensity" is hard to define. If a kid gets strong as fast as his work sets increase, a 10-pound jump is not really heavier relative to his improved strength. The key to maintaining this rate of improvement is the careful selection of the amount of weight that you increase each time.

Work-set weight increases will vary with the exercise, your age and sex, your experience, and the consistency of your adherence to the program. For most male trainees with good technique, the squat can be increased 10 pounds per workout, assuming three workouts per week for two to three weeks. When you miss the last rep or two of your last work set, the easy gains are beginning to wane, and you can take 5-pound jumps for several months; back up 5 pounds and start with 5-pound jumps. For very young kids, older trainees, and most women, 5-pound jumps are sufficient to start with, and then smaller jumps will be required, as will the lighter barbell plates (lighter than the standard 2½ lb plates) that make smaller jumps possible.

If it is important for women and kids to make progress – and why would it not be? – it is important to have the right equipment to train them correctly. You might need to make the plates out of 2-inch flat washers, or have some 2½ lb plates milled down, but it is obviously necessary, so get it done. Small plates are available from various sources on the Web, and baseball bat weights will usually fit the bar quite well. It will be useful at some point for everybody to have access to light plates, since progress on the lifts will eventually slow to the point where they will be useful even for advanced men. Don't be afraid to take small jumps – instead, do be afraid to stop improving.

Some very genetically gifted, heavier men can take bigger jumps of 15 or 20 pounds for the first two weeks. Anything more than this is usually excessive, even for the most gifted athlete, since an increase of 60 pounds per week in the squat is not going to be realistically sustainable for very long. Don't be in a big hurry to find your sticking point early in your training progression. It is always preferable to take smaller jumps and sustain the progress than to take bigger jumps and get stuck early. Getting stuck means missing any of the reps of the prescribed work sets, since the weight cannot be increased until all of the reps have been done as prescribed. **It is easier to not get stuck than it is to get unstuck.**

In the bench press, the muscles used are smaller, so the increases will be smaller. If the first workout has properly determined their initial strength level, most men can do 5-pound jumps for a while, perhaps three to four weeks, if they are alternating bench presses and presses. Some talented, heavier men can make a few 10-pound jumps, but not many. Older guys, the very young, and women will need to start with small jumps, and the special light plates are particularly important for these trainees to keep making progress on the bench. Do not be afraid to slow the increases down to very small jumps on the bench; remember that an increase of even 2 pounds per week means a 104-pound increase in a year, not a shameful amount of progress for the bench press.

The press will behave similarly to the bench press, since the muscles involved in moving the bar are small relative to the squatting and deadlifting muscles. The press uses lots of muscles, true, but the limiting factors are the strength and the efficiency of the mechanics of the smaller upper-body muscles, and no chain is stronger than its weakest link, as the saying goes. The same jumps used for the bench can usually be used for the press, although the press will start off at somewhere between 50% to 70% of the weight used in the bench press. Since you are alternating the two exercises, they will stay about the same weight apart as they increase.

The deadlift will progress faster than any of the other lifts, because the start position, basically a half-squat or above, is very efficient mechanically, and because virtually every muscle in the body is involved in the movement. Most men can add 15 pounds to the deadlift each workout for a couple of weeks, with the very young, women, and older guys taking a more conservative approach. But 5-pound jumps in the deadlift should be sustainable for several months. This being the case, the deadlift will start out with heavier weights than the other lifts for all trainees, should get stronger faster, and will continue to be stronger than the other lifts (unless you become an advanced powerlifting competitor). A trainee who benches more than he deadlifts needs to stop avoiding his deadlift workouts. But since the deadlift involves more muscles and more weight than the other lifts, it is easier to overtrain. **For a novice, the deadlift should not be trained using sets across.** It is really easy to get really beat-up doing a lot of heavy deadlifts. One work set at the intensity of a real work set is quite sufficient to produce improvement.

It is interesting that the power clean behaves more like the bench press than like the squat or deadlift, in terms of the way it increases over time. The reason for this involves the biomechanical nature of the movement and the factors limiting its progress. The power clean is explosive and technical, and it involves more than just absolute strength. It is limited at the top of the movement by the lifter's ability to get the bar on the shoulders, and the heavier the weight, the more the power clean depends on the lifter's ability to generate enough momentum to get the bar high enough to rack. This momentum is controlled by the lifter's ability to explode – to recruit lots of motor units into contraction instantly – a physical attribute that is largely dependent on genetics and thus is less responsive to training than strength is. The power clean will move up maybe 5 pounds per workout for most men. If the power snatch is used, it will also move up slowly for the same reasons, albeit with a lighter weight than that used in the power clean. Women and younger, older, and lighter trainees will need to introduce smaller plates earlier in the progression.

Ancillary exercises, which are by their nature inefficient isolation-type exercises, produce very slow progress. Anybody claiming rapid gains on triceps extensions or barbell curls is not utilizing particularly strict form and should be criticized for such foolishness.

When these smaller jumps can no longer be sustained, a trainee can be considered an intermediate, and the fun begins with more complicated manipulation of training variables. This variation in exercises, tonnage, and intensity for the purpose of ensuring continued progress is referred to as *periodization*. It is unnecessary for rank beginners, since they get strong as fast as they can increase the weight every workout, and it is indispensable for advanced lifters, who cannot continue to make progress without it. Intermediates are, like the name says, somewhere in between, with some degree of training parameter manipulation necessary to allow for continued but slower progress. Programming beyond the novice phase is beyond the scope of this book and is dealt with in detail in *Practical Programming for Strength Training, Second Edition* (Aasgaard, 2009).

And all these guidelines apply only to committed trainees who do not miss workouts. Failure to train as scheduled is failure to follow the program, and if the program is not followed, progress cannot predictably occur. If you have to miss a couple of workouts due to severe illness, or possibly the death of a parent, spouse, or good dog, allowances can be made, and the last workout you completed should just be repeated set for set. But if you continually miss workouts, you are not actually training, and your obviously valuable time should be spent more productively elsewhere.

Likewise, trying to increase the weight faster than prescribed by the program and by common sense is also failure to follow the program. If you insist on attempting unrealistic increases between workouts, it is your fault when progress does not occur. Ambition is useful, greed is not. Most of human history and the science of economics demonstrate that the desire for more than is currently possessed drives improvement, both personally and for societies. But greed is an ugly thing when

Novice
Example

Young Angus McSnort

Mon
8/2/04

Squat
45X5X3
65X5
85X5
105X5X3

Press
45X5X2
55X5X3

Deadlift
88X5X3

Age: 17
Bodyweight:
158

Wed
8/4/04

Squat
45X5X2
65X5
85X5
105X5
120X5X3

Bench
45X5X2
65X5
85X5
95X5X3

Deadlift
88X5X2
110X5
132X5
154X5X2

Fri
8/6

Squat
45X5X2
75X5
95X5
115X5
125X5X3

Press
45X5X2
55X5
60X5X3

Deadlift
88X5
110X5
132X5
154X2
165X5
(back
rounding)

Mon
8/9

Squat
45X5X2
75X5
95X5
115X2
135X5X3

Bench
45X5X2
65X5
85X2
95X1
100X5X3

Deadlift
88X5
110X5
132X2
154X1
165X5X2
better

Wed
8/11

Squat
45X5X2
75X5
105X5
125X2
145X5X3

Press
45X5X2
55X5
65X5X3

Power
Clean
Bar X3
X many
reps
55X3X2
65X3
75X3
88X3X3

Fri
8/13
(Be careful)

Squat
45X5X2
75X5
105X5
135X2
155X5X3

Bench
45X5
65X5
85X2
105X5X3

Deadlift
88X5
110X5
132X5
154X1
176X5

Figure 8-5. *This page and facing page,* An example of the first few days of a typical beginner's program.

Y. A. McS.

Mon 8/16	Wed 8/18	Fri 8/20	Mon 8/23	Wed 8/25	Fri 8/27
Squat	**Squat**	**Squat**	**Squat**	**Squat**	**Squat**
45×5×2	45×5×2	45×5×2	45×5×2	45×5×2	45×5×2
75×5	85×5	85×5	95×5	95×5	95×5
105×2	115×3	125×5	135×5	135×5	135×5
135×1	145×2	155×2	165×2	175×2	195×2
165×5×3	175×5×3	185×5×3	195×5×3	205×5×3	215×5×3
Press		**Press**	**Bench**	**Press**	**Bench**
45×5×2	**Bench**	45×5×2	45×5×2	45×5×2	45×5×2
55×5	45×5×2	55×5	75×5	60×5	75×5
65×2	75×5	65×5	95×5.	70×2	105×2
70×5×3	95×3	70×2	110×2	80×5×3	125×5×3
	110×5×3	75×1	120×5×3		
Power Clean	115×5	78.5×5×3		**Power Clean**	**Back Ext.**
55×3×3	120×5		**Back Ext.**	55×3×2	BW×10×3
75×3×2		**Deadlift**	BW×10×3	75×3	
88×3 (40k)	**Back Ext.**	88×5		40k×3	**Chins**
42.5k × 3×3	BW×10×3	132×5	**Chins**	45×3×5	BW×7
		154×2	BW×7		BW×6
Bodyweight: 165	**Chins**	176×1	BW×5×2		BW×5
	BW×6	198×5			
	BW×5		**Bodyweight: 169**		
	BW×3				

uncontrolled and untempered with wisdom, and it will result in your program's progress coming to an ass-grinding halt. The exercises must increase in weight in order for progress to occur, by definition. But if you allow yourself to succumb to the temptation of 10-pound jumps on the bench press, or 50-pound increases on the squat, just because the heavier plates were handy (or the correct plates were inconvenient), you are going to get stuck. Too much weight on the bar is just as bad as no increase in weight at all or, for that matter, missing workouts. Take the time and care necessary to ensure that the right weight gets on the bar and gets lifted the right number of times the right way.

It is understandable that you want your program to show results. But please understand this, if you miss everything else in this entire book: *stronger does not necessarily mean more weight on the bar.* Resist the temptation to add weight at the expense of correct technique – you are doing no one any favors when you sacrifice form for weight on the bar. Progress stops, bad habits get formed, injuries accumulate, and no one benefits in the long run.

Nutrition and Bodyweight

It is common to want what you cannot have. But you must keep in mind that the phenomenon of cause and effect cannot be argued with or circumvented by your wishes and desires. Everyone who has been a kid or has raised kids is familiar with the phenomenon of the "growth spurt," which happens naturally during all stages of normal development. Growth occurs sporadically as we develop and mature; it is not smooth over the course of the whole infant/child/adolescent/teenager continuum, but within the growth spurt itself, a period of smooth linear increase does occur. We are creating an artificial growth spurt with our training, and if the stress is sufficient and the diet is adequate to facilitate recovery, amazing progress can occur. This is why proximity in age to the normal growth window makes for a more efficient response to this stimulus: the processes by which growth is accomplished are still functioning, and the system is not yet cemented in its final form. The older the trainee, the further the remove from the capacity to generate a growth spurt. But the stimulus/response relationship is axiomatic – you get out of it what you put into it, within the context of your ability to respond. You maximize this ability by training, eating, and resting in the most effective way possible.

A program of this nature tends to produce the correct bodyweight in an athlete. That is, if you need to be bigger, you will grow, and if you need to lose bodyfat, that happens, too. It is possible, and quite likely, that skinny kids on this program will gain 10–15 pounds of bodyweight in the first two weeks of a good barbell training program, provided they eat well. "Well" means four or so meals per day, based on meat and egg protein sources, with lots of fruit and vegetables and lots of milk. Lots. Most sources within the heavy-training community agree that a good starting place is one gram of protein per pound of bodyweight per day, with the rest of the diet making up 3500–6000 calories, depending on training requirements and body composition. Although these numbers produce much eyebrow-raising and cautionary statement-issuing from the registered-dietetics people, it is a fact that these numbers work well for the vast majority of people who lift weights, and these numbers have worked well for decades.

One of the best ways to move in the direction of these numbers is to drink a gallon of milk a day, most especially if weight gain is a primary concern. A gallon of whole milk per day, added to the regular diet at intervals throughout the day, will put weight on any skinny kid. Really. The problem is getting them to do it. It is apparently a persistent tendency, since about 1990, for boys to think they need a "six pack," although most of them don't have an ice chest to put it in. The psychology of this particular historical phenomenon is best left to others to investigate and explain. Aesthetics aside, heavier is eventually necessary if stronger is to occur, and once most people see that weight gain actually makes them look better (amazingly enough), they become less resistant to the idea.

Milk works because it is easy, it is available, it doesn't need any preparation, and it has all the components necessary for growing mammals, which novice lifters most definitely are. There also seems to be something special about milk that the equivalent amount of calories, protein, fat, and carbs can't duplicate in terms of growth enhancement. It may be the fact that milk has very high levels of *insulin-like growth factor 1* (IGF-1), a peptide hormone that has been shown to have some relationship to accelerated growth in mammals. But that research is far from conclusive; suffice it to say that experience has shown that people who drink lots of milk during their novice phase get bigger and stronger than people who don't. This time-proven method works for everybody who can digest milk – though the truly lactose-intolerant might not be able to take advantage of its benefits without supplementing with lactase, the enzyme needed for the breakdown of this milk sugar. Most other people are fine with a gallon per day if they start out with a quart and work up over two weeks.

Weight gain occurs the same way strength gains occur – fast at first, then more slowly as training progresses. It is quite possible for genetically favored individuals – for example, a broad-shouldered, motivated 5'10" kid, weighing 140 pounds – to gain as much as 60 pounds in a year of good steady training, good diet, and milk. This is actually not that unusual a result for this type of trainee, although when it occurs, there will always be talk of steroids, because this is human nature – as a general rule, anybody stronger than you is taking steroids. What is unusual is finding a genetically gifted athlete who will actually do the program – all of it. It is far more common to see 20-pound increases in bodyweight over a four-month period, with only a very few diligent trainees doing much better. But most guys who will eat even a little better than they did before will gain several pounds the first few weeks.

Fat guys (not used here disparagingly) see a different result entirely, as their bodyweight doesn't change much for the first few months. What they notice is looser pants in the waist; legs and hips staying about the same; shirts that are much tighter in the chest, arms, and neck; and faster strength

increases compared to their skinny buddies. Their body composition changes while their bodyweight stays close to the same, the result of a loss in bodyfat due to their increasing muscle mass.

So if you do the program as written, and you are a novice male between the ages of 18 and 35 with a starting bodyweight of 160–175 pounds, the first five or six squat workouts will see the work sets going up 10 pounds every time. If your first day is 115 x 5 x 3 sets across, then 165 x 5 x 3 will be the sixth workout. A novice in this demographic who is eating and resting correctly and who is otherwise healthy will be able to do this. Eating correctly may mean 6000 calories/day, including a gallon of whole milk, or it may mean 3500 calories/day on a Paleo-type, lower-carb, no-dairy diet, depending on your initial body composition. If this or its equivalent training result did not happen, you're not doing the program. During this period of time, it is common to gain 5–10 pounds of bodyweight if you are underweight, or to stay about the same if you are in need of bodyfat loss. In this demographic, you're too fat if you're over 20% bodyfat and underweight if you're less than 10%. Bodyfat under *about* 10% is not usually the level that a performance athlete carries, and growing a significant amount of muscle mass will entail an increase in bodyfat. A bodyfat level over *about* 20% means that you're headed in the direction of carrying around more than is required for an anabolic environment and more than is efficient for moving either the bar or an opponent.

It is potentially slipshod to assign an underweight or overweight designation on the basis of bodyfat, but it usually works pretty well, and in the absence of currently non-existent height/weight/bodyfat tables that take all three variables into account, it's about the best we can do. It is true that many people who want or need to gain bodyweight are also in love with their visible abs, and will not appreciate the advice to increase bodyfat if they are below 10%. The fact is that the dietary habits necessary to sustain *about* 10% or lower *for most people* is too low to sustain the metabolic environment required for a novice to gain muscle mass. And 10% bodyfat – if you do not have genetically low bodyfat (you know who you are) –

is not healthy; the conditions that are required to produce and maintain it are not compatible with high strength and power performance levels; and those levels are necessary to get big and strong. Or rather, strong and thus big.

This probably means you. Make up your mind that at least for the first year or two, you're not going to worry about bodyfat levels if you're already lean, because lean is easier to reacquire than strong is to build. This current emphasis on being lean at the expense of all other things is the direct result of Joe Weider's having done his job very well. You have seen pictures of big bodybuilders at 6% bodyfat in contest shape so often that you think it's normal, desirable, and always possible. Don't forget that there are drugs involved, along with enough other odd dietary behavior that Mr. Weider should be flogged for forgetting to mention that part. It would be much better to become realistic about these things and to stop letting the physique magazine and supplement industries make you stupid.

On the other hand, if you're a little fluffy around the belly, you have obviously already created the conditions necessary for growth. You'll usually start out stronger than the skinny guy, and because your body hasn't got the problems with growing that skinny guys do, strength gains can come more easily for you if you eat correctly. You'll still eat a lot, but don't drink the milk, and cut your carb intake if you don't see bodyfat levels drop during these first couple of weeks. You'll first notice that your pants fit looser in the waist.

So, if you correctly chose the work-set weight for your first workout and your squat didn't go up 40–50 pounds between the first and sixth workouts, either you're not in that demographic (a novice male between the ages of 18 and 35 with a starting bodyweight of 160–175) or you're not doing the program. If you're one of these guys who thinks you gained a lot of strength because your squat went up 30 pounds in three months, you're not doing the program (which I shall henceforth abbreviate as YNDTP). If you think the program is hard because your bodyweight at 5' 8" went from 148 down to 146 and you got stuck on the third workout, with

your squat having gone up 15 pounds, YNDTP. If you're a fat guy who has decided to go on the Atkins diet at the same time you started the novice progression, is continually sore, and is stuck at 30 pounds of squat increase, YNDTP.

After the first couple of weeks, the increase of 10 pounds per workout becomes unsustainable and 5-pound jumps become the rule. This jump provides for a long, steady linear increase in strength that has the potential to go on for months. It translates to a 15-pound-per-week increase in squat strength, half as fast as the first two weeks but still very significant at about 60 pounds per month. This progression adds up to a 205–225 x 5 x 3 squat workout after six or seven weeks of training for our novice male, **if he has been eating correctly.** And eating correctly is part of the program. If he started the program at a bodyweight of 165, he should probably weigh 185 at this point, more if he's taller. If you're squatting 30 pounds more than you started, at six weeks into the program, YNDTP. If you started at 5' 9" and 155, and six weeks later you weigh 160, YNDTP. If you started at 5' 9" and 235, and six weeks later you're only squatting 50 pounds more than you started with, still at a bodyweight of 235, YNDTP.

Realistically, gains on the squat will slow after this period to an *average* of about 10 pounds per week due to the fact that most people will get sick occasionally, miss a workout or two because of school, work, family, etc., or get a minor injury that will need to be dealt with. Ideally, these interruptions do not occur, but you'll find that in most cases, the extremely rapid growth in strength and size experienced during the first six to eight weeks is not sustained. But the program does not change, because 5-pound jumps are theoretically possible for this entire novice period. The bumps are dealt with on a case-by-case basis, and the diet is held constant as long as things are improving predictably. This will therefore usually mean that after 10–12 weeks on the program, another 40 pounds has been added to the squat, resulting in about 245–265 x 5 x 3 for our generalized guy's squat. During this period, your bodyweight should be continuing to increase if you're the skinny guy, or your bodyfat should be continuing to moderate if you were the fat guy. Skinny guys by now have added perhaps 40 pounds, and fat guys might have started to actually gain bodyweight after the initial loss, depending on how fat they were when they started.

So, if you're three months into the program and your squat has gone up 50 pounds, YNDTP. If you're three months into the program at 10% bodyfat and you have gained only 6 pounds, YNDTP. If you're three months into the program at 30% bodyfat, your waistline has not gone down 4 inches, and your squat is not up at least 150 pounds, YNDTP. Again, the program uses a diet that facilitates progress, and not everybody will use the same diet to progress toward the same goal of more muscle mass, since we don't want to let bodyfat get out of control. And out of control is not the same thing as a moderate, necessary, healthy increase.

After the first three or four months, a change will be necessary for most guys who started off skinny. If you have done the program correctly, you will have gained quite a bit of weight, about 60% of it being lean body mass (LBM) – muscle, tendon, and bone. This means that your bodyfat may have gone from ~10% to 18–19%. This is fine; it was necessary to produce the LBM increase. But now it's time to modify the diet to reflect your body's approach to its limit of fast LBM growth. All improvement rates taper off; improvement obviously can't go on forever, but it must occur at first to get our goal accomplished. Now, we need to drop the milk down to a half-gallon a day for a while, and then perhaps less than that. At the same time, daily caloric intake should drop to about 4000 calories/day, which you accomplish by cleaning up the carb intake and focusing on dietary quality instead of quantity like you did at first. This adjustment will allow your bodyfat levels to drop back to where they need to be, in the range of 15–17%, normal for athletic males in our demographic. The fat guys should be approaching 20% by now as well, since their diet has been about the same since the beginning; but their body*weight* should have started back up by now, as bodyfat loss has slowed and LBM increases have begun to exceed the loss. In this way, the two extremes converge at about the same dietary intake levels, with the guys who were skinny maintaining a slightly higher caloric intake that reflects their natural tendency toward being skinny.

Along with these changes have come another 30–40 pounds of squat. The program has not changed significantly, but the gains have begun to taper as the complexities of life and adaptation have accumulated to further interfere with your good intentions. But if you have persisted on the program and have not used these tapering results as an excuse to drop it and move "on" to super-slow, or HIT, or this year's Pre-Olympia Contest Preparatory Routine, you'll still be accumulating progress. This will mean that your squat may be up 200 pounds.

So, if you're still drinking a gallon of milk a day eight months into the program, YNDTP. If you have gained only 8 pounds, either as a skinny guy or above your low point when you were losing bodyfat, YNDTP. If your squat has increased only 50 pounds, YNDTP.

Training drives strength acquisition, the strength increase drives mass gain, and the mass gain facilitates the strength increase. They are all intimately related, and they approach a limit asymptotically. The younger you are, the steeper the curve. You need a caloric and protein surplus, which will produce some bodyfat accumulation that you can deal with later. The training stress has to constantly increase by as much as you can tolerate every workout. The variable is the load, not the number of exercises, sets, or reps. The ability to tolerate a rapid increase in load and to continue to quickly adapt slows after a few months. But during this period, don't waste your opportunity to grow quickly. After this, the program and diet must change to reflect the reality of slower progress.

Equipment

A lot of money has been wasted on weight rooms and gyms since the 1970s. Commercial exercise machines, as a general rule, are expensive, single-purpose devices, delivering one exercise per footprint on the floor at a very high price per square foot of training space. Home gym equipment is usually multi-station, using various elastic media to provide adjustable resistance for a variety of silly exercises. Barbells, on the other hand, are cheap. They can be used for lots of different exercises. The upright support bench for the bench press, a single-purpose device, is not an absolutely necessary piece of equipment, since the exercise we use it for can be done with a flat bench and a power rack. All of the exercises in this program can be done with a minimum of equipment, which allows for the better use of resources. Instead of the hundreds of thousands of dollars spent on an average 15-station circuit of machines, a third of that amount could be spent on the best barbell room in the world, with bumper plates, good bars, and platform space to accommodate lots of lifters, all in the same space. At home, a good free-weight gym can be built in the garage with brand new equipment for the price of three years' gym dues. You may decide to build your own gym, and the following guidelines can apply to your garage or to any gym you might decide to join.

THE POWER RACK AND PLATFORM

The training facility should be organized around the power rack. The rack should have a floor built into it, and a platform attached to it, so that the inside floor of the rack is perfectly flush with the surface of the platform. An 8' x 8' platform works well, providing plenty of room for every purpose it will serve. The rack and platform unit will use about 96 square feet, and in this space, all the exercises in this program can be performed. A bench press and bar assembly uses about 36 square feet if this equipment is available separately. The layout of the room around this equipment accommodate the amount of space needed for loading and spotting the bars used on the stations.

The power rack is the most important piece of equipment in the room, second only to the plate-loaded barbell as the most useful piece of gym equipment ever invented. All five primary exercises can be done with a correctly designed rack, barbell, and flat bench. The rack should be wide enough between the uprights to just safely accommodate the bar without a lot of extra room between the

Figure 8-6. A simple and functional platform/rack/flat-bench station. All basic barbell exercises can be done using this equipment.

sleeves and the uprights (about 48 inches). The wider the rack, within safe limits, the more easily it can be safely used by taller, bigger lifters, thus accommodating everyone. A 7½- to 8-foot-tall rack allows the crossbar at the top to be used for chin-ups and pull-ups by tall trainees. The depth of the rack may need to accommodate squatting inside it occasionally; for most people, an inside dimension of 22 inches works well and allows them to do dips inside the rack. The base depth should be greater (about 36 inches) for tipping stability. The optimum setup is to have the rack bolted to the floor at the corners so that pull-ups and chin-ups can be done without tipping the rack if they happen to swing.

The rack should be fitted with a heavy plywood floor, reinforced with a welded crossmember under the wood. The floor will extend all the way to the front and rear edges of the rack base so that it can be made flush and continuous with the platform surface. There should be a hook assembly for the bar to hang from outside the rack – my hook assemblies consist of two very large shoulder bolts with stops welded on them about halfway down the bolt at the edge of the unthreaded shoulder. Four heavy pins should cross the depth of the rack from front to back, with 4 inches or so extra on each side. These pins and hooks will adjust in height using the holes drilled in the channel iron that forms the uprights of the rack. The closer together the holes are, the finer the adjustments can be to accommodate lifters of various heights; 3 inches center to center is good, but 4 inches does not work well. The holes should extend from top to bottom. The entire rack should be correctly welded together, with no bolted components to loosen.

Plywood is the most commonly used material for the platform. It is relatively cheap and very tough, and six sheets make a perfect 8' x 8' platform. The layers are alternated so that the seams do not penetrate the whole platform, and the unit is made very strong when the layers are glued and screwed together. Be sure to buy plywood without any void spaces in the layers, because they WILL collapse if you drop a loaded barbell on top of them, anywhere in the stack of layers. This means that you have to buy B-grade or better, where all the knotholes are plugged.

Particle board makes a very good, very flat, solid hard surface with no void spaces, but it has some drawbacks. It comes in 49" x 97" sheets, so it doesn't overlap perfectly when three layers are laid in alternate directions – the edges will be off by an inch

Figure 8-8. The best power racks are heavy. This one is welded, and it has uprights of 4-inch channel with holes drilled on 3-inch centers, heavy 1¼-inch pins and chin bar, a heavy plywood floor reinforced with channel, and heavy bolts for hooks. The plan for this rack is on the next page.

Figure 8-7. The rack should have a floor flush with the surface of the platform, so that racking and unracking weights is safe when trainees are squatting outside the rack.

Figure 8-9. The layers of an inexpensive and durable plywood platform.

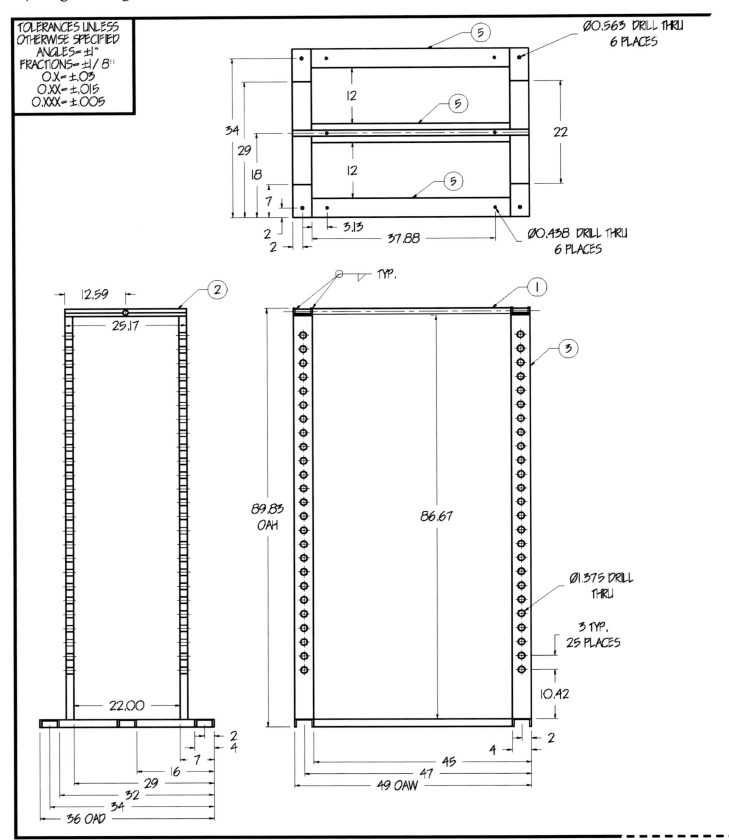

Figure 8-10. Power rack plan.

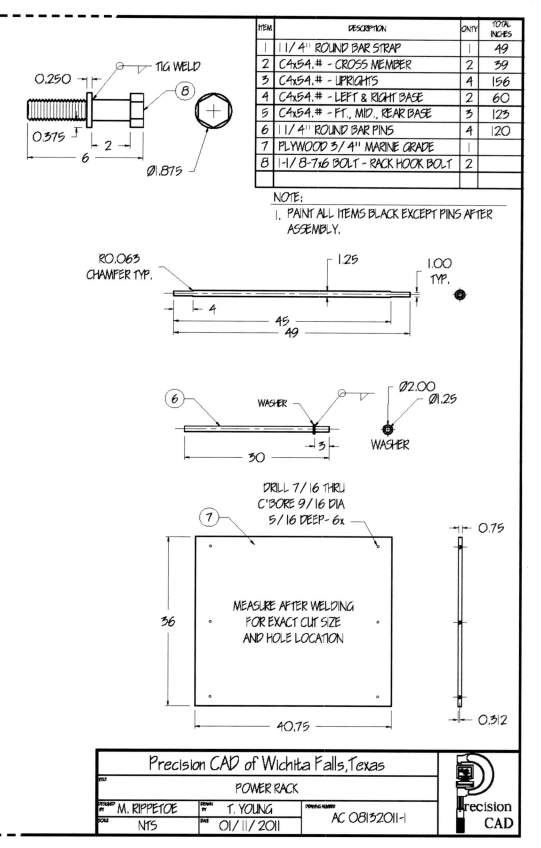

ITEM	DESCRIPTION	QNTY	TOTAL INCHES
1	1 1/4" ROUND BAR STRAP	1	49
2	C4x54.# - CROSS MEMBER	2	39
3	C4x54.# - UPRIGHTS	4	156
4	C4x54.# - LEFT & RIGHT BASE	2	60
5	C4x54.# - FT., MID., REAR BASE	3	123
6	1 1/4" ROUND BAR PINS	4	120
7	PLYWOOD 3/4" MARINE GRADE	1	
8	1-1/8-7x6 BOLT - RACK HOOK BOLT	2	

NOTE:
1. PAINT ALL ITEMS BLACK EXCEPT PINS AFTER ASSEMBLY.

TIG WELD

0.250
0.375
2
6
Ø1.875

R0.063 CHAMFER TYP.

1.25
1.00 TYP.
4
45
49

WASHER
Ø2.00
Ø1.25
WASHER
30
3

DRILL 7/16 THRU
C'BORE 9/16 DIA
5/16 DEEP- 6x

MEASURE AFTER WELDING
FOR EXACT CUT SIZE
AND HOLE LOCATION

36
40.75
0.75
0.312

Precision CAD of Wichita Falls, Texas

TITLE: POWER RACK

DESIGNED BY	M. RIPPETOE	DRAWN BY	T. YOUNG	DRAWING NUMBER	AC 08132011-1
SCALE	NTS	DATE	01/11/2011		

Precision CAD

every two sheets. And even though the material is very smooth and hard (the ¾" board feels like sheet concrete), it is extremely sensitive to moisture; one leak anywhere around it and the whole platform is useless. But if the room can be kept dry and you don't mind ripping the edges, particle board makes a damned good platform. It is even a little cheaper than plywood, since A/B plywood is very pricey these days.

Rubber horse-trailer mats finish the surface, making it virtually indestructible. These are available in farm stores and vary in thickness from ½ to ¾ inch. These mats are important to protect your platform and your plates when weights are dropped, which will occur no matter your intentions. The thickness of the whole platform assembly is about 3 inches, assuming ¾-inch plywood and ¾-inch rubber (see example Figure 4-48, page 140). The rack and the platform surface need to be flush to eliminate the tripping hazard, and invariably either the rack or the surface of the platform will need to be shimmed, since racks and platforms usually won't match. Shim the floor under the rack with rubber, plywood, or some other dense, flat stuff to make the dimensions agree, or use extra rubber on the platform or rack floor surface. Custom platforms are available from several sources; these are usually designed for the Olympic lifts and will be expensive but good-looking. They are unnecessary, but nice if the budget permits.

UPRIGHT SUPPORT BENCHES

An upright support bench for the bench press should be sturdy as hell, fully welded with no bolted joints to loosen, and may or may not have adjustable hooks. If the hooks are not adjustable, the fixed hook should be about 19 inches above the surface of the bench. This equipment should always have wide uprights, about 48 inches apart, to minimize the risk of bar-loading imbalances and racking accidents involving the hands. The surface of the bench will be 17 inches high with the padding compressed, 12 inches wide, and 48 inches long. The feet of the bench should not interfere with your foot placement; i.e., the bench feet should not be so wide that your feet touch them. The bench should be built in such a way that it does not tip back when heavy weights are racked hard. There should be no obstruction for a center spotter standing at the bencher's head. Some benches are equipped with safety hooks, fixed below the top hooks, to give a stuck solo bencher a way to get the bar off his chest without having to dump it on the floor or wait till the First Responder arrives. If these safety hooks are present, they should be right above chest height, about 9–10 inches above the bench.

Most commercial gyms will have bench-press benches, since having them frees up the power racks for other exercises (assuming that the gym has power racks and knows how they're used for this purpose), but again, they are not actually necessary since the power rack and a flat bench can be used for bench presses. Your garage gym will not need anything but a flat bench, which should have the same dimensions and simple construction as the support bench without the uprights. Too much padding will increase the effective height of the bench; that is not good for shorter lifters, annoying to taller ones who have used proper equipment

Figure 8-11. A standard upright support bench for the bench press. Note the safety hooks at the lower position on the uprights.

Figure 8-12. A flat bench can be used with a power rack as a bench press station, as shown in Figure 8-6. The flat bench should be as sturdy as an upright support bench.

before, and bad for everybody trying to get a firm plant against the bench. Too wide a bench is a bad problem at the bottom of the movement, where it interferes with the shoulders and arms as the bar touches the chest.

Most benches are upholstered with vinyl for ease of cleaning. This material wipes off well, but fabric upholstery lasts *many* times longer, especially auto upholstery fabric. Fabric also provides better traction for the back during lifting. Fabric can be cleaned with a wire brush and a shop-vac, and stains can be removed with mineral spirits and a rag.

BARS, PLATES, AND COLLARS

Bars are the place to spend money, if you have it. If you don't, raise it somehow, because cheap bars are potentially dangerous, unpleasant to use, and a bad investment. Cheap bars will bend. Even expensive bars can bend under the wrong circumstances, if they are dropped loaded across a bench, for instance. But cheap bars will always bend, even under normal use. Cheap bars should be – but somehow never are – an embarrassment to their manufacturers and the gyms that keep them. You can do better, and you should.

Standard "Olympic" bars – the general term for a bar with a 2-inch sleeve that accepts plates with a 2-inch hole – should weigh 20 kilos or 44 pounds, within a tolerance of just a few ounces. The tradition in the United States is to round the bar weight up to 45 pounds since our plates have traditionally been manufactured in pounds (even if the bars were actually 20 kg to satisfy the competitive standards of the international barbell federations). The weight on the bar will always be referred to as "135" even though it actually weighs 134 pounds. Cheap bars are occasionally produced that weigh below spec, so be careful, again, with cheap bars.

A good bar should be properly knurled and marked, should be put together with roller pins or snap rings, not bolts, and should require little maintenance beyond wiping it off occasionally and putting a drop of oil on the bushings or bearings every six months. It should be made to international competition specs, not because you'll be competing internationally (although you might) but so that the sleeves will accommodate the different brands of plates that all weight rooms eventually accumulate. Above all, a good bar is made of excellent steel bar stock, which will not deform with normal use. Expect to pay $250 or more for a good bar. There are lots of cheap imported bars available for less than $150. They are junk. Do not buy them. And do not hesitate to send back a good bar that bends under normal use, since it is not supposed to do that. A reputable company will replace a bar that fails, since their manufacturer will stand behind them in this event. If they don't, tell all your friends.

All real weight rooms are equipped with standard barbell plates with a 2-inch center hole. The little plates with a 1-inch hole are referred to as "exercise plates," and are not useful since no good bar is commercially produced for them. Standard barbell plates come in 2.5-, 5-, 10-, 25-, 35-, and 45-pound sizes. Of these, all are necessary except the 35s. Any loading that involves a 35 can be done with a 25 and a 10, and the space saved on the plate racks can be used for additional, more useful plates. Plates lighter than 2.5 pounds should be provided for use by women, kids, and everybody who wants to maintain linear progress on the bench press and press. Lighter plates can be made from 2-inch flat washers glued or taped together in the appropriate

Figure 8-13. Standard Olympic plates are the best choice. They come in a wide variety of denominations and constructions. Metal plates as light as a quarter-pound are very useful, and bumper plates up to 25 kg (55 pounds) allow heavy bar loads with fewer plates.

groups. Metric plates are 1.25, 2.5, 5, 10, 15, 20, 25, and occasionally 45 kg, with lighter plates down to 0.5 kg used in weightlifting competition.

Good plates are milled to be close to the weight named on the casting, and they should be well within a half-pound, or 0.25 kg. Metric bumper plates go up to 25 kg, and bumper plates calibrated in pounds are available from a few sources. Bumpers are useful for power cleans, and save a lot of wear and tear on bars and platforms. All plates bigger than 25 pounds, and all bumper plates (since they

won't bump if they don't touch the floor), should be 17.5 inches (45 cm) in diameter. Good plates should also have a correctly sized inside diameter (ID) – the size of the hole in the middle where the bar goes. A sloppy, loose ID in a plate limits its usefulness to merely hanging from the bar in a rack for a squat, bench, or press. Bad plates are quite aggravating to use for a deadlift because the slack between plate and bar sleeve lets the plates lean sideways as they support the bar on the ground, resulting in the plates continually "walking" off the bar if it's uncollared.

Figure 8-14. Plate racks are essential for weight room organization. An A-frame plate rack (left) and two types of tray racks are available commercially, or can be manufactured by clever, talented lifters.

Figure 8-15. The most common type of inexpensive spring collar is available from most sporting goods stores. They can be doubled up for extra security.

Plate racks are available in two main styles: the A-frame tree and the plate tray. If the A-frame is used, it should have two pins on each side, spaced so that 45s or other full-diameter plates can be loaded on the bottom and smaller plates can be loaded on the top pins. Such a rack can accommodate more than 650 pounds of standard barbell plates. The pins themselves should be made from at least 8 inches of 1-inch rod, so that the 2-inch hole in the plate fits over it with an inch of slop. This is very important for ease of racking the plates – if the pins are made from 2-inch material, you'll have to use both hands every time you rack a plate. This can become annoying. Tray-style racks are easy to use since there is no center pin, but they usually do not hold as many plates as an A-frame rack does, and their design is not as sturdy.

Collars are usually thought of as necessary safety equipment in the weight room. Although collars are important on occasion, it is much more useful to learn to keep the bar level so that plates don't slide off it. Plate slide is often a problem during squats, since walking a bar out of the rack unavoidably involves some side-to-side movement when you step back. Collars are useful when you're squatting, but they are less important when you're benching and pressing since the bar theoretically stays level during the movements, and you take only one step out of the rack for the press. In the event of an uneven elbow extension, collars are quite handy.

If it becomes apparent that you have problems with uneven extension, it would be prudent to use collars. It would also be good to correct this error if possible. Collars are useful in the deadlift, since they help keep sloppy plates from "walking" down the bar during the pick-up/set-down cycle. The same holds true for the clean, although bumper plates aren't as bad about this as standard plates because they are thicker across the ID and more plate is in contact with the bar.

Collars come in many designs, from inexpensive spring clips (which are very serviceable and reliable unless worn out or sprung), to expensive, very sturdy plastic types, to set-screw sleeve types, to adjustable competition collars. Collars used in powerlifting and weightlifting competitions weigh 2.5 kg, while the other styles will vary quite a bit. Springs work fine for most training purposes. If security is a problem, two springs can be used on each side. The weight of the collars will have to be calculated into the load if precision is necessary.

CHALK, CLOTHING, TRAINING LOGS, AND GYM BAGS

Chalk should be provided in the weight room, by either the gym or you. Chalk increases traction between the bar and the hands, reducing the likelihood of grip accidents. It reduces callus formation, since the folding of and friction against the skin of the palms and fingers are functions of the movement of the bar, and calluses form in response to this stress. It should be kept in a chalk box in a strategic location in the weight room. If the gym does not provide the chalk, for whatever misguided reason, you should bring your own, in a plastic bag or a can that stays in your gym bag. It can be purchased at most sporting goods stores or ordered over the Internet. If the gym is nice enough to provide the chalk, be nice enough back to use it sparingly; don't bathe in it, don't drop chunks on the floor, don't put clouds of it in the air, or otherwise waste it. Gyms that provide chalk have decided that training is more important than their housekeeping concerns, and you should appreciate this attitude.

Each trainee should have proper clothing, i.e., a cotton T-shirt, stretchy sweats or shorts, and a pair of shoes suitable for squatting and pulling. Some facilities provide belts, but not many, and you'll probably want your own anyway. One of the wonderful things about strength training is that minimal personal equipment is actually necessary, especially compared with other sports. The money spent on shoes is about the only significant expenditure the trainee has to make, belts being cheap and quite shareable between buddies.

Another thing each trainee should have is a training log – a journal in which to record each workout. No one can remember all the numbers involved in all the exercises in this program. Maybe the numbers for a couple of weeks of workouts can be remembered, but a person's entire training history constitutes valuable data that should be recorded for future use. This is information that will be used each workout and over the course of your training career to determine the nature of problems and to analyze the productivity of various training periods. Training information should be written in a format that can be easily read by both you and any coach you might have, since you will have to consult your training log on a regular basis. A composition book works just fine, and the price is certainly right. A spiral notebook tears up too easily in the gym bag. The best training book would be a bound ledger, with enough pages for years' worth of training notes. *All people who are serious about their training write down their workouts.*

Speaking of gym bags, get one, put all your stuff in it, and keep it with you. That way you'll always have your shoes, belt, chalk, training book, Band-Aids, tape, Desenex, spare shoelaces, extra shirt, towel, knee wraps, straps, and lucky troll doll. Don't worry about making a fashion statement with your bag. Just get one and take it with you every time so that I don't have to spot you a towel.

Soreness and Injuries

There are two more things that everyone who trains with weights will have: soreness and injuries. They are as inevitable as the progress they accompany. If you work hard enough to improve, you will work hard enough to get sore, and eventually you will work hard enough to get hurt. It is your responsibility to make sure that you are using proper technique, appropriate progression, and safe weight room procedures. You will still get hurt, but you will have come by it honestly – when people lift heavy, they are risking injury. It is an inherent part of training hard, and it must be prepared for and dealt with properly when it happens.

Soreness is a widely recognized and studied phenomenon. Despite the fact that humans have experienced muscle soreness since the Dawn of Time, its cause remains poorly understood. It is thought to be the result of inflammation in the basic contractile unit of the muscle fiber, and the fact that it responds well to anti-inflammatory therapy tends to support this theory. Since muscular soreness has been experienced by so many people for so long, many misconceptions about it are bound to develop, and they have. What is certain is that lactic acid (a transient byproduct of muscle contraction) has nothing whatsoever to do with it.

Soreness is usually produced when the body does something to which it is not adapted. A good example of this would be your first workout if it's not properly managed. Another example would be your first workout after a long layoff, which can, if handled incorrectly, produce some of the most exquisite soreness a human can experience. Anytime you change a workout program, either by increasing volume or intensity or by changing exercises, soreness normally results.

The onset of the perception of soreness is normally delayed, anywhere from 12 to 48 hours, depending on the age and conditioning level of the athlete, the nature of the exercise being done, and the volume and intensity of the exercise. For this reason, it is referred to in the exercise literature as DOMS, or *delayed-onset muscle soreness.* Many people have observed that certain muscle groups get sore faster and more acutely than others, and that certain exercises tend to produce soreness, while others, even when done at a high level of exertion, produce very little.

The part of the rep that causes most of the soreness is the eccentric, or "negative," phase of the contraction, where the muscle is lengthening under the load rather than shortening. The eccentric contraction probably causes most of the soreness because of the way the components of the contractile mechanism in the muscle fibers are stressed as they stretch apart under a load. And this explains why some exercises produce more soreness than others. Exercises without a significant eccentric component, like the power clean, in which the weight is dropped rather than actively lowered, will not produce nearly the soreness that the squat will. Squats, benches, presses, deadlifts, and many assistance and ancillary exercises have both an eccentric and concentric component, where the muscles involved both lengthen and shorten under load. Some sports activities, like cycling, are entirely concentric, since all aspects of pedaling involve the shortening of the muscles involved. Cycling and exercises like sled pulling or pushing can therefore be trained very hard without causing much, if any, soreness. Since soreness is an inflammatory process, the harder an athlete can train without producing high amounts of muscle inflammation and the attendant unfriendly hormonal responses, the better that is for recovery. Exercise methods that produce very high levels of soreness as a constant feature of the program – due to random exercise selection that precludes adaptation to the stress – can contribute to long-term systemic inflammation, the kind that produces poor health instead of fitness and strength. Soreness is an unavoidable part of training, but it should not be sought after as a primary objective and worn as a badge of honor for its own sake.

Occasional acute soreness, unless it is extreme, is no impediment to training. In fact, many records have been set by sore athletes. If you are not training hard enough to produce occasional soreness, and are therefore not having to train while sore, you are not training very hard. Waiting until soreness subsides before doing the next workout is a good way to guarantee that soreness will be produced every time, since you'll never get adapted to sufficient workload frequency to stop getting sore. Extreme soreness that interferes with the normal range of motion must be dealt with on a case-by-case basis, and you will need to decide whether to train through the soreness after you have warmed up carefully and thoroughly. But in general, if the warm-up returns the movement to the normal range of motion, you can do the workout. Some alterations in programming and recovery strategies might have to be made if it is determined that the soreness is the result of an accumulated lack of recovery from the preceding several workouts.

In contrast to normal soreness, which by its nature is delayed for several hours after the workout, an *injury* can be defined as something that happens to the body that causes pain in a way that is not the normal consequence of a correctly performed exercise. An *acute injury* is immediately perceived as pain or discomfort in an identifiable structure and persists after the movement has stopped. The injury could be a disruption of the structure of a muscle belly, tendon, or ligament, or, less commonly, of an intervertebral disc, a knee meniscus, or an articular cartilage. Most training-associated injuries affect the soft tissues; bony fractures are extremely rare weight room events. If pain occurs immediately in response to a movement done during training, it should be assumed to be an injury and should be treated as such. *Chronic injury* is usually an inflammatory response to the overuse of a joint or its associated connective issue due to poor technique or excessive training volume. Tendinitis and bursitis are common diagnoses and are usually the result of repeated exposures to maladaptive stress. It is extremely important to develop the ability to distinguish between injury pain and normal soreness, since your health and long-term progress depend on it.

When you return to training after some time off, you must consider your de-trained condition. Depending on the duration of the layoff, different approaches are taken. If you have missed just a few workouts (fewer than five or six), repeat the last workout you did before the layoff. You should be able to do this, although it may be hard. This approach results in less progress lost than if significant backing-off is done, and the following workout can usually be done in the order it would have been had the layoff not occurred.

If the layoff has been a long one, a couple of months or more, take care when planning your first workout back. If you have been training with weights for long enough to get very strong, adaptations have occurred in more than just your muscles. The neuromuscular system – the nervous system and its interface with the muscles – has adapted to training by becoming able to recruit motor units more efficiently, and it is slower to detrain than are the muscles it innervates. It remembers how to lift heavy weights even if the muscles are out of shape. This neuromuscular efficiency is quite useful when you are in shape, but when you are de-trained, it allows you to lift more than you are actually in condition to do without incurring adverse effects. Spectacular soreness, as mentioned earlier, will always be the result unless you use restraint in determining your volume and intensity. Hubris, not heroism, is demonstrated when a guy comes back after a year's layoff and tries to repeat his PRs that day. Unless you have absolutely nothing else important to do for several days afterward, please exercise good judgment when doing your first workout back in the gym.

Barbell Training for Kids

A whole lot of people are under the erroneous impression that weight training is harmful for younger athletes, specifically the pre-pubescent population. Pediatricians are a wonderful group of folks as a whole, but very often they are woefully uninformed regarding the data pertaining to the injury rates of various sports activities. They may also be reluctant to apply some basic logic to an analysis of those numbers.

Table 8-2 lists the injury rates of various sports. Note that organized weightlifting activities, at 0.0012 injuries per 100 participation hours, is about 5100 times safer than everyone's favorite organized children's sport, soccer, at 6.2 injuries per 100 player hours. Gym class, at 0.18, is more dangerous than supervised weight training. Yet it is still common for medical professionals to advise against weight training for kids. The most cursory glance at the actual data renders this recommendation foolishness.

So why does this mythology persist, and how did it get started? Most often cited as the primary concern is the chance of epiphyseal fracture that damages the growth plate, leading to growth asymmetry in the affected appendage. The entire body of the sports medicine literature contains six reports of growth-plate fractures that occurred in kids and were associated with weight training; none of these reports were detailed enough to determine whether the injury occurred under the bar (or if there even *was* a bar), occurred as the result of a fall due to faulty technique or improper instruction, or occurred as the result of injudicious loading. And even in these six isolated examples, none of the kids subsequently displayed *any* long-term effects that would indicate that a growth-plate injury does not heal just like any other injury. You know this yourself because fractures involving joints are common in kids, and the world is not crawling with roving gangs of asymmetrically-armed or -legged people seeking revenge for their misfortune.

The most intensely silly argument of all is that weight training stunts a kid's growth. *But hauling hay does not?* Such nonsense is not really worthy of response. Not only does weight training at a young age *not* harm developing bones and joints, but it produces thicker, more durable articular cartilage surfaces that persist into adulthood, and likely contributes to long-term joint health. The mechanical and biological conditions produced by full-ROM barbell training affect the skeletal components of both adults and children in a positive way (Carter, Dennis R. and Gary S. Beaupré, *Skeletal Function and Form*, Cambridge University Press, 2001).

Here's the bottom line: weight training is precisely scalable to the age and ability of the individual lifter. Soccer is not. We have 11-pound bars – or even broomsticks – for kids to start lifting with, but a full-speed collision on the field with another 80-pound kid is an inherently unscalable event. This logic also applies to every group of people who might be viewed as a "special population" – the frail elderly, people with skeletal and muscular disease, the completely sedentary, the morbidly obese,

Sport or Activity	Injury Rate
Soccer	6.2
Rugby	1.92
Basketball	1.03
U.S. Track-and-Field	0.57
Cross-country	0.37
U.K. Track-and-Field	0.26
Physical Education	0.18
Football	0.1
Squash	0.1
Tennis	0.07
Badminton	0.05
Gymnastics	0.044
Weight Training	0.0012
Powerlifting (competitive)	0.0008
Weightlifting (competitive)	0.0006

Injury rate = injuries per 100 participation hours

Table 8-2. Injury rates per 100 participation hours in various sports. From Hamill, B. "Relative Safety of Weightlifting and Weight Training," *Journal of Strength and Conditioning Research* 8(1):53-57, 1994.

distance runners, and the lazy. Note that women are not listed as a special population: they are *half* of the population. Anyone who claims that women are so different in their physiological response to exercise that the principles of basic barbell training do not apply to them is thinking either irrationally or commercially. In fact, the adaptation to weight training is *precisely* the adaptation that these special populations need, and aerobic-type long slow distance exercise is only a tiny bit more useful than playing chess.

Blind obedience to the uninformed and obviously incorrect opinion of a professional who should know better represents lost opportunity and wasted time and money. For lots of marginally gifted kids, weight training is often the difference between a scholarship opportunity and a prohibitively expensive advanced education. Many people who could have benefited from improved strength, power, bone density, balance, coordination, flexibility, and confidence have instead done what they were told and have not benefited at all. Not all expensive advice is worth the money.

AUTHORS

MARK RIPPETOE is the author (rather obviously) of *Starting Strength: Basic Barbell Training, Practical Programming for Strength Training 2nd edition, Strong Enough?, Mean Ol' Mr. Gravity,* and numerous journal, magazine and internet articles. He has worked in the fitness industry since 1978, and has been the owner of the Wichita Falls Athletic Club since 1984. He graduated from Midwestern State University in 1983 with a Bachelor of Science in geology and a minor in anthropology. He was in the first group certified by the National Strength and Conditioning Association as a CSCS in 1985, and the first to formally relinquish that credential in 2009. Rip was a competitive powerlifter for ten years, and has coached many lifters and athletes, and many thousands of people interested in improving their strength and performance. He conducts seminars on this method of barbell training around the country.

JASON KELLY is an Illustrator and personal trainer in New York City. He graduated from the Savannah College of Art and Design with a Bachelor of Fine Arts in Illustration in 2007. He has over 15 years of weight training experience.

STEF BRADFORD, PHD is the operations manager of The Aasgaard Company and Community Organizer for www.startingstrength.com. She received her doctorate in pharmacology from Duke University in 2004. She has been strength training most of her life and a competitive Olympic weightlifter for several years. She teaches barbell training throughout the country.

CREDITS

PHOTOGRAPHS

All photographs by Thomas Campitelli unless otherwise noted.

Photographs by Torin Halsey: Figures 2-16, 2-17, 2-20, 2-21, 2-24, 2-34, 2-40, 2-57, 2-58, 2-60, 3-15, 4-6, 4-45, 4-48, 4-49, 4-50, 4-51, 5-4, 5-5, 5-6, 5-10, 5-21, 5-22, 5-27, 5-28, 5-29, 5-32, 6-17, 6-39, 6-42, 6-44, 6-45, 6-46, 7-3, 7-13, 7-14, 7-21, 7-25, 7-36, 7-37, 7-38, 7-39, 7-40, 7-41, 7-42, 7-48, 7-49, 7-50, 7-51, 7-53, 7-59, 8-6, 8-7. 8-8, 8-11, 8-12, 8-13, 8-14, 8-15.

Photographs in Figures 7-43, 7-45, 7-57, 7-58, 7-61 and 7-62 by Lon Kilgore.

Photographs in Figures 4-1, 4-39, and 5-1 courtesy of Mike Lambert and Powerlifting USA magazine.

Photographs in Figures 2-56 and 7-31 by Stef Bradford.

Photographs in Figures 3-1, 3-2 and 6-1 courtesy of Bill Starr.

Photograph in Figure 7-23 by Bruce Klemens.

Photograph Figure 4-47 by Treva Slagle.

Photograph in Figure 6-37 by Tom Goegebuer.

MODELS

Ryan Huseman, Andrea Wells, Justin Brimhall, Carrie Klumpar, Stef Bradford, Josh Wells, DeLisa Moore, Damon Wells, Matt Wanat, Ronnie Hamilton, Roland Conde, Paul Ton, Joel Willis, Tara Krieger, Miguel Alemar, and The Orangutan.

ILLUSTRATIONS

All illustrations by Jason Kelly unless otherwise noted.

Figures 6-5, 8-1, and 8-5 from *Practical Programming for Strength Training 2nd edition*, The Aasgaard Company,
    2009.

Figure 2-19 by Lon Kilgore and Stef Bradford.

Figure 6-3 by Stef Bradford.

Illustrations and proof in Figure 4-45 by Matt Lorig.

EMG and force diagrams for figure 8-3 courtesy of Jaqueline Limberg and Alexander Ng of Marquette
    University.

Power rack plan in Figure 8-10 by Terry Young.

INDEX

Index

Index

D

Index

Index

defined, 42-43, 109
development of your, 70
effective athletic performance &, 50
efficient force transfer &, 50
lack of, 42-43, 51, 109
lumbar curve awareness &, 51
Kinetic chain, *see under Bench press & Press biomechanics*
Kipping pull-ups/chin-ups, warning for, 271
Knee, forces on the squatting, 19
Knee angle, 37, 44, 45, 46
Knee-control techniques, 52-56
Knee extension, isometric, 167
Knee meniscal cartilage
    disrupted structure of the, 321
    front squat & damage to the, 52, 245
    impingement of the, 52
    weight training for kids & durable, 322
    wedging of posterior, 245
Knee safety, bounce &, 50
Knee structures, inner, 281
Knee wraps, why & how to use, 67
Knurling & rings
    power bar, 23-24
    standard bar, 105, 147-148
Kono, Tommy ("core strength"), 9
Kuc, John (powerlifter), 145

L

Law of mechanics & system of levers, 30-37
Layback
    clean & snatch, 119-120
    excessive, 92, 93, 211, 241
    moderate (Tommy Suggs), 74
Layoff, first workout after, 320, 321, 322
Learning the bench press, **148-153**
    bar in balance, 150
    eye gaze, 149, 151
    foot and leg position, 149
    grip, 150, 153
    moment arm to work with, 150
    sequence of movements, 152
Learning the deadlift, **103-108**
    Step 1: stance, 103-105
    Step 2: grip, 105
    Step 3: knees forward, 105
    Step 4: chest up, 105-106
    Step 4.5: weight off your toes, 106
    Step 5: pull, 106-108
Learning the lifts, **295-308**
    progression, 303-308
    warm-up sets, 297-300
    work sets, 300-303
    workout order, 296-297
Learning the Power Clean, **183-194**
    1. hang, rack, & jumping positions, 184-191
    2. adding weight to the bar, 191-192
    3. using the hook grip, 192-194
    teaching method, 194
Learning the Power Snatch, **220-230**
    Step 1: hang position, 222-224
    Step 2: rack position, 224-226

Step 3: jumping position, 226-228
Step 4: after the jump, 228
Step 5: the drop, 228-230
Learning the Press, **81-88**
    setting up, 81-85
    Step 1: big breath and lockout, 85-86
    Step 2: driving the bar to lockout, 86-88
Learning to Squat, **19-29**
    generating hip drive, 19-23
    adding the bar, 23-27
    important things done wrong, 27-29
Leg curl, bodyweight, **279-282**
    knee sheer force &, 281
    poor conditioning &, 281
Leg press, 64-65, 252
Leg & trunk length variation, squat, 51
Lever, Class 1, 112, 113
Lever arm defined, 30, 32-33, 111-113, *see also Moment arm*
Leverage, isometric stress & bad, 13
Leverage & moment, 29-37
Leverage system, 35-37, 113, 209
Levers, law of mechanics & the system of, 30-37
Lifter/barbell system, *see under lift's biomechanics*
Lifting heavy, *see also under lift's biomechanics*
    ACL missing &, 18
    awkward object &, 264
    back injuries &, 110, 192, 203
    back strength &, 203
    bar path &, 90, 114, 117-120, 128, 198
    barbell curls &, 262, 286
    barbell rows &, 277
    barbell shrugs &, 235, 236
    behind-the-neck presses &, 265, 266
    California front squat &, 249
    calluses &, 101
    center of mass &, 11
    cervical overextension under the bar when, 69
    cervical rotation under the bar when, 69
    decline press & danger of, 252
    exploding with high level motor units &, 182
    foot slip when (bench press), 168-169
    hormonal responses to, 10
    injury from, 320
    isometric stress when, 13
    lying triceps extension (LTE) &, 287, 288
    mirror &, 69
    neuromuscular system &, 182, 322
    normal anatomical position &, 21
    one-rep set versus 20 reps when, 301
    power & velocity when, 182, 183
    powerlifter compared to weightlifter when, 180
    pulling mechanics & scapulae when, 16
    rack height for, 23
    rack pull grip & straps when, 234, 235
    recovery from, 98
    rounded lower back &, 125, 136
    spotters when, 62, 63, 175, 255, 288
    squat belt for, 65, 66, 67
    straps (loop-ended) &, 140
    strength versus power when, 179
    Valsalva maneuver &, 59, 61, 62, 89, 264
    warm-ups for, 298, 300

N

O

Index

Index

Q

R

S

Index

Index